AF342340

The Foreign
Invention
of British Art

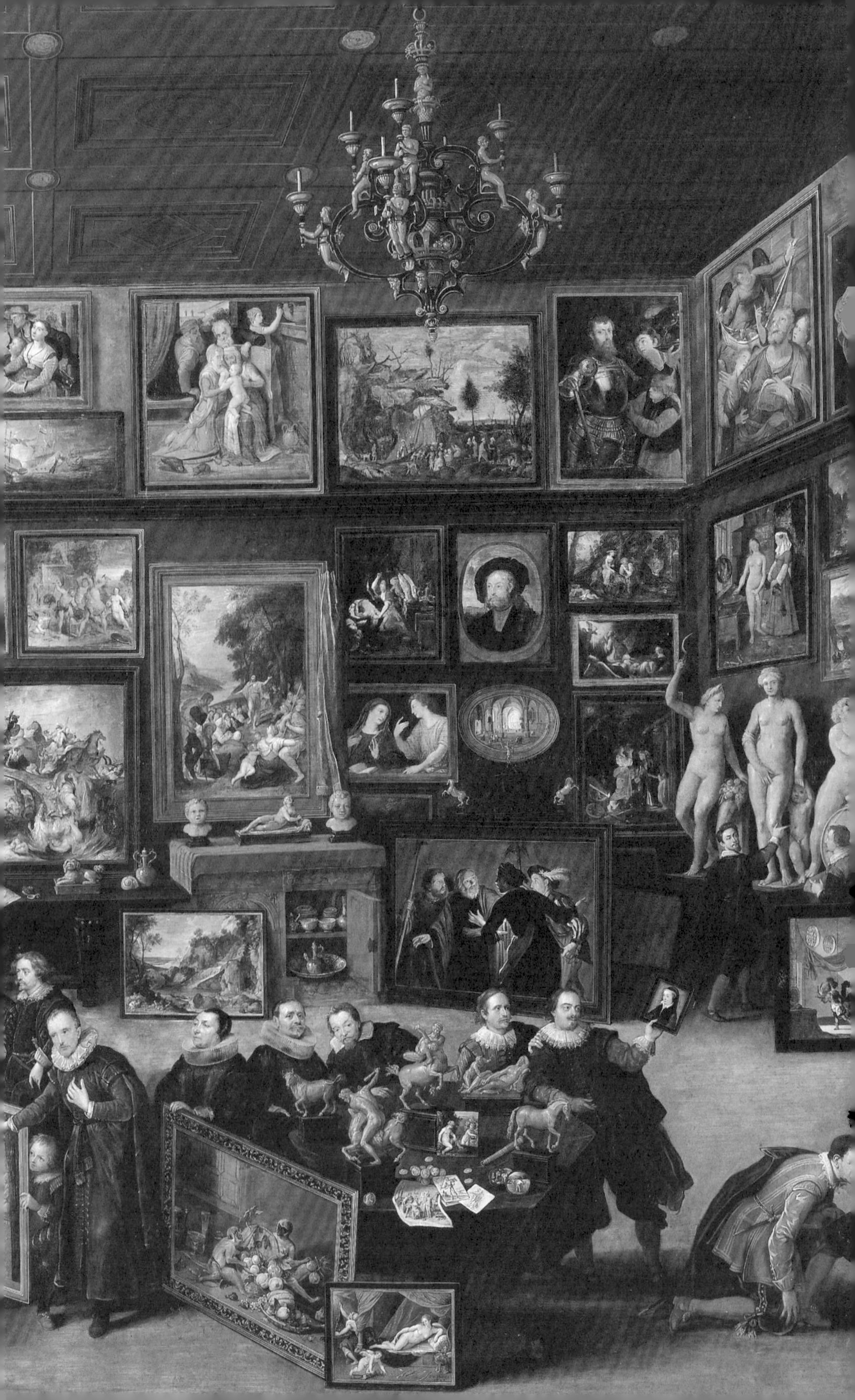

The Foreign Invention of British Art

LESLIE PRIMO

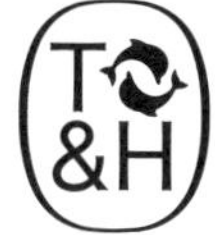

*To my partner Clair O'Leary for her love, support and
companionship throughout, and to my mother Olive*

FRONTISPIECE: Willem van Haecht,
The Cabinet of Cornelis van der Geest, 1628.

First published in the United Kingdom in 2025 by
Thames & Hudson Ltd, 181A High Holborn, London WC1V 7QX

First published in the United States of America in 2025 by
Thames & Hudson Inc., 500 Fifth Avenue, New York, New York 10110

The Foreign Invention of British Art © 2025 Thames & Hudson Ltd, London

Text © 2025 Leslie Primo

Development edit by Felicity Maunder

Designed by P D Burgess

All Rights Reserved. No part of this publication may be reproduced
or transmitted in any form or by any means, electronic or mechanical,
including photocopy, recording or any other information storage
and retrieval system, without prior permission in writing from
the publisher.

British Library Cataloguing-in-Publication Data
A catalogue record for this book is available from the British Library

Library of Congress Control Number 2024943719

ISBN 978-0-500-02401-0

Impression 01

Printed in China by Shenzhen Reliance Printing Co. Ltd

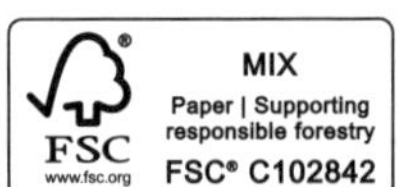

Be the first to know about our new releases,
exclusive content and author events by visiting
thamesandhudson.com
thamesandhudsonusa.com
thamesandhudson.com.au

Contents

Introduction

In 1526 Sir Thomas More, soon to be chancellor to the English King Henry VIII, received a letter from his close friend Erasmus of Rotterdam, one of the most influential thinkers of his day. In the letter, Erasmus informed More that the German-born artist Hans Holbein the Younger, whose fame had already spread across Europe, was coming to England. The painter's arrival, with a letter of recommendation from Erasmus to More in hand, would herald the start of an artistic revolution at the English court, with Holbein producing works of a quality never seen before in the British Isles. He would be among the first of many artists to come to Britain from abroad, bringing with them new technical knowledge, talent and innovation that would revolutionize the cultural life of the nation.

This book tells the story of how these artists played a massive, often unsung role in the invention of what would come to be known as the British school of art. It is a personal narrative in which I aim to demonstrate that the international nature of British art, a feature it still enjoys today, owes an enormous debt to immigration and integration, a fact that I do not believe is sufficiently recognized or celebrated when we speak of great British art.

The mission statement for the Yale Center for British Art, as set out on its website, notes that it 'accepts implicitly the transnational character of British painting', while Tate outlines that its collection of British art 'is represented by artists chosen for their contribution to its history and development, rather than for their own nationality alone'.[1] As two of the world's leading repositories for British art, neither institution overlooks its international nature. Nevertheless, if we are to accept these statements on face value, does this not call into question the whole idea of a style of art being particular to a single nation, and indeed the very existence of 'British art'? To answer this question, we might consider that many periods of art have been described under various labels over many centuries and, in common with British art, many of these definitions were invented after the fact. For instance, while the Italian biographer Giorgio Vasari first mentioned the word *rinascita* (rebirth) in his *Lives of the Artists* in 1550, it was only in 1860 that the term 'Renaissance' was first used, by the Swiss historian Jacob Burckhardt, exclusively to describe the visual arts in Italy in the period roughly from the 1420s to 1600. In doing so Burckhardt embedded this period into the artistic canon as a coherent cultural movement.[2] This so-called Renaissance was clearly not exclusive to Italy, however, as innovations in art, science and literature were being paralleled in Northern Europe by the likes of Holbein and Albrecht Dürer, whose artworks travelled across the Continent, as did the artists themselves. In a similar way, 'British art' is a term that serves to group together artists who practised in Great Britain while circumventing the reality that many of the artists who created our most notable works of art were in fact incomers. But while what is termed Renaissance art transcended national borders and morphed into local manifestations in every country it reached, British art is firmly a national invention, one that has little meaning outside of Britain, America and some former colonial (now so-called Commonwealth) countries.

I am often asked why foreigners were employed in Britain in the first place, and frequently preferred over native-born artists. Clues can be found in the words of the seventeenth-century clergyman Henry Peacham, tutor to the sons of the Earl of Arundel, who lamented, 'I am sory that our courtiers and great personages must seeke farre and neere for some Dutchman or Italian to draw their pictures, and invent their devices, our Englishmen being held for Vaunients.'[3] Such comments both confirm the influx and popularity of foreign artists in the period and illustrate the antipathy that was felt towards the valuable innovations they brought to Britain, with Peacham seeming to provide a possible answer to his own question in using the word 'vaunients', meaning a worthless or unskilled person, to describe homegrown artists.

We can gain an early insight into the cultural value of foreign arrivals into England from *The Annales of England*, produced by the sixteenth-century historian and intellectual John Stow, whose work was continued after his death by the English chronicler Edmund Howes. In the 1615 edition of Stow's *Annales*, published by Howes, it is noted that in 1564 the Dutchman Guylliam Boonen had introduced the first coach to England, while in the same year a woman from Flanders called Mistress Dinghen set up a business teaching English women how to make starch and use it to stiffen garments. Although there was much talk of foreigners allegedly depriving the native population of housing, this was not the view of Howes, who argued that they were in fact responsible for improving the housing market.[4] Howes went on to extol the economic benefits of the foreigners' arrival, pointing out that increased commerce and trade could not succeed without them.[5]

Other arguments for the benefits of immigration were offered in 1593 by the Member of Parliament Sir John Wolley, who spoke on behalf of immigrant communities in London against a parliamentary bill preventing incomers from selling foreign products in their shops.[6] It was not only London that benefited from the foreign influx. In 1564 the *Norwich Dutch and Walloon Strangers Book of Orders* noted that the Dutch had brought trade and valuable materials to this part of England and employed the native population in these areas, while further appreciation of foreign influence on local trade came from Colchester, with James I's 1612 *Letters of Patent* highlighting again how foreigners had lifted the local populations out of poverty.[7]

The artists I have chosen to include in this book have all in my view made pivotal contributions to the art and culture of Britain, and so are representative of British art. Reflecting the well-known idiom that 'travel broadens the mind', what they all have in common is the effect that travel had on their artistic practice and their lives. Many of the artists included have had major international exhibitions in the last twenty to thirty years, meaning they are still alive in the public consciousness. While some are well known to the international public at large, the names of others have not retained the European reputation they held in their own lifetime. I have therefore tried to balance my approach by including artists who may be less well known to a wider audience, such as Marcus Gheeraerts the Younger, Wenceslaus Hollar, Lucas Horenbout and Daniel Mytens. Also discussed is the ubiquitous and subsequently tragic Polynesian figure Mai, painted by Sir Joshua Reynolds, who was treated as an exotic novelty on his arrival in England. Yet all the individuals discussed made a tangible and long-lasting contribution to the amorphous persona we now associate with the notion of Britishness. We will see also that the flow of traffic was not necessarily in one direction, with native-born artists such as John Bettes the Elder and Nicholas Hilliard assimilating the lessons they learned from the incoming artists who practised in England before them. Equally, the reputation of some British artists reached well beyond their native shores. William Hogarth, for instance, can be seen to have influenced his European counterparts within his lifetime, with his innovative contributions to the genre of the conversation piece; the Dutch artist Cornelis Troost is known to have borrowed motifs from Hogarth's works.

Over the four hundred or so years this narrative spans – from the mid-fifteenth to the early nineteenth century – we will see time and again how emigration, immigration and diversification are at the heart of the competition that drives innovation, prosperity and, ultimately, creativity. We will observe the profound effects of international innovation on the artistic style of generations of pan-European artists, including Hans Holbein the Younger, Artemisia Gentileschi, Peter Paul Rubens, Anthony van Dyck and Angelica Kauffman. They and many others travelled widely across the Continent, witnessing the work of Italian Renaissance masters such as Masaccio, Brunelleschi and Michelangelo, along with the obsessive verisimilitude of Netherlandish masters such as Jan van Eyck, Rogier van der Weyden and Robert Campin, before bringing the knowledge they had accumulated with them to Britain.

The arrival of these artists often represented a clash of cultures on every level, bringing the foreign interlopers into direct conflict with British-born artists and craftsmen. Alongside their creative influence, this book will look at the tensions that arose between foreign artistic communities and guilds representing the interests of native-born artists, focusing in particular on the work of Robert Peake the Elder, George Gower, Nicholas Hilliard and John Bettes the Elder. We will observe how centuries of European artistic styles introduced by incoming foreign artists coalesced into a fledgling and as yet undeveloped native painting practice, and witness British artists realize that emulation of these foreign styles would inevitably progress their practice and ultimately result in their own success. These developments led towards a new artistic sensibility that formed the beginnings of what would eventually become known as the British school of art.

In re-examining artists who came from abroad and made a positive impact on the nation's culture, this book will look closely at some of their most celebrated works, those that helped to cement their reputations and ultimately led to their inclusion among the pantheon of great British artists. But it will also feature stories of xenophobia, racism, misogyny and resentment of foreigners and the perceived harm they caused. By including such details, our journey through the centuries in the footsteps of these adventurous craftspeople will inevitably highlight striking parallels with our contemporary lives and familiarity with tales of the interloper who ignites in the native population fear of the other and their supposed negative impact on society.

In short, this book tells a complex historical story that demonstrates the interconnectivity of artists, subjects, patrons, fiefdoms and king-doms, moulding the oeuvres of both foreign- and British-born artists and producing the works of art we recognize today. While Britain's rewriting and repackaging of its artistic heritage into the 'British school' is clearly a propagandistic attempt to lay claim to an exceptional and exclusive cultural heritage for the nation, it is not so far removed from the endeavours of past writers such as Vasari, who successfully placed Florence at the heart of the Renaissance. An often-quoted axiom is that 'history is written by the victor'. But often history is also *invented* by the writer; we now know that the Renaissance was not led by Florence, nor did it originate there. Equally we shall discover that Britain did not achieve its current cultural and artistic prominence purely through its own internal nationalistic creativity. Nevertheless, the style we know as British art does exist and is no less important than other artistic styles, thanks to those innovators who arrived and made vital contributions, the foreigners who refashioned and invented British art.

1

Hans Holbein
the Younger

*The Beginnings of Immigrant Art
in Tudor England*

Images of Henry VIII (r. 1509–47) and his court by Hans Holbein the Younger have become so synonymous with Tudor England that it can be difficult to see this period through any other lens. Of those many images, the iconic painting in the Museo Nacional Thyssen-Bornemisza in Madrid is one that can be said to be as exquisite as it is imposing in its detail, composition and likely verisimilitude (fig. 6). It is almost as though the panel on which the sitter is painted strains to contain not only his physicality but also his larger-than-life personality. As was common for many artists of his time, it was travel that aided Holbein's success, enabling him to absorb new techniques and adapt his work to the varied needs of his wealthy patrons as he encountered them on his European travels. To give us some idea of what drove Holbein's artistic journey across Europe, and eventually brought him to England, we must first explore the socio-political milieu that gave birth to his art, making Holbein one of many artists whose work would eventually contribute to the invention of British art.

In the late Middle Ages and the years leading up to the Reformation of 1517, a vast amount of art made in Europe served a devotional purpose. Church interiors were richly adorned with decorative schemes that included stained glass, side-chapel altarpieces and carved wooden altarpieces combined with painting. Almost without exception, the carved part of the altarpiece was placed at the centre and usually considered more important than the painted sections because of its three-dimensionality and thus closeness to reality. Occasionally, a painted altarpiece such as the *c.* 1501 altarpiece made for the high altar of a Dominican church at Frankfurt am Main by Hans Holbein the Elder would be allowed to hold centre stage among the carved wooden sections. However, the oncoming Reformation would see many such examples destroyed.

The over-familiarization of the laity with religious images to the point of displaying idolatrous tendencies would make the Reformists' uncomfortable relationship with images and the role of paintings within the religious world more and more precarious. The humanist scholar Desiderius Erasmus Roterodamus, aka Erasmus of Rotterdam, was one of those who signalled this oncoming iconoclasm (destruction of images) when in 1504 he heaped criticism on popular Christian practices such as the worship of saints, fasting rituals, and the purchasing of indulgences to shorten one's time in purgatory. Erasmus quite pointedly warned against the consequences of a perceived idolatrous manner of worship, with its painful associations with paganism, more than a decade before an outbreak of iconoclasm reached Germany in the sixteenth century.

Though himself opposed to iconoclasm, Erasmus objected to the so-called medieval *cultus divorum* – the practice of worshipping saints and the belief in their intercession on one's behalf – seen by him as a return to the idolatrous pagan past, as spelled out in his *Handbook for the Christian Soldier* (in Latin, *Enchiridion militis Christiani*) written in 1503: 'This kind of piety, since it does not refer either our blessings or trouble to Christ, is hardly a Christian practice. As a matter of fact, it is not very different from the superstitions of the ancients…The names have been changed, indeed, but the purpose is the same in both cases.'[1] Erasmus would voice these condemnations in his work *Praise of Folly*, written in 1509 and first published by Gilles de Gourmont in Paris in 1511.

In some of his later works such as the *Colloquies* of 1518, Erasmus was even more direct with his attacks on the Church in Rome. These attacks were far more pointed and scholarly, and in the long term they would have a devastating effect on the unity of the Church, the results of which are arguably still with us today. *Praise of Folly* was quite particular in demonstrating that Erasmus had a deep contempt for the people who underpinned Catholic doctrine, the scholastic theologians. These pillars of the Church were pilloried as being intellectually flawed in their belief that they were able to fathom the deeper mysteries of the Trinity. Erasmus characterized them as having no such insight, and suggested they may as well dispute whether God could have come to save mankind in the form of a woman, a devil or an ass.

It was into this atmosphere of perceived decadence that Hans Holbein the Younger came of age. He was born in Augsburg, Germany, probably during the winter of 1497–98. His father, Hans Holbein the Elder, was a painter and draughtsman, and this would become the business of both Hans the Younger and his older brother Ambrosius. It is clear that Holbein the Elder was successful in business because records show that he ran a large and busy workshop in Augsburg. There is precious little evidence of him training his two sons, but there is at least an extant well-executed drawing of the young Hans and his older brother that gives us further indications of the father's skill as an artist (p. 17). It is not known who trained the brothers before they moved on to Basel; one theory is that they were taught by the Augsburg-based painter Hans Burgkmair the Elder.

An existing document seems to indicate that one of Holbein the Elder's sons assisted him in the workshop. The record of payment in the account books of the collegiate church of St Moritz in Augsburg, dated 16 March 1508, says that the artist's son was given a one-guilder tip when his father received final payment for an altarpiece painted for the church, but unfortunately it does not say which son. Some reference to this event may be that which is seen acted out in a c. 1504 altarpiece triptych made for the Basilica of San Paolo fuori le Mura in Rome, in which Holbein the Elder seemingly points, in a gesture of acknowledgment or favouritism, to Hans the Younger, who is alongside his brother Ambrosius in the lower right section of the left-hand panel (fig. 1). But this painting, containing the crucial pointing gesture, is not the one related to the previously mentioned one-guilder tip; the known finished altarpiece by Holbein the Elder that is directly related to the guilder was unfortunately destroyed in the iconoclastic riots of 1537.[2]

By that time, in England, a new art form had arrived that would change the face of English art. According to the print historian Richard T. Godfrey, 'In one aspect, and one alone, did English art outshine all other schools, and that was in the art of the miniature[, a] tradition founded by Holbein and refined in the mannerist Elizabethan elegance of Nicholas Hilliard (1547–1619) and Isaac Oliver (*c.* 1565–1617)'.[3] Hilliard was indeed a pre-eminent English miniaturist, born in Exeter, but Oliver was in fact born in Rouen, France, and came to England as a Huguenot child refugee. In his eagerness to claim the English refinement of this art form as superior to foreign schools, Godfrey not only fails to acknowledge that the artist he cites as its founder was himself foreign, and died four years before Hilliard was born, but also neglects to mention that an artist family from Ghent in fact preceded Holbein, Hilliard and Oliver in establishing it. One can only speculate that Godfrey was perhaps inspired by the courtier and writer Sir John Harington, who voiced a similar sentiment in some later notes to his 1591 translation of Ludovico Ariosto's *Orlando Furioso*.[4] The historian Mary Edmond did, notably, mention the Horenbout family and their arrival in England, and quoted Sir Roy Strong's 1981 publication *The English Miniature* in her own 1983 publication.[5] In both instances, the increased activities of Flemish illuminators and the rise of miniatures at the English court of Henry VIII are mentioned as predating Hilliard. In fact, Holbein would learn much from one particular Horenbout miniaturist, later establishing himself in the tradition and producing miniatures in the 1530s.[6]

The miniaturist in question was Lucas Horenbout (*c.* 1490–1544), who arrived in England at some unknown point in the 1520s, along with his father, Gerard Horenbout, a famed manuscript illuminator, his mother, Margaret Svanders Horenbout, and his sister, Susanna Horenbout (1503–*c.* 1554). It is most likely that Susanna and Lucas were trained in the tradition of manuscript illumination by their father, who had been court artist to Margaret of Austria, Governor of the Habsburg Netherlands. Clearly, manuscript illumination was already present in England before the arrival of this family, but miniature painting as a stand-alone genre was not. This family repurposed their skills to produce the first stand-alone miniature portraits in English painting and thus were responsible for introducing the new art form of the miniature, which took its name from the Italian word *miniatura*, originally referring to a small image within an illuminated manuscript.[7]

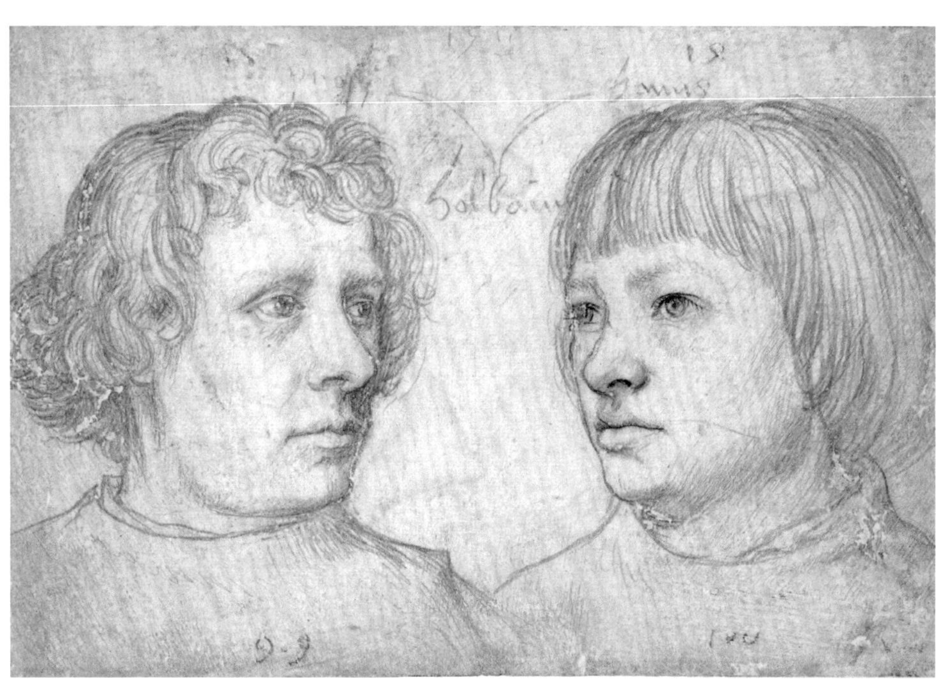

Hans Holbein the Elder, *Ambrosius and Hans, the Sons of the Artist*, 1511.
Silverpoint on white primed paper, reworked with quill,
10.3 × 15.5 cm (4⅛ × 6⅛ in.)

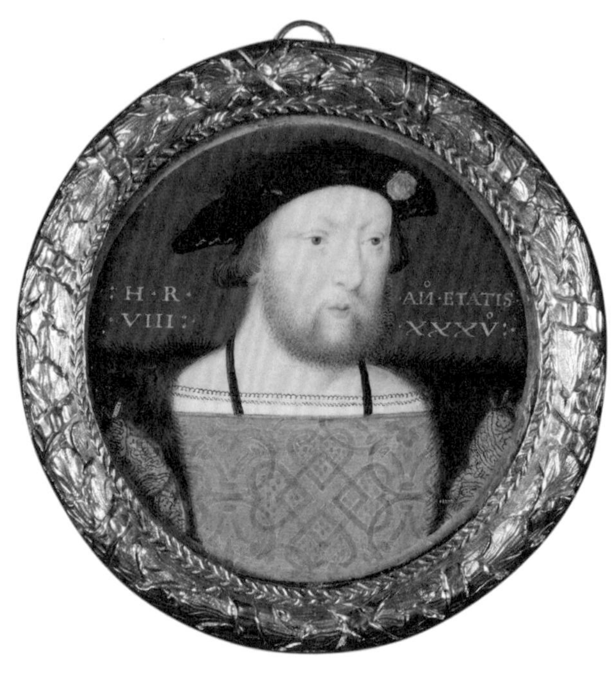

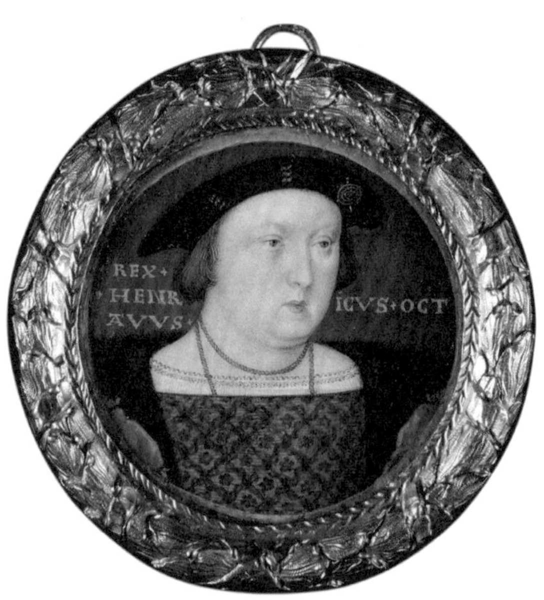

TOP Lucas Horenbout, *Henry VIII*, 1526–27.
Watercolour on vellum laid on playing card, diameter 4.7 cm (1⅞ in.)

ABOVE Lucas Horenbout, *Henry VIII*, 1526–27.
Watercolour on vellum, diameter 4 cm (1⅝ in.)

It is also important to note that Susanna Horenbout is now regarded as the first known female artist in England. Unfortunately, corroboration of this is difficult, given that the only documentary information we have is from royal accounts detailing the activities of her father, Gerard, and her brother, Lucas. Court documents record that between October 1528 and April 1531 Gerard Horenbout was in the service of Henry VIII.[8] Missing from these detailed accounts is any mention of Susanna Horenbout, although it is possible that she painted some miniatures, and perhaps one of the two that are thought to be the earliest surviving *ad vivum* (directly from the life) portraits of Henry VIII. One portrait features a clean-shaven Henry and is attributed to Lucas Horenbout; the other shows a bearded Henry and is believed by some to be Susanna's work. As her name is not listed in the King's account records, it is generally thought unlikely that she had a hand in this miniature, and both are usually attributed to her brother. However, factors relating to the social mores of the day, such as distinctions of class and whether or not women were paid for their professional work, mean that the lack of records in the account books cannot be seen as definitive evidence of Susanna's exclusion from this work. Such cases of discrimination could have irreconcilably skewed the historical record, were it not for a comment made about Susanna Horenbout by the artist Albrecht Dürer in Antwerp in 1521, after he purchased an illuminated image of Christ from her for one gulden: 'Amazing that a woman should have done something like that.'[9]

Returning to the previously mentioned *ad vivum* portraits, the inscription on the bearded Henry shows him to be thirty-five at the time it was made, but it does not shed light on why he chose to break with tradition and sit for these portrait miniatures. It is known that Henry experimented with his facial hair, regularly growing and then shaving off his beard, and these two works, made roughly around the same time, demonstrate how frequent an occurrence this was. However, it is also thought they may have been made as a deliberate vanity comparison so the King could quickly determine what he looked like bearded and clean-shaven (p. 18).[10] It is now believed that the compositional precedent set by the Horenbout miniatures may have served as the foundation on which other artists could base their own portraits of Henry VIII; indeed, there would be many such copies by artists whose names are long since lost and only survive as generic categorizations.

Lucas Horenbout clearly managed to stand out from the other foreign competition at court and was evidently held in high esteem by Henry, who employed him from around 1524 or 1525 until Horenbout's death in 1544. His status among the King's painters was evidently important, because in the accounts of Henry VIII from September 1525 he is listed as a 'pictor maker' in receipt of a yearly salary of £33, compared with the £30 a year that Holbein would receive when he arrived around 1531; in fact, by 1531 we see Horenbout being described as the King's painter.[11] He was appointed to this position for life in June 1534, whereupon he was also made a denizen of England, a naturalized English subject.[12] It is hard for us to imagine five hundred years hence what £33 a year could buy, but we do know that the average curate working in England at this time was well-housed and lived a comfortable middle-class existence on that sum. Indeed, the denization that Lucas Horenbout was afforded meant he was now officially an English citizen, and with this new status he was entitled to housing.

Accommodation in London was as much sought-after then as it is now, yet we know that Lucas Horenbout was given lodgings in the well-to-do Charing Cross area. Perhaps of more importance, his change in status meant he could officially become an employer. Although no information survives regarding the identity of those he employed, it is known that he took on four foreign assistants, most likely journeyman artists (*Wandergesellen*), who helped him in his workshop. Such apparent luxuries and privileges would soon become a bone of contention, as native-born painters became more and more angry and resentful about the success of foreigners relative to their own (see Chapter Three). But, despite this growing hostility, Lucas and possibly Susanna Horenbout continued to prosper, and are now widely assumed to be responsible for the first portrait miniatures produced in England (the portrait miniatures of the King are among the very earliest that exist). When Hans Holbein the Younger eventually arrived in England to settle, around 1531, demand was such that he produced a series of portrait miniatures for a variety of clients throughout the 1530s and thus found himself in direct competition with Lucas Horenbout.[13]

In the year 1515, by which time both Holbein sons had completed their apprenticeships, they moved as journeyman painters to the city of Basel. As painters, Hans and Ambrosius were certainly part of the journeyman tradition that had its roots in the early medieval period and encompassed many trades, including mason-architects and goldsmiths. The tradition of journeyman years (*Wanderjahre*) was mostly prevalent in France and German-speaking countries, and it required participants to ply their trade in other cities and countries for approximately three years and a day, or for the same amount of time they had served as an apprentice.[14] Although not strictly enforced, there was an additional requirement for the journeyman to be debt-free and unmarried, and both Hans and Ambrosius were unmarried when they set out on their journey. Indeed, so too was that other great journeyman artist Dürer, who only married on his return to Nuremberg in 1494. Traditionally, the journeyman was expected to seek work outside of a sixty-kilometre (thirty-seven-mile) radius of his hometown, and this practice would have certainly contributed to the spread of artistic styles and techniques across Europe. At the time of the Holbeins' arrival in what was then the territory of the Swiss Confederation, work producing Catholic images was still very much available to them, and Basel was also a city known for its university and the burgeoning print trade.

That same print trade would become the driver behind the events following 31 October 1517, when Martin Luther is said to have nailed his 'Ninety-Five Theses' to the door of the Castle Church in Wittenberg, Saxony. This document contained a raft of protests against Church practices such as the sale of indulgences, which at the time partly funded the rebuilding of the Church of St Peter's in Rome (begun in 1506). Of course, Luther could not have anticipated the effect that the newly invented printed type would have on the dissemination of his writings; eventually, circulation of printed copies would ensure a far greater audience reception across Europe. In time, Luther would become the most published person in Wittenberg, developing into a virtual one-man publishing industry, with his works stretching to numerous volumes.

The year 1515, which saw the arrival of Hans and Ambrosius Holbein in Basel, also saw the arrival of Erasmus of Rotterdam. He had come to

Basel to meet Johann Froben, who had successfully founded a printing workshop there in 1491. Froben quickly became by far the most prolific printer of Erasmus's works, publishing somewhere between 230 and 235 of them right up until Erasmus's death in 1536. Among Erasmus's works published by Froben in Basel was a 1515 edition of *Praise of Folly*, first owned by the Protestant reformer Oswald Geisshüsler of Lucerne. It was probably Geisshüsler's idea to illustrate this copy with seventy-nine marginal drawings by Hans Holbein the Younger and three by his brother Ambrosius, and it is possible that Erasmus saw these drawings.[15] Hans Holbein became very well acquainted with both Erasmus and Froben, painting their portraits on numerous occasions, and designing a personal printer's device for Froben. The device, with its Renaissance motifs, features the caduceus (a staff intertwined with two snakes) of the Roman messenger god Mercury, who was also the god of trade and commerce.

The years leading up to Holbein's success marked the beginning of the end for Church unity in Europe, all triggered by the Reformist Martin Luther in 1517, and by 1520 Luther had published three Reformation treatises. Luther believed that the Church had surrounded itself by and explicitly promoted a culture of materialism by supporting the production of material objects in the form of pictures and sculptures that could not, according to the Reformists, serve any real use. In 1521 Luther was excommunicated by Leo X. This act was followed by a publication written by Henry VIII, possibly assisted by Thomas More, entitled *Assertio Septem Sacramentorum* (The Defence of the Seven Sacraments), which also opposed Luther. These seismic events would have far-reaching effects on the production of devotional Christian works of art, manifesting first in a proliferation of images, mostly woodcut prints, representing the foundational Reformation distinction between Law (or God's Law) and Gospel (or the Gospel of Jesus Christ), also called Law and Grace. Such depictions sought to remove non-scriptural subjects from the pictorial narrative, including veneration of the saints, Marian worship (including the Coronation or Assumption of the Virgin), the Birth of Christ and the Adoration of the Magi. These images proliferated particularly in Northern Europe: from 1529 the German artist Lucas Cranach the Elder and his workshop notably produced a number of 'Law and Grace' paintings, and Holbein also made one during his first visit to London.

In 1563 the Council of Trent (the nineteenth ecumenical council of the Catholic Church, held between 1545 and 1563) endeavoured to address Reformist concerns regarding the probity of images by issuing a decree entitled 'On the Invocation, Veneration and Relics of Saints, and on Sacred Images', which set out the role of religious imagery in Catholic worship 'to cultivate piety' among viewers.[16] Ultimately the council instructed that individual bishops were responsible for policing the correct production of Christian art in their dioceses. A guide published in 1582 by the Bishop of Bologna, Gabriele Paleotti, is helpful in outlining what was considered acceptable in the representation of religious imagery in response to the council's decrees.[17] Elements singled out by Paleotti as inconsistencies in the production of art included an overabundance of distracting ornament; nudes in complicated poses; wild gesticulations surplus to the requirements of accurate and realistic emotions commensurate with the painting's narrative; and a lack of tonal range, relating to his belief that vibrant colours contributed to the beauty of paintings, which was the aspect – being perceived purely through the senses – most easily accessible to the uneducated masses ('gli idioti' or the ignorant, as he called them). The rhetoric of both the Council of Trent and Paleotti had a profound effect on painting south of the Alps, just as Luther's did in the north.

In 1515 the Holbein brothers joined, as apprentices, the workshop of the successful Basel painter Hans Herbster and also found work as designers of woodcuts and metalcuts for printers. The Holbeins' arrival in Basel coincided with the arrival of Lutheranism in the university town, but by 1517 the family was on the move again. Hans Holbein the Elder and Younger went to Lucerne, where they worked together on a commission to paint internal and external murals at the house of a local magistrate called Jakob von Hertenstein. While working on this commission, Holbein the Younger also produced a portrait of Jakob's eldest son, Benedikt (p. 24). The text on the wall behind, together with the direct gaze, is intended to read as though the sitter is directly addressing his audience: 'When I looked like this, I was twenty-two years old.' Directly following these words is the declaration, 'H.H. painted this 1517'. This early foray into the genre of portraiture would give an indication of the high-quality work that would establish Holbein's reputation in Britain.

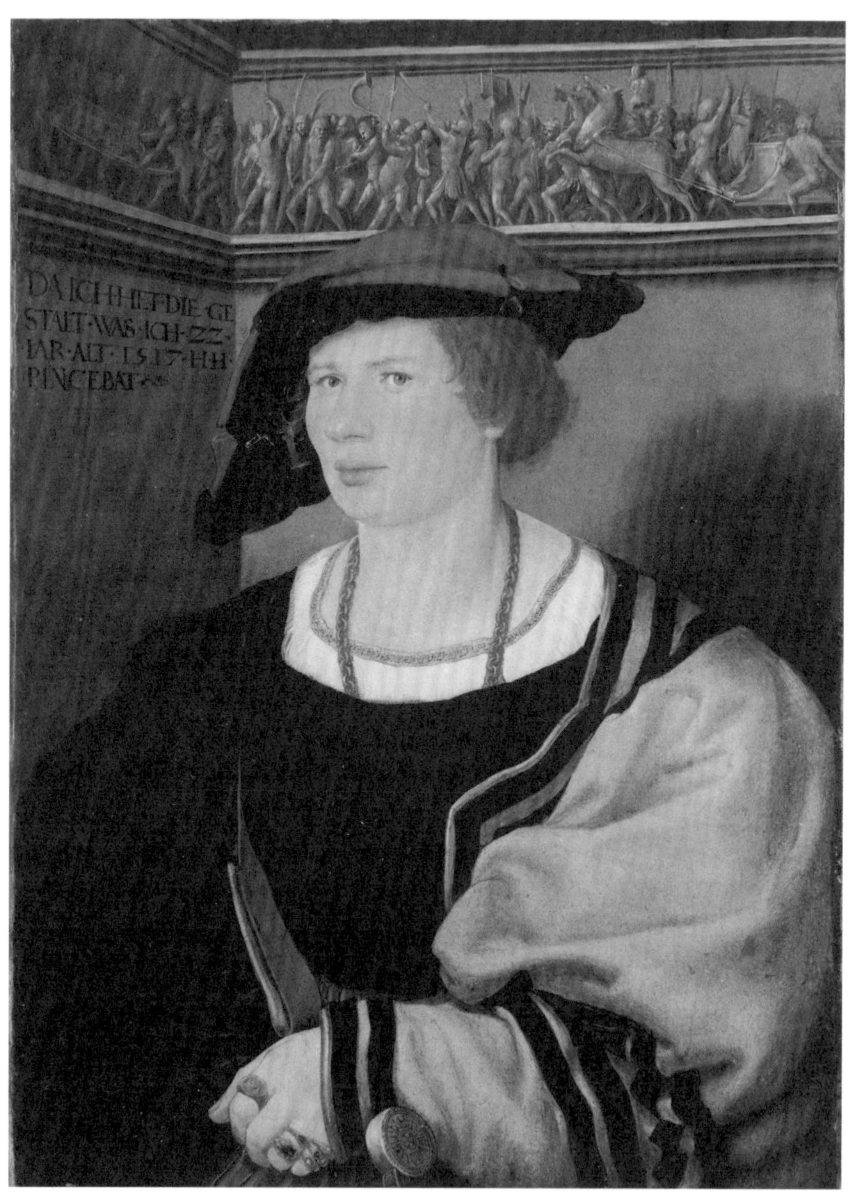

Hans Holbein the Younger, *Benedikt von Hertenstein*, 1517.
Oil and gold on paper, laid down on wood, 51.4 × 37.1 cm (20¼ × 14⅝ in.)

While inscriptions rarely appear on the portraits Holbein later painted for his English patrons, such works were the forerunners to those he would execute for his German clients in England, mostly London-based members of the Hanseatic League, an organization of northern German towns and merchants dedicated to protecting their commercial interests. In particular, the inscription on Holbein's 1532 portrait of the London Hanseatic merchant Hermann von Wedigh III features the date of the picture, the age of the sitter, the initials 'H H' inscribed on the front of the sitter's book, and the sitter's name beneath the clasp along the page edging. Further identifying features include the ring that he wears on his left hand, which bears the arms of the Wedighs of Cologne.

Meanwhile, Ambrosius Holbein remained in Basel, where he became a citizen in June 1518. On completion of their work in Lucerne, Hans Holbein the Elder and Younger returned to Basel. Here, both brothers paid to be admitted to the Zunft zum Himmel, the local painters' guild: Ambrosius on 24 February 1517 and Hans on 25 September 1519. However, soon after these events, all records concerning Ambrosius cease and therefore we must assume that he died around this period. Thereafter Holbein the Younger plunged himself into his work, setting up and running a workshop, and producing his earliest known work as an independent master, a portrait of Bonifacius Amerbach, son of the Basel-based printer Johannes Amerbach and a very close friend of Erasmus. In the prominently Latin-inscribed plaque, we are left in no doubt not only of Holbein's education and the precise date of the painting's inception, but also of the near-reality of the image portrayed (fig. 3).[18] Holbein would become a citizen of Basel in July 1520. It was usual for this to incur a fee, but it seems that on this occasion Holbein did not have to pay. It is more than likely that his connections may have afforded him this exemption. As was customary on returning from one's *Wanderjahre*, Holbein settled down.

It is not known precisely when, but it may have been in this year that he married Elsbeth Binzenstock, the widow of a local tanner. Holbein would eventually paint a portrait of Elsbeth with two of their children, Philipp and Katharina, shortly after he returned from London around 1528 (fig. 2).[19] There are various speculative explanations for the apparent extreme grief on the faces of Holbein's wife and children, one of which suggests sadness at Holbein's constant and long absences from his family, and another which posits that Holbein's wife was suffering from a recent eye infection, but nevertheless it is recognized as one of Holbein's most personal paintings.

Holbein's status as citizen of Basel would be confirmed on his receiving a now-celebrated commission to paint the portraits of Basel's mayor Jakob Meyer zum Hasen and his wife Dorothea (fig.4). Completed just before Holbein departed for England, the painting features Hasen, who had also been the mayor of Darmstadt, but was removed from office in 1521, accused of corruption, and thereafter imprisoned. The mayor's isolation was further compounded by his continued adherence to the Catholic faith right up until his death in 1531. In the painting known as the *Darmstadt Madonna*, Hasen appears at the altar together with his first wife, Magdalena Baer (the woman closest to the Madonna), who died in 1511; his wife at the time of the painting, Dorothea Kannengiesser; and their daughter, Anna, who is dressed in white and wears a *Jungfernschapel* headdress, commonly worn by young Basel women of marriageable age. The naked baby and the richly adorned young boy at lower left are yet to be identified. The rigorous attention to detail which characterizes his work at this time would stand Holbein in good stead for what was to come – a successful career as a portrait painter to those in positions of power in London.

Before travelling to England Holbein seems to have made a brief visit to France, in either 1523 or 1524, which was around the time that his father died. His purpose for visiting France may well have been to seek work at the French court or at least to gain new commissions from wealthy courtiers. Here he would have undoubtedly had his first encounter with portrait works in miniature by Jean Clouet who, like Lucas Horenbout, came from the Low Countries and was a manuscript illuminator.[20] Despite setting up his workshop in Basel a few years earlier, Holbein was clearly still a *Wandergeselle* at heart and could not pass up this lucrative opportunity. Indeed, it does seem that Holbein's visit yielded results, in that France appears to be where Holbein first acquired and perfected the use of coloured chalks, which he employed for the first time in compositional drawings. One such drawing that survives from this period is of French poet and reformer Nicholas Bourbon (p. 28), who described Holbein as 'the Apelles of our time'.[21] Despite this accolade, it is clear from the briefness of his visit that long-term success in France was not to be, or perhaps he thought there was more lucrative work to be had in England. In any event, his newly acquired skill served him well in the genre of portraiture and would soon come to dominate his output in England.[22]

But the accomplishments and subsequent success that Holbein achieved in England would not have come to fruition were it not for the advocacy of Erasmus of Rotterdam. In 1499 a twenty-one-year-old scholar by the name of William Blount (4th Baron Mountjoy, Henry VIII's boyhood tutor and, in 1509, Master of the Mint) invited the thirty-three-year-old Erasmus to England for the first time, where he would meet William Warham (Archbishop of Canterbury from 1504) and Thomas More, who would become a lifelong friend. During this visit he would also teach at Oxford University.

By 1506 Erasmus was in Italy, which enjoyed a vibrant economic and artistic trade with Augsburg, the town of Holbein's birth. Erasmus's visit to the university town of Bologna in 1506 coincided with the triumphal entry into the town by the all-conquering warrior pope, Julius II, described by many as being more like Julius Caesar than Pope Julius II. This was the same pope that would go on to commission not only Michelangelo's Sistine Chapel frescoes (1508–12) but also Raphael's School of Athens fresco (*c.* 1509–10). Erasmus returned to England in 1509 and lived there until 1514, although little is known of his activities during this time.

Erasmus's interest in the power of the image is evident in the many extant portraits of him by artists including Quinten Massys, who painted him in 1517, and Dürer, who made an engraving of him in 1526. However, it is the numerous portraits of him by Holbein and Holbein's workshop, made over a decade or so between 1523 and 1532, that are the most well-known, and consequently it would be Erasmus, with the help of Thomas More, who promoted Holbein's career in England.

Often, what is not documented in the historical record is just what the sitters in portraits thought of their images. Did they believe their

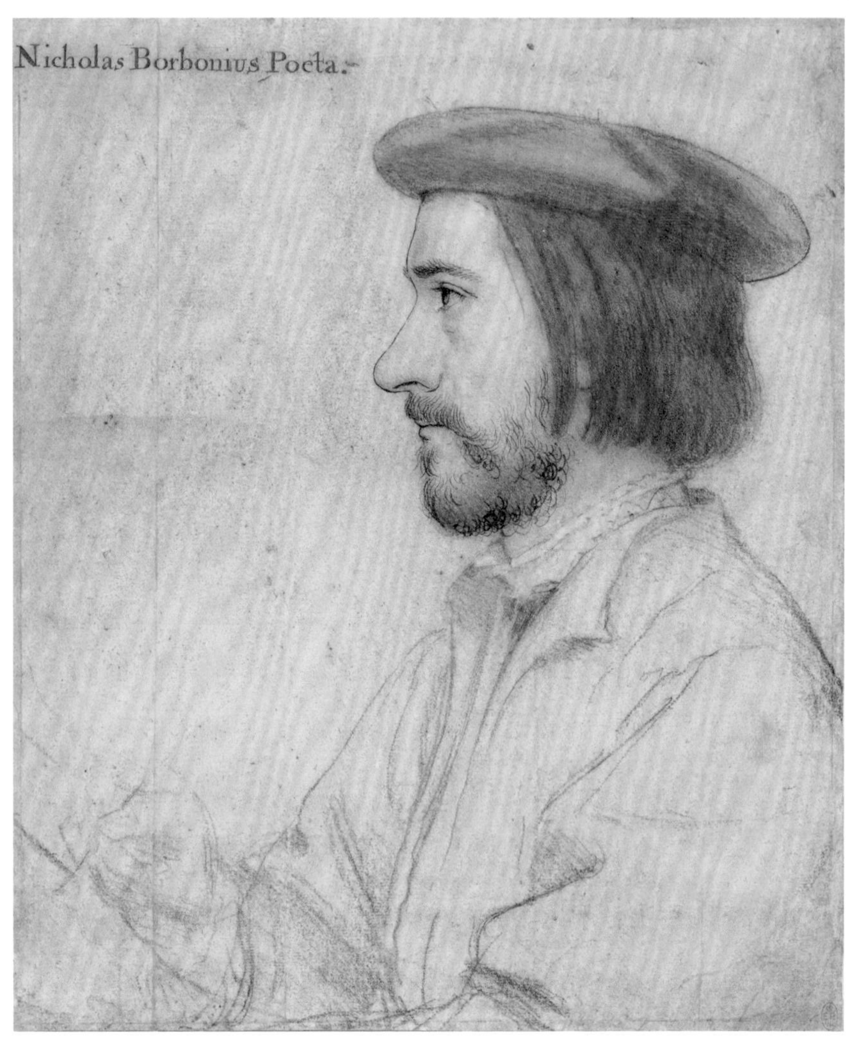

Hans Holbein the Younger, *Nicholas Bourbon*, 1535. Black and coloured chalk on pink prepared paper, 30.8 × 25.9 cm (12¼ × 10¼ in.)

portraits to be a true reflection of their physiognomy, or were they simply not as concerned as we might be in today's image-obsessed society? The collaboration between Holbein and Erasmus would give us a rare insight into the reception of such works, when in 1524 Erasmus sent a portrait of himself by Holbein from Basel to London, to his friend and patron William Warham; that portrait was almost certainly the one now on loan from a private collector to the National Gallery (p. 30). In his text accompanying the portrait, Erasmus explains that it was sent as a reminder of himself, so that, 'should God summon me from here, you might have some part of Erasmus'. In describing it so, Erasmus not only indicates that the image is an authentic lifelike facsimile, but also powerfully endorses Holbein's illusory powers. Indeed, Erasmus's joy at the accuracy of the portrait allowed Holbein to insert into it a boastful statement along the page edging of the book behind Erasmus's head, which reads, 'I am Johannes Hans Holbein, whom it is easier to denigrate than emulate'. Such high-profile endorsements served much as they do today: they set a quality assurance standard of what is considered to be great art and, in doing so, dictated the style and look of British art that was to some degree inevitably led and invented by foreigners. The exportation of Holbein's work saw to it that his fame would spread throughout Europe and pave the way for his arrival in England.

Two years later, on 29 August 1526, Erasmus wrote to his close friend and fellow humanist Sir Thomas More, who was at this point a rising figure at the English court, that Holbein was 'coming to England to pick up some angels'. This somewhat cryptic, or perhaps colloquial, use of language – a pun on the word for English coins and Anglo-Saxons – brought with it an explicit endorsement of Holbein's work that was clearly based on Erasmus's satisfaction with the numerous portraits that Holbein had produced of him. The letter eventually garnered a reply from More, written on 18 December 1526, which was positive yet tentative: 'Your painter, my dear Erasmus, is a wonderful artist, but I am afraid that he will not find England such a fruitful and fertile land as he had hoped…however, lest he find it quite barren, I shall do what I can.'[23]

Holbein had not been known as a specialist portrait painter before coming to England and had produced relatively few works in this genre.

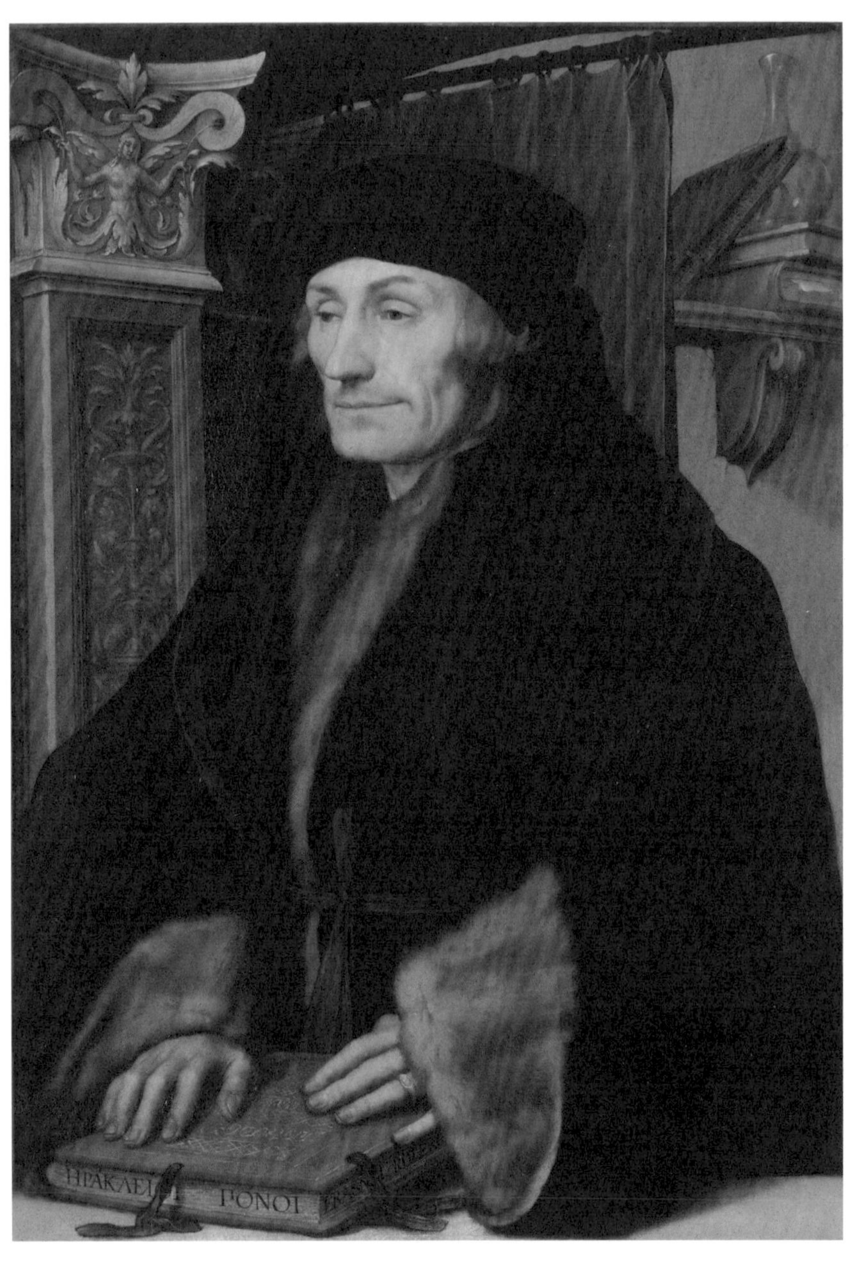

Hans Holbein the Younger, *Erasmus of Rotterdam*, 1523.
Oil on wood, 73.6 × 51.4 cm (29 × 20¼ in.)

Nevertheless, he arrived in England in the autumn of 1526 and was in London by 1527, bringing with him a letter of recommendation from Erasmus to More. Holbein would enjoy two successful working years in London, producing portraits of high-profile figures such as More and Warham, who lauded his work. However, the strict Basel guild rules, which Holbein was beholden to, permitted him only two years' leave of absence, otherwise he risked losing his membership and status in the town. Before his departure, Holbein completed an enigmatic portrait of a woman with a starling at her shoulder and a squirrel on her arm (fig. 5). The sitter seems to be from a well-to-do family, judging by her mode of dress, but her identity remained a mystery to modern audiences from the time of the painting's purchase in 1992 by the National Gallery until 2004, when its mysteries slowly began to be unravelled. In an article that year, the stained glass historian David King demystified the conundrum of the squirrel and the starling on noticing that the coat of arms of the well-connected Lovell family in the church of East Harling in Norfolk includes three squirrels, crouching and eating nuts, just as the single squirrel does in Holbein's painting, and further to this he suggested that the starling could be a pun on East Harling, which in local dialect was commonly spelled 'Eastharling'.[24] This would lead to the suggested identity of the woman as highly likely to be Anne Lovell, wife of Sir Francis Lovell, a personal attendant to Henry VIII.

The completion of this painting marked the end of Holbein's first stay in England, and he returned to Basel for approximately four years, from the summer of 1528 to 1532. Here, Holbein completed works he had begun before he left, and on 29 August 1528 he deposited 100 florins in cash for a sumptuous home for himself and his wife Elsbeth and their four children. This was a clear demonstration of just how much he had earned in England. It was also at this point that Holbein produced the family portrait mentioned earlier, though unfortunately only the part of the painting that features Elsbeth, son Philipp and daughter Katharina remains. It is clear that at this stage of his career Holbein was held in high esteem in his adopted hometown, since the Council of Basel made considerable efforts to persuade him to remain this time. However, these negotiations failed, perhaps not through any fault of the council.

In February 1529 Holbein would have witnessed the *Bildersturm* ('image storm' or 'statue storm'). These violent iconoclastic riots led to the mass destruction of images by Reformists, who forced the town council to declare Basel an officially Protestant town.

Although Holbein produced many portraits, his production of religious paintings arguably outstripped this work, and though the artist's works had a much better chance of surviving because of his fame, in reality precious few were spared. In fact, almost no religious paintings by any contemporaneous Basel painters survived the Reformation. Much of what artists had produced in the period prior to this was destroyed on huge pyres, so it seems reasonable to assume that we may have also lost a large quantity of work by Holbein.[25] The impact these scenes of mass destruction had on Holbein, and the decimation of the market for religious paintings, cannot be underestimated and would have been a significant factor in persuading the artist to return to England around 1531.

Holbein's arrival in England was well received because of growing interest in his portraiture skills by a great number of wealthy courtiers who were eager to have their likenesses immortalized for posterity. Such figures included William Reskimer and Robert Cheseman. Holbein also painted numerous members of the Hanseatic League, mostly between 1532 and 1536. Just as Giorgio Vasari did much to immortalize the lives of artists in the Italian Renaissance, so too did writers in England promote Holbein. They included humanist writers and poets such as John Leland, Sir Thomas Wyatt and Sir Thomas Elyot, who – like Nicholas Bourbon – described Holbein as the Tudor Apelles.[26] But it was not just Holbein's skill that was celebrated. A significant factor was his foreign credentials. As Elyot, the English writer and prominent courtier, observed in his 1531 work *The Boke named the Governour*, people were inclined, 'if we wyll have any thinge well paynted, kerved, or embrawdred, to abandon our own countraymen and resorte unto straungers [foreigners]'. The statement clearly implies a qualitative preference on the part of his fellow countrymen for the work of foreign artisans over that of native-born English artists, and Elyot and his wife would themselves have their portraits painted by Holbein in the early years of his return to England. The preference as far as royal and aristocratic patrons were concerned seems to have been about style and quality. While little is known about the reception given to English-born painters in the sixteenth century, it is quite possible that semi-resentful opinions like this one gave voice to a general malaise regarding their work that cannot have been helpful to their progress and chances of receiving commissions from the English aristocracy.

Just two years after Elyot's remark, Holbein again demonstrated why he was lauded as the Apelles of his time with his production of the full-length double portrait now known as *The Ambassadors* (fig. 8). The work is characterized by Holbein's obsessive attention to detail, which brings alive textures, colours and materials with a heightened reality that England had scarcely seen before. It is still the largest surviving autograph work by Holbein, precisely dated to 1533. Painted on ten vertically aligned oak planks, the painting was commissioned by the sumptuously dressed French diplomat Jean de Dinteville, seen in the picture on the left.

As with *A Lady with a Squirrel and a Starling*, the identity of those in the picture was lost over the five-hundred-year period of the work's existence, and for quite some time the sitters were known as 'Two English Gentlemen'. Without the identity of the sitters, the reason for its production and the reason for the inclusion of so many objects in the picture also remained a mystery, leading to speculation that Holbein's famous double portrait was more than just a decadent portrayal of the lifestyle of the rich and famous, and was ultimately about the meaning behind the objects.

Over the years this led to numerous investigations, and it was not until the turn of the twentieth century that the identities of the sitters were confirmed, beginning with the discovery in 1890 of the Château de Dinteville in Polisy, France, by the English curator, art critic and keeper of prints and drawings at the British Museum, Sir Sidney Colvin. This discovery at last revealed why the terrestrial globe in the lower half of the painting was turned around to the château's location and placed in close proximity to Dinteville. Then in 1900 the historian Mary Frederica Sophia Hervey identified the second sitter as Georges de Selve, Bishop of Lavaur from 1526 to 1540. Her discovery of a French document, dated 1653, listing both sitters' names in the context of the composition, finally solved at least this mystery of the iconic painting.[27]

The sum of the various objects and iconography has yet to be formed into a cohesive narrative applicable to the painting as a whole, but individual objects have been ascribed meaning, such as the distorted skull beneath the table, a *memento mori*, intended to remind the viewer of the brevity of life; the broken string on the lute, meaning discord; and the Cosmati-style pattern on the paved floor, which echoes a similar one still extant in Westminster Abbey, perhaps referencing the place where a royal couple would stand for a wedding. The significance here could be of one marriage coming to an end, such as that of Henry VIII and Catherine of Aragon, which lasted from June 1509 until May 1533, and the beginning of another, Henry's marriage to Anne Boleyn in 1533. Holbein may have left behind the Protestant uprisings and iconoclastic destruction of images in Basel, but he and the French ambassadors would now find themselves in the midst of upheavals in England. Henry VIII's break with the Catholic Church took place around this time and would prove to be one of the most far-reaching events in British history, and this painting was made right in the middle of it all.

On the surface, the painting could be read as a warning against valuing the material trappings of life in the face of its transience (or as we would say now, 'you can't take it with you'), but the political environment and its impact on Holbein's approach to this painting cannot be ruled out, including the appropriately visible word 'Dividirt' (Divide) that appears on the open page of the arithmetic book. To this end, detailed analysis of the painting made by the National Gallery in 1993 adds a further level of complexity to the story, with the discovery, after cleaning, that the hymn book on the right-hand lower level of the table could not only be read as actual music notation, but could also be identified as a first edition of Johannes Walther's Lutheran *Holy Hymn Book*, published in 1524 in Wittenberg, the very city that saw the beginning of the Protestant uprising. The pages shown, displayed on the two facing pages, are the hymns 'Veni Sancte Spiritus' (Come Holy Spirit) and the 'Ten Commandments': both were age-old Catholic hymns, but in this case are Lutheran German translations rather than the original Latin. Although it would seem that Holbein has taken some artistic licence, because the pages shown are not displayed consecutively in the original publication, this is still a significant discovery. Along with the overtly Reformist 'Law and Grace' painting he produced in London, it almost certainly confirms Holbein's Protestant allegiances (he is also known to have attended Protestant services in a Reformed Basel some years earlier, and to have produced a charity design for the Protestant community in London, much used by Reformists in the Netherlands).[28] While such connections did not necessarily put him in a better position than other artists to be welcomed into Britain, given the ensuing political climate they could not have done his prospects any harm.

As for the hymn book itself, it is clear that it could not have been included in the painting without the explicit agreement of the sitters, and in this case the proximity of the book to de Selve suggests that he requested its inclusion. It is known that de Selve expressed a wish to end the division in Germany brought about by the Reformation, and perhaps this inclusion was a signal of his continued optimism towards this cause. Yet the cryptic nature of this painting, which makes no bold statement in any obviously decipherable iconography, contrasts with the vast majority of Holbein's works and entrenches the atmosphere of secrecy and mystery that continues to surround this painting.

By the time *The Ambassadors* was painted in 1533, Holbein had already secured an international reputation on the Continent and gained the high-profile clients that often accompanied such an itinerant lifestyle. Praise for his work from respected figures such as Erasmus, Warham and More cannot have gone unnoticed by those with the means to secure his services, and it is no surprise that the artist established a successful portraiture business in England. But this painting's impact on British art has been mostly retrospective, symbolizing a crucial moment in English history that has been an endless source of inspiration for countless books, plays and films. It has been embraced as a quintessentially British painting, loved by the public because it is about the nation's own history. For a painting like this by a foreign artist to be so highly regarded reveals much about what leads to certain artworks – and indeed artists – being claimed as 'British'.

With the beheading of Anne Boleyn in 1536, Holbein would be tasked with producing a portrait of Henry VIII's new wife, Jane Seymour (fig. 7), as well as a portrait of the King himself (see fig. 6). Both were painted around 1537 and were probably conceived to hang together as pendant portraits. If viewed together, the Queen does indeed look as though her gaze is directed upon the King, but the scale does not seem to match, with the King being much larger and in bust-length rather than three-quarter-length. Jane Seymour would not live long enough to fully admire Holbein's exquisite portrait of her, as she died on 24 October 1537 while giving birth to Edward, Prince of Wales. This left a vacancy for a new queen, and once again Holbein was sent on his travels, this time to Brussels in March 1538 at the behest of his patron, to take the likeness of the sixteen-year-old Christina of Denmark as a prospective wife for Henry (fig. 9). The finished full-length portrait depicts her in mourning attire in respect of the death of her first husband, the Duke of Milan. It is more than likely that Holbein did not finish the picture while he was abroad, but instead took sketches and drawings from life and finished the painting on his return to London. The marriage never took place, partly because of objections by Christina and her family. Nevertheless, it is significant that Henry chose to keep the resulting painting in his personal collection, demonstrating how very enamoured he was with it. This speaks volumes of how much Holbein's works had – and have – become greatly admired beyond their original functions, far outliving both their subjects and their times.

By 1543, Holbein was forty-five and had spent much of his life travelling. He had now passed that tipping point that many émigrés eventually reach, in that he had lived away from the town of his birth longer than he had lived there. While now a citizen of nowhere in particular, he had become a true European. There would be no going back: the place he had left would literally now be, to him, a foreign country. It had been a meteoric rise and perhaps also a lonely one, away from his family for such lengthy periods of time. Forever the *Wandergeselle*, Holbein died in London in 1543, most likely of plague; his patron, Henry VIII, died four years later. But Holbein left an indelible mark on British painting that would pave the way for future artists. He succeeded in bringing to Britain an artistic style and sophistication that had hitherto only been seen on the Continent, in the work of early Netherlandish artists and the great painters of the Renaissance. In Holbein's work we can recognize the veri-similitude of Jan van Eyck, the intellectual sensibilities and use of colour of Titian, and the sensitivity and poise of Raphael. With the introduction of these innovations, Holbein set British art on a new path that would lead to the nation being able to stand as an equal among the international intelligentsia, part of – and now a contributor to – the great European Renaissance.

2

Marcus Gheeraerts the Younger

The Impact of Netherlandish Painting

During the fifteenth and sixteenth centuries Netherlandish painting came to dominate European artistic taste and was exported across the Continent, to the Burgundian courts in France and wealthy families in Italy, the Habsburgs in Spain and the royal courts of Scandinavia and England. Indeed, the close geographic proximity of the British Isles to the Low Countries facilitated the import not only of works of art, but also of artists.[1] Their arrival fed a growing demand for the skills these artists possessed, particularly the well-developed and sophisticated use of oils that had been underway in the Netherlands since at least the 1430s, well ahead of Italian Renaissance painters. Even the Renaissance biographer Giorgio Vasari acknowledged in his *Life* of Antonello da Messina (*c.* 1430–1479) that the Dutch, in particular Jan van Eyck (*c.* 1390–1441), had invented oil painting.[2] But Vasari's assertion that the technique was personally imparted to Antonello by the elderly Van Eyck clearly cannot be the case, as is evident from both artists' dates, which in turn leads us to doubt the validity of the entire story. While Vasari brings us no closer to knowing precisely who invented the oil painting technique, it nevertheless enabled artists to create illusionistic effects in the depiction of texture, textiles and flesh tones not previously seen to this extent in most parts of Europe, and certainly not in native English painting.

By the time Marcus Gheeraerts the Younger arrived in England these techniques were already thoroughly absorbed into the painting culture of Northern and subsequently Southern Europe. Gheeraerts was born at an unknown location in the Low Countries in 1561 or 1562, into an age of religious warfare. A staunchly Catholic nation up to the 1540s, since 1482 the Netherlands had been part of the Catholic Habsburg Empire, and since the introduction of Calvinism, one of many Protestant sects, in the 1540s, religious persecution of its adherents had been rife throughout the Low Countries. Following the popular Protestant uprisings of 1566, Philip II of Spain sent the notorious Fernando Álvarez de Toledo y Pimentel, 3rd Duke of Alba, to the Netherlands with a large army to punish the rebels, root out heresy and re-establish the King's shaken authority. As governor-general of the Habsburg Netherlands from 1567 to 1573, Alba arrested the Protestant opposition leaders and set up a new court, the so-called Council of Troubles, which would become widely known to the local population as the Council of Blood. The court ran roughshod over all local laws and condemned to death approximately twelve thousand people said to be rebels; many had already fled the country. In Protestant countries thereafter, Alba's name was synonymous with cruelty and religious persecution.[3]

These tumultuous events formed the backdrop to Gheeraerts's early life and would lead to him escaping from Bruges with his Protestant father. They reached London in 1568, when the young Gheeraerts would have been about six or seven years old. Like many immigrants who arrived under such circumstances, he would eventually spend more of his life in England than he ever did in his native country, but although by adulthood he could easily pass as an Englishman, and was certainly a Londoner, that does not mean he ever forgot his heritage. With the arrival of such skilled and talented artists, it seems that, at least at this time, the creative industries in England benefited from the persecution and discrimination of the other by those in power in mainland Europe. The diversity of this incoming talent would play a large part in changing the style of English art from provincial to European, and by the late sixteenth century Netherlandish painting techniques and practices were gradually being assimilated into English artistic production and becoming the norm. Their impact was seen not only in technical aspects, such as the preparation of panels and canvas to paint on, but also in stylistic differences such as the naturalism seen in Renaissance art, achieved through the use of linear perspective to compose realistic spatial arrangements, along with the use of modelling to imitate the fall of light on sitters' faces.[4] The proliferation of these innovations would eventually result in native English painters' work being almost indistinguishable from that of the incomers.[5]

Gheeraerts's father, Marcus Gheeraerts the Elder, was a painter and engraver, himself the son of an artist. In 1558 he married Johanna Struve and we know that seven weeks later he became a member of the artists' guild in Bruges. But when Gheeraerts fled to England with his son in 1568, his Catholic wife stayed behind in Bruges, where she died a few years later. Evidence of the father and son's arrival in England is recorded in the Return of Aliens, a register of people born overseas and residing in England. An entry for Marcus Gheeraerts the Elder, dated 1568, makes implicit reference to his reasons for coming to England: 'Markus Gerott of Bridgis [Bruges], painter, Ducheman, came for relygyon; Phillippus de la Valla, his seruant [servant]; Markus Gerott, his sonne [son]; all theas goe to the Douche churche [Dutch Church]. Dutche persons iij [three].'[6] Just as we may find our own various registered addresses tracked by national censuses through our lives today, so further Return of Aliens documents register the location of father and son in May 1571 in the parish of St Stephen, Coleman Street (now in the City of London). In July 1576 they are registered at a new City location, the parish of St Dionis Backchurch.

Although the document does not go into details such as working practices, it is safe to assume that Gheeraerts the Younger initially received artistic training from his father after their arrival in England. However, there is still no clear evidence as to the extent of this training, and it is quite possible that the younger Gheeraerts could also have been trained by other immigrant painters in his father's circle at the time. Despite taking place in England, the training passed on to the young Gheeraerts could not have been steeped in any other tradition than a Netherlandish one; indeed, it has been suggested that his training may have included a brief apprenticeship with the Flemish painter and poet Lucas de Heere, a Protestant refugee from Ghent thought to have arrived in England by 1566 or 1567, having also escaped religious persecution.

We can surmise from the existing documentation that Marcus Gheeraerts the Elder was part of a sophisticated humanist elite of Netherlandish poets, painters and exiles resident in London in what appears to have been a tightly knit immigrant community.[7] A modern parallel might be the many British people living abroad who interact only with their fellow 'expats' rather than with the local indigenous population, but when similar communities travel from abroad to live in Britain they are usually described as 'foreign', or else an antiquated legal term such as 'aliens' is used, certainly not 'expats'. The equivalent applies here in sixteenth- and seventeenth-century England.

Despite their alienation from the wider population, this community nevertheless thrived, and would go on to include other artists such as John de Critz the Elder, who also came to England as a boy escaping persecution, this time from Antwerp. De Critz learned his trade as a painter in London and, like Gheeraerts, it was not from an indigenous artist. By the late 1590s he had established himself as an independent painter. He was evidently successful given the extent of his activities in England, which can be traced through bills detailing the restoration of decorative elements, the gilding of royal coaches and barges, and individual tasks such as painting the signs and letters on a royal sundial. He also painted for court masques and dramatic spectacles, which required elaborate scenery and scenic effects. Such tasks are known to have been carried out by de Critz under James I (r. 1603–25) and Charles I (r. 1625–49), but unfortunately these works – by their very nature ephemeral – have not survived. Together with the lack of demand for religious paintings in a Protestant country and the fact that English patrons had little or no interest in genres such as landscape and still life, this ensured that the vast majority of surviving works are in the area of portraiture.[8] From 1603 de Critz held the post of Serjeant Painter to the King, from 1607 sharing it with the English-born artist Robert Peake the Elder (see Chapter Three).[9] Despite the ubiquity of his works, John de Critz never signed any of them, and although many paintings survive from this period, there is very little documentary evidence regarding the precise circumstances of individual pieces. Contemporary court letters that do survive make little, if any, mention of paintings and none of artists, as neither subject was considered to be of any interest, even as gossip.

It should be noted that in this period in England the custom of artists signing their works as a form of authentication did not exist as standard practice, and even Gheeraerts, despite his growing popularity, rarely signed any of his works; the habit would not become de rigueur until the nineteenth century.[10] But on the rare occasions that Gheeraerts did sign his name, he would deliberately refer to the city of his heritage, Bruges, even though he had spent only the first six or seven years of his life there.[11] This suggests there was an advantage to be gained in highlighting a foreign name and origin, perhaps indicating a skill and quality superior to the work of English-born artists. The narrative was also to the advantage of the client, who could demonstrate sophistication in their ability to procure work from international artists. In certain quarters in England, foreign art was becoming a byword for quality and must have carried a certain cachet. It is an attitude that is still part of British culture even to this day – when we speak of sophisticated Italian fashion, wonderful French cuisine or German efficiency and precision, we are echoing sentiments like those expressed by Thomas Elyot in 1531 (see p. 32).

The way in which the life of this community of foreigners in London played out was not unusual; in common with many immigrant communities, this one looked after its own, with members marrying within the group and giving each other jobs, helping it to survive and flourish. Indeed, when Marcus Gheeraerts the Elder remarried in London in 1571, his new wife, Susanna, was a member of the immigrant de Critz family from Antwerp. In 1590 his son continued the family tradition, marrying Magdalena de Critz, sister of both his stepmother Susanna and the painter John de Critz, at the Dutch Church in London.[12]

Marcus Gheeraerts the Younger is an artist for whom – unlike many others of the period – we have documented sources, including extant works. His earliest paintings are known to date from the early 1590s, just after his marriage. They include a half-length portrait of a woman now thought to be Mary Rogers, Lady Harington (p. 43). Inscribed at the top left-hand corner 'Aetatis suae 23 Ano 1592' (aged 23 in the year 1592), it is a painting replete with iconography, with strings of pearls threaded into a shape of four knots known to reflect a design from the Harington heraldry and a black and white pattern on the sitter's sleeves that is also

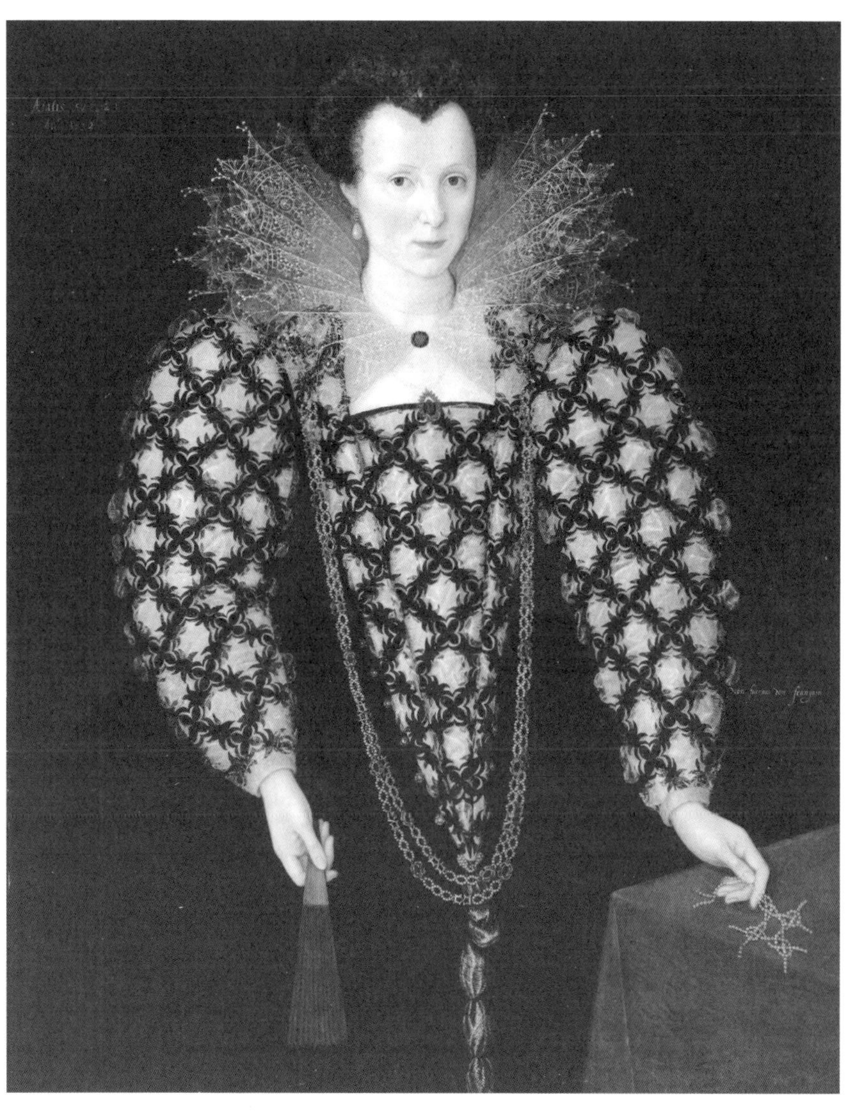

Marcus Gheeraerts the Younger, *Mary Rogers, Lady Harington*, 1592.
Oil on panel, 113 × 85.1 cm (44½ × 33⅝ in.)

a feature of the family arms.[13] The ability to accurately represent these important elements, following a Northern tradition of verisimilitude, was a clear advantage to artists such as Gheeraerts, whose influence on painting in England cannot be underestimated.

Also dating from this early period is Gheeraerts's full-length portrait of Captain Thomas Lee (fig. 10), now thought to be one of the earliest full-scale English paintings to feature a landscape background. This is supposed to represent Ireland, where Lee served rather unsuccessfully on behalf of the English Crown to repress and subdue the local population.[14] He stands under the shelter (or lee) of an oak tree, a reference to the family name, in particular his far more successful and influential cousin Sir Henry Lee, one of Elizabeth I's most important couriers and a royal champion who continued in favour under James I and was granted a pension of £200 per annum. The costume of elaborately embroidered shirt and expensively decorated armour, largely of Lee's own invention, is loosely based on native Irish military dress in a poor attempt to demonstrate his credentials in that country. Unfortunately, rather than demonstrating any practicality or accuracy, it serves only to highlight the subject's wealth and nobility.[15] It is clear Lee took advantage of the fact that Gheeraerts seems to have been one of the few painters both to regularly place his subjects in landscapes and to understand how to pictorially render iconographical ideas that delighted his patrons.

The crowning achievement of Gheeraerts's career, also from this early period, is the full-length portrait of Elizabeth I (r. 1558–1603) known as the 'Ditchley portrait' (fig. 11), still considered the embodiment of the Elizabethan age. It is a work that clearly uses art as propaganda, portraying the Queen as one who forgives, emphasized by the appearance of the sun, a symbol of the monarch, emerging from a dark and stormy sky to shed the light of benevolence on her realm. The picture is thought to have a dual purpose: first, to mark the Queen's forgiveness of Sir Henry Lee for becoming a 'stranger lady's thrall' (lover to a banished lady),[16] and second, to commemorate an entertainment organized for the Queen by Lee at his house in Ditchley, Oxfordshire (on a map of England she stands specifically on that county).

Some documentary evidence of Gheeraerts's activities as a portraitist comes in the form of a now lost letter of around 1597 written by Sir Robert

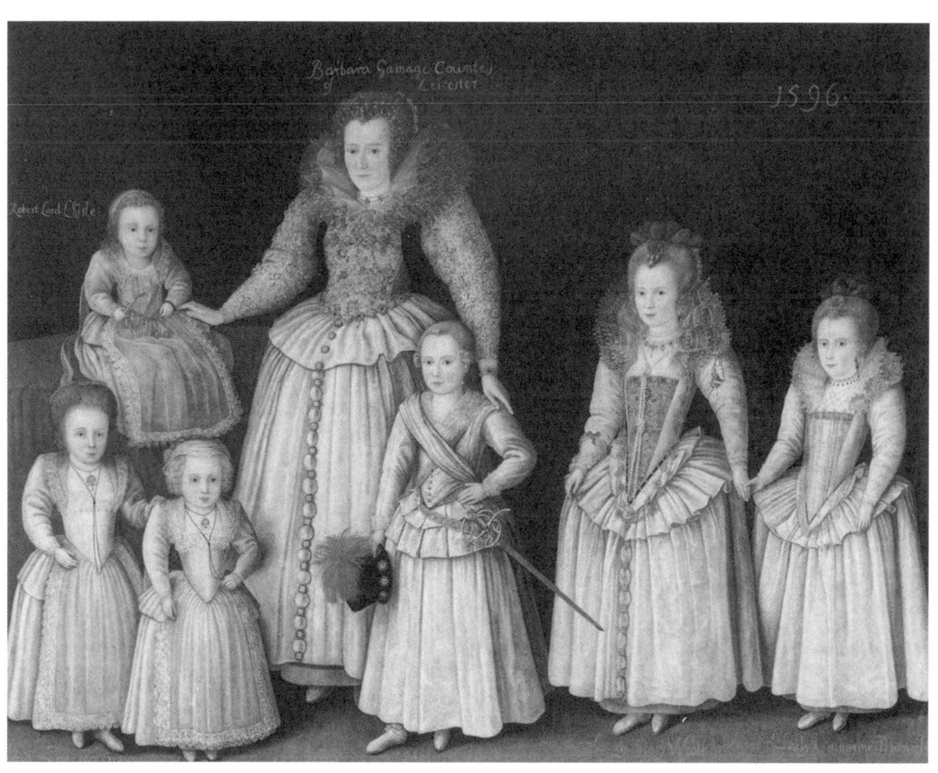

Marcus Gheeraerts the Younger, *Barbara Gamage, Lady Sidney with her Six Children*, 1590s. Oil on canvas, 203.2 × 259 cm (80 × 102 in.)

Sidney, later 1st Earl of Leicester, and referenced by the eighteenth-century engraver and writer on art George Vertue. In the letter, Sir Robert asks his wife to pay 'Mr Gerrats' for a painting of herself and their children, which had been completed and not yet paid for.[17] This letter is now taken as referring to the large group portrait of Lady Sidney, Sir Robert's first wife, with six of their children (p. 45). Considering its innovation, the painting now looks incredibly formal to modern eyes, enhanced by the fact that the children resemble miniature adults. In an age when the teenager was yet to exist this was the reality of children's lives, though the patriarchal construct of favouring the male children, with the mother's hands resting on them only, is one we unfortunately still understand. The painting remains in the family collection to this day at Penshurst Place, Kent.

The group portrait was by no means an unknown format in England before Gheeraerts's arrival; earlier examples had been made by other incoming artists, including Holbein's *Sir Thomas More and Family* of *c.* 1527 (subsequently lost in a 1752 fire) and the painting of *The Family of Henry VIII* made in the style of Holbein, *c.* 1545. The mysterious Master of the Countess of Warwick also made group portraits that predate Gheeraerts's works. As the name implies, this painter's identity and origins are yet to be determined, but a convincing argument has been made that he may be unmasked as Arnold Derickson, whose family name is perhaps an anglicization of Derksen, Dircksen or Dircksz; if this is indeed the case, it would also make him an incoming artist from the Low Countries, possibly Delft-born.[18] But while Gheeraerts did not introduce the group portrait into English painting, he can take some credit for popularizing it among a wider clientele. Soon his major commissions would include paintings of figures such as Sir Henry Lee and Robert Devereux, 2nd Earl of Essex, as well as Elizabeth I and several other members of the royal family.

Further developments by Gheeraerts would see him become one of the first artists working in England to paint in oil on canvas, a far more suitable support for full-length portraits than panel, and it is entirely possible that he may have introduced this method to England.[19] It must be stressed that Gheeraerts was by no means its inventor; by the late 1490s, when Titian was training as a young artist, canvas was already widely used as a support medium, showing up at least as early as 1500 in the work of Gentile Bellini and by 1515 in the work of Giovanni Bellini and Vittore Carpaccio. But there was very little, if any, use of oil on canvas in England before it was popularized by Gheeraerts.[20]

There had of course been earlier examples of full-length portraits in oil on panel, like the one of Sir Francis Drake painted *c.* 1581 by an unknown, possibly English-born artist (p. 48), as well as works by Guillim Scrots. This much-travelled painter (whose first name would soon be anglicized to William) is credited with helping to popularize full-length portraiture, which was becoming much more common in England than on the Continent. Scrots came to England via the Netherlands, where he had been appointed painter to Mary of Hungary, Regent of the Netherlands, in 1537. Although the documentary evidence for this artist is sparse, to say the least, we do have records that pick up on his activities in Antwerp, where he is said to be living in 1544. By September 1545 he is documented as being in England, though in fact he may have arrived even earlier, by Christmas of 1544. His arrival was clearly occasioned to take up the post of painter to Henry VIII following Hans Holbein's death in 1543. Very few works can be fully documented to Scrots, and just two paintings can be attributed to him from his time in England; there is documentary evidence of payment received by him for two full-length portraits of Edward VI (r. 1547–53), which were commissioned to be sent to the English ambassadors abroad. Unfortunately, there is still considerable doubt as to whether two full-length portraits of Edward VI that survive in the Royal Collection and the Musée du Louvre in Paris are by Scrots.[21]

Although Scrots probably spent less than ten years in England he apparently received an annual salary of £62 10s, more than double Holbein's annual salary of £30.[22] But this exorbitant salary lasted only until 1553, which marked the death of Edward VI. Following this event there is a dearth of activity recorded in his name; in fact, little is known about Scrots's life after this date, and it is assumed he returned to the Netherlands, probably dying there the same year. If this is indeed how his time in England concluded, it makes an important point that many immigrant painters did not necessarily arrive for reasons of religious

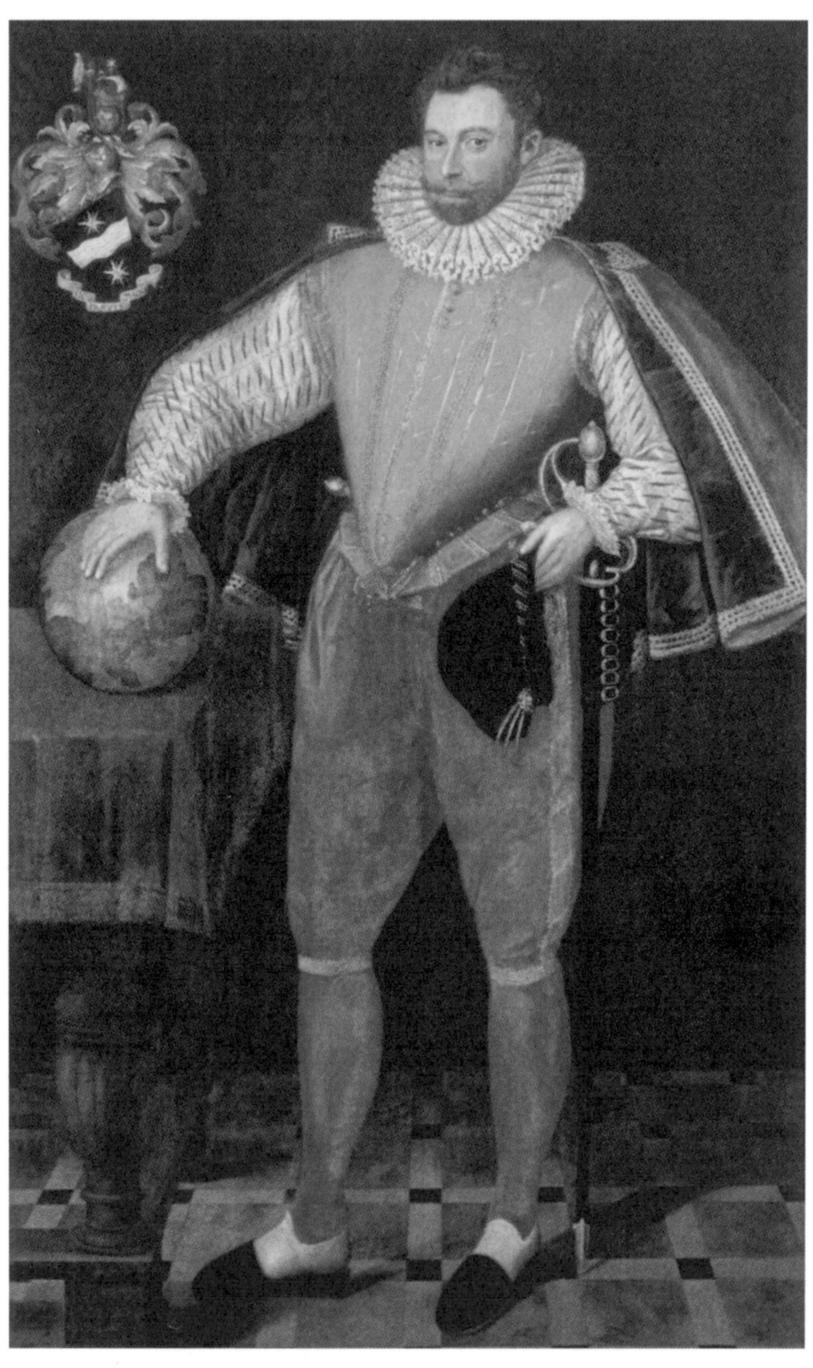

Unknown Artist, *Sir Francis Drake*, *c.* 1581. Oil on canvas,
181.3 × 113 cm (71½ × 44½ in.)

persecution. Instead, they were more likely to have been economic migrants than refugees and so were not inclined to settle down and live out their lives in England.

Those who did stay, like the immigrants of today, were a minority who were arguably very visible and therefore vulnerable to persecution and unfair treatment by the indigenous population. In this period a considerable number of Black people (estimated at 156,000 between 1441 and 1521) were living in European countries such as Spain, Portugal and the Atlantic Islands, most of them enslaved.[23] In contrast there were relatively low numbers in Britain during the same period, though some Black people had been living there since Roman times. It was only with the start of Britain's involvement in the international slave trade from 1562 that enslaved people from Africa were brought to England in greater numbers, increasing from the 1570s onwards as they became popular as household servants. But crucially, there is no existing evidence of commodification of these individuals in England at this time, surely because there was no recognition of the state of slavery in English law.[24] These people would find themselves the unwitting subject of racially discriminatory ideas that had circulated widely since ancient times, which posited that the human personality could be fathomed simply by observing differences in facial features, theories that resulted in a particular kind of persecution.[25] Gheeraerts's principal patron, Elizabeth I (who used Black slaves at her own court), would write an open letter on 11 July 1596 to the Lord Mayor and Aldermen of London and the mayors and sheriffs of smaller towns, voicing her dismay at the 'diverse blackamoors brought into this realme, of which kinde of people there are allready here too manie'. She would go on to comment on the 'great numbers of negars and Blackamoors which are crept into this realm'.[26]

Even though many foreign craftsmen arrived in this period, their numbers were very few in comparison to native people in similar professions. The ratio of foreign to English-born painters and craftsmen is thought to have been one to ten, which includes glassmakers, goldsmiths, cloth workers and glovers living in London during the 1570s.[27] But if this period tells us anything, it is that foreign artists were in demand. The quality of their work commanded premium prices, with high expectations in return, and there was clearly money available to meet these sometimes exorbitant sums. This growing wealth and conspicuous consumption fuelled the need for wall decoration to furnish the ever-larger rooms, great chambers and long banqueting galleries that were being built. In the 1580s a new genre of life-size, full-length portrait painting, virtually unknown before that decade, started to become fashionable, especially the more showy and decorative examples exhibited by artists such as Gheeraerts and de Critz. In fact, documentary evidence leads us to believe that in some cases the paintings existed before the chambers they were hung in, and may have even precipitated their construction, as witnessed in surviving correspondence between Thomas Howard, 1st Viscount Howard of Bindon, and Robert Cecil, Earl of Salisbury. A letter, dated 29 April 1609, gives us a glimpse of how it was now considered socially important to own a long gallery filled with contemporary portraits of one's circle. In the letter Howard asks if he may have a portrait of Cecil in garter robes, 'to be placed in the gallery I lately made for the pictures of sundry of my honourable friends, whose presentation thereby to behold will greatly delight me to walk often in that place where I may see so comfortable a sight'.[28] Such a request would have been satisfied with a copy of a previously made portrait, this one probably by John de Critz. In an earlier age the walls of these houses would have been mainly decorated with smaller pictures and tapestries; even through the Renaissance, Italian tapestry was considered much more prestigious – and consequently more expensive – than painting. In fact, the decorative patterning and general flatness of paintings in this period seem to be trying to emulate the effect of tapestry, in turn giving them an expensive look; this may account for the decorative style of these full-length portraits, which in many cases included exotic floor coverings.[29]

By the early seventeenth century we gain a fairly good idea of Gheeraerts's achievements from the sheer volume of commissions for paintings he had received from the Queen and the aristocracy, and the importance and meaning of those works. As previously mentioned, some paintings of the monarch were made to convey specific messages about the persona she wanted to project, and again it was primarily Gheeraerts who would be called on for the task. A case in point is the 'Rainbow

Portrait' (fig. 12), although it must be acknowledged that some attribute this work to his fellow émigré, the miniaturist painter Isaac Oliver. The painting itself, made sometime around 1600–2, shows Elizabeth with her hand resting on a rainbow. The Latin inscription above her hand on the left side of the painting – 'Non sine sole iris' – reminds the viewer that there can be 'no rainbow without the sun'; in other words, only the Queen's wisdom and benevolent rule can ensure peace and prosperity.

In a royal account of 1609, it is possible to discern not only Gheeraerts's growing wealth but also the circles in which this pan-European painter was moving. Records from this period relate to a payment made to him for a posthumous portrait of Philip II of Spain, although no such portrait has yet come to light. Further records of 1611 from James I's treasurer refer to Gheeraerts as 'His Ma[jes]ties Paynter'. This seems to relate to a commission for four paintings, of the King, the Queen, Princess Elizabeth and the future Charles I, the payment for all four amounting to £79. Although we do not have precise dates for the timescale over which these paintings were executed, this was a substantial sum of money for the time.

The artist's fame can also be gauged through the influence of writers and intellectuals. Around 1609 Gheeraerts painted a portrait of the English historian William Camden (p. 53), whose fame had been established in 1586 with the publication of the first chorographical survey of the islands of Great Britain and Ireland, which was also the first detailed historical account of the reign of Elizabeth I. On the opening page of the book, Camden declared his intention 'to restore antiquity to Britaine, and Britaine to its antiquity'. The popularity of this Latin publication eventually saw it reach seven editions by 1607, with the first English-language edition published in 1610, probably about the time Gheeraerts made his portrait of Camden. Although the artist's signature, at bottom left, was moved from the bottom centre to accommodate a different signature,[30] this is another rare example of a signed work by Gheeraerts. Surely the reason behind this exception to the rule is that the fame of both sitter and artist was of mutual benefit in this transaction.[31]

Following the death of Elizabeth I on 24 March 1603, Gheeraerts continued as court artist, becoming the favoured large-scale painter to

James I's queen, Anne of Denmark. The records list further payments to Gheeraerts for portraits up to 1618, which are followed a year later by an account that includes him among those who attended Anne of Denmark's funeral in 1619. That the artist attended such an event speaks volumes about his position at the royal court in this period, and therefore his status in the royal household. Yet the elevation of painters up the social hierarchy was not universally accepted by all, especially some writers, with the historian and intellectual John Stow asserting in 1580 that: 'Painting is a meere mestier of an Artificer and handy Craftsman, certainly no business for a gentleman, and clearly not amongst the liberal arts – a tradesman's job.'[32]

By 1618 the Return of Aliens record has Gheeraerts listed as living in 'Faringdon Within' as 'noe free denizen picture drawer to his Majesty, professing the Apostolick faith taught & held by the Church of England'.[33] This record suggests the artist's Anglican faith and, more importantly, that his status was not yet secure, since he had not been given indefinite leave to remain in England, despite all he had achieved. This last detail was resolved in February 1619 when Gheeraerts was finally made denizen. After his denization the artist is thought to have become a freeman of the Painter-Stainers' Company, a London guild that had complained vociferously regarding the presence of foreign painters arriving in the city (see Chapter Three).

By 1619 it seems that Gheeraerts was gradually being superseded in the royal favour by a new wave of Netherlandish artists who arrived at the Jacobean court between 1616 and 1618. Among them were Daniel Mytens (see Chapter Five) and Paulus (or Paul) van Somer, born in Antwerp, whose style was soon sought after by the aristocracy. From his arrival in 1616 Van Somer became the preferred painter of Queen Anne and then James I, and would soon eclipse other foreign artists such as Gheeraerts's brother-in-law John de Critz.[34] But in what seems to have been a final rally against this new foreign onslaught, Gheeraerts (who now considered himself English) produced a flurry of signed works in the final decade of his career, including a half-length portrait of Lucy, Countess of Huntingdon, as a girl in 1623, a full-length portrait of Lady Russell in 1625 (together with an unsigned companion portrait of her husband),

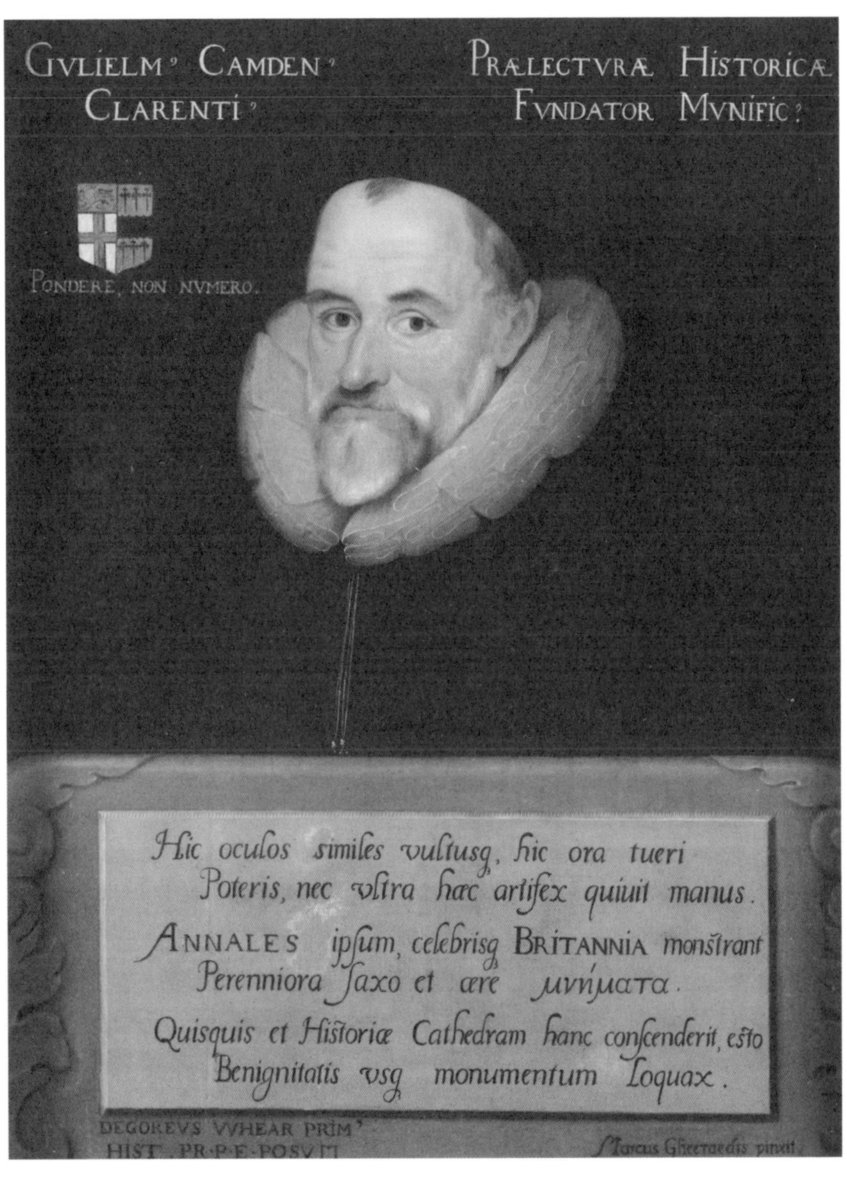

Marcus Gheeraerts the Younger, *William Camden*, 1609. Oil on panel, 76.2 × 58.4 cm (30 × 23 in.)

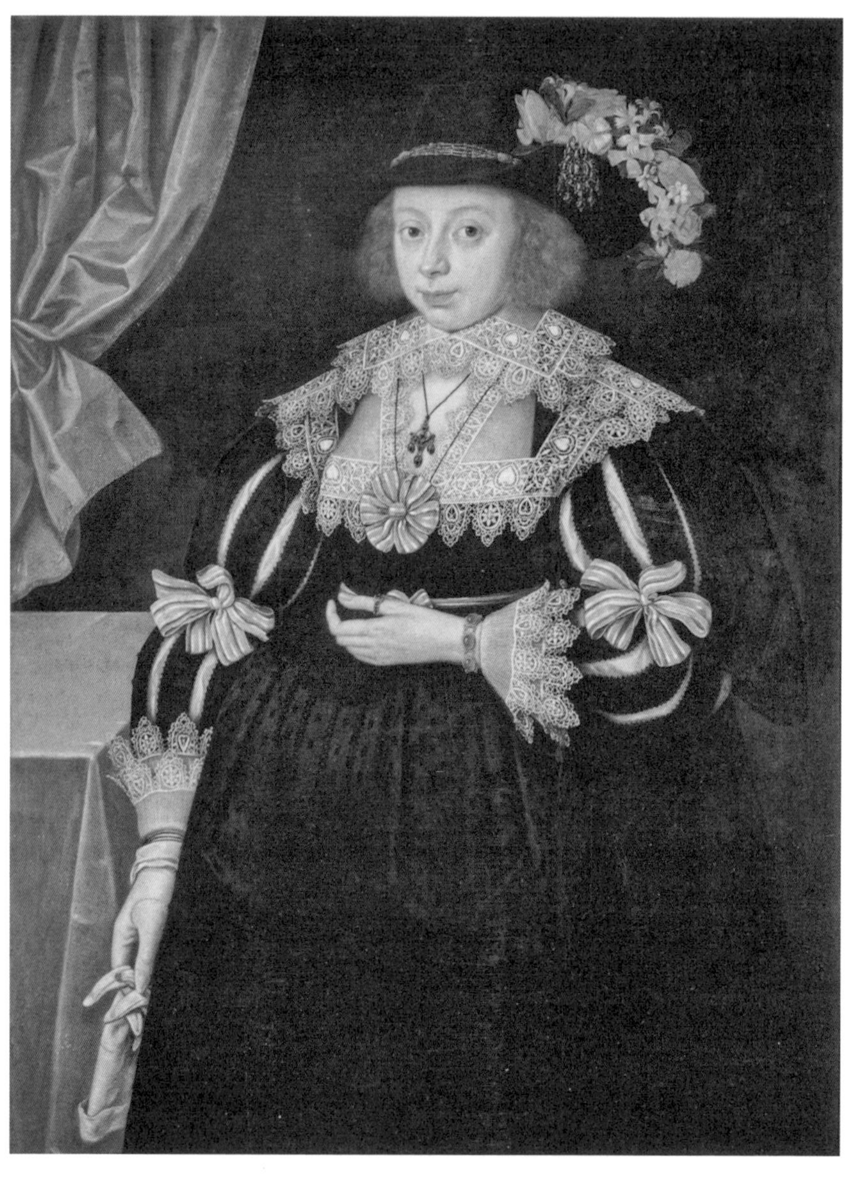

Marcus Gheeraerts the Younger, *Anne Hales, Mrs Hoskins*, 1629.
Oil on panel, 111.7 × 82.5 cm (44 × 32½ in.)

and a three-quarter-length portrait of Mrs Hoskins in 1629 (p. 54) (also with an unsigned companion portrait of her husband).[35]

But time eventually caught up with Gheeraerts; the Return of Aliens records state that he died at the age of seventy-four in the parish of Christchurch Newgate Street, London, on 19 January 1636. Significantly, in 1644 one of the new wave of foreign artists, an etcher from Bohemia called Wenceslaus Hollar (see Chapter Eight), produced an engraving of a Gheeraerts self-portrait. The text on the engraving not only praises Gheeraerts's status and achievements but also makes clear in a Latin inscription that both he and his father were of foreign origin: 'Marcus Garrardus the painter, in the service of the most illustrious and serene Princes, Elizabeth and Anne, of blessed memory, Queens of Great Britain, France and Ireland, was the son of the outstanding artist Marcus Garrardus of Bruges of Flanders, where he was born.' Like many foreigners who leave their native lands, whether fleeing persecution or seeking their fortune, Gheeraerts never returned to his homeland; though clearly proud of his heritage, England was just as much if not more of a home to him than the place of his birth, proving once again that both identities can coexist within an individual comfortably and without conflict.

In assessing the origins of the techniques and style of painting in England during the second half of the sixteenth century, a straight line can be drawn from the work of Marcus Gheeraerts the Younger and John de Critz – along with English-born painters such as Cornelius Janssen (born to parents from the Low Countries), William Larkin and Robert Peake the Elder (see Chapter Three) – back to the Netherlands, and the term 'Anglo-Netherlandish' continues to be used as a convenient way of describing such artists and their work.[36] Regardless of what the native population thought of their foreign status, Gheeraerts and his fellow émigré artists had introduced new and innovative ideas to England and, whether or not they were acknowledged in their lifetimes for these invaluable contributions, the historical record would eventually catch up with their achievements, confirming that they had altered the very idea of what English art could be, and changing its course and standing forever.

3

John Bettes to
Robert Peake the Elder

Foreign Influences on
Indigenous English Art

Across a period spanning just over a century, from 1530 to 1650 a significant number of foreign artists came to England and made a substantial contribution to its cultural landscape. Many of these incoming artists settled and achieved varying degrees of success, including Hans Holbein, Hans Eworth, Orazio and Artemisia Gentileschi, Daniel Mytens, Peter Paul Rubens and Anthony van Dyck. With such a stellar roll-call of names it might appear that there was little room for native-born artists to flourish, but this was clearly not the case: English-born artists active across this period include John Bettes the Elder, George Gower, Robert Peake the Elder, Nicholas Hilliard, William Larkin, Sir Nathaniel Bacon and William Dobson. But such was the success of the incomers that the contribution of native-born artists to English art often becomes buried over time, obscured by the growing fame of those foreign painters. The result can be that the names and/or works of the homegrown artists all but disappear from the popular historical record. Indeed, such erasure is not uncommon and has been known to affect the stories and lives of entire sections of some populations. Yet we know that English-born painters were not left out of the picture entirely and were making their own contribution to the history of English art, mostly in the genre of portraiture. It is clear from the art that does survive that in this stage of artistic practice in England, from the mid-sixteenth century through to the mid-seventeenth century, native-born painters were able to survive and even prosper.

As we saw in the previous chapter, the introduction and popularity of full-length portraiture in England, along with the ability to build large spaces to house such works, no doubt fuelled by rising wealth and prosperity in the nation at this time, opened up the market for paintings. But the good fortune that came with this wealth was not an exclusive monopoly for the incoming artists. Rising wealth and prosperity also ran concurrently with the beginnings of the English slave trade in 1562, the proceeds of which ever since have been inextricably linked with the building of property and can be said to have played a substantial part in the development of Western European capitalism. The mania for collecting art, and indeed the steady accumulation of wealth from this trade, cannot be ruled out as a contributing factor in financing the large banqueting halls and long galleries constructed to house these collections of works painted by native-born and foreign artists alike. In fact, both patrons and artists became increasingly reliant on this steadily growing wealth for their livelihoods in the years and centuries to come.

A painting in the Tate collection is described as the earliest work by a named English-born artist. That artist is John Bettes the Elder, about whom there is very little documentation in the historical record. The works that do survive have only been attributed to this Tudor-period artist, active between *c.* 1531 and *c.* 1570, on the basis of stylistic similarities, rather than being definitive autograph works. His one surviving autograph work, the Tate painting, is a portrait of an unknown man in a black cap (fig. 14), signed on the back in French 'faict par Johan Bettes Anglois' (done by John Bettes, Englishman), while on the front is inscribed 'ANNO D[OMIN]I 1545' (in the year of our lord 1545) and the sitter's age, given as twenty-six. The most plausible explanation for the first inscription being in French is that the picture was painted abroad, which could open up the possibility of the English-born Bettes being another itinerant artist, perhaps absorbing new techniques on his travels in much the same way as many foreign artists of the time.[1]

The painting's style makes it evident that Bettes was very much working in the manner of Holbein and may even have had some limited contact with him, further corroborated by his use of a pink primer on the canvas and the characteristic bluish-teal background, both used by the German artist. Unfortunately, for his background Bettes used a pigment known as smalt, made from ground glass, which would have produced a rich and vibrant blue at the time but was later discovered to be unstable. The result is that prolonged exposure to light has turned that vibrant blue into the muddy brown colour we see today, which is beyond retrieval with current restoration techniques.

The art historian Susan Foister has highlighted some crucial details regarding Bettes's technique, such as the loosely painted fur, the limited range of tones in his flesh painting and the flat and decorative nature of his beard painting, which suggest he is unlikely to have had the sort of close contact with Holbein that one would associate with an assistant.[2] But the close correlation in the style of his work with that of Holbein must surely have benefited Bettes's position, because he is recorded as working for Henry VIII at Whitehall Palace from 1531. Later, following the deaths of Holbein and Henry's chief miniaturist Lucas Horenbout, Bettes is recorded in the accounts of Queen Katherine Parr as receiving payments in 1546/47 for six painted portraits and some work in the art of 'lymning' (miniature painting). It is clear from these records and the few attributed works that survive not only that Bettes owed much to his foreign antecedents in terms of his success and the direction of travel in his work, but that, generally, success as a portrait artist in England at this time was predicated on emulating the style and fashion of these foreign artists. It is not known precisely when Bettes was born, but he is thought to have died in or before 1570.[3]

The English-born painter George Gower is a similarly elusive figure; we do not know when he was born and have little knowledge of his early life, except that he was a gentleman by birth, the grandson of Sir John Gower of Stittenham in Yorkshire. We do, however, have what is said to be the only known surviving self-portrait in large size by an English-born artist of the sixteenth century, dated 1579 (p.59).[4] The English obsession with both class and pictures of themselves furnished Gower not only with a living as a portrait painter but also the privilege of being one of the few English-born painters able to compete with the foreign incomers. Indeed, when text appears in his work it betrays a more than comfortable grasp of Latin, French and Italian, suggesting attendance of a very good school, commensurate with a well-to-do upbringing.[5] Such privilege clearly gave Gower the confidence to declare himself foremost

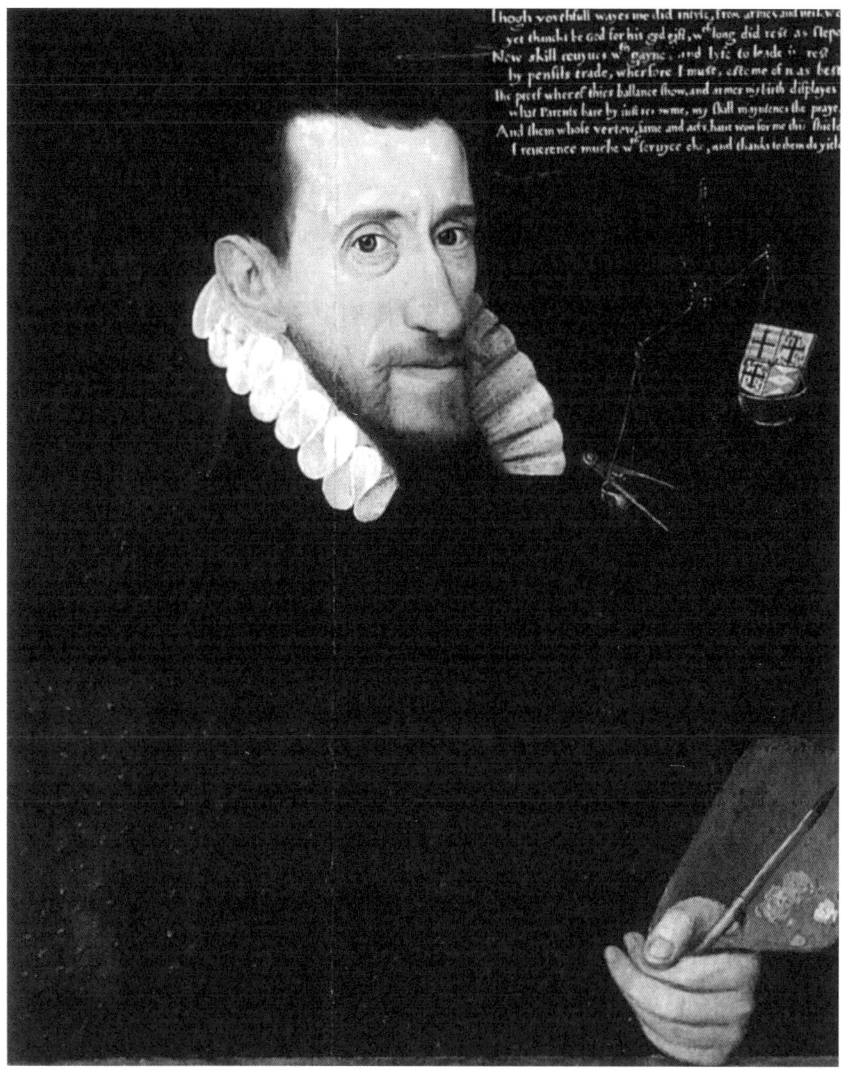

George Gower, *Self-Portrait*, 1579. Oil on canvas, 56.4 × 49.6 cm (22¼ × 19⅝ in.)

as an artist, above his rank as a gentleman, in his self-portrait. This kind of open declaration was unprecedented at a time when painters were viewed as little more than craftsmen dabbling in decorative interior design work, as was the duty of a Serjeant Painter. Gower depicts himself with paintbrush and palette in hand, and shows his family coat of arms outweighed in a balance by a pair of dividers, a symbol of the painter's craft. This is qualified further by an inscription that declares his pride in the profession of painting, comparing it to the military victories obtained by his forefathers, from which they gained their status. Needless to say, when one is in a position of privilege such modesty in the face of strict social hierarchies is not too difficult to achieve. So it comes as no surprise that just two years after painting the portrait of Elizabeth I known as *The Plimpton 'Sieve' Portrait* (fig. 13), in July 1581 Gower was made Serjeant Painter to the Queen.

The iconography of the sieve in Gower's portrait of the Queen alludes to the ancient Roman tale of the Vestal Virgin Tuccia, falsely accused of unchasteness, who set out to prove her virginity by carrying a sieve full of water from the river Tiber to Vesta's Temple without spilling a single drop; parallels with the Virgin Queen were clearly being drawn. The concept and format were picked up by foreign artists active at the Tudor court, including Quinten Massys the Younger, who later produced his own version of the sieve portrait. This proves that it was not just foreigners who were bringing innovation to English painting at this time.

Prior to Gower's appointment the main duties of the Serjeant Painter (a relatively new position, created around 1527) were mostly decorative painting, including an astronomical clock, coaches and furniture. Individuals who held the post before Gower included a Florentine artist, Antonio di Nunziato d'Antonio, called Anthony Toto, identified by Vasari as having worked with the Renaissance painter Ridolfo Ghirlandaio.[6] Toto arrived in England around 1519 to work as an assistant to his compatriot, the sculptor Pietro Torrigiano, who was already in the country; he was later naturalized and appointed Serjeant Painter by Henry VIII in 1543. But significantly, Gower appears to have been the first artist assigned to the office who specialized in portraiture.[7] His appointment acknowledged the progress and popularization of the portrait format by those foreign artists who had come before him; the portrait was now so mainstream as a genre that the Serjeant Painter was required to have this skill. That said, a draft patent of 1584 granting Gower a virtual monopoly in respect of producing all forms of royal portraits (except for miniatures, which were reserved exclusively for Nicholas Hilliard) is now suspected to have been penned by Gower himself.[8]

There also exists an undated commission that not only authorizes Gower to obtain via the royal purse all necessary materials for his work, but crucially grants him special permission to employ workmen and labourers, be they native-born or foreign.[9] The success afforded by such benefits arising from his documented position at court can be measured by the few, but important, works that remain, including a 1588 image of the Queen called the *Armada Portrait*, which survives in three versions (National Maritime Museum, London; National Portrait Gallery, London; and Woburn Abbey); unfortunately none of these portraits has so far been securely linked to Gower. There are, however, approximately a dozen or so portraits of various members of the aristocracy, some of which are considered autograph works. Gower's earliest surviving pictures, his portraits of Sir Thomas and Lady Kytson, only date back to 1573, payment details for which are confirmed in Kytson's accounts of September 1573 as twenty-five shillings each (pp. 62 and 63).[10] Most of Gower's portraits are busts or half-lengths, with the notable exception of a full-length portrait of Sir Thomas Cornwallis. The majority use a formulaic composition with the left shoulder nearest to the viewer as the sitter turns to look at them (this is reversed in the *Plimpton 'Sieve' Portrait*). There is little or no attempt to introduce any background, let alone landscape, with the odd exception such as the 1584 portrait of Sir Charles Somerset attributed to Gower (p. 64), in which the sitter's family coat of arms hangs from a nearby tree with a landscape beyond.

While it is important to note that there is debate surrounding the attribution of some of these works to Gower, the artist clearly held a privileged and favoured position, which in turn lessened the impact of foreign incomers on his practice while greatly enhancing his success in such a febrile environment. That said, recent evidence has come to light that Gower was perhaps not able to make a choice about whether

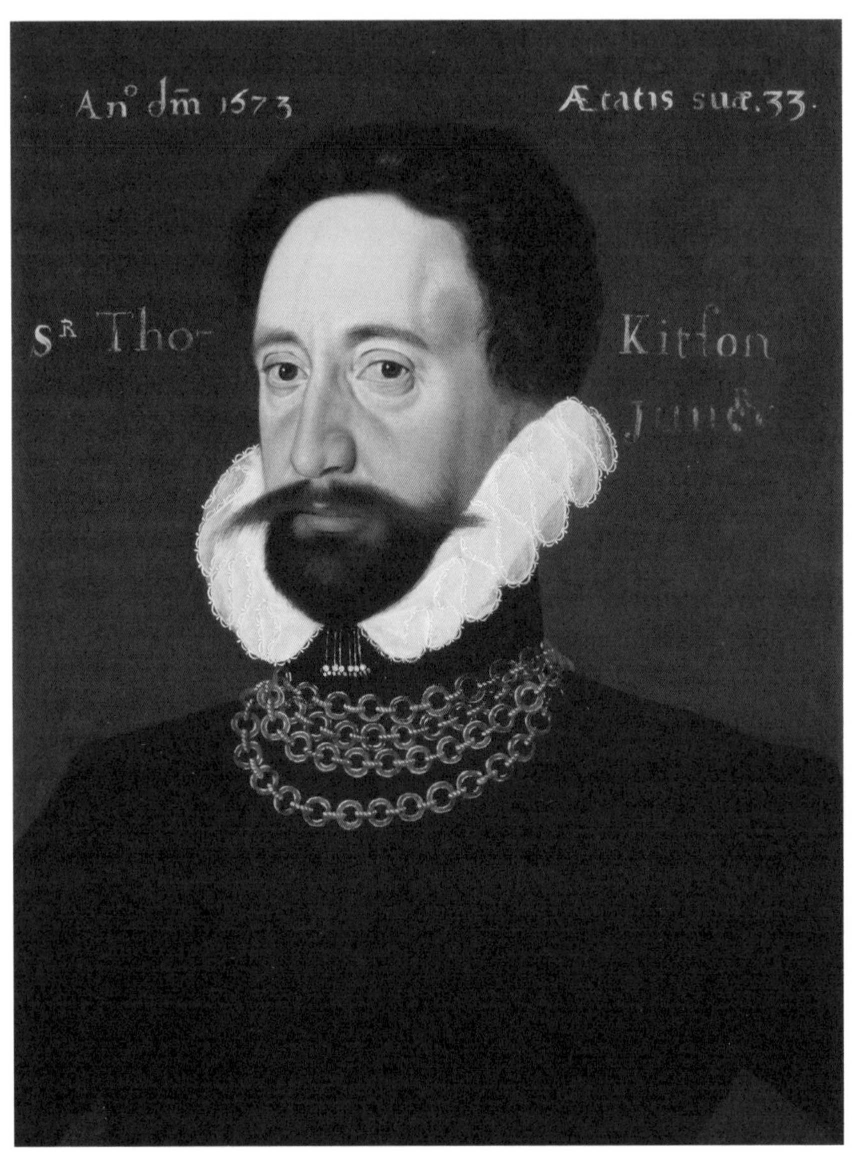

George Gower, *Sir Thomas Kytson*, 1573. Oil on oak, 52.7 × 40 cm (20¾ × 15¾ in.)

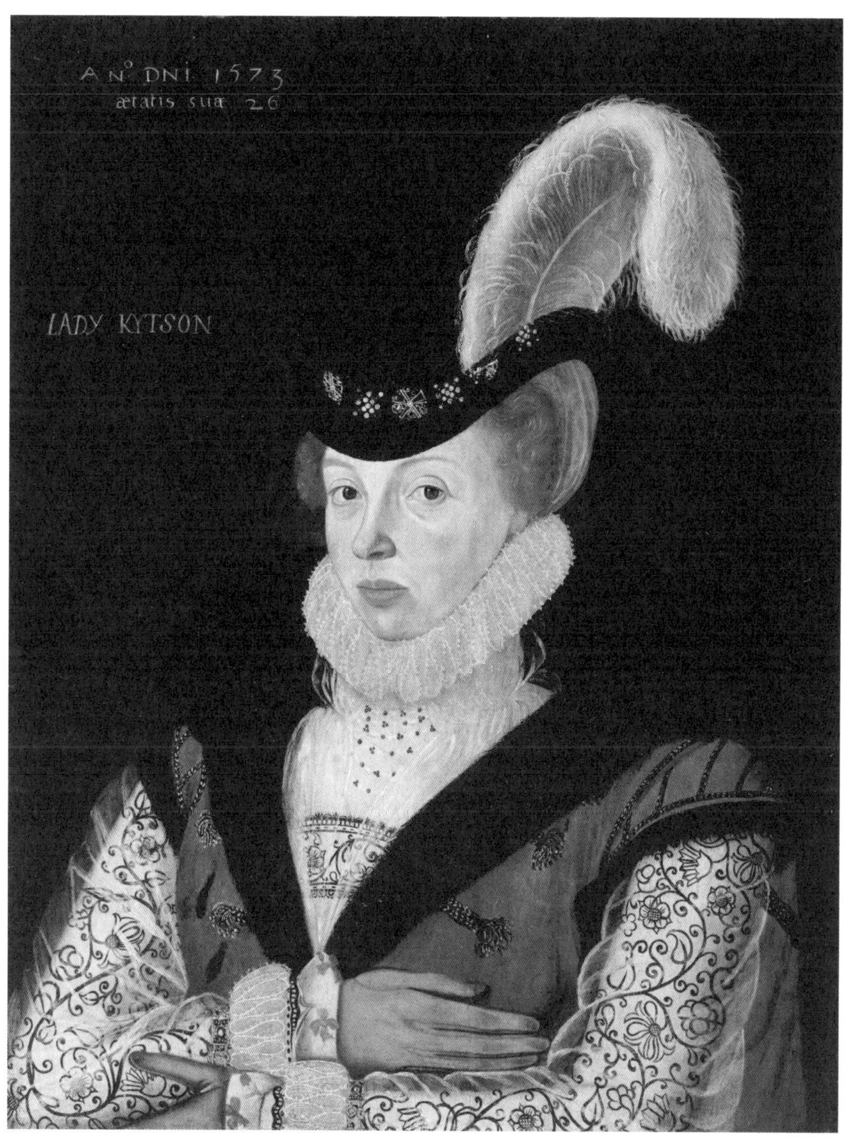

George Gower, *Elizabeth Cornwallis, Lady Kytson*, 1573.
Oil on oak, 68.5 × 52.2 cm (27 × 20⅝ in.)

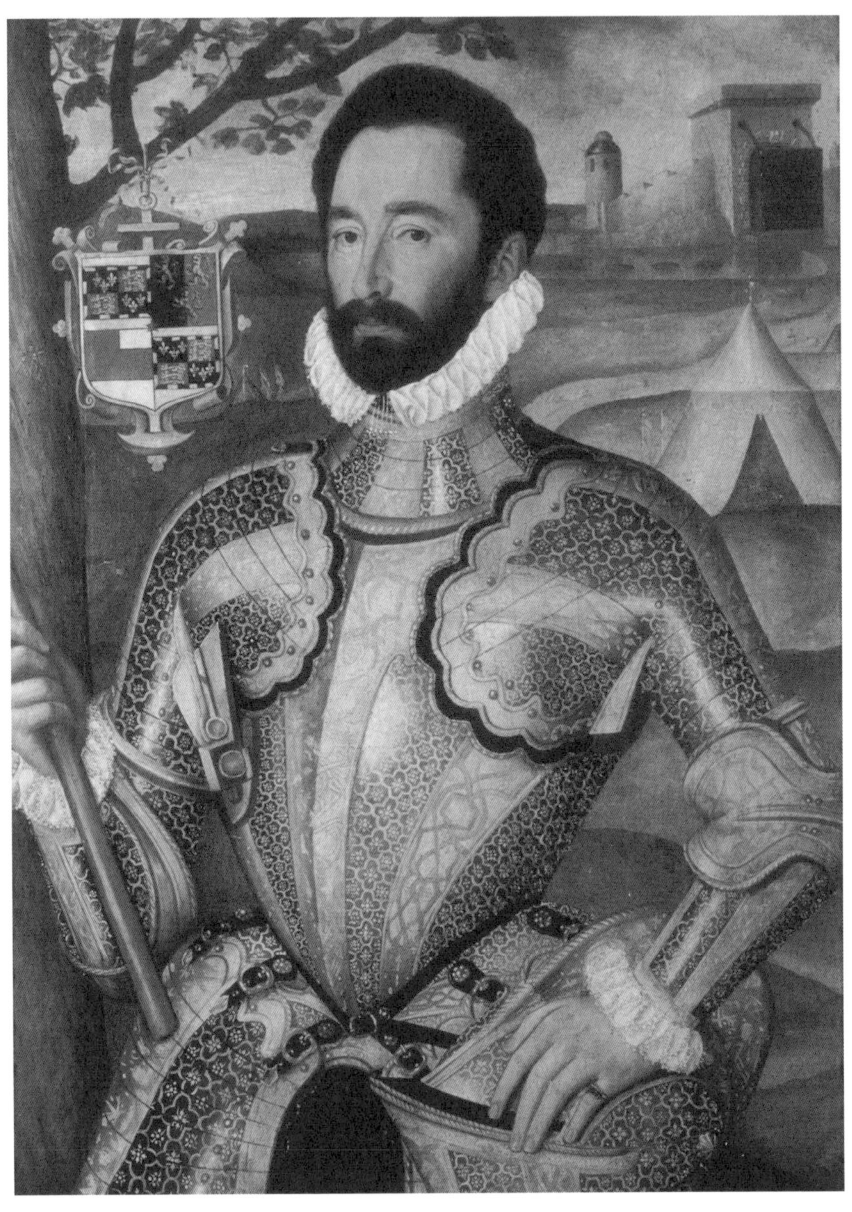

George Gower, *Sir Charles Somerset*, 1584. Oil on canvas, dimensions unknown

to work after all, because the bequest left to him in his father's will did not allow such a luxurious position.[11] He would remain in the service of the monarch until his death in the London parish of St Clement Danes in August 1596.[12]

In 1547, three years after the death of the miniaturist Lucas Horenbout, Nicholas Hilliard was born in Exeter, Devon. He is probably the first great English painter for whom we have not only a name but also a good deal of documentary evidence, along with surviving works. Hilliard was born the year Henry VIII died, marking the end of an intensely tumultuous period but a lucrative one for foreign artists. Nicholas trained with his father, Richard, as a goldsmith, a profession in which many of the great artists of the Italian Renaissance had also trained, including Andrea del Verrocchio, tutor of Leonardo da Vinci, the celebrated architect Filippo Brunelleschi and the famed sculptor Donatello. Unlike them, Hilliard would continue to practise this art throughout his professional life, alongside the work that made his name, the art of making miniatures. In Hilliard's time this was known as the art of limning, a term that drew on the art form's roots in illuminated manuscript production. From the early fifteenth century 'to limn' – from the Latin *luminare* – was used to describe the act of illumination, and later used to describe both manuscript illumination and making miniatures; within Hilliard's lifetime it was eventually overtaken by the word 'miniature'.[13]

The young Hilliard's introduction to the arts was enhanced by early experience of foreign travel, albeit under difficult circumstances. In 1549 his father, Richard, had been among those who defended the town of Exeter against a siege led by Catholics protesting the introduction of a Protestant prayer book. The accession of the Catholic Queen Mary I (r. 1553–58) to the English throne soon drove some Protestants into exile, including Richard and his son Nicholas, who travelled in the household of John Bodley, a wealthy Exeter merchant who had helped fund the Protestant cause. On the Continent the young Nicholas found himself part of a diverse international community, learning French as the Bodley retinue visited various European destinations including Wesel, Frankfurt, and eventually Geneva by 1557.[14] By the time it was safe to return to England with his father in 1559, following the 1558 accession of the Protestant Queen Elizabeth I, Hilliard was still only ten years old, having been away from home for just four years. They were undoubtedly formative ones, though, having an enormous impact on his life, and without this diverse international experience Hilliard arguably would not have become the artist he did.

By 1562, at the age of fifteen, Hilliard had taken up a goldsmithing apprenticeship with the royal goldsmith, Robert Brandon. Working with him would have given Hilliard his first contact with the art of the recent past in the royal collection. There he would have seen the work of Holbein and, crucially, miniaturist works by Lucas Horenbout and the Bruges-born Levina Teerlinc (1510s–1576), which would set Hilliard on a path that determined the direction of his art for the rest of his life. As the only limner from the Low Countries employed at Henry VIII's court after Holbein and Horenbout had died, Teerlinc, though much overlooked in recent years, represents an important chapter in the history and evolution of English art. Invited to England by Henry VIII (her name first appears in the court account books as 'king's paintrix' in January 1546), Teerlinc's success can be measured not only by her £40 annuity from the Crown for her services in the art of limning (a greater amount than Holbein and, for a time, Hilliard), but also by her continuing employment as court painter to the subsequent monarchs, Edward VI, Mary I and Elizabeth I. Like Horenbout, her background was in illuminated manuscript production, and she is likely to have first received training in this area from her father, Simon Bening, a seasoned practitioner in this profession. Teerlinc's work and influence on the art of miniature painting in England is crucially brought to bear in the period immediately preceding the arrival of Hilliard. Her importance is such that it was once thought she may have even been the tutor of the younger Hilliard, though that cannot be confirmed owing to the generic painting techniques used in this period, along with the condition and paucity of surviving works attributable to Teerlinc.[15] While much documentation regarding the commissioning of work from Teerlinc has survived, the difficulty of identifying extant works has been compounded, perhaps unsurprisingly, by the rise of the male, English-born limner Hilliard, whose reputation has eclipsed Teerlinc's contribution to British art right up to the present day.[16]

Following the end of Hilliard's apprenticeship, he was made a freeman of the Goldsmiths' Company in July 1569, which allowed him to practise independently. The earliest extant work from this period is a portrait of an unknown man dated 1571 (Portland Collection), but it is highly likely that he produced other works at this time that have not survived due to these objects' fragility and sensitivity to light. Some of this work must have garnered royal attention because he was swiftly appointed the official limner to Elizabeth I around 1570, the first English-born artist to assume this role. Hilliard made the earliest known miniature of Elizabeth I in 1572 (fig. 15).[17] In producing this work he was effectively continuing what by now had become an English tradition of *ad vivum* (from the life) monarch portraits. In his treatise of around 1600, now called *The Art of Limning*, Hilliard claimed he had learned his art from Holbein, who in turn had learned the art of limning from Lucas Horenbout. Although Holbein had died in 1543, and Horenbout a year later in 1544, the influence and legacy to English painting of these two important foreign artists still very much represented the height of taste and fashion among the aristocracy and nobility, a situation from which Hilliard's future career would benefit.

As well as these foreign influences at home, in September 1576 Hilliard ventured abroad to France as part of an English embassy led by Sir Amias Paulet, of whom Hilliard would produce a three-quarter-length portrait in the same period. His duties there appear to have included producing a good likeness of François, Duke of Anjou and Alençon, the youngest of Catherine de' Medici's sons and Elizabeth's suitor at the time. To achieve this, he had to become part of the duke's household and so was temporarily appointed in the standard role of *valet de chambre*, giving Hilliard the opportunity to set up a workshop in Paris specializing in miniatures and goldsmithing.[18] His experiences at the French court would have a lasting impact on Hilliard's art, and like Holbein before him, Hilliard perfected and excelled in the use of chalks in his portrait drawings there. The embassy to France must have been important for both painter and patron alike, and in fact he extended his stay, remaining there until 1578. However, this was not purely for artistic reasons, but rather was a desperate attempt by Hilliard to be properly remunerated for his services.

In a letter from Paulet to the Queen's secretary, Francis Walsingham, on 19 February, possibly 1577 or 1578,[19] the explanation given was that he wished to stay 'upon hope to get a piece of money of the lords and ladies here for his better maintenance in England'.[20] The letter foreshadows the financial problems that would plague Hilliard throughout his life.

Once back in England, Hilliard rose to be a court favourite, producing portraits of the Queen and numerous portrait miniatures of other prominent figures. These included a 1581 miniature of the English privateer Francis Drake, one of numerous portraits created of him around this time that were likely commissioned to aggrandize what would have been seen as the heroic exploits of Drake and his cousin, the naval commander John Hawkins (fig. 16). In 1562 Hawkins had embarked on his first slaving expedition, selling around three hundred enslaved people (either bought from African merchants on the Guinea Coast or hijacked from Portuguese slave traders) to Spanish colonizers in the Caribbean. Just two years after that first voyage, in 1564 Hawkins received royal endorsement of his activities when Elizabeth I loaned him her own seven-hundred-ton vessel *Jesus of Lübeck* along with three hundred men, expressly for the purpose of slaving. Later he was joined by his younger cousin Drake, and their subsequent expeditions established a slave trade that would contribute substantially to Britain's wealth and prosperity.

Other individuals at court whose likenesses were captured by Hilliard included Sir Walter Raleigh, then the Queen's favourite, in a miniature made around 1585 (p. 69). Raleigh's wife, Elizabeth, Lady Raleigh, was one of the first to popularize a fashion, driven by the exploits of Hawkins and Drake, for bringing Black slaves to Britain to work as domestic servants. Along with her husband, Lady Raleigh had her portrait painted in 1595 by the English-born artist Sir William Segar (p. 69).[21] Such was the quality of Segar's painting that he was previously thought to have been born in Holland, again reinforcing the idea that fine work could only be achieved by foreign artists. These works clearly demonstrate the enchantment of the English aristocracy with the genre of portraiture at this time.

Hilliard's rising fame at court, both at home and abroad, resulted in an increasingly busy workshop to supply the numerous commissions

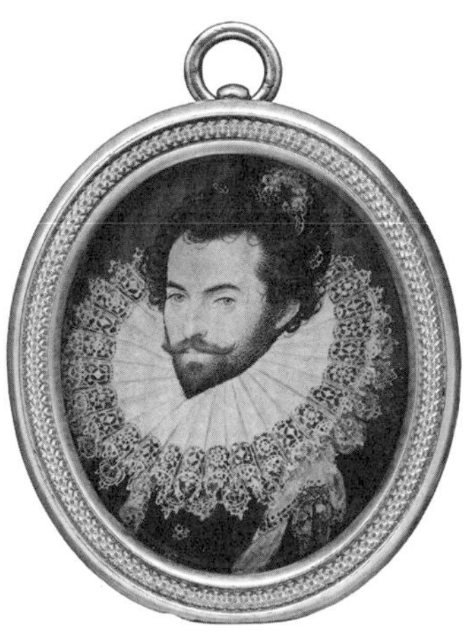

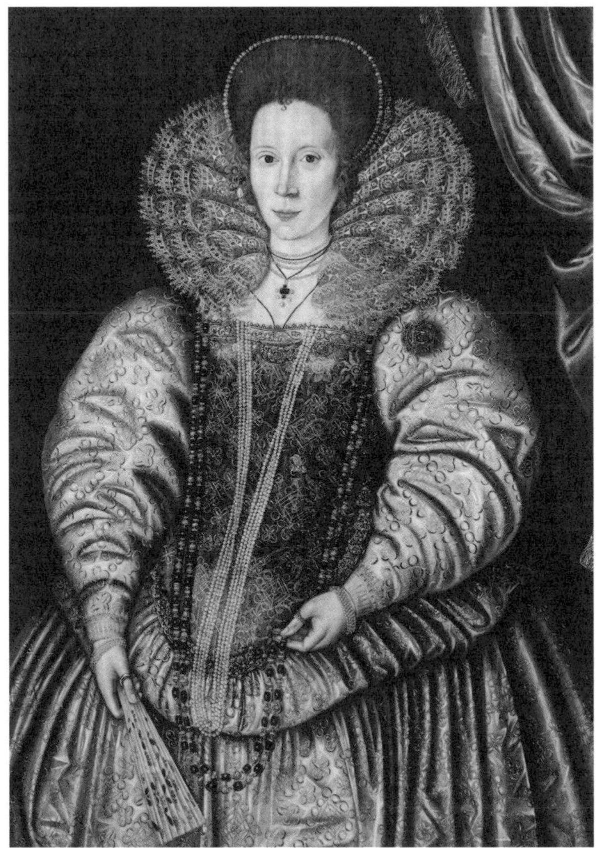

TOP Nicholas Hilliard, *Sir Walter Raleigh*, *c.* 1585.
Watercolour on vellum, 4.8 × 4.1 cm (2 × 1⅝ in.)

ABOVE Sir William Segar, *Elizabeth 'Bess' Throckmorton,
Lady Raleigh*, 1595. Oil on panel, 110 × 79 cm (43⅜ × 31⅛ in.)

from those in powerful positions, including the Queen herself, but this did not shield Hilliard from mounting debts. His financial problems were not helped by a series of ill-judged investments, including one in which he went into business with two Dutch artists, Cornelis de Vos and Arnold van Bronckhorst, which saw him lose his entire stake in a failed gold-prospecting venture in Scotland. This was followed by involvement with a discredited goldsmith called William Laborer, with whom he pitched for a government contract to make road repairs; this scheme also failed.[22] Making financial investments requires a cool head and a lack of desperation, neither of which Hilliard seems to have been blessed with. Unfortunately, the art historical record is littered with creatives who suffered from a chronic inability to manage their financial affairs, and Hilliard was no exception.

There were, however, other mitigating factors that fuelled Hilliard's increasingly precarious situation; despite being in such high demand, incredibly he was not in receipt of a regular wage from the Crown and so was forced to make money in any way he could to support his family and household. In 1595 a failed attempt to redeem the mortgage on his house resulted in the artist being bailed out by one of his patrons, Robert Devereux, 2nd Earl of Essex. In the following years Hilliard's work expanded to include collaborations with Derrick Anthony, chief engraver at the Royal Mint, where he designed Elizabeth I's second Great Seal; however, his payment of £40 for this was what is known as 'a lease in reversion', a promise of a yearly payment on his death. After years of hardship, Hilliard petitioned the Queen's senior minister, Sir Robert Cecil, despairing that his lack of salary had 'brought him into great extremes', and in August 1599 he finally received a salary of £40 a year. However, this payment clearly came too late and was not enough to alleviate Hilliard's financial problems, because he subsequently fell behind with his rent and had to be bailed out again, this time by the Privy Council. Once more he sought an escape from his financial woes through travel to France, a clear measure of the high regard in which his talents were held in that country. In 1601 he wrote again to Cecil seeking permission to travel to remedy his debt problems, but unfortunately the request was refused, the suggestion being that Hilliard was in danger of being poached by the French court. The refusal proves just how important an artist Hilliard was to the Queen, despite his poor remuneration.[23] This could also be said to demonstrate, however, that when it came to recognizing the need to properly renumerate talented craftspeople, clients on the Continent were more appreciative and forthcoming with their patronage. When Hilliard attended the funeral of Elizabeth I at Westminster Abbey in April 1603, he received four yards of black cloth for his livery.[24]

On the accession to the throne of James I, Hilliard maintained his position and for the first time received a regular annual pension of £40, which was paid quarterly. This sum did not include individual payments for works commissioned from his workshop by royal and non-royal patrons.[25] But the Queen Consort, Anne, and her eldest son, Henry, Prince of Wales, chose as their principal miniaturist Isaac Oliver (*c.* 1565–1617), whom Hilliard had trained, immediately paying the younger artist a salary that was equal to Hilliard's hard-fought settlement. Oliver had arrived in London as a Huguenot child refugee and as he grew up he retained his links with the Continent, reflected in a style that was seen in England as avant-garde and more fashionable than that of native-born artists. Once again, the penchant for foreign-born artists, including those who retained their international connections, trumped indigenous painters. It has been plausibly suggested by the art historian Elizabeth Goldring that Hilliard's spiralling descent into financial ruin resulted in part from the death in 1612 of his fabulously wealthy protector, Sir Robert Cecil, 1st Earl of Salisbury, Lord Treasurer and Secretary of State to James I. The situation would severely compromise Hilliard's financial stability; in fact a late payment of £104 made by Cecil's son William, relating to outstanding payment owed for commissioned work, was eventually paid after Hilliard's death to his son Laurence, which serves to underline how unfortunate the artist's financial situation was.[26]

There are, of course, many examples of inequitable pay among incoming artists, some detailed in this book, but such competition served only to further undermine the status of English-born artists. Paradoxically, Hilliard's treatment at the hands of the English Crown proved that the French Crown was clearly more appreciative of his skills; indeed, the physician and amateur artist Richard Haydock commented on the foreign appreciation of Hilliard's work, remarking that he was 'much admired amongst strangers'.[27] Such financial travails were faced by many artists across the centuries both in Britain and on the Continent, and were indicative of the perceived low social status of painters, often termed craftspeople or manual labourers, unlike writers who were viewed as intellects. However, with the championing of the visual arts, at least on the Continent, by writers such as Vasari, the position of artists in society began to improve, and as artists themselves studied classical literature not only to meet the creative needs of their educated patrons but also to improve their own station in life, a slow but inevitable transformation took place in the societies in which these artists plied their trade.

In fact, across a period spanning the 1490s to the 1650s, England witnessed a flourishing of English-born humanist writers, including the antiquarian and historian William Camden and playwrights and poets such as Ben Jonson, William Shakespeare and John Ford. This was a period of immense homegrown literary and artistic activity that could easily be characterized as an English Renaissance, eventually morphing into a period of Baroque excess. Even before the arrival in Britain of artist intellects such as Rubens and Van Dyck, Hilliard had signalled in his own treatise his admiration of the artists of the past such as Holbein and Dürer, along with his interest in the writings of Alberti. But unlike works by Italian writers, Hilliard's treatise would remain in manuscript form until it was finally published in 1912, suggesting there was little interest in this aspect of his work. Hilliard was somewhat ahead of his time: it was not yet the moment, at least in Britain, for artists also to be writers and intellectuals. Yet, although not widely acknowledged in the period, his treatise could at least be identified as an early attempt to lend further intellectual respectability to the visual arts in Britain, as the earlier Renaissance writers had achieved in Italy.[28]

The extent to which skilled craftsmen like Hilliard were entirely dependent on the benevolence of royalty and those in inherited positions of power was laid bare in the final tumultuous years of the artist's life. On 11 July 1612, just weeks after Cecil's death, in a seemingly desperate situation Hilliard signed a bond with William Pereman, a yeoman usher of the King's Chamber, in which he promised to pay back a £40 loan. Given that this was an entire year's wage for Hilliard, there seemed little prospect that he would be able to return such a sum, which he had spent in full by at least September that year. He was forced to borrow again, this time the sum of £2 from a fellow goldsmith, Sir William Herrick, Jeweller to the Crown. He could only repay this loan by pawning some of his miniatures. Hilliard would spend the last few years of his life firefighting his way out of mounting debts; so much so that, at the age of seventy, he found himself suffering the indignity of imprisonment at the debtors' prison Ludgate, from which he was released in January 1618. Hilliard died around the age of seventy-two, and although his will stipulated that he would leave a sum of £80, in reality this was based on the amount owed to him in lieu of pension instalments and the predicted sale price of his household goods. Actual cash assets amounted to twenty shillings, left to his sister Anne.[29] He was buried at St Martin-in-the-Fields in January 1619.

Living almost exactly concurrently with Hilliard, and firmly embedded among a coterie of foreign artists in London, was the English-born artist Robert Peake the Elder. Like Hilliard he also trained as a goldsmith and was apprenticed at the same time. Once qualified as independent masters, they established their workshops in close proximity to each other in Goldsmiths' Row, Westcheap, an area in the City of London now known as Cheapside.[30] Although we have no firm information concerning his date of birth, there are details about Peake's artistic life as a portraitist and decorative painter active in the later part of Elizabeth I's reign and for most of James I's. He achieved a measure of success, possibly owing to his association with artists such as Marcus Gheeraerts the Younger, Isaac Oliver and John de Critz the Elder, all of whom had workshops in London drawing on each other's expertise. In 1604 Peake was appointed picture maker to Henry Frederick, Prince of Wales and heir apparent of James I and VI; unfortunately the Prince died tragically in 1612, aged just eighteen. But significantly Peake's most important appointment, as Serjeant Painter to James I in 1607, was shared with de Critz.[31]

In surviving court records and royal accounts, English-born painters frequently seem to be mentioned in connection with decorative tasks such as the painting of interiors, furniture, banners or a royal boat. But on his appointment as Serjeant Painter to James I, Peake's duties would mainly be the execution of royal portraits, while de Critz was in charge of a large department responsible for managing all decorative projects within the royal court, palaces and other residences, effectively making him Peake's line manager.[32]

It is worth noting at this point that the local painters were very xenophobic, jealously guarding their right to operate within the area of the City of London as laid out by the Painter-Stainers' Company of London, which fiercely protected its members. Company records show that in 1488 a painter petitioned the mayor to deal with 'the multitude of foreyns repairing daily to the said citee'.[33] In this context 'foreyns' (foreigners) meant anyone from outside of the City of London, whether English or from abroad. The move against all foreign encroachment on lucrative City of London trade was further consolidated in 1492, when the Painter-Stainers' Company demanded that no painters within the City were permitted to employ foreigners (from beyond the City) if they could not in the first instance acquire equivalent painters at the same cost within the City of London. We could argue that such attempts to preserve 'British jobs for British workers' (a rallying cry used by a former prime minister) have always been deeply flawed, achieving little more than damage to economic prosperity.

But from a positive perspective, like many such systems this one was inherently porous, and foreigners clearly found ways around the restrictions because the records show that there were many immigrants living in London in this period, specializing in a variety of trades such as goldsmithing, fabric manufacture and painting.[34] And those with a newly acquired status as denizen, such as Lucas Horenbout, were allowed to take on assistants in their now permitted establishment of workshops. But it is interesting to note that, of the four assistants Horenbout employed, none was a native-born Englishman. Such employment opportunities could only lead to improvement and innovation in the workshops of the foreign painters, as those assistants and journeymen brought with them the latest techniques from abroad, which would then be incorporated into the master's style and proliferate widely, becoming the predominant painting style in Britain. If this indeed is taken to be the case, the opposite could be said to be true of English-born painters and their workshops, which were not permitted to employ foreign workers. This surely meant that the unforeseen result of protectionism was the prosperity and success of the foreign painters' workshops to the detriment of the English ones.

By this time dissent against foreign workers had been growing in England for well over a century; in 1470 Kentish rioters had descended on the capital attacking the homes of Flemish and German immigrants,[35] while the so-called 'Evil May Day' anti-alien riots in the spring of 1517 saw hundreds of Londoners ransacking the homes and businesses of immigrants in an attempt to destroy their livelihoods and create a hostile environment for aliens, as they were called, most of whom were from the Low Countries and France, with some from Italy and various German states. The extent of the unrest stretched from Newgate Prison in the west of the city, where the rioters freed men who had previously attacked immigrants, to Blanchappleton near Aldgate in the east. It was eventually brought to an end, and the next day hundreds of rioters were arrested, charged with treason and hanged for attacking foreigners who were considered under the protection of the King, Henry VIII, though some were pardoned. The events were later chronicled and published in 1548 by Edward Hall, a Member of Parliament.[36]

The 1560s and 1570s saw an influx of around 2,200 foreigners into London, fuelled by the Spanish persecution of Protestants in the Netherlands (see Chapter Two) and to a lesser extent the St Bartholomew's Day massacre of French Protestants in August 1572; by the 1570s the foreign population in London is thought to have swelled to between 9,000 and 10,000, representing at least a tenth of the city's total population.[37] Rather than the negative impact irrationally feared by those who had rioted, this immigration resulted in a long-term positive contribution to British culture and the economy. The Dutch and Flemish communities of artisans and craftspeople in London significantly increased the production and range of luxury goods available in the city, which in turn forced the native workers to up their game to compete with the incomers. To avoid the strict guild rules that favoured English-born artists and citizens, the foreign artists set up their workshops beyond the City limits, in places such as Southwark. Much like immigrant communities in modern London, a visit to these areas would open the senses to a multitude of new ideas and experiences, as though one was actually in the Low Countries. Eventually the new artistic skills brought by the settling foreigners and their offspring soon seeped into native practice. Such an outcome was inevitable, because although the Painter-Stainers' Company tried its very best to segregate the foreigners' painting practice from that of their own native members, both communities still had to source the same supplies such as oils, pigments, canvas and panel from the same purveyors, and so would come into daily contact with each other, leading to the native-born artists wanting to emulate the successful style of the foreign ones.[38] Indeed, by the first decade of the seventeenth century the Anglo-Netherlandish tradition in painting would start to meld with the indigenous style, becoming indistinguishable from what would come to be called the 'British school'.[39]

Nevertheless, these positive gains were seldom acknowledged or even recognized by the native population, the result of which was growing resentment, represented by the Painter-Stainers' Company, which became increasingly vocal over the influx of foreign painters, which it characterized as 'the tide of foreign painters entering London and threatening their livelihoods'. These tensions came to a head on 15 November 1575 when the Company petitioned the Queen, remarking that over the past twelve years they had witnessed a visible decline in the painters' craft, 'by such as never have bene brought vp in the knowledge of painting as well in counterfeyting of your majesties picture and pictures of noblemen and others'.[40] In another petition, this time addressed to Lord Burghley, the Painter-Stainers accused heralds of attempting to rob them of their livelihood.[41] With a historic role announcing knights at jousting events, heralds were also the disseminators and record-keepers of coats of arms, which amounted to being gatekeepers of the nobility. Their responsibilities included the painting of arms, but they were also itinerant free lances (from where the term freelancers derives) hired for jousting occasions.[42] The Painter-Stainers' complaint derived from the fact that the heralds were actually a subsect of the Company and were encroaching into areas of interior design that were the province of the painters.

The Painter-Stainers' Company also worked with local government to make it as difficult as possible for outsiders from France and the Low Countries, as well as those Englishmen not in their guild, to take work from them.[43] In 1578 two hundred London painter-stainers signed a petition against the operation of foreign artists in the city. In essence the guilds were incensed that their members were not able to practise their trades without the irritation of competition.[44] Eventually the Painter-Stainers' Company acted without any laws in place and began to ban the opening of any new shops or workshops by anyone other than English-born painters, or at least denizens, going so far as to blacklist English painters who dared to employ foreign-born apprentices. The complaints would eventually lead to a full charter and licence being granted to the Painter-Stainers in 1581, allowing them to enact measures against the outsiders.[45] This piece of legislation, what we would now call positive discrimination, would eventually give native-born artists opportunities to obtain much more prestigious commissions.

The dominance of the foreign style could not have been lost on native painters such as Robert Peake, whose decorative effects and use of landscape in the background of his portrait of Princess Elizabeth of Bohemia (p. 78), more than likely painted as a pendant to his portrait of Henry Frederick, Prince of Wales (fig. 17), demonstrate the clear influence of his foreign contemporaries. Not only did Peake embrace the burgeoning popularity of the full-length portrait, no doubt made fashionable by foreign artists such as Gheeraerts the Younger, but he was also clearly enamoured of the Netherlandish artist's innovation of placing his sitters in landscaped surroundings. Also seen in Peake's work, no doubt due to patronal interest, is a clear leaning towards exploiting his ability to render realistic decorative effects in both fabrics and interior surroundings. Peake and Hilliard had been closely linked in their practice throughout their lives, and both died in the same year, 1619. But Hilliard left no dynasty to carry on his legacy, with his son Laurence never achieving the heights of his father, whereas Peake's son William went on to be a successful painter and printseller, and his grandson, Sir Robert Peake, was also a successful printseller.

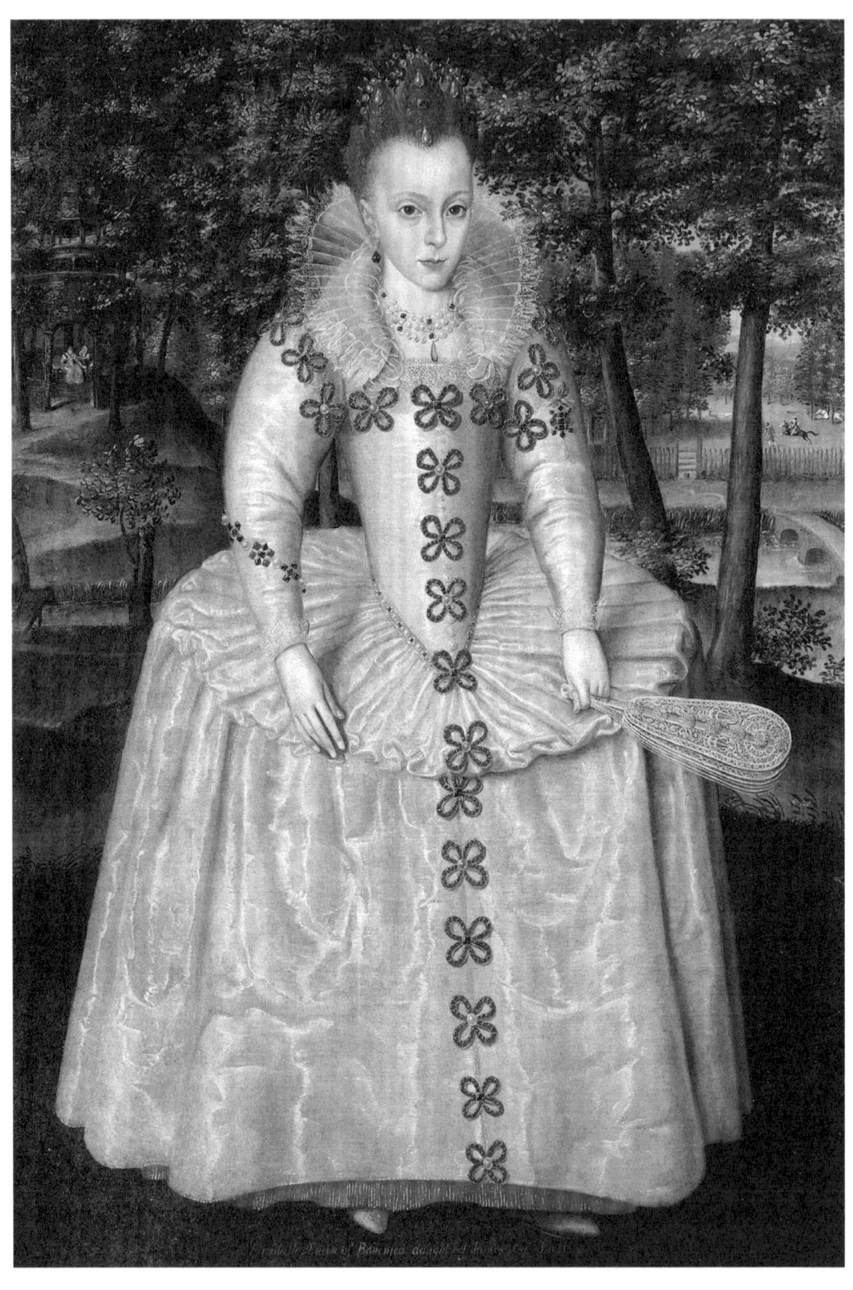

Robert Peake, *Princess Elizabeth of Bohemia, The Winter Queen aged 7*, 1603.
Oil on canvas, 135.9 × 95.2 cm (53⅝ × 37½ in.)

So far this period of innovation, integration and foreign influence on English art has been mostly concentrated around the practice of portraiture. But an exception is Sir Nathaniel Bacon, who was responsible for producing what is currently acknowledged to be the earliest surviving landscape painting by an English-born artist. The small oil painting, on unprimed copper backed with oak panel, has no precise date but could have been made any time between 1600 and the artist's death in 1627. Remarkably it precedes the advent of Dutch landscape painting, which only began to rise in popularity from the 1630s onwards; unusually for an English artist of this period, it is known that Bacon travelled frequently to the Low Countries, including a recorded visit to Antwerp in late 1613. In an age when landscape painting was in its infancy, it is possible that with this solitary survival Bacon may have even managed to steal a march on the great Dutch landscape painters who would come to dominate the genre only a few decades later. Indeed, the newness of the genre was made clear by the limner, musician and writer on art Edward Norgate, who bemoaned the fact that no word in the English language was adequate to describe this new mode of painting; he did acknowledge that the genre came from abroad, specifically from the Low Countries, when he used the Dutch word *landschap*, which would later be anglicized to landscape.[46]

Further Continental influence can be recognized in Bacon's most well-known work, *Cookmaid with Still Life of Vegetables and Fruit*, made around 1620–25 (fig. 19). The painting owes a great deal to the sixteenth-century Flemish artist Joachim Beuckelaer, from whom Bacon certainly drew inspiration for this work (fig. 18). Indeed, Beuckelaer himself drew on an existing tradition of paintings practised by his master Pieter Aertsen. These works presented themselves as mere market or kitchen tableaux, but in fact functioned as sophisticated moral narratives, with biblical scenes in the background indicating that the abundance displayed in the foreground should not be taken for granted.[47] Bacon's work contains no such religious allusions, but rather indulges in the English preoccupations of satire coupled with sexual innuendo. The association of large breasts with melons is difficult to miss, with the strategically placed fruit cut open and propped on the table at just the right angle to echo the cookmaid's plunging cleavage (the artist is in fact known to have grown melons on his East Anglia estate Brome, which probably offered him the perfect excuse). That aside, the subject is just as it purports to be: a woman at a market stall. This allegorical picture, neither landscape nor portrait, is certainly unusual for an English artist of this period, but increasingly not so among Continental artists.

Paradoxically, Bacon's status as an amateur artist makes it difficult to claim him as a successful early example of indigenous English art, despite his innovative landscape painting. Nor was he the earliest English-born painter to be knighted for artistic talent: it is clear that the knighthood afforded to him in 1626, Charles I's coronation year, resulted instead from his marriage to Jane, Lady Cornwallis, widow of Sir William Cornwallis and mother of Frederick Cornwallis, 1st Baron Cornwallis. Even before this Bacon was well connected: his grandfather, Sir Nicholas Bacon, was the Lord Keeper under Queen Elizabeth I and he was also related to the influential politician and philosopher Sir Francis Bacon. Bacon's aristocratic status is mentioned by Henry Peacham in *The Gentleman's Exercise* of 1622, where he is described as a prime example of an upper-class Englishman with the ability to paint, later adding that no one 'deserveth more respect and admiration for his skill and practice herein…not inferiour in my judgement to our skilfullest Masters'.[48] He died at the age of forty-two on his other East Anglia estate, Culford Hall, where he was buried on 1 July 1627. It would not be until Sir James Thornhill, William Hogarth's father-in-law, was knighted in May 1720 that a native-born English artist would obtain the accolade for services to the visual arts.

As we have seen throughout this chapter, this was a period of exciting artistic innovation, driven by immigration and integration but also coloured by tensions, fear and conflict. The long view demonstrates a wide-ranging advantage to English commerce and culture, but this did not come without a cost, especially to those who did not reap any of the rewards or benefits resulting from the influx of prosperity. The growing wealth accumulated from the burgeoning trade in enslaved people created fertile ground for consumerism through exploitation, which increased exponentially over the following centuries. Nevertheless, against a background of defensive prejudice and perceived protectionism, the valuable

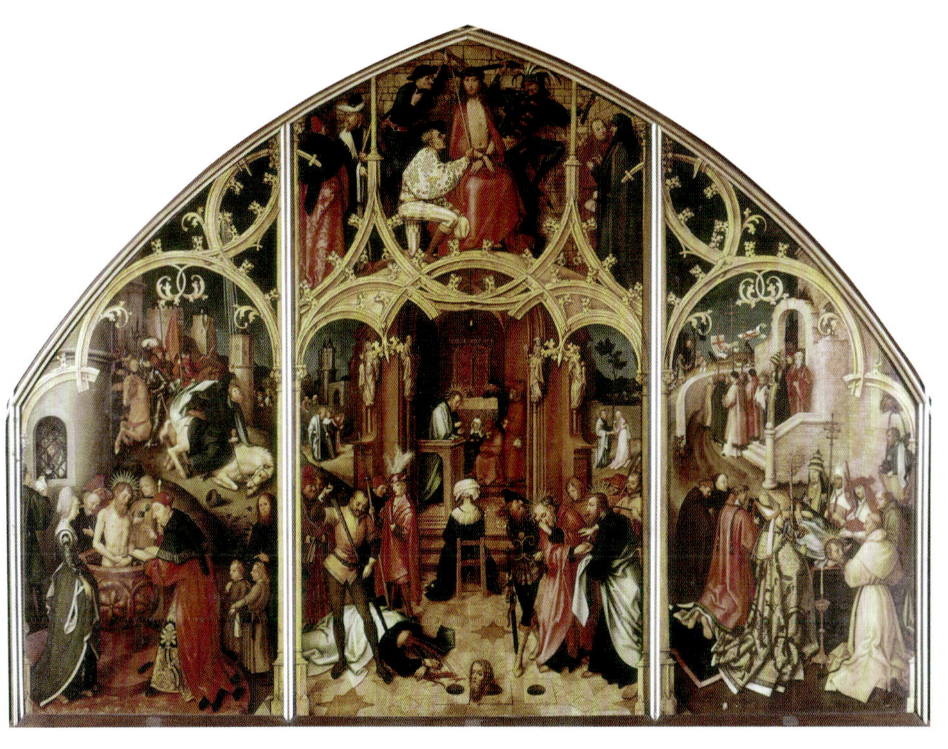

1 Hans Holbein the Elder, *Basilica of San Paolo fuori le Mura*, central panel: *Scenes from the Legend of St Paul*, *c.* 1504. Oil on wood, 217.2 × 125.5 cm (85⅝ × 49½ in.)

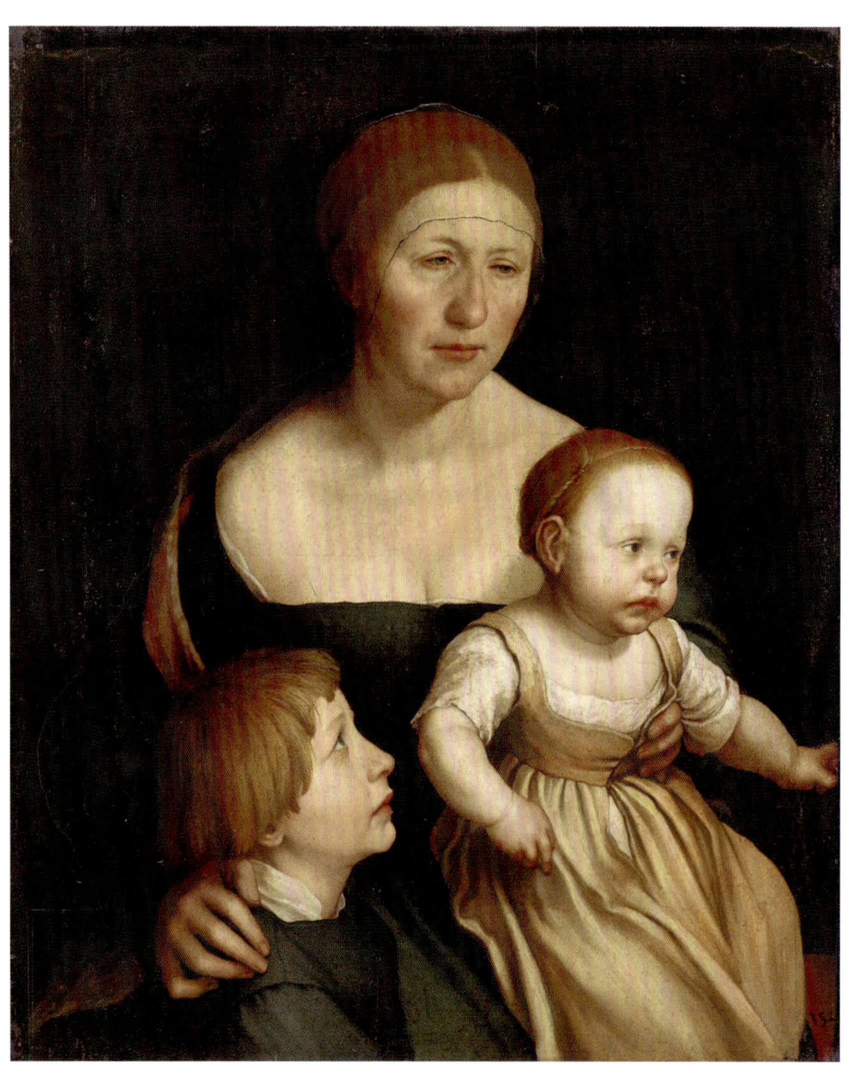

2 Hans Holbein the Younger, *The Artist's Wife with their Two Elder Children*, 1528–29. Mixed media on paper, cut out at the figure contours and mounted on wood, 79.4 × 64.7 cm (31⅜ × 25½ in.)

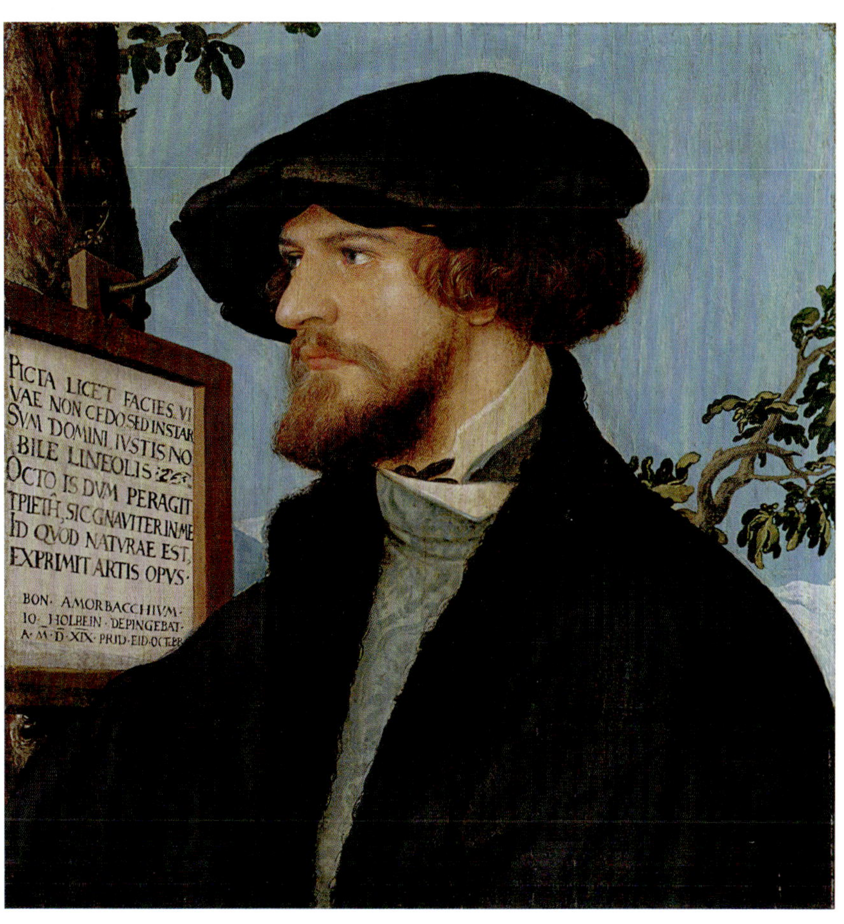

3 Hans Holbein the Younger, *Bonifacius Amerbach*, 1519.
Mixed media on wood, 29.9 × 28.3 cm (11⅞ × 11¼ in.)

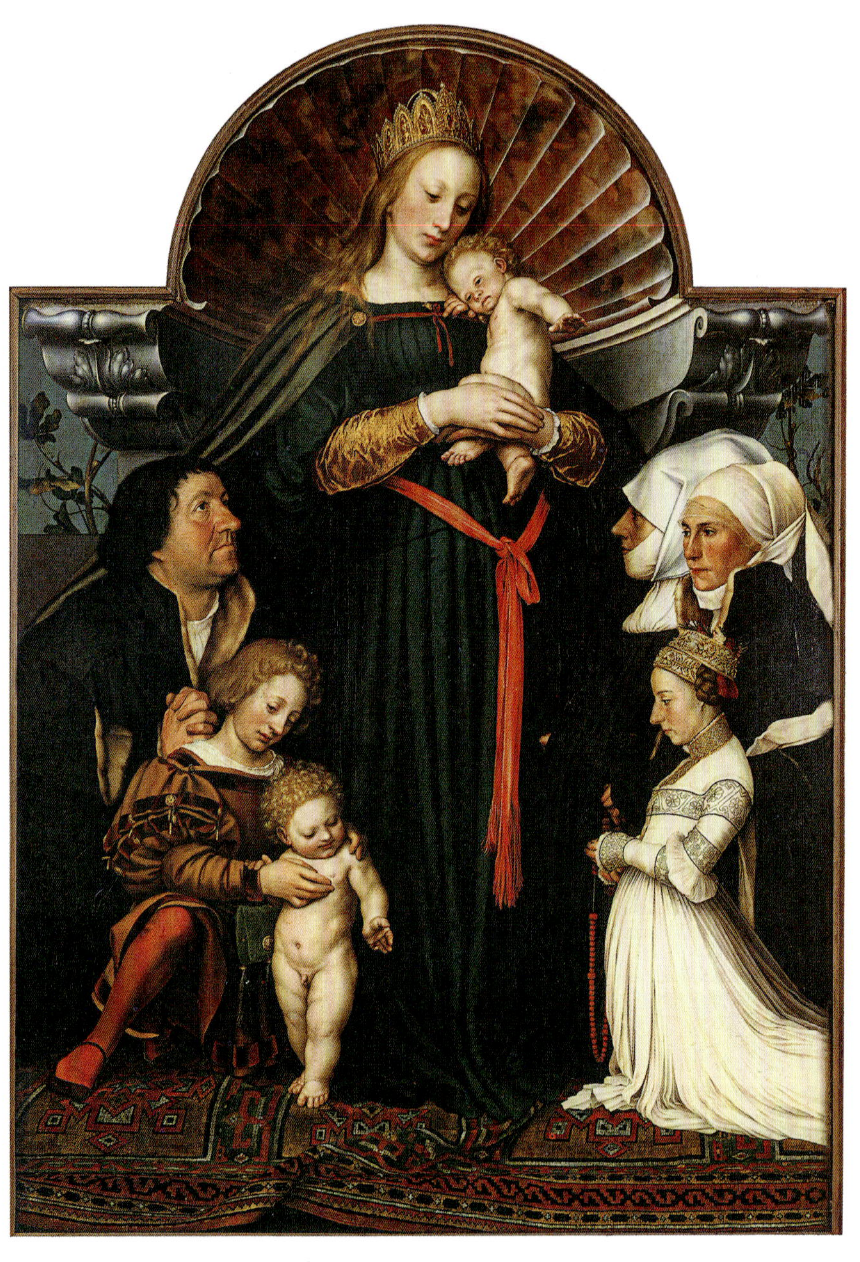

4 Hans Holbein the Younger, *Madonna of the Lord Mayor Jakob Meyer zum Hasen (Darmstadt Madonna)*, 1526–28. Oil on wood, 146.5 × 102 cm (57⅝ × 40 in.)

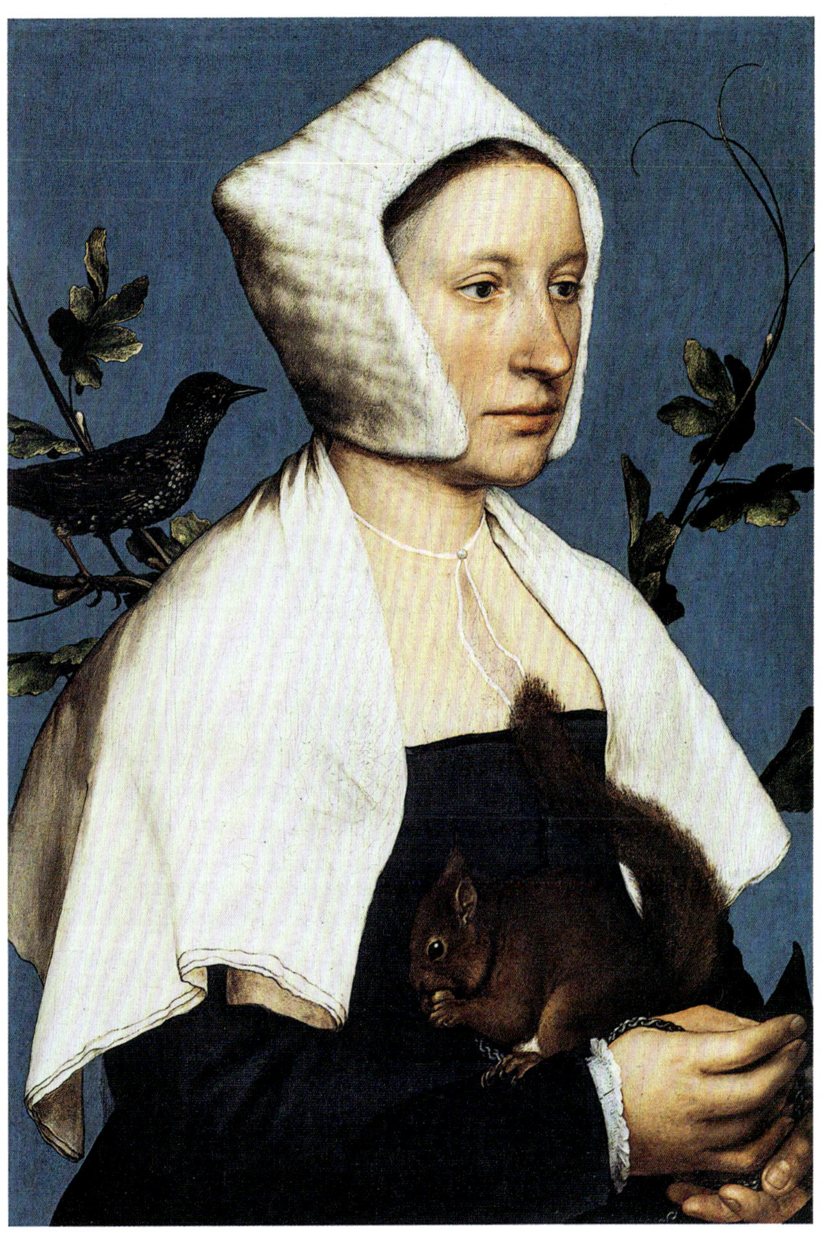

5 Hans Holbein the Younger, *A Lady with a Squirrel and a Starling, probably Anne Lovell*, *c.* 1526–28. Oil on oak panel, 56 × 38.8 cm (22⅛ × 15⅜ in.)

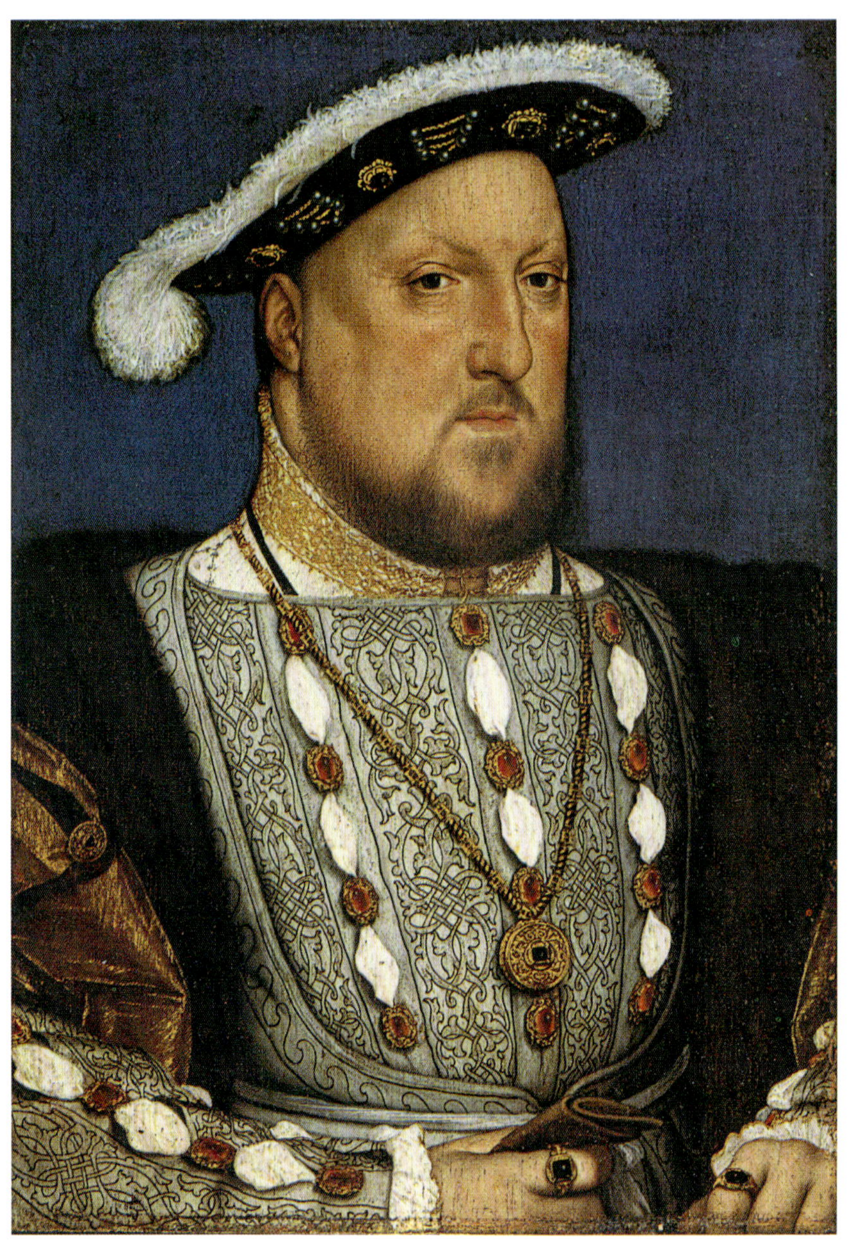

6 Hans Holbein the Younger, *Henry VIII*, *c*. 1537.
Oil on panel, 28 × 20 cm (11⅛ × 7⅞ in.)

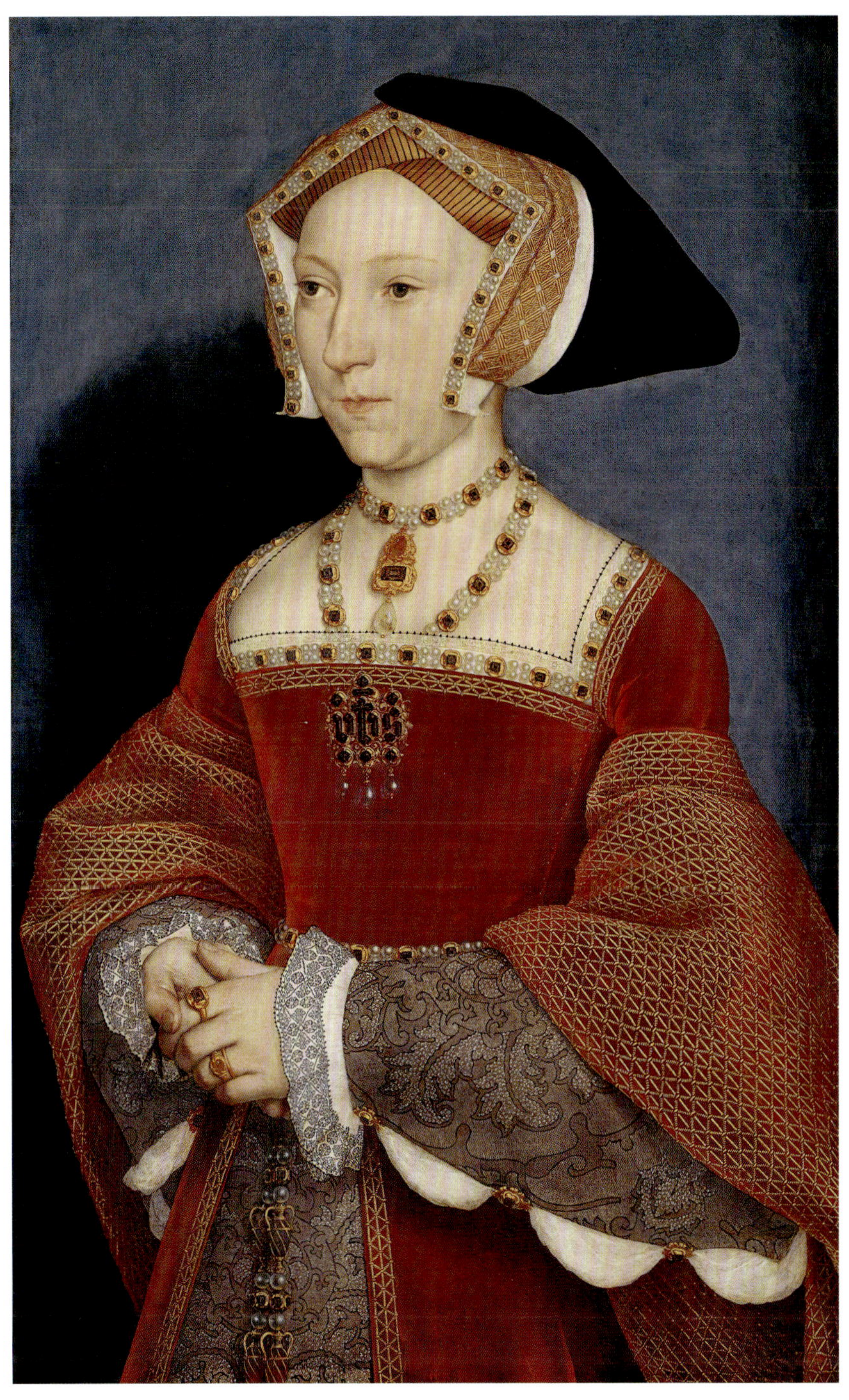

7 Hans Holbein the Younger, *Jane Seymour*, *c.* 1536–37.
Oil on oak, 65.5 × 47 cm (25⅞ × 18⅝ in.)

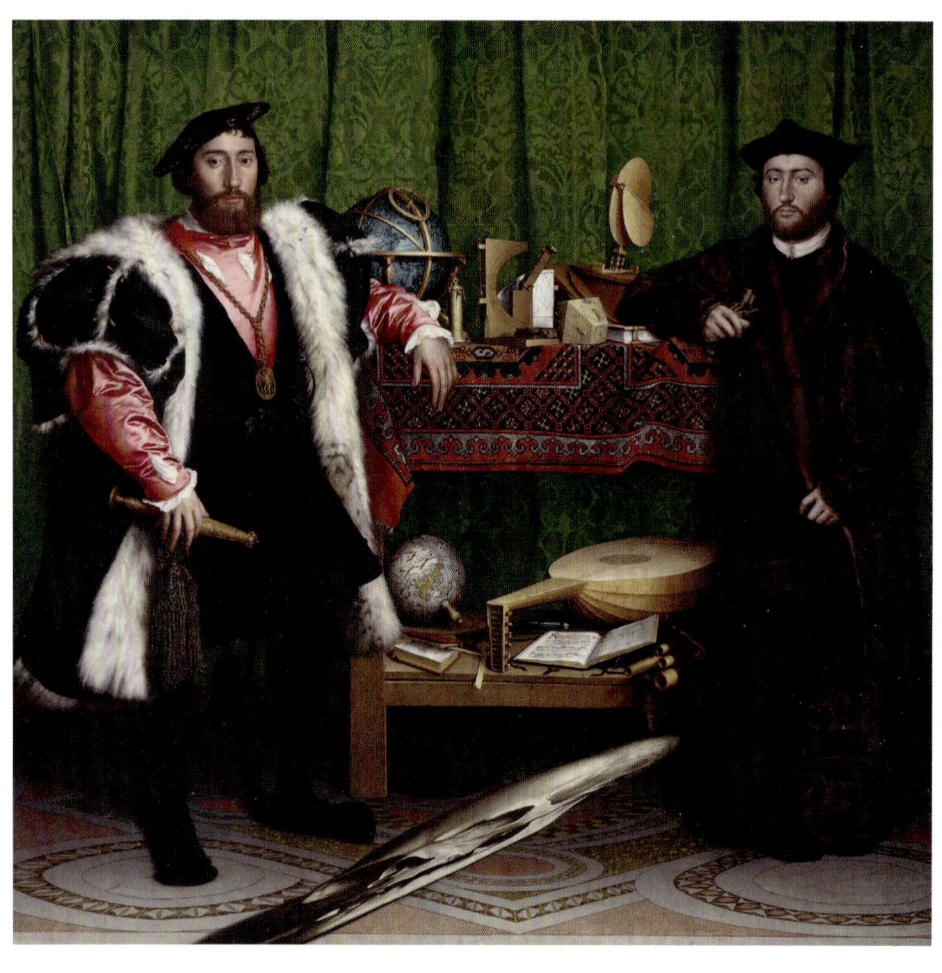

8 Hans Holbein the Younger, *The Ambassadors*, 1533.
Oil on oak, 207 × 209.5 cm (81½ × 82½ in.)

9 Hans Holbein the Younger, *Christina of Denmark, Duchess of Milan*, 1538.
Oil on oak, 179.1 × 82.6 cm (70⅝ × 32⅝ in.)

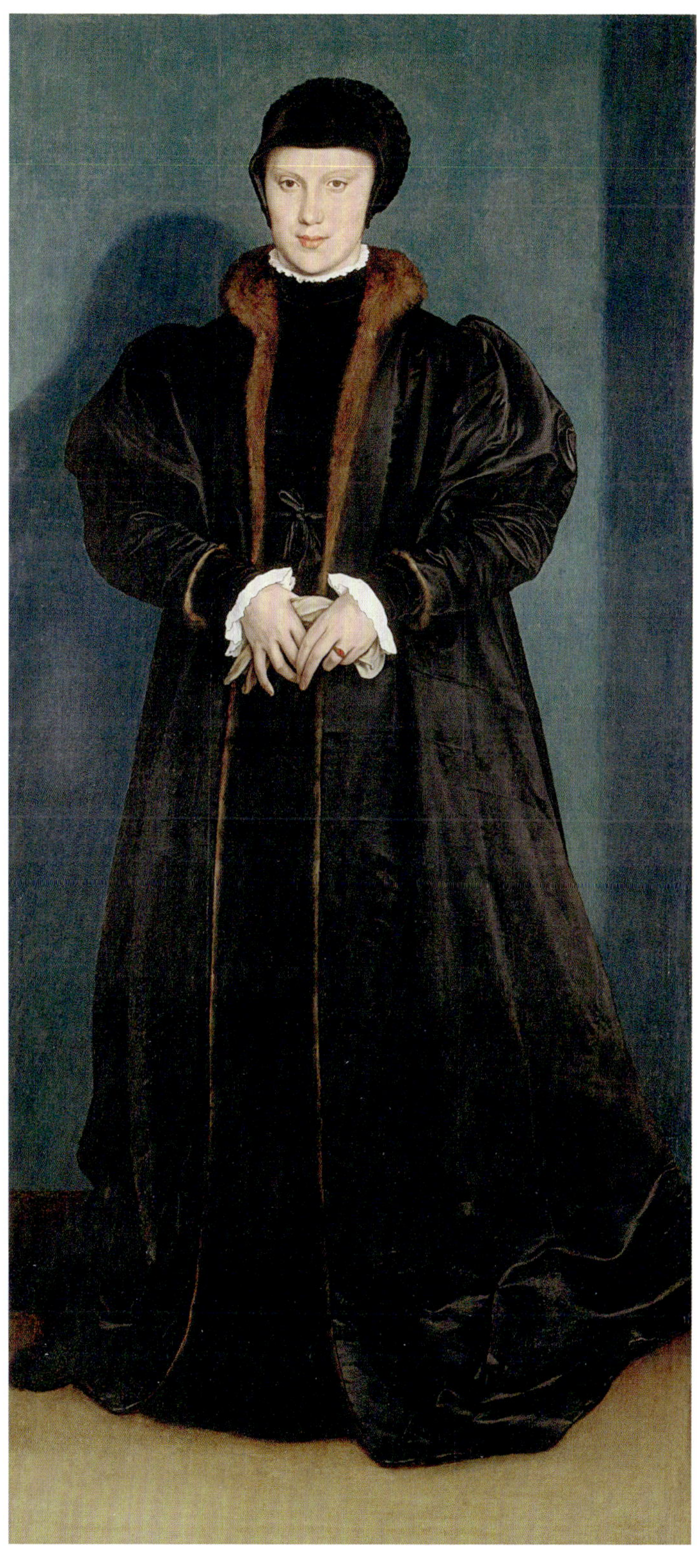

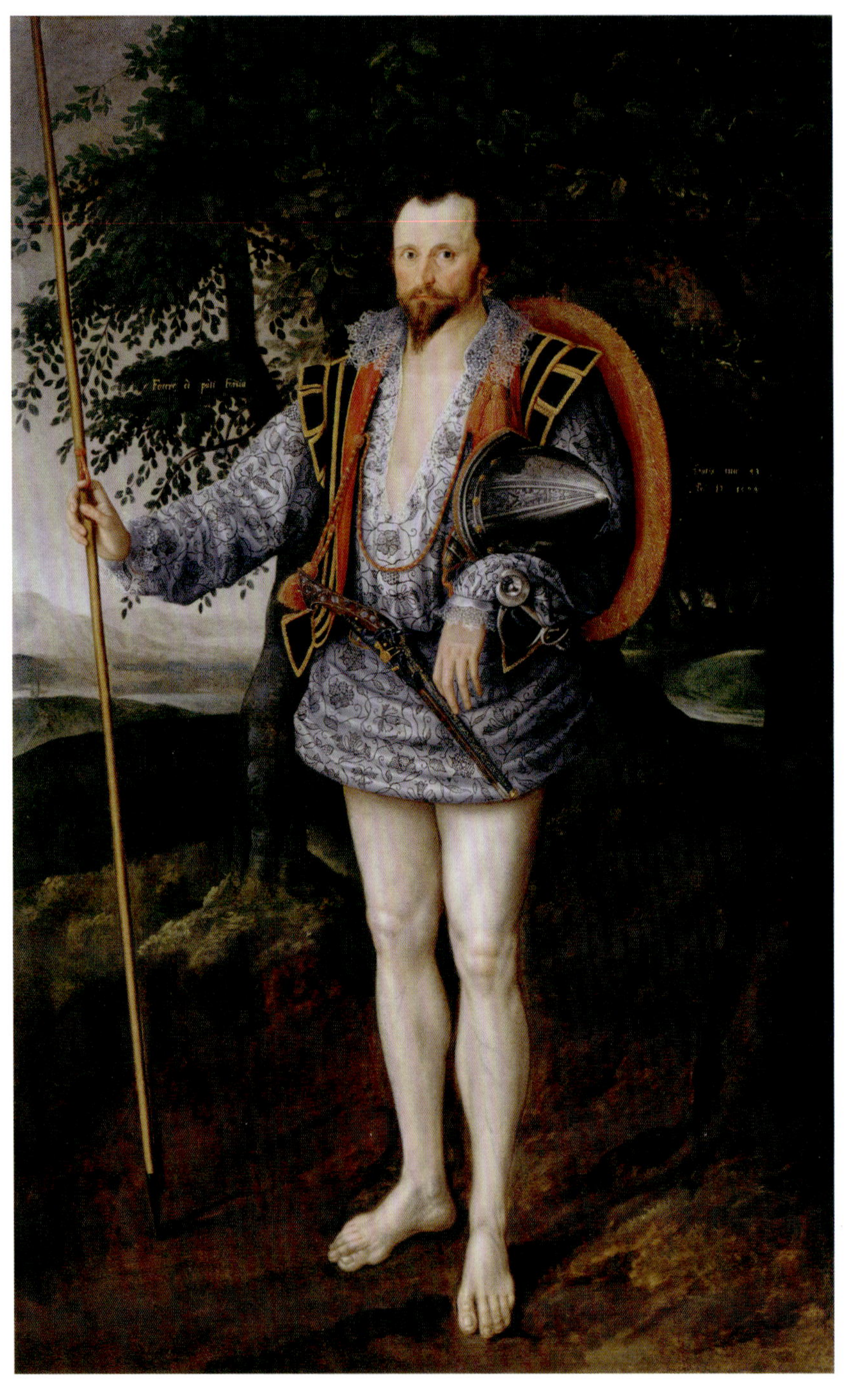

10 Marcus Gheeraerts the Younger, *Captain Thomas Lee*, 1594.
Oil on canvas, 230.5 × 150.8 cm (90¾ × 59⅜ in.)

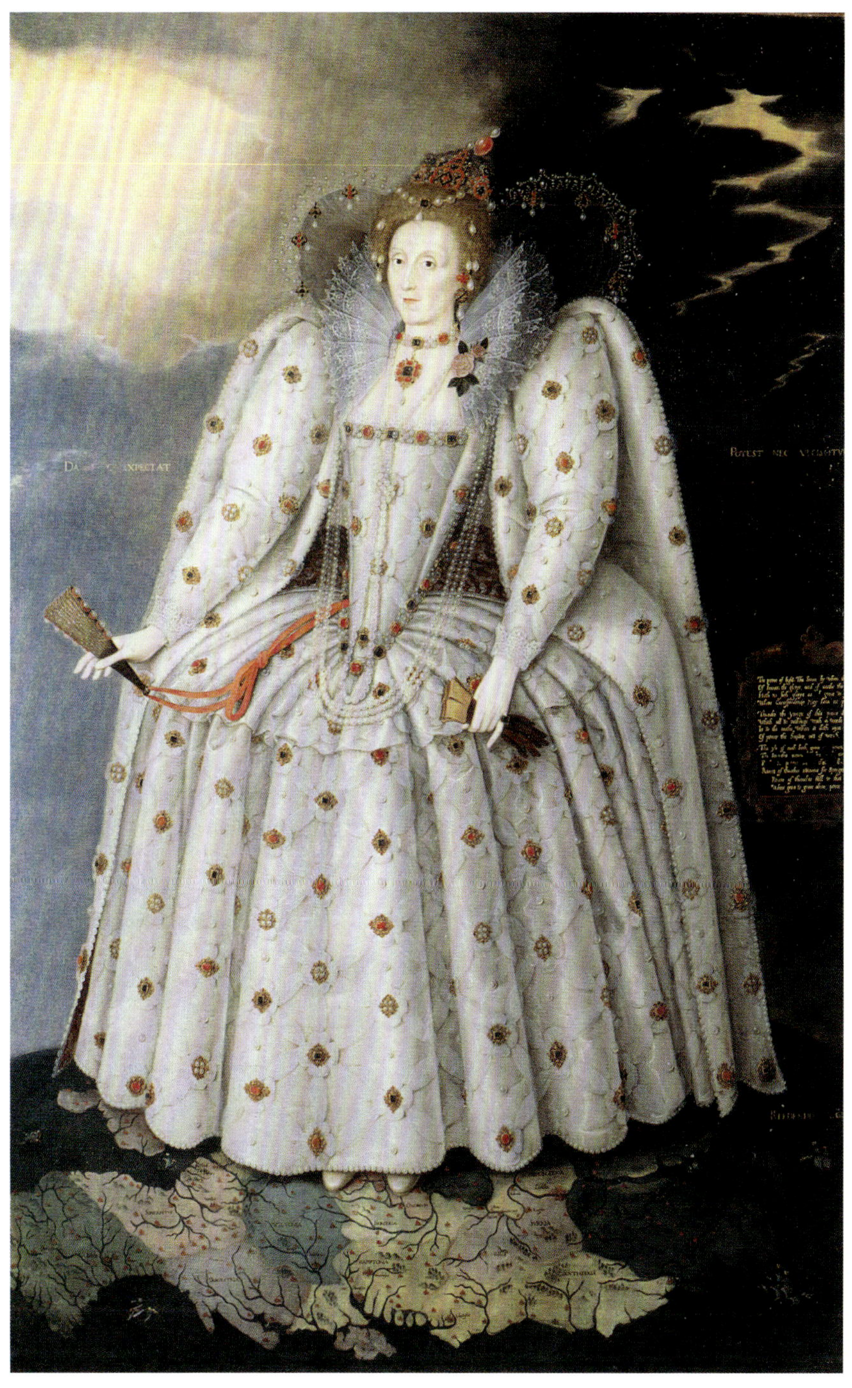

11 Marcus Gheeraerts the Younger, *Queen Elizabeth I* ('Ditchley Portrait'), *c.* 1592. Oil on canvas, 241.3 × 152.4 cm (95 × 60 in.)

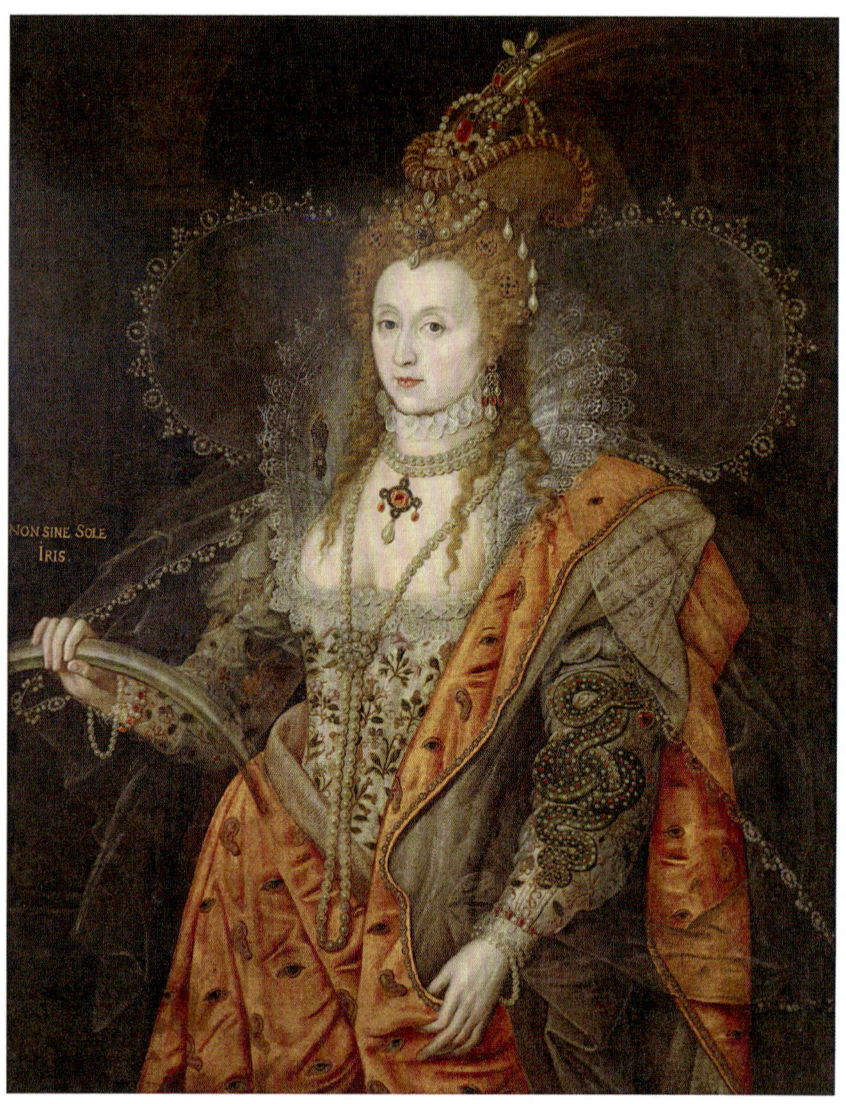

12 Marcus Gheeraerts the Younger (also attributed to Isaac Oliver), 'Rainbow Portrait', *c.* 1600–2. Oil on canvas, 127 × 99.1 cm (50 × 39⅛ in.)

13 George Gower, *The Plimpton 'Sieve' Portrait of Elizabeth I*, 1579. Oil on panel, 104.4 × 76.2 cm (41⅛ × 30 in.)

14 John Bettes the Elder, *A Man in a Black Cap*, 1545. Oil on oak, 47 × 41 cm (18⅝ × 16¼ in.)

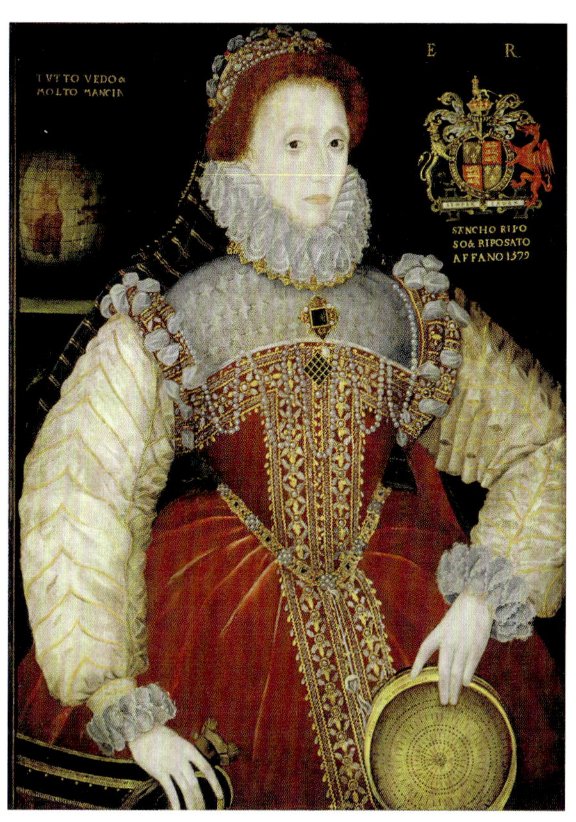

E R
TVTTO VEDO &
MOLTO MANCIA
SANCHO RIPO
SO & RIPOSATO
AFFANO 1579

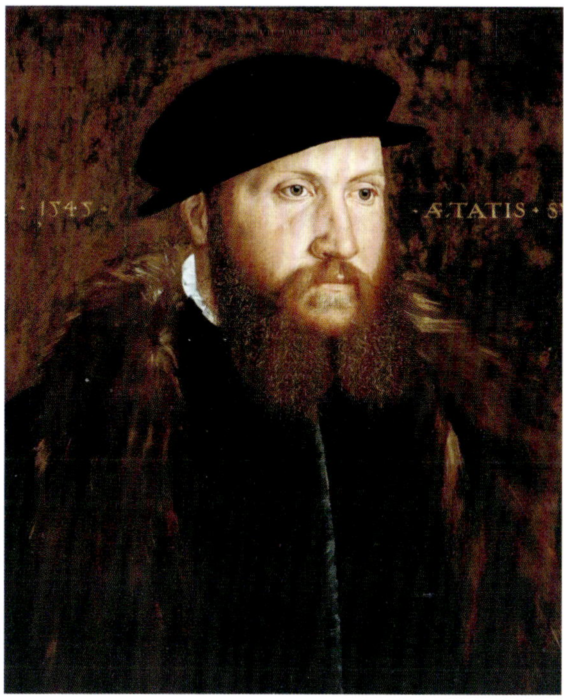

· 1545 ·
· ÆTATIS · S·

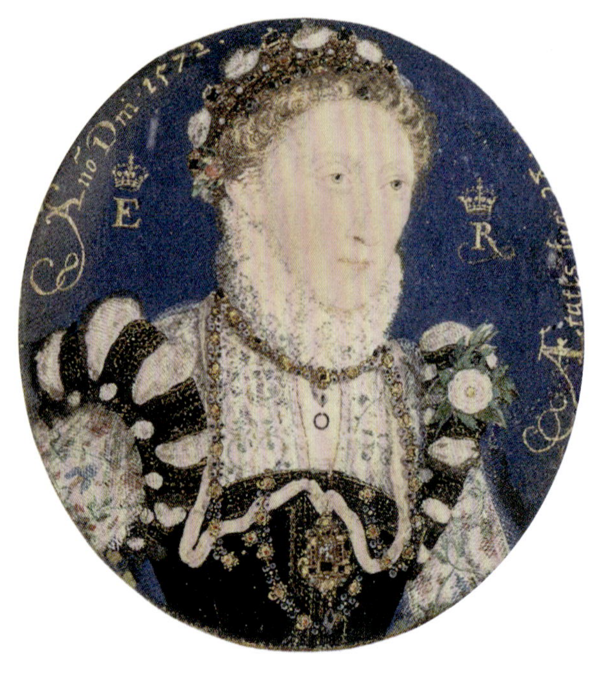

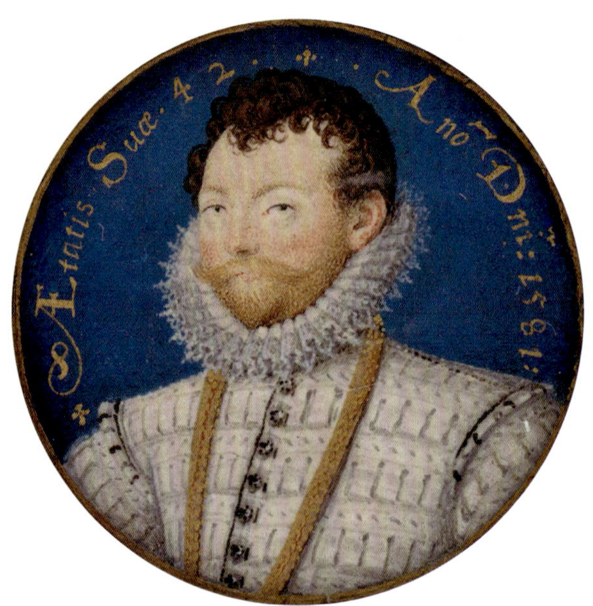

15 Nicholas Hilliard, *Queen Elizabeth I*, 1572.
Watercolour on vellum, 5.1 × 4.8 cm (2⅛ × 2 in.)

16 Nicholas Hilliard, *Sir Francis Drake*, 1581.
Watercolour on vellum, diameter 2.8 cm (1⅛ in.)

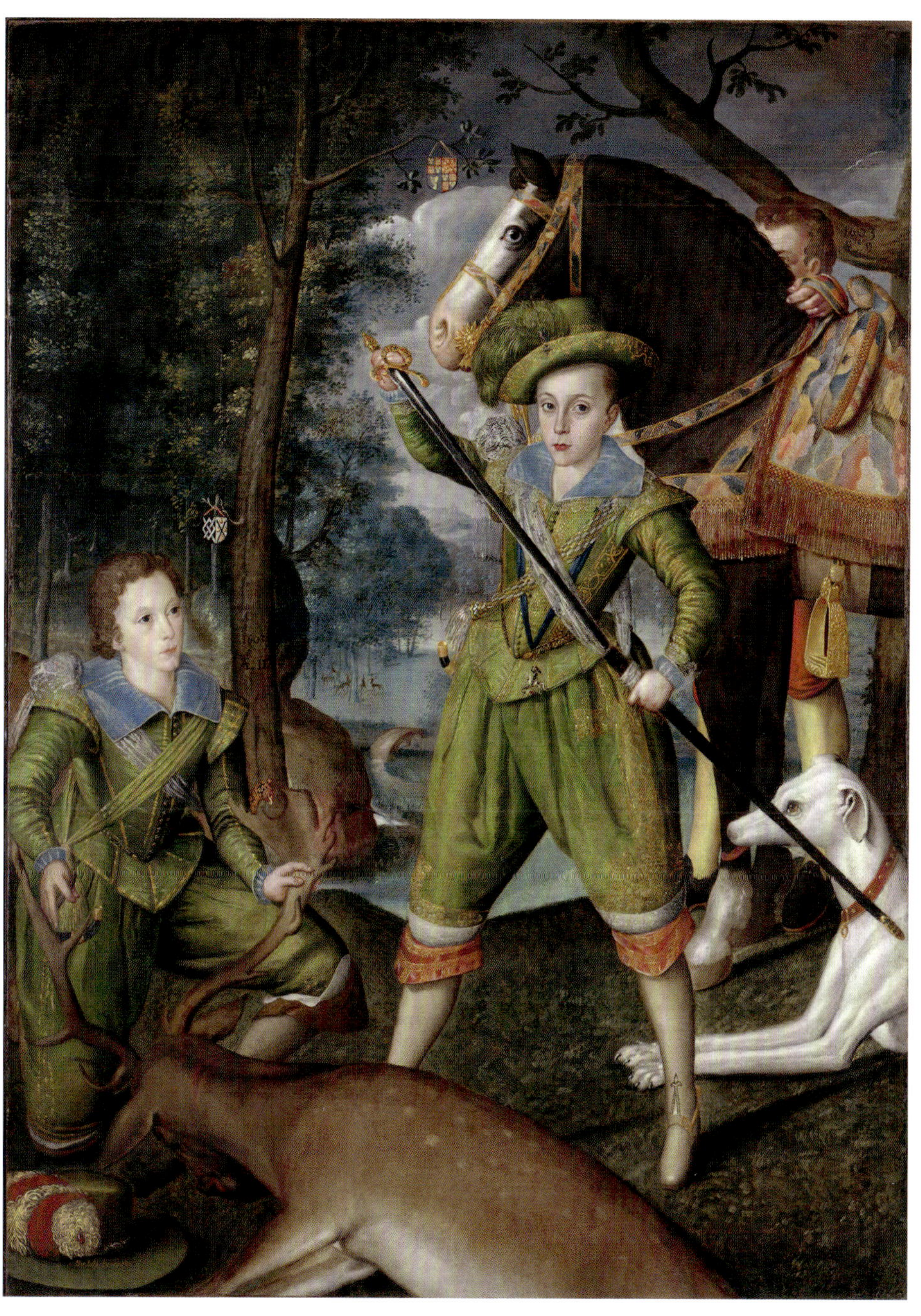

17 Robert Peake, *Henry Frederick, Prince of Wales, with Sir John Harington, in the Hunting Field*, 1603. Oil on canvas, 201.9 × 147.3 cm (79½ × 58 in.)

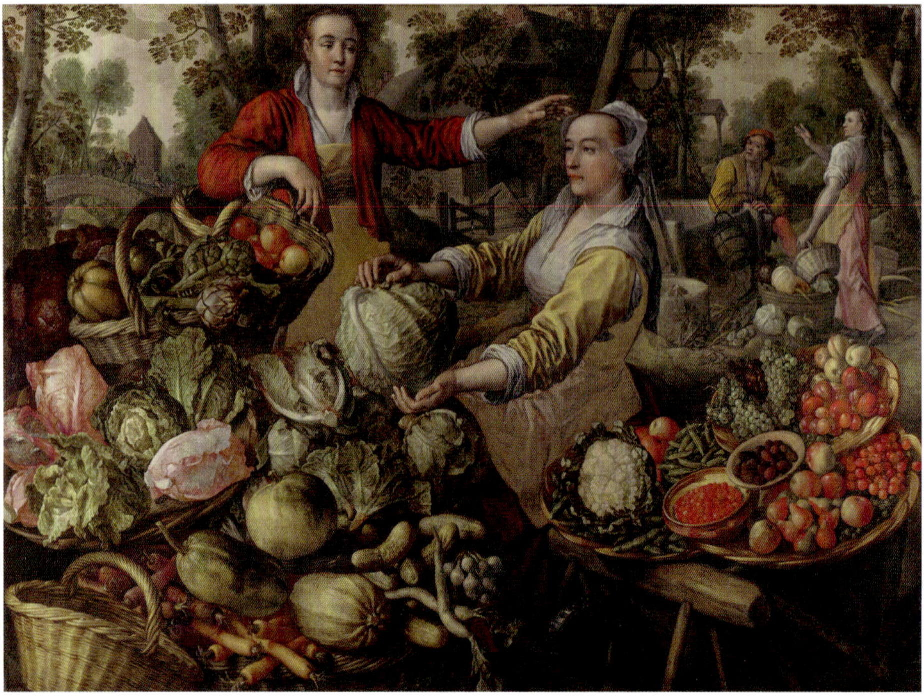

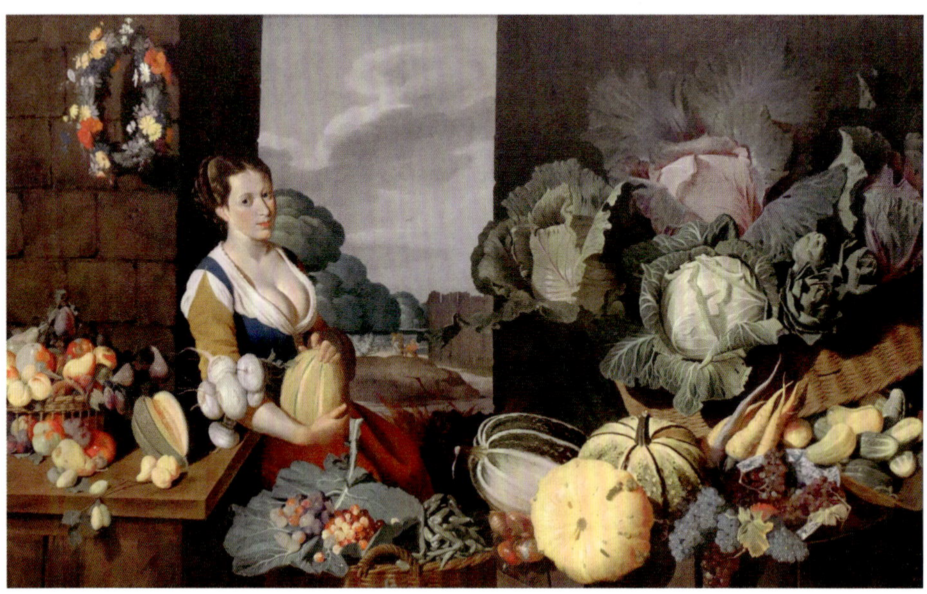

18 Joachim Beuckelaer, *The Four Elements: Earth*, 1569.
Oil on canvas, 158 × 215.4 cm (62¼ × 84⅞ in.)

19 Sir Nathaniel Bacon, *Cookmaid with Still Life of Vegetables and Fruit*,
c. 1620–25. Oil on canvas, 151 × 247.5 cm (59½ × 97½ in.)

contributions made by foreign artists, and those native-born artists who emulated them, significantly enhanced Britain's cultural heritage (it could be said, in spite of itself). Nevertheless, a profound amnesia seems to have taken place in the British consciousness, so that over the intervening centuries these foreign artists have been claimed as belonging to the 'British school' of painting. Perhaps this is effectively a more palatable means of downplaying the contribution of these foreigners, and in the process retaining an exceptionalist belief in the British being 'world-beating' in all fields.

4

Orazio and Artemisia Gentileschi

English Baroque at the Court of Charles I

When the Italian painter Michelangelo Merisi da Caravaggio died in Porto Ercole in 1610, he left behind no obvious successor because, unlike his Renaissance predecessors, he had not taken the traditional path of running a workshop or studio populated by pupils and apprentices.[1] But his many followers would nevertheless go on to spawn a new style of painting that favoured naturalism over the classicism of Caravaggio's contemporary Annibale Carracci or the clean aesthetic beauty of Renaissance artists like Raphael. This soon morphed into a style – widely popular across Europe – known as Caravaggism, characterized by Caravaggio's trademark chiaroscuro technique, which used the illusion of a single light source to create deep shadows and dramatic effects. The legacy of Caravaggio's style would eventually be absorbed into British painting, brought to the English court by followers of the artist who arrived to work for wealthy patrons, including the Dutch artist Gerrit van Honthorst and the Italian artist Orazio Gentileschi.

Like most great international cities of this time, Rome flourished in the seventeenth century thanks to the influx of a large immigrant population. This included itinerant painters who had travelled all over Italy and France, along with an increasing contingent of Flemish, Dutch and German artists who joined and enlarged established communities of their fellow countrymen. This multicultural melting pot led to fierce competition between incoming and native artists, resulting in the rapid development and dissemination of new artistic styles not only in Rome itself but beyond the papal states and ultimately across Europe. The

82

febrile activity of all these artistic comings and goings gave the city a rather transient air, a feature we still recognize in major international metropolises to this day, especially around transit hubs. Such pockets of diversity more often than not have a substantially positive effect on a city's wealth, and this was true in Rome.[2]

Many of Caravaggio's followers and imitators had never actually met him, a case in point being the Dutch Caravaggisti painters, such as Gerrit van Honthorst, Hendrick ter Brugghen and Cornelius van Poelenburgh, who arrived in Rome just over a decade after the artist's death, mainly from Utrecht.[3] One devoted follower who did meet Caravaggio though, and operated within his circle, was Orazio Gentileschi. The two artists first encountered one another in 1600, some eight years after Caravaggio arrived in Rome probably in the summer of 1592. Orazio's daughter, Artemisia, born in 1593, would almost certainly have met Caravaggio as well, perhaps sometime before her twelfth birthday.[4]

Orazio was born in 1563 and brought up in Pisa, the son of a Florentine goldsmith, Giovanni Battista di Bartolomeo Lomi. The young Orazio must have been proud of his father's roots in Florence, a city that had been made famous by great Renaissance artists of the recent past; this heritage encouraged Orazio to visit Florence with his older brother, Aurelio, and it is likely that he received some training as a painter during the short period that he was there. The brothers moved to Rome sometime around 1575, probably after the death of their father, when Orazio was about twelve. Aurelio later returned to Pisa, and Orazio, still a young adolescent, was left in the care of a maternal uncle, whose surname, Gentileschi, he eventually adopted.[5] In 1588–89, a decade or so after his arrival in Rome, Orazio was working in a large workshop on decorative schemes for the Biblioteca Sistina, and by 1593 he was paid for the design of medals for the feast of St Peter. Such work would suggest he was following in the footsteps of his father as a goldsmith, but he left that profession behind early in his career and is documented as having turned to painting at least by his twenties. In October 1593 he took part in one of the first meetings of the newly established painters' guild, the Accademia di San Luca, and Orazio and his wife, Prudentia, baptized Artemisia, the eldest of four children, the same year.[6]

Orazio's own distinctive artistic style began to develop with projects such as a 1596 commission for a large altarpiece of the *Conversion of Saul* for the Basilica of San Paolo fuori le Mura in Rome (the original was destroyed and the work is now known only from a 1610 print by the French-born printmaker and draughtsman Jacques Callot). By about 1600 he was again working on decorative schemes, this time in the basilicas of Santa Maria Maggiore and San Giovanni Laterano. His prodigious output soon gained the attention of a number of patrons in Rome, including Pope Paul V's nephew Cardinal Scipione Borghese, and such patronage inevitably led to Orazio crossing paths with Caravaggio around 1600, though there is no firm indication that they were close friends. We know that Caravaggio apparently expressed his admiration of Gentileschi's work as an artist, while Gentileschi claimed that he had lent some studio props to Caravaggio.[7] While they may not have worked together directly, from this point onwards it is clear that Orazio, though eight years older than Caravaggio, was falling more and more under the influence of the younger artist's style.

But when does imitation become plagiarism? The intense and fierce rivalry among artists in Rome erupted into ugly scenes in 1603, when one of Caravaggio's imitators, Giovanni Baglione, unveiled his painting of the Resurrection commissioned for the Gesù, one of the most important churches in Rome. The painting was immediately singled out by the artistic community for ridicule, most of all by Caravaggio and Orazio Gentileschi. The abuse would circulate through Rome via a number of verses that contained some of the most derogatory language that had ever been committed to print at this time: 'Giovan Bagalia, you are a know-nothing; Your pictures are mere daubs…I'll warrant that you will not earn so much as a brass farthing from them. Not even enough cloth to make yourself a pair of breeches, so you'll have to go round with your arse in the air. So, take your drawings and cartoons round to Andrea Pizzicarolo [the grocer], or maybe wipe your bum with them, or stuff them up Mao's [nickname for Tommaso Salini, a supporter of Baglione] wife's cunt, so that he can't fuck her any more with his great mule's prick.'[8]

As far as Baglione was concerned, he knew immediately who his detractors were, pointing the finger at Caravaggio, Orazio Gentileschi and the architect Onorio Longhi. He wasted no time in obtaining copies of the offending verses for evidence and brought a libel suit against the three, singling out Orazio as a personal friend of Caravaggio and author of the verses.[9] Caravaggio would testify that he had not seen Orazio for at least three years, and that he did not consider him to be one of the most competent painters in Rome.[10] For his part Orazio testified from prison that they had not spoken for months.[11] Could Caravaggio have been lying to protect Orazio by positioning him as a possible enemy, and was Orazio's statement an attempt to distance himself from a friendship with Caravaggio and so authorship of the scurrilous texts? There is certainly the whiff of a cover-up on the part of both artists, contemporary intrigue that ultimately muddies the historical record. We can never be sure whether Caravaggio's statement reflected his true feelings about Orazio's work or was just subterfuge, nor can we know just how close their friendship was and so how strong was Orazio's devotion to Caravaggio's style in his own work.

Following the death of his wife in childbirth in 1605 at the age of thirty, Orazio was left to raise his daughter and three sons. As the only girl, it is likely that much of the caring responsibilities for the younger children fell on Artemisia, aged just twelve at this time,[12] with perhaps some help from Orazio's widowed sister Lucretia, who was living with the family in Rome from at least 1607.[13] Orazio trained his daughter as a painter for at least some of her early years, encouraged by the example of successful woman artists such as Sofonisba Anguissola and Lavinia Fontana, and in 1610, at the age of seventeen, Artemisia signed and dated her painting *Susanna and the Elders* (fig. 20). A letter of July 1612 written by her father to Christina of Lorraine, the dowager Grand Duchess of Tuscany,[14] both gives us an idea of when Artemisia began accepting commissions and demonstrates just how proud Orazio was of her achievements: 'Having been active in the profession now for three years, [she] has learnt so much that I can dare to say that there are few equal to her, and that some major painters of our time cannot match her skills.'[15] When Artemisia depicted women, like in *Susanna and the Elders*, she did so in a manner that men had scarcely been able to achieve across the centuries. Taking Caravaggio as her model, she produced figures of women in a realistic style directly taken from life. Here at last were authentic depictions of women's bodies, in contrast to the heavy, muscle-bound female figures of Michelangelo or Sebastiano del Piombo in the Renaissance. But in an atmosphere of normalized yet rampant misogyny, as a woman artist she was always going to face a difficult path. From 1611 to 1612 her father had formed a successful and no doubt lucrative working relationship with the artist Agostino Tassi, painting various decorative schemes together in Rome. Either unable to take her training any further himself or finding that access to the all-male painting academies was denied to Artemisia, Orazio seems to have enlisted Tassi's help in tutoring his daughter privately. The situation would result in the rape of Artemisia by Tassi.

In the ensuing seven-month trial of 1612, it emerged that Tassi had form, having attempted to murder a prostitute whom he had made pregnant, as well as being tried for incest in 1610. The major issue of the trial was the fact that Tassi had, in the language of the day, 'deflowered' Artemisia, meaning that if she had not been a virgin before the rape took place, the Gentileschi household would not have been able to press charges. During the trial, to corroborate the truth of her allegation, Artemisia was given a gynaecological examination and made to repeat her story under torture, using a device made of rope wrapped around the fingers and tightened by degrees. After the initial rape, it seems that Artemisia continued to have sexual relations with Tassi, under the expectation that they would marry, which would have effectively annulled the crime in an age when rape within marriage was not recognized. But Tassi reneged on his promise to marry her after hearing a rumour that she was having an affair with another man. The art historian Patrizia Cavazzini has put forward a plausible argument that Orazio pressed charges against Tassi to force his hand in marrying Artemisia, or at least to gain a dowry payment, and it was only after the failure of this strategy that the charge of rape was levelled at Tassi and the trial went ahead.[16]

In the aftermath of the rape, Artemisia produced her now famous *Judith Beheading Holofernes* (fig. 21). The painting must have been influenced by her experiences, with the physicality of Judith's attack on the Assyrian general Holofernes perhaps echoing not only Artemisia's own ordeal at the hands of Tassi, but also the trial. Pent-up violence and revenge are unleashed against a man at the hands of a woman who, with the help of her handmaiden, possesses both the mental and physical strength to carry out this gruesome act. At the end of the trial Tassi was found guilty, but reports of his punishment range from eight months' to two years' imprisonment along with a period of five years' exile from Rome;[17] most agree that, whatever the initial sentence, he did not serve the full term and certainly did not stay away from Rome for the length of time stipulated.[18] Orazio then faced an age-old problem: how to marry off a woman who in the eyes of society was now seen as 'damaged goods'? The answer came in the form of a financial incentive: Orazio promised an impoverished Florentine artist by the name of Pierantonio Stiattesi a 1,000 scudi dowry, to be paid in instalments. With this arranged marriage Orazio hoped to draw a line under the whole sorry affair, which had seen his business with Tassi collapse and his public reputation in tatters.

The marriage took place in Rome in November 1612, and by the beginning of 1613 the couple were probably in Florence, where Artemisia began her life as an itinerant artist. Establishing a studio in the house of her father-in-law, she started to receive lucrative commissions from wealthy Florentines, including the Grand Duke Cosimo II de' Medici. Her success in the city led to her being the first woman to enter the Accademia delle Arti del Disegno. Her admission in July 1616 to this by now fifty-year-old institution – helped by a lower entry fee because her father was already a member – enabled her to claim professional status as a painter for the first time in her career, despite the fact that she had been taking commissions for some time.

For the first time Artemisia established a studio outside her home.[19] A self-portrait as St Catherine of Alexandria, now in the National Gallery, London, another as a lute player and a third as a martyr all date from this period and reflect an ongoing theme in her work of martyrdom or women scorned. The self-portraits were made at a harrowing period of her life, in a particularly difficult marriage that resulted in the birth of five children between 1613 and 1618, only two of whom lived beyond childhood. One can almost see the anguish and exhaustion etched into her face in the self-portrait as St Catherine (fig. 22); like the *Judith Slaying Holofernes* paintings, it could not have been infused with such realism were it not for her current hardships. Together with her arranged marriage, these circumstances would lead Artemisia to embark on an affair with the wealthy nobleman Francesco Maria Maringhi.

By 1620 Artemisia and her husband were in Rome. Her fascination with the story of Susanna and the Elders continued throughout this time, as did her passion for Maringhi, with what would appear to be the tacit approval of her still financially challenged husband. But by 1623 all records regarding her husband cease and at this point we have to assume he was no longer in her life.[20] In late 1626 or perhaps early 1627, Artemisia left Rome and appeared in Venice, where she was invited to become a member of an informal literary group, the Accademia dei Desiosi.[21] Numerous pieces of documentary evidence in the form of poems speak not only of her time in the city but also make reference to artistic works she made there, including a *Judith and Holofernes*, a *Lucretia* and a *Susanna and the Elders*, none of which have been traced.

As we can see from a later version of Judith and Holofernes (p. 89), Artemisia's works became darker and more Caravaggesque in their intensity. But unlike Caravaggio, and in keeping with the Dutch Caravaggisti painters, the light source in her paintings is revealed. This darker and increasingly more dramatic work evidently did not deter patrons, who were clearly enamoured with Caravaggism. Artemisia would go on to produce work for a number of international clients, including a painting of Hercules and Omphale (whereabouts unknown), commissioned by Iñigo Vélez de Guevara y Tassis on behalf of Philip IV of Spain and intended to hang alongside *Achilles Discovered by Ulysses and Diomedes* by Peter Paul Rubens and Anthony van Dyck. In having her work placed alongside that of two of the most revered and successful artists operating in Europe at the time, Artemisia could now claim to have truly arrived as a professional painter equal to any of the great artists.[22] Her list of notable clients would grow to include Manuel de Acevedo y Zúñiga, Count of Monterrey, Karl Eusebius, Prince of Liechtenstein, the French nobleman Charles de Lorraine, 4th Duke of Guise, and Charles I of England.

Despite documentary evidence of works produced in this period, only one can be positively attributed and securely dated to her time in Venice. *Esther before Ahasuerus* (p. 90) depicts the Jewish heroine attempting to

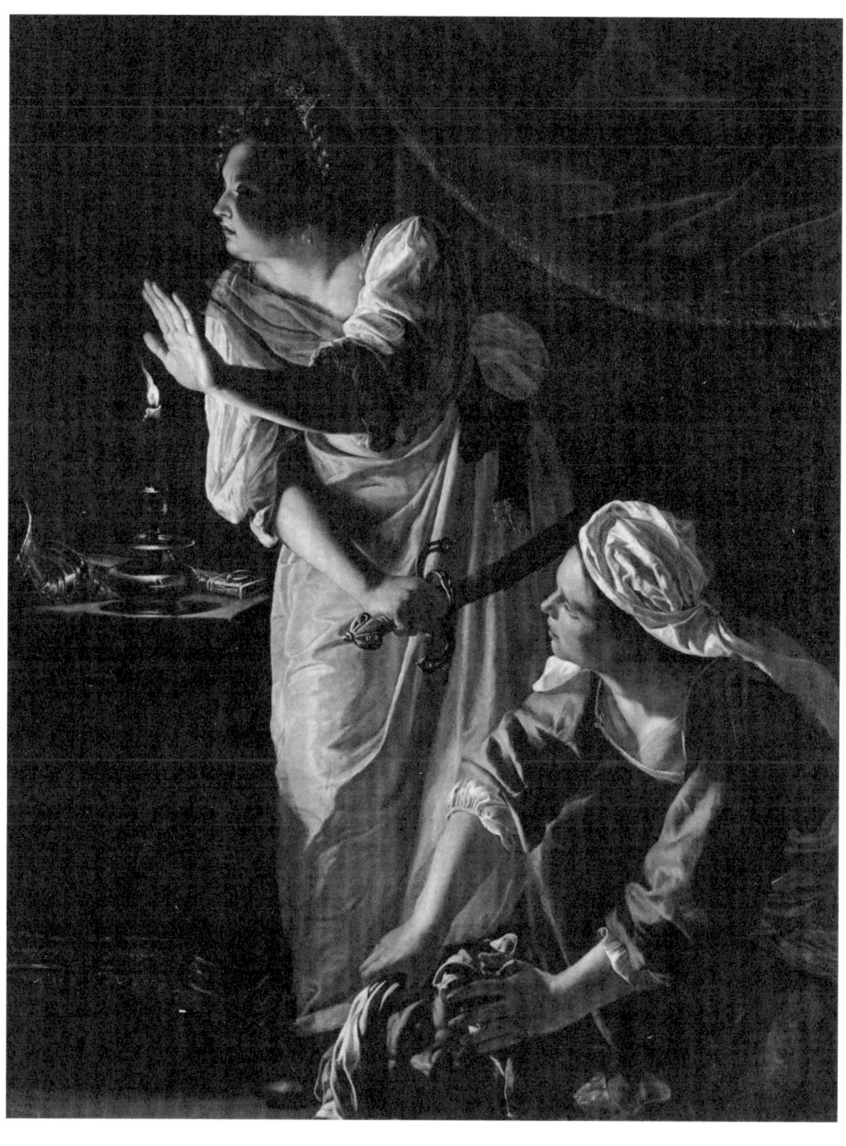

Artemisia Gentileschi, *Judith and her Maidservant with the Head of Holofernes*, *c.* 1623–25. Oil on canvas, 187.2 × 142 cm (73¾ × 56 in.)

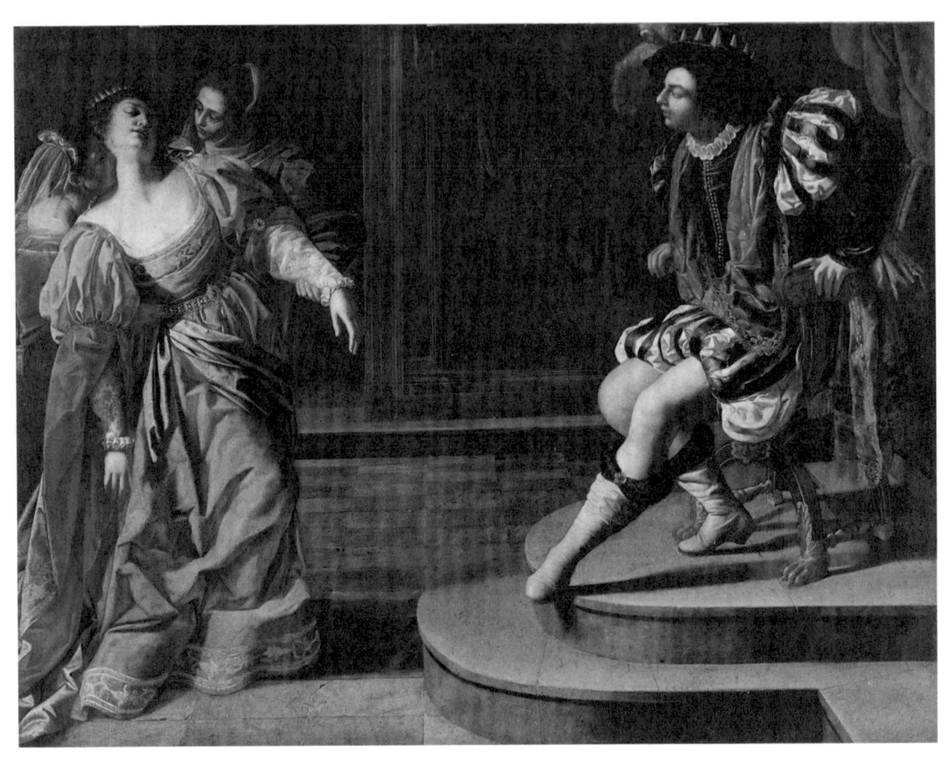

Artemisia Gentileschi, *Esther before Ahasuerus*, c. 1628–30.
Oil on canvas, 208.3 × 273.7 cm (82⅛ × 107⅞ in.)

convince her husband, the King of Persia, not to massacre the Jews living in his lands, once again casting a woman heroine as the principal protagonist triumphing against the might of a patriarchal world.[23] It is one of Artemisia's largest and most ambitious paintings, with accomplished perspectival views that give it the feel almost of a stage-set, along with beautifully rendered fabric effects and theatrical costumes clearly not contemporary to fifth-century BCE Persia.

Around 1630 Artemisia left Venice and headed for Naples, at this time under Spanish rule and the second largest city in Europe after Paris.[24] She was no doubt aware that more lucrative work was to be found there, and indeed she probably went at the invitation of the Spanish nobleman and diplomat Fernando Afán de Ribera, 3rd Duke of Alcalá. Having watched Rubens's success with Spanish patrons, Artemisia's ambition to succeed artistically was no less unbridled than that of her male counterparts. But another motivation that hastened her departure was the plague, then raging across the north of Italy, which would go on to take the lives of at least a third of the Venetian population.

Artemisia's ability to escape this calamity speaks volumes about her international credibility, wealth and influential friends. In this period, moving from city state to city state within or outside Italy was just as important as travelling to France, Spain, England or the Low Countries; however, visitors were not immune to the jealousy and rivalry of local artists. When the Bolognese painter Guido Reni attempted to set up shop in the lucrative territory of Naples, it resulted in him fleeing in apparent fear for his life, while fellow Bolognese artist Domenichino, who arrived there just after Artemisia in 1631, apparently died of poisoning ten years later.[25] But Artemisia managed to avoid such dangers. One can only imagine that, as a woman, the predominantly male art fraternity did not see her as a threat, and for once the discrimination she experienced throughout her career worked in her favour. Aside from a fleeting visit to London at the end of the 1630s, Artemisia would spend almost twenty-five years in Naples, yet it is clear that, despite receiving many plaudits for her work, she was still not satisfied with her circumstances, and much of the work she produced there in 1635–37 was made to curry favour with patrons elsewhere.

Artemisia's father, Orazio, was also on the move around this time. His ability to gain lucrative commissions in Rome had been significantly curtailed by the trial, with Tassi probably under the protection of his patron Pope Paul V. Underestimating Tassi's influential contacts, Orazio found himself offered very little work in Rome beyond a couple of documented altarpiece commissions. This scarcity of work contributed to Orazio's increasing itinerancy and he left Rome around 1620, working first in Fabriano and then in Genoa from 1621 to 1623. By this time Caravaggio had been dead for over a decade and Orazio had to rely on the artist's works for inspiration, rather than the man himself. We can see that a painting from his time in Rome, *The Rest on the Flight into Egypt* (fig. 23), owes much of its tenderness and humanity to an earlier work of the same subject by the earlier artist (fig. 24). But at last Orazio's fevered artistic activity began to attract the attention of patrons further afield.[26] By 1626 he was in Paris at the service of the French Queen Mother, Marie de' Medici, where he came to the notice of Charles I's closest advisor, George Villiers, 1st Duke of Buckingham. With the offer of a completely refurbished apartment within his own residence at York House on the Strand, Buckingham persuaded Orazio to come to England.

He arrived in London around early October 1626 at the age of sixty-three, accompanied by two of his sons, Giulio and Marco. Like Rome, London was a melting pot of foreign artisans who, despite their itinerant status, were nevertheless successful and able to build on the reputation of artistic quality and innovation established by previous incomers who had arrived at least a century earlier. During Orazio's time in London the taste for foreign artists among royalty and the aristocracy was still very much alive, leading to the success of Dutch and Flemish artists such as Gerrit van Honthorst and Hendrick van Steenwyck the Younger, who is documented in the city from about 1615. Just as the French Gothic style of architecture was refashioned into what became known as the English Perpendicular style, so Renaissance and Baroque styles in European painting were adapted by these incoming artists to suit an English court style. To please his English patrons and be successful, Orazio would have to adopt this style. Ironically, it would be fellow foreigners he was competing with, not native-born artists; they too would ultimately have to adapt their style to compete.

The itinerant lifestyle of these visitors underlines the fact that artists travelled to England not only for reasons of religious persecution, but also because there was an economic imperative to do so. In fact, the two motivations are not always separate, even today, although contemporary society often wants them to be just that, questioning whether foreigners are economic migrants or persecuted refugees, who some fear may be successful at the expense of our own people. But such circumstances are never quite so simple because they could be both; indeed, the success of immigrants frequently has a positive economic ripple effect throughout society. Unfortunately, these benefits are often intangible, and history demonstrates that we can fail to recognize such positive contributions, many of which remain in the very fabric of our culture and institutions today.

Now in the autumn of his life, Orazio's work, which had so successfully adopted the chiaroscuro style of Caravaggio in that artist's absence from Rome, started to give way to a cooler, more flamboyant court style displaying rich colours and opulent fabrics. The days of high drama in Rome, especially in projects he had worked on with his former colleague Tassi, such as the Casino delle Muse, were firmly behind him by the time he arrived in London. But the move seems to have been a success as he was now essentially at the service of the Duke of Buckingham, as corroborated by two early mentions of him at the court of Charles I. The first was provided by the French courtier François de Bassompierre, who was in London to negotiate the composition of the household of Queen Henrietta Maria, sister of Louis XIII, following her marriage to Charles I in 1625. Bassompierre noted in his diary that on the evening of 21 November 1626, the King had hosted a dinner for the Duke of Buckingham, which was attended by several high-ranking courtiers including Orazio Gentileschi, the earls of Suffolk, Carlisle and Holland, and the diplomat Sir Dudley Carleton.[27] Very soon after this event, Orazio seems to have been at the service of the King on an annuity of £100, and not only as a painter. A letter written in December 1626 by Amerigo Salvetti, ambassador of the Grand Duke of Tuscany, suggests that Orazio had been sent on a secret mission to Brussels to engage in diplomatic meetings with the Spanish rulers in Flanders, prior to which he held several meetings with Buckingham and the King.[28] By the first half of the seventeenth century, it was becoming not uncommon for painters to act as diplomatic agents. The portrait painter and miniaturist Sir Balthazar Gerbier, a French Huguenot born in the Dutch Republic who had arrived in London in 1616, served as Buckingham's advisor on artistic matters and as the keeper of his art collection acted as a courier and diplomat, eventually becoming Charles I's ambassador in Brussels; it is almost certain that Orazio also acted as an art advisor to Buckingham until the duke's assassination in August 1628.

While Charles was seemingly pleased to have acquired Orazio, said to have had first-hand experience of working with Caravaggio, the King's developing taste for European artists had seen him try in vain to lure to London several other prominent Italian painters of the day. Francesco Albani and Francesco Barbieri, aka Guercino, had both declined offers. Guercino, who was at the time working under the papal patronage of Gregory XV in Rome, declined Charles's invitation, saying that he did not want to live among Protestant heretics and – probably more importantly – that he had heard the English weather was terrible. It is quite clear from these failed overtures that not every itinerant artist was travelling because of difficulties in their own countries, and that quite a few of them were doing well enough to turn down even seemingly lucrative offers. But, as we will see, the choice made by some artists to work for English royal patrons would turn out to be well judged.

Despite his Caravaggesque credentials, Orazio's move to England would see him leave behind the earthy realism of his mentor. The change in his work is evident from two paintings of *The Finding of Moses* from the 1630s, which reveal a style that was becoming more and more refined and courtly. He often repeated compositions, in the process simply altering the colours of the sumptuously rendered silk drapery while keeping its pattern and style; indeed, virtually all the major figures in these two paintings are repeated with just a few minor changes. His wealthy clients were not concerned about receiving a copy as long as it was made by the hand of the master. The earlier version (p. 96) was made for Queen Henrietta Maria, wife of Charles I, and the second was sent by the artist as a gift to Philip IV of Spain (p. 97). This method of working was not new for Orazio, as can be seen from three versions of *Lot and his Daughters* dating from his time in Genoa, at least one of which was commissioned in 1621 by the nobleman Giovanni Antonio Sauli for his palazzo (fig. 25). The Sauli version seems to have been a pendant commission with a *Danaë and the Shower of Gold* (fig. 26). It seems odd that such a subject – the rape of the mythological princess Danaë by Zeus disguised as a shower of gold – should have been commissioned as a pendant to a religious painting, but given that the Old Testament narrative also dealt with themes of rape and incest, perhaps one subject was not considered more distasteful than the other.

Despite his successful integration at court, it is clear that after all the trials and tribulations of his life Orazio had become weary of England. In a letter written in 1633 to Ferdinando II de' Medici, Grand Duke of Tuscany, he appealed to him for employment and revealed a longing to return to his native Italy, producing a small painting to accompany his letter: 'to transmit to Your Highness this small example of my painting… in order to perceive if with it I am able to merit employment in your service, for the little that remains of my life, for this weak talent of mine, with which could be fulfilled my very ardent desire to return to my country, submitting myself to the smallest instruction of Your Very Serene Highness, to whom with devoted affection I make a reverent bow from London this day of July 18, 1633.'[29]

But Orazio was persuaded to remain in England when in 1629 Queen Henrietta Maria was granted Greenwich Park and within it the Queen's House, former residence of Charles I's mother, Anne of Denmark. This was to be the setting for Orazio's largest commission, this time from the Queen herself rather than the King. The major project involved decorating the ceiling of the Great Hall in the Queen's House with nine canvases depicting twenty-six women, a work entitled *An Allegory of Peace and the Arts* (fig. 27), probably intended by Henrietta Maria to represent a realm of womanly virtue. Sadly, Orazio gained this prestigious commission far too late in life, at seventy-two years old when the project began in 1635.

Although much of the necessary work would not have been carried out in situ, the prospect of an elderly man climbing scaffolding, perhaps on a daily basis, over a period of three or more years was clearly daunting

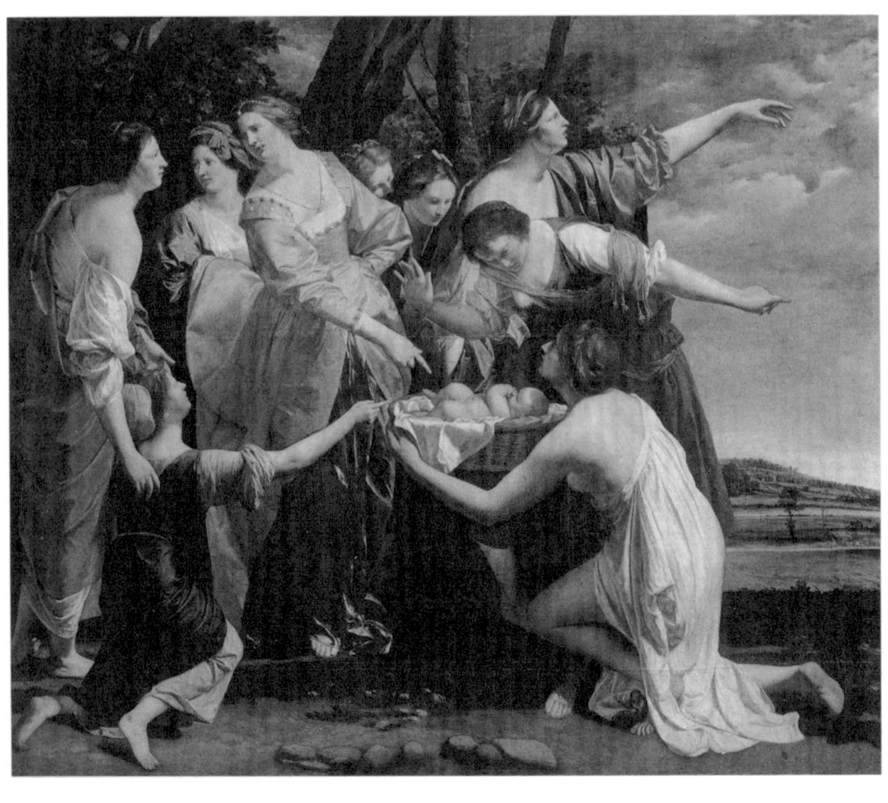

Orazio Gentileschi, *The Finding of Moses*, early 1630s.
Oil on canvas, 257 × 301 cm (101¼ × 118⅝ in.)

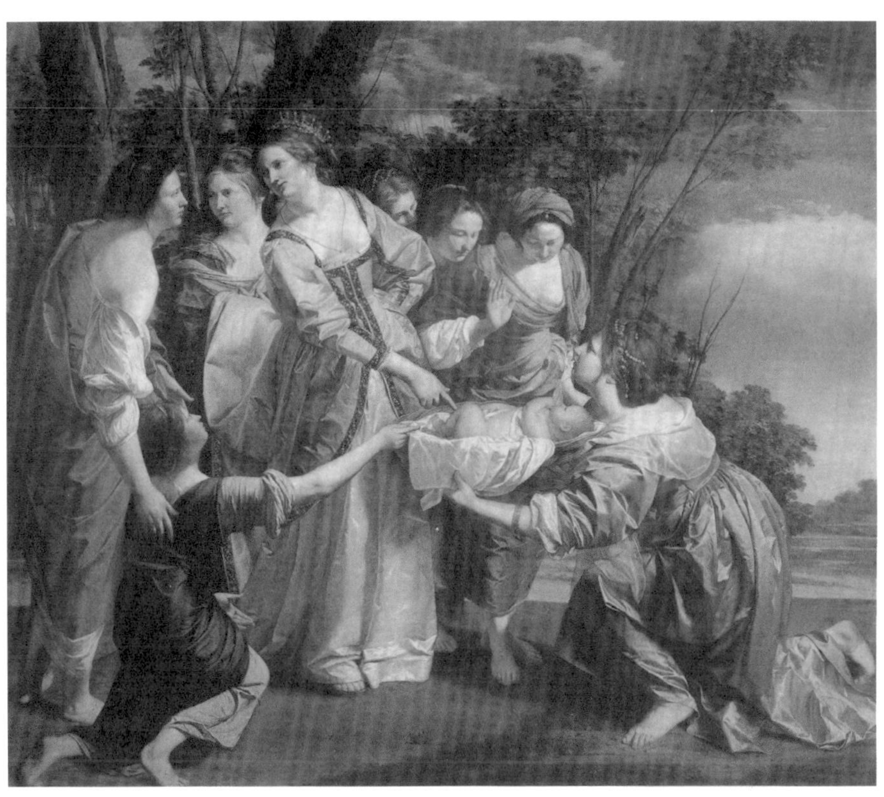

Orazio Gentileschi, *The Finding of Moses*, 1633.
Oil on canvas, 242 × 281 cm (95⅜ × 110¾ in.)

for Orazio, especially as he had rarely been involved in such large-scale decorative projects on his own, instead working either as part of a workshop or with his former partner Tassi. So in the first year of the project, 1635, Orazio managed to procure a royal invitation for Artemisia to join him in London and hopefully assist in this major undertaking. By this late stage in Orazio's life, Artemisia had not seen her father, let alone worked with him, for decades. It seems safe to say that the time apart amounted to an estrangement, no doubt a result of the fall-out from the Tassi tragedy and her clearly forced marriage to Pierantonio Stiattesi. So it is not surprising that, despite her professed closeness to her father, emphasized in letters to him, Artemisia seems to have done her utmost to avoid coming to England by attempting to gain court positions across Italy. In a further attempt to bolster her international credentials, she even used word of her invitation to London to inform the Duke of Modena, Francesco I d'Este, that her brother Francesco had been sent by Charles I to escort her there.[30] This procrastination continued for three years before she finally acquiesced to her father's invitation. Although Artemisia is recorded as being in Naples only up to November 1637, she was no doubt keen to avoid travelling in the winter months, so it is likely that she would have come to London in the spring of 1638.

By the time she arrived the ceiling project was nearing its end. Her arrival at such a late stage has long led to speculation as to the extent – if any – of Artemisia's involvement in the project. But Cavazzini has argued, quite plausibly, that figures from the ceiling such as Apollo, Astronomy, Strength and some of the muses seem to be by her hand, though we must acknowledge that this assessment has not been proven beyond doubt.[31] Unfortunately the question of attribution was seriously compromised by the brutal removal of the ceiling paintings from the Queen's House to Marlborough House in the early eighteenth century, which damaged them beyond repair.[32]

This was to be one of Orazio's last works. He finally brought the ceiling project to an end in 1638 and died in London on 7 February 1639 at the age of seventy-six, just a year after completing it. Artemisia would remain in London for at least another year. Surveyor of the King's Pictures Abraham van der Doort recorded several works by Artemisia in his

1638–40 inventory of the King's collection, and a subsequent inventory drawn up in the wake of the King's execution in 1649 counted seven paintings by her; sadly, few of these have survived to the present day. One rare survival is a *Self-Portrait as the Allegory of Painting* (*La Pittura*), which remains in the Royal Collection (fig. 28). It is a dynamic and accomplished portrait of an artist in full command of her medium, and demonstrates drapery effects equal to those of her father. She also employs a confident use of the Renaissance technique of foreshortening, creating an illusory effect as though she is leaning beyond the picture plane which, along with dramatic chiaroscuro light effects, makes the image the epitome of an independent woman successfully working on her own terms. Until recently it was thought to be the only surviving work from Artemisia's time in England, but another work has now been identified by the Royal Collection as dating from this period, a *Susanna and the Elders*, most likely painted between about 1638 and 1640. Both pictures demonstrate a sophisticated and confident style, the legacy of which can be seen in the work of William Dobson and Peter Lely.

Artemisia returned to Naples around 1639 or 1640, when she would have been about forty-seven. In a series of thirteen letters written between 1649 and 1651 to her last major patron, the Sicilian collector Antonio Ruffo, we get a glimpse of how her determination to be judged on an equal footing with her male counterparts had not dimmed with age, but if anything had increased: 'I will show Your Illustrious Lordship what a woman can do'; 'you will find the spirit of Caesar in the soul of a woman'; 'never has anyone found in my pictures any repetition of invention, not even a single hand'; 'if I were a man this could not have happened'.[33] But by 1652 she had been in ill health for some time, and that year she signed her last painting, another version of *Susanna and the Elders* (fig. 29). The subject she had made her own, which had started her career, would also end it.

While the precise date of Artemisia's death has never been certain, recent research has determined that a tax payment made on 12 August 1654 is the last official document in her hand, meaning that she must have died soon after this date, in her early sixties.[34] Although she made only a small direct contribution to British art with her part in her father's ceiling project, it can be argued that works she executed abroad but which were recorded by Van der Doort as being in the Royal Collection – including *Tarquin and Lucretia*, an *Allegory of Fame* and another *Susanna and the Elders* – remained an inspiration for artists who saw them, both on the Continent and in England.

Orazio Gentileschi was buried in the Queen's Chapel in Somerset House, beneath Rubens's Crucifixion altarpiece. In his will he left £1,638, not a lot to show for a life considering how much work he had done for the royal couple, but this may be related to the fact that by 1630 the artist had to petition the King for three years of his annuity in arrears. The amount left was distributed among his sons, with Giulio getting the most because he had children, and the rest going to Francesco, who was made executor of his estate. Like many immigrants who never really feel at ease in their adopted country, Orazio had longed to go home, but never got the chance to return to his native Italy. English painting, though, was all the richer for the contribution of the Gentileschi, and some semblance of their styles would go on to influence generations of English artists long after their lifetimes, making a significant contribution to the British school of painting.

5

Daniel Mytens

Citizen of The Hague,
Denizen of England

In many ways the artist Daniel Mytens can be seen as a missing link in the story of British art, sandwiched as it were between the period that saw the rise of Marcus Gheeraerts the Younger and the sweeping artistic changes brought about by Mytens's near contemporary Anthony van Dyck. Although Mytens had much in common with these artists, having origins in the Low Countries, he was not a refugee fleeing persecution, nor was he seen as a gentleman painter, and despite being intimately connected with the courts of both James I (r. 1603–25) and Charles I (r. 1625–49), little has been written about him in the way of stand-alone biographies compared with other artists of the period such as Van Dyck and Rubens.

Little is known of Mytens's early life beyond the fact that he was born in the Low Countries, probably in Delft, around 1590. He came from a family that was widely involved in the creative arts, and many of his relatives – either by blood or marriage – were artists or involved in the art trade. His uncle, Aert Mijtens, was a history and portrait painter in Naples, and his father, Maerten Mijtens, was an art dealer as well as a seller (and perhaps maker) of saddles. Daniël Mijtens (later known in England as Daniel Mytens) became a master of the painters' guild in The Hague in 1610, but his career as a painter must have begun some years earlier to have accumulated the skills that were undoubtedly needed to be accepted into the guild. It is probable that he acquired some instruction in the art of painting from an older master. In a 1944 article, the historian and art critic Emile Cammaerts states that Mytens 'very probably worked in Rubens's studio', perhaps picking up on a rumour that may have been circulating since the artist's youth.[1] But the absence of sources for this information both in the article and in the historical record might suggest that the idea originated from Mytens himself, in an attempt to boost his own reputation by aligning himself with the great Flemish master, who was already enjoying significant fame in Europe at this time.

A more plausible notion is that he studied under Michiel van Miereveld (1566–1641), court painter to the Prince of Orange and the leading artist in The Hague at the time. In fact, Miereveld may have inadvertently played a part in bringing Mytens to the attention of his English patrons. The art historian Karen Hearn relates an attempt to secure Miereveld's services in England as painter to James I's eldest son, Henry Frederick, Prince of Wales.[2] The brokering of this arrangement in January 1611 was led by the governor of Brill, Lord Conway, and involved a suggestion from Miereveld that he was amenable to a three-month stay in England, but by February 1612 the deal had failed and it never came to fruition. Hearn plausibly suggests, however, that this failed deal may have highlighted to potential patrons the presence of other painters closely associated with Miereveld, including Mytens.[3]

Here it is worth taking a moment to acknowledge the influence exerted on English painting by those artists who did not travel to the British Isles, Miereveld among them. Hostilities between Spain and the Northern Netherlands were brought to a temporary halt between 1609 and 1621, in a period known as the Twelve Years' Truce, and the presence in The Hague of prominent English ambassadors involved in the negotiations gave Miereveld ample opportunities to acquire prestigious clients. These included Sir Ralph Winwood and, significantly, Sir Dudley Carleton, who commissioned a late portrait from the artist in 1628 (fig.30). It depicts Carleton resplendent in courtly black dress, made fashionable by the Spanish aristocracy, and the latest flat collar, which had superseded the larger ruffs of old. In fact, Carleton had ordered nine portraits from the artist prior to this, only six of which survive, as evidenced by a bill drawn up by Miereveld detailing an outstanding 596 guilders owed to him by the ambassador.[4]

At least twenty-five Englishmen of varying ranks, including ambassadors, diplomats, governors and the nobility, commissioned portraits from Miereveld between 1608 and 1634. Although he had originally trained as a history painter, the artist clearly had his eyes on the prize and seized the opportunity afforded by the much more lucrative genre of portraiture. That said, he did not charge his English clients any more than his Dutch ones and did very little to adapt his practice to accommodate an English sensibility, other than perhaps giving his female sitters a paler complexion.[5] His interest in the genre is confirmed by the early seventeenth-century painter and biographer of artists Carel van Mander in his 1604 *Schilderboeck*, where he praises Miereveld's mastery in the field of portrait painting.[6] This, coupled with the evident interest in his work by the well-resourced English abroad, ensured that Miereveld made a significant impact on English painting without ever setting foot in that country.

The success of foreign-born artists and those born in London of foreign parentage was as much about timing as it was about the new ideas they brought to English painting. Writing at the beginning of the seventeenth century, Van Mander alludes to political and economic unrest as a reason why artists may have wanted to leave the Netherlands, and cites profit and necessity as motivations for moving their practice towards portraiture. Although Van Mander was in general disparaging of the genre and, by extension, the English lack of taste and sophistication in matters of art appreciation, he nevertheless made an exception for Miereveld.[7]

The downturn in artists' fortunes in the Netherlands coincided with an increased possibility of earning good money in England for those willing to make the journey, and the accession of James I to the English throne in 1603 saw a rise in painters arriving from the Low Countries for purely economic reasons.[8] Another factor that aided their success was the death in 1619 of three prominent English-born painters, Robert Peake the Elder, William Larkin and Nicholas Hilliard, creating a talent vacuum into which artists from abroad could introduce a contemporary Continental approach.[9]

In 1618 Daniel Mytens wrote to Sir Dudley Carleton in apparently excellent English (it would appear then, as anecdotally it does now, that the Dutch tended to have an excellent grasp of the English language, and better grammar in fact than much of the English population!). The brief correspondence seems to mark the beginning of Mytens's career in England, with Carleton describing Mytens in August that year as 'your Lordship's painter' in a letter to Thomas Howard, 14th Earl of Arundel.[10] A collector of both art and artists, Arundel is credited with fostering the career of the Palladian architect Inigo Jones, as well as introducing to England artists such as Van Dyck, Rubens and Wenceslaus Hollar. By then established in London, one of Mytens's earliest commissions was a pair of pendant portraits of Arundel and his wife, Alethea Howard, Countess of Arundel. Arundel was one of the most prolific collectors of the age, and Mytens portrays him showing off his collection of classical sculpture (p. 106), the first major example in London, in the sculpture gallery at Arundel House, which formerly stood on the Strand overlooking the Thames. In the pendant portrait (p. 107), Lady Arundel is shown in the family portraits gallery there.

The art historian Anastassia Novikova has proposed that Arundel may have commissioned these portraits as a gift to Carleton, to persuade him to sell his collection of sculptures. She also suggests that the interiors depicted are a fanciful exaggeration of those at Arundel House, backing up her argument with contemporary documentation of visitors' accounts and prints by Hollar. If Arundel did indeed want Carleton's sculpture collection, one can perhaps understand why he might seek to show an embellished version of his property in order to demonstrate that the sculptures would be going to a good home.[11] Whatever the truth behind these portraits, they demonstrate the artist's imagination and skilful use of Renaissance-style perspective, which must surely have put Mytens and his fellow incomers in an advantageous position when it came to acquiring important English clients who had toured abroad.

Given Arundel's significant influence in artistic matters, his introduction of Mytens to James I in 1619 was all but inevitable, and records detailing official payments to the artist for portraits ordered by the Crown begin that year. One of these, for the sum of £32, relates to a portrait of Lord Howard of Effingham, 1st Earl of Nottingham, and includes a gilded frame (p. 108).[12] This marked the beginning of the artist's transition from a previously somewhat formal style towards an English sensibility, combining what he had learned in his Hague period with the tradition of the full-length portrait that had been developed in England by an earlier generation of immigrant artists such as Marcus Gheeraerts the Younger and Guillim Scrots.

The year Mytens completed his portrait of the Earl of Nottingham, Anthony van Dyck arrived in England for a brief period. Mytens cannot have known that Van Dyck would eventually undermine his comfortable position as a court artist, although the two were acquainted (as evidenced by a lost portrait of Mytens by Van Dyck, which now survives only in an engraved version). Nevertheless, along with other compatriots who preceded him, such as Abraham van Blijenberch and Paulus van Somer, Mytens is credited with introducing a more three-dimensional naturalism into English painting. Works like his portrait of Robert Rich, 2nd Earl of Warwick (p. 109), marked a revolution in the art of portraiture. Compare Mytens's work with the formal court portraiture of thirty or forty years earlier, such as the *c.* 1581 portrait of Sir Francis Drake by an unknown English artist (see p. 48), in which one struggles to imagine a body underneath Drake's costume and the head somehow does not belong to the torso. Although such portraits were made to serve a different purpose from the ones Mytens was producing, it is clear that Dutch painters were bringing a fresh, less stuffy approach to formal English portraiture in this period, along with new technical proficiency.

Another work that can be placed within the early years of Mytens's employment in the royal household is the portrait of James I dated 1621. It is unique in its realistic depiction of the aged and frail King nearing the end of his reign (fig. 31). Such realism was uncommon in English painting and highlighted the King's vulnerability, not a trait that monarchs were generally keen to advertise. But the portrayal reveals much about Mytens and his position at court, reflecting a closeness and trust between painter and sitter. It shows a king comfortable in the knowledge that he was leaving an heir to the throne in his second son, Charles, following the tragic early death from typhoid fever of his eldest son, Henry Frederick, Prince of Wales, in 1612.

Mytens's integration as a valued member of court was ratified in July 1624, when James I awarded him a grant of £25 and an annual

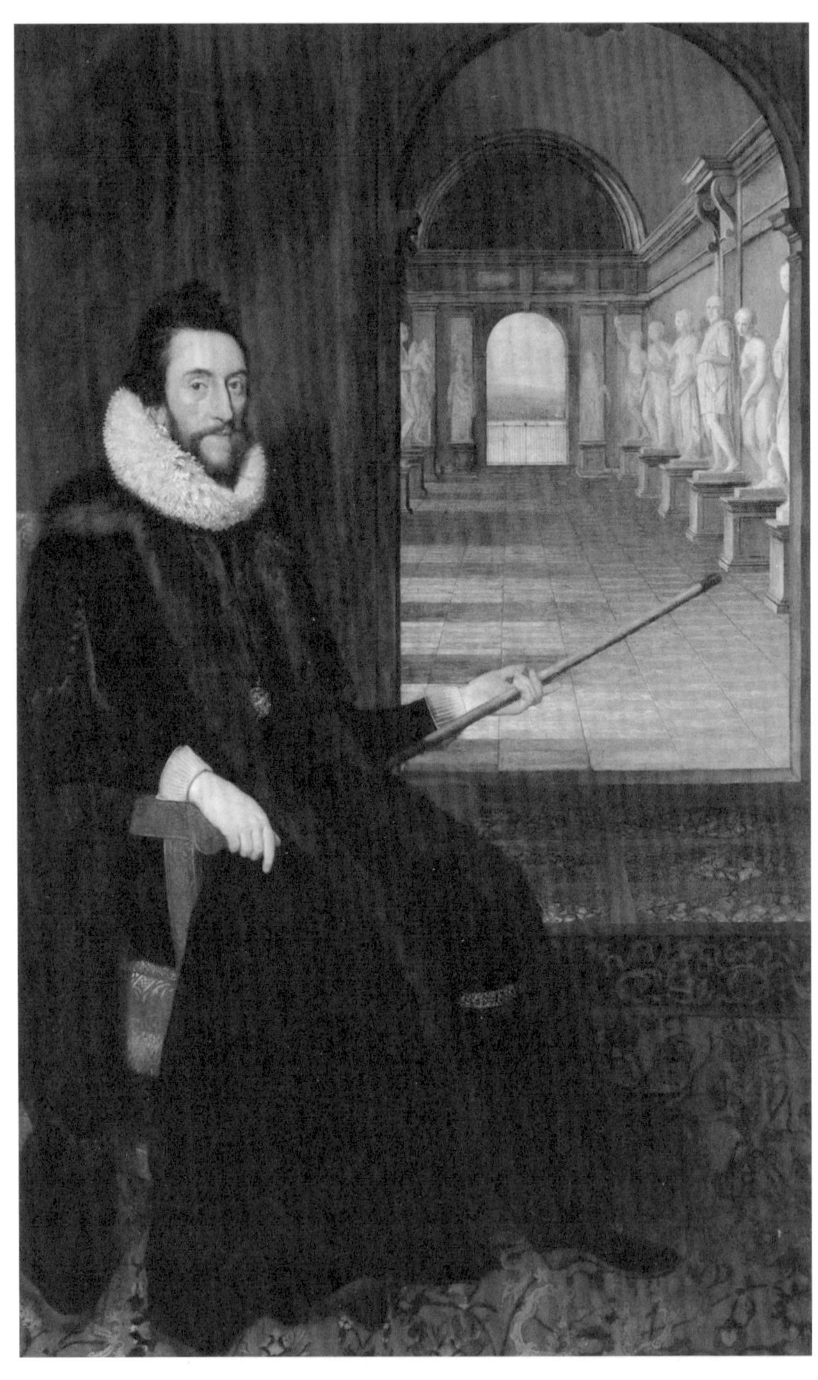

Daniel Mytens, *Thomas Howard, 14th Earl of Arundel,*
c. 1618. Oil on canvas, 207 × 127 cm (81½ × 50 in.)

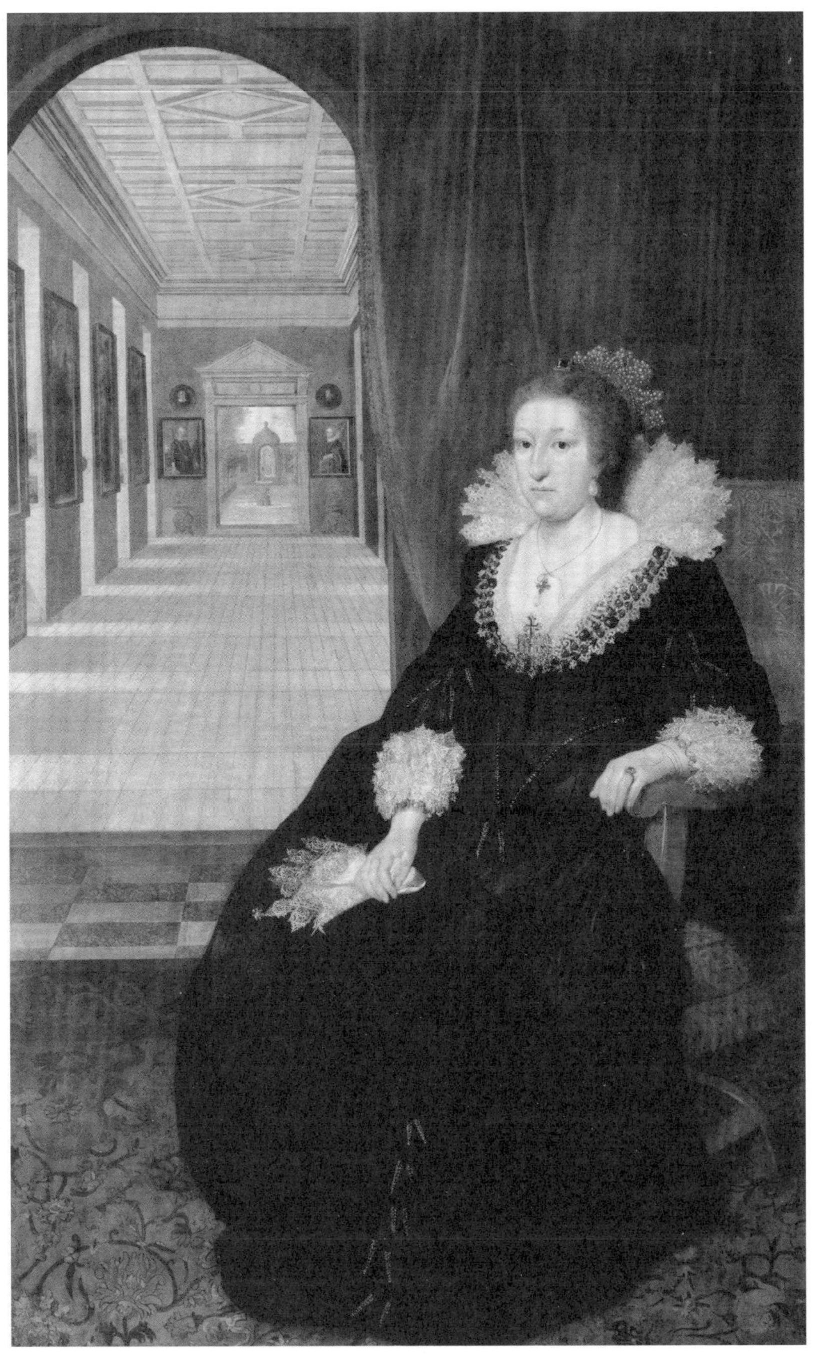

Daniel Mytens, *Aletheia Talbot, Countess of Arundel,*
c. 1618. Oil on canvas, 207 × 127 cm (81½ × 50 in.)

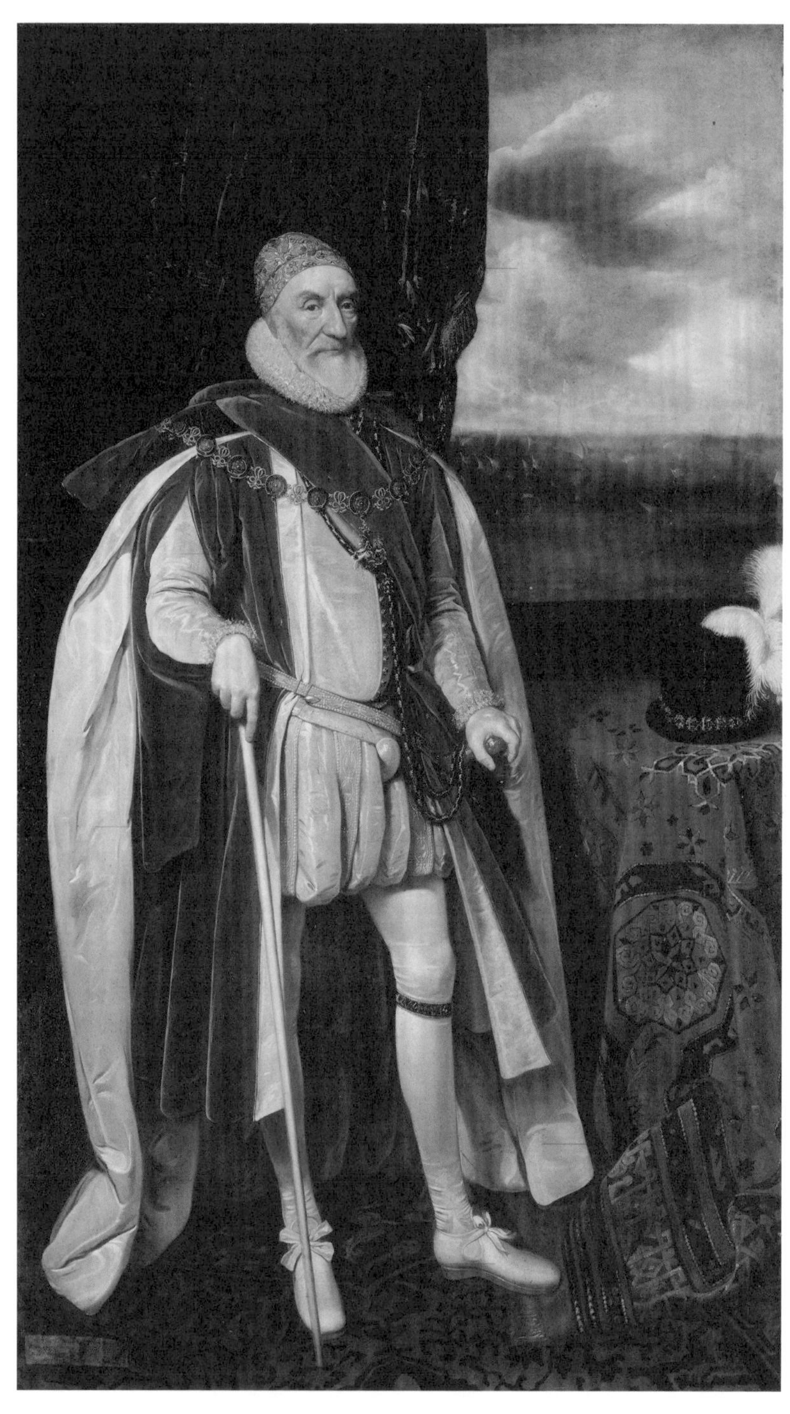

Daniel Mytens, *Charles Howard, 1st Earl of Nottingham, c.* 1620.
Oil on canvas, 208.5 × 139.5 cm (82 × 55 in.)

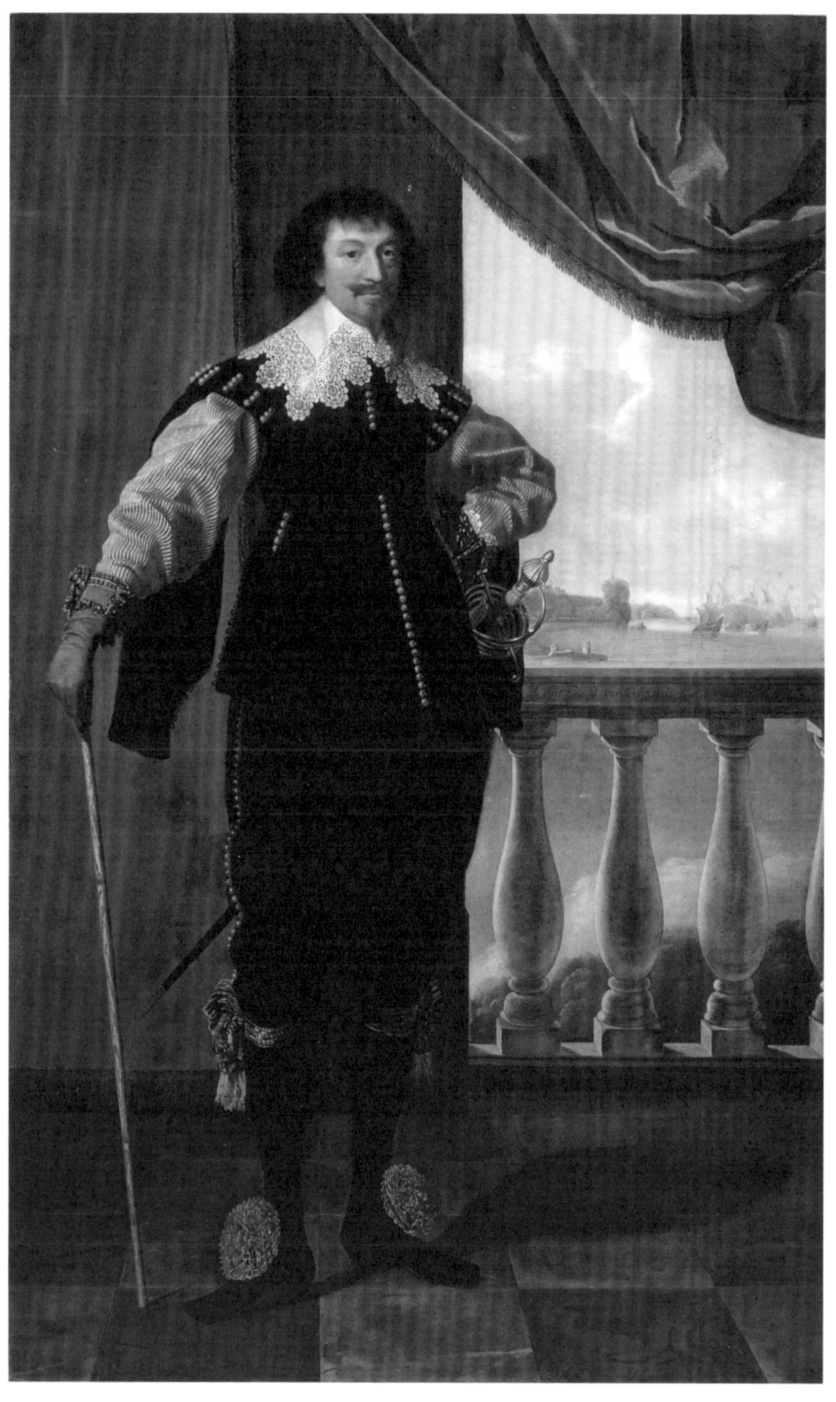

Daniel Mytens, *Robert Rich, 2nd Earl of Warwick, c.* 1632.
Oil on canvas, 221 × 139.5 cm (87⅛ × 55 in.)

pension of £50, equivalent to a yearly income of about £3,000 in today's terms. The payment documents spell out the reasons for such recognition: 'In consideration of the good service done unto us…and for his encouragement in his art and skill of Picture-drawing.' Nevertheless, the award came with quite specific stipulations 'on condition that he do not depart from the realm without a warrant from the King or the Council, and that he do not refuse such service and employment in his art as shall be reasonably required of him'.[13] The next month, in August 1624, Prince Charles supported the recommendation that Mytens be made a denizen of England. The artist was furnished with a leasehold property on St Martin's Lane in London; the deeds for the transaction are dated 30 December 1624 and co-signed by the King's chancellor, Sir Henry Hobart, who just a week earlier had sat for Mytens to paint his own portrait.[14]

In the final years of James I's life, Mytens was clearly in a comfortable position and able to earn decent sums of money.[15] On the death of his father in 1625, Prince Charles became Charles I of England, at which point it was but a formality to appoint Mytens 'one of our picture drawers of our Chamber in ordinarie'. However, the situation reveals the somewhat precarious position that artists like Mytens were in, because they could not guarantee the retention of a similar financial position in the household of the subsequent ruler; with this appointment for life, Mytens was awarded an annual pension of £20, £30 less than the pension awarded to him by Charles's father.[16] The man responsible for brokering the deal was the highly influential diplomat and courtier Endymion Porter, who signed a letter of patent on 4 June 1625.[17] A staunch Royalist, appointed to the position of Groom of the Bedchamber to Charles I, Porter was described by the seventeenth-century English antiquarian Anthony Wood as 'a great man and beloved by two kings, James I for his admirable wit and Charles I (to whom…he was a servant) for his general learning, brave stile, sweet temper, great experience, travels and modern languages'.[18] Like the Earl of Arundel, Porter was a major patron of the arts, represented by the most important artists of the day. His portraits reflect changes in both clothing and painting style. While Mytens's beautifully detailed, crisp rendition of 1627 (fig. 32) hides its means of production, Van Dyck's portrait of just a year later (fig. 33) has a looser application of paint (in what is known as a painterly style) and reveals its means of production, presenting a more relaxed and nonchalant sitter who feels natural to the viewer. The modern attire worn by Porter in the Van Dyck portrait not only gives it a fresher and more contemporary look, but also allows the artist the opportunity to bring to life textural contrasts in materials, skin tone and hair, generating a dynamic feeling of movement while enhancing his sitter's personality and stature. The two approaches would eventually be synthesized just a few years after Van Dyck's death in a late portrait of Porter by the English-born artist William Dobson, who would depict his subject, somewhat lost in his copious garments, in an aggrandizing tableau of antiquity featuring a bust of Apollo, god of the arts (fig. 34).

The shape of things to come, and the eventual demise of Mytens's position at court, was heralded by a warrant, issued on 2 July 1625, 'to pay Daniell Mittens the King's Picture Drawer £120 for a copy of Titian's Great Venus'.[19] While on face value this was a significantly lucrative commission, it also signalled Charles I's interest in a style of Continental painting steeped in a Venetian Renaissance sensibility. This would become the dominant English style of painting, and Mytens would never really adapt to it. Nevertheless, since 1618 the artist had enjoyed a golden period spanning almost seven years, during which time he was the chief provider of royal portraits, as confirmed by documents including a 'Warrant to the Exchequer to pay to Daniell Mittens, His Majesty's Picturer, the sum of £125 for divers pictures by him delivered to sundry persons by His Majesty's special direction, July 31, 1626' and a 'Warrant to pay Daniell Mittens the King's painter £100 for 3 pictures, one of James IV of Scotland, one of Mary the last Queen of Scotland, another of His Majesty's own royal person. July 10th, 1627'.[20]

By the late 1620s, Mytens was firmly ensconced in his post at court, but he could not afford to rest on his laurels since he could be usurped at any moment by incoming rival artists with new and potentially more fashionable ideas in the field of portraiture. Competition from these arrivals was much more of a threat to him than native-born painters. Knowledge of the latest styles and innovations in Flemish portraiture was clearly not yet strong enough in England for Mytens to learn what he needed to remain unchallenged in his post, or it would not have been necessary for him to return to the Netherlands.

The Acts of the Privy Council records give notice in August 1626 of a 'passe for Daniell Mitten, his Majesty's picture drawer, to goe over into the Low Countries and remain there for the space of six months'.[21] The King must have thought such a journey necessary in order for his court artists to learn the latest Continental techniques and hold their own in the face of work commissioned by other great European leaders. In other words, Charles, like most citizens of certain means, was subject to the vagaries of fashion or, as we would say today, the fear of missing out. Two portraits by Mytens of James Hamilton, Earl of Arran, perhaps best illustrate just what the artist gained from his six-month sojourn. The first was made in 1623, when the sitter was just seventeen years old, and the second six years later (figs 35 and 36). The earlier portrait is a beautiful bravura work in Mytens's handling of the gradations of black in the costume; the brushwork is pristine and the detailing picked out in the cuff, collar and shoes exquisite, all set off by the vibrant red of the stockings. But despite these wonderful qualities, the costume seems to be wearing the sitter, rather than the other way round, resulting in a somewhat stiff appearance. In fact, this kind of fixed, rigid pose was made for ease of copying, as confirmed by the existence of more than twenty versions of this work.

In contrast, the later portrait is much more relaxed, both in Hamilton's countenance and in the way the costume reveals the body beneath. Mytens's modelling of the light falling on the costume deftly picks out the brocading, along with the subtle modulations of the silver-grey tonality, while the detail on the collar beautifully communicates the light silkiness of the material, giving the viewer a real sense of the texture of these fabrics. Mytens had learned much on his travels in the Low Countries to justify his short leave of absence and had brought these new skills back to England, where they would be disseminated to his workshop assistants and eventually absorbed into the wider British school of painting. But no sooner had he established himself in England than the writing was already on the wall; although he was not yet aware of the imminent return of a triumphant Anthony van Dyck, in 1629 – the same year

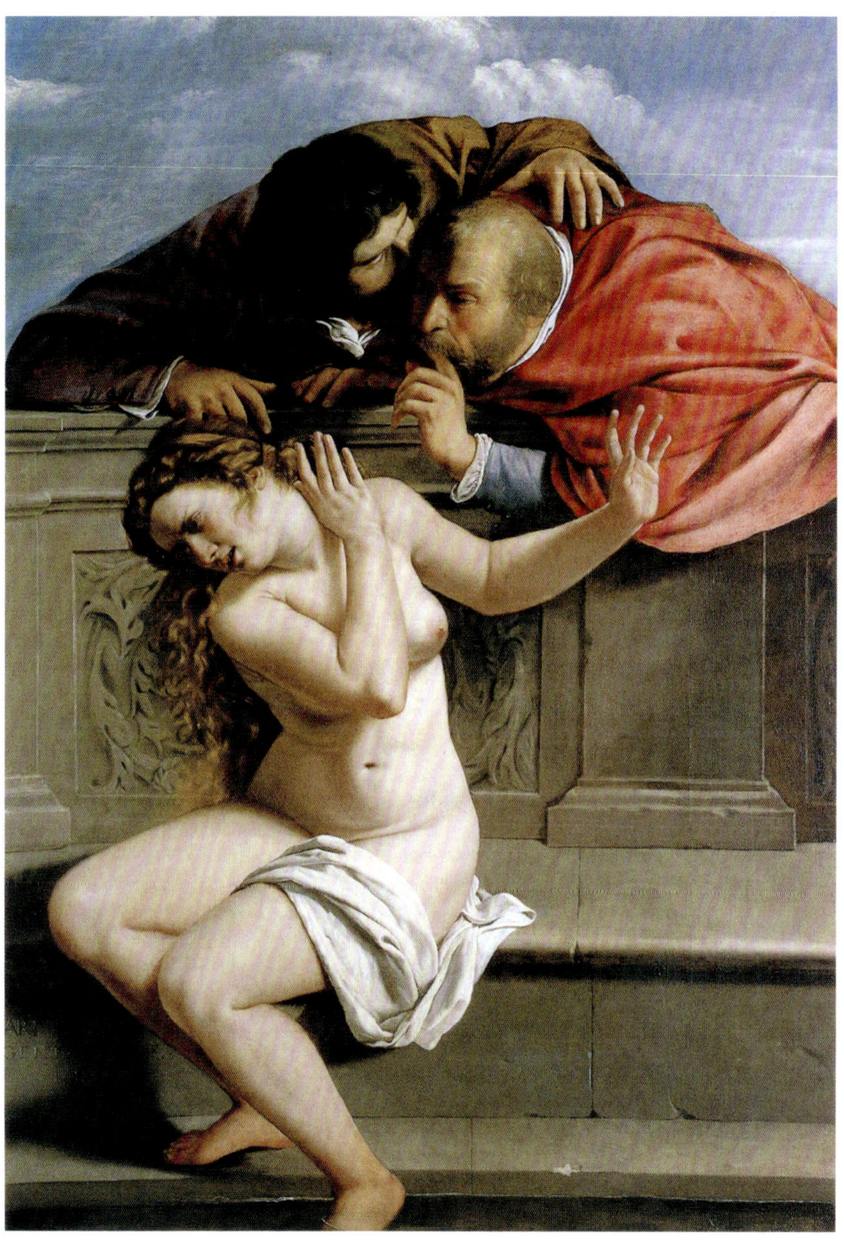

20 Artemisia Gentileschi, *Susanna and the Elders*, 1610.
Oil on canvas, 170 × 119 cm (67 × 46⅞ in.)

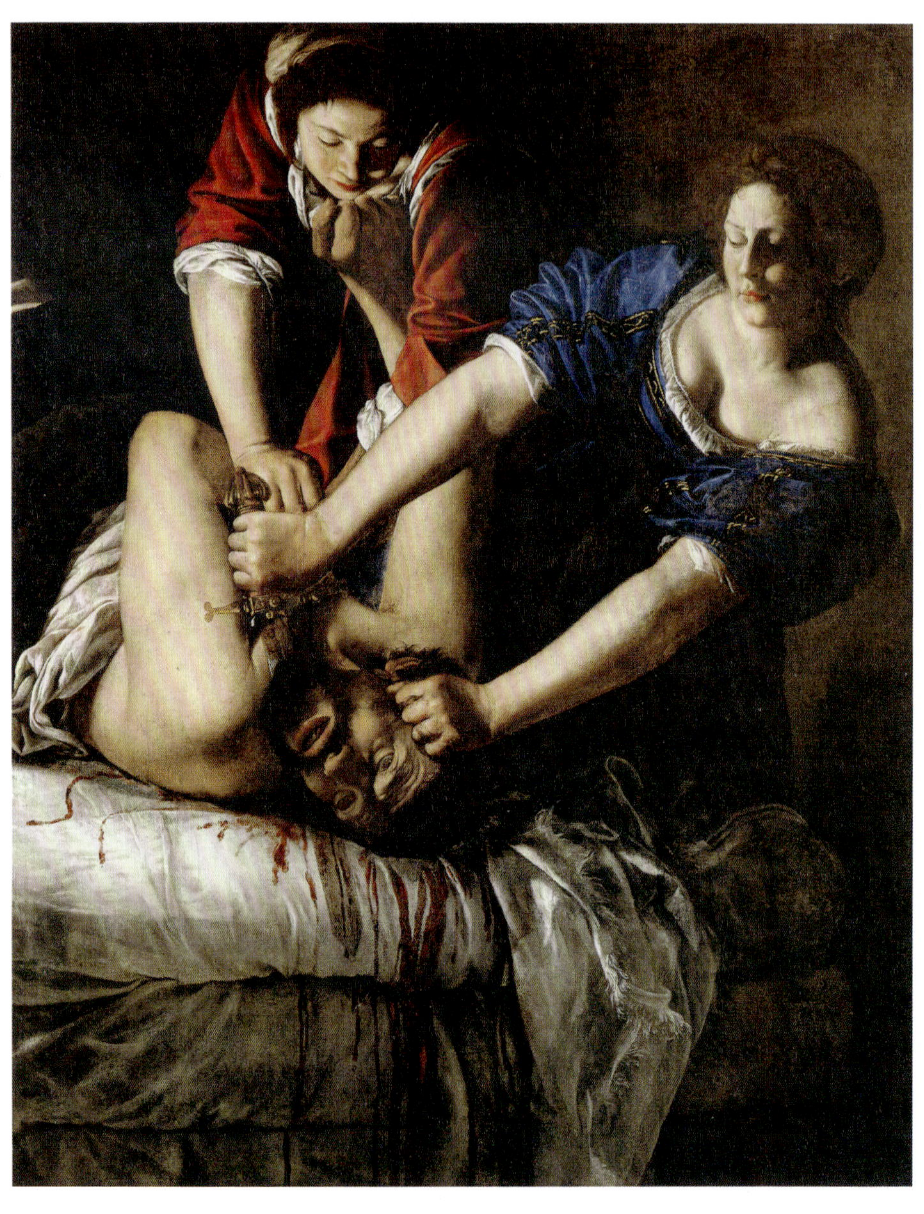

21 Artemisia Gentileschi, *Judith Beheading Holofernes*, *c.* 1613.
Oil on canvas, 158.8 × 125.5 cm (62⅝ × 49½ in.)

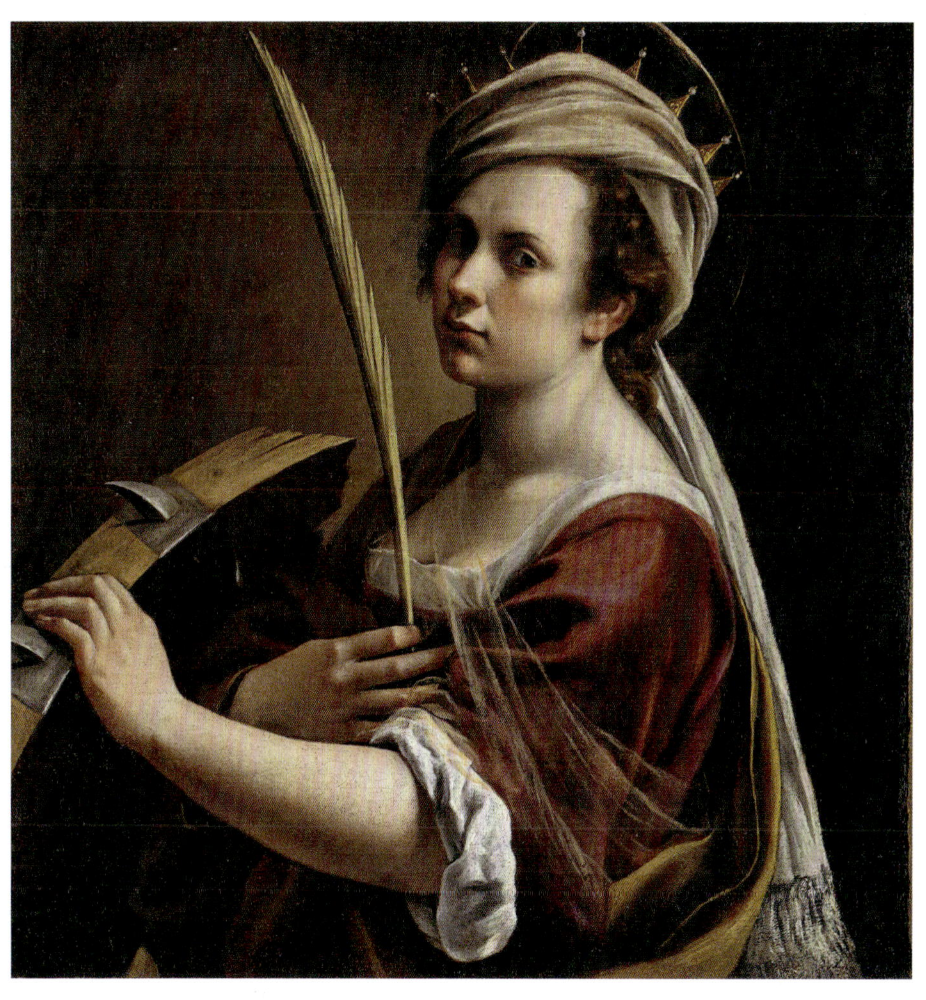

22 Artemisia Gentileschi, *Self-Portrait as St Catherine of Alexandria*, *c.* 1615–17. Oil on canvas, 71.4 × 69 cm (28⅛ × 27¼ in.)

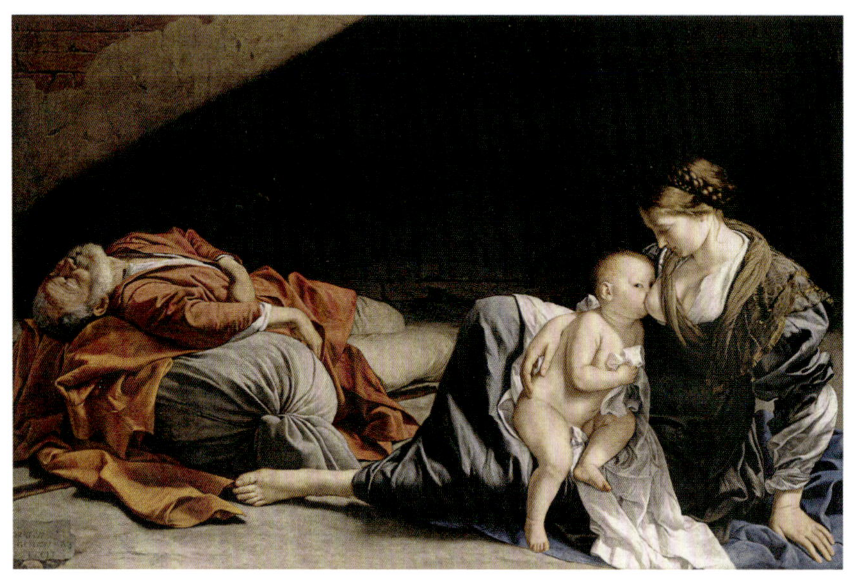

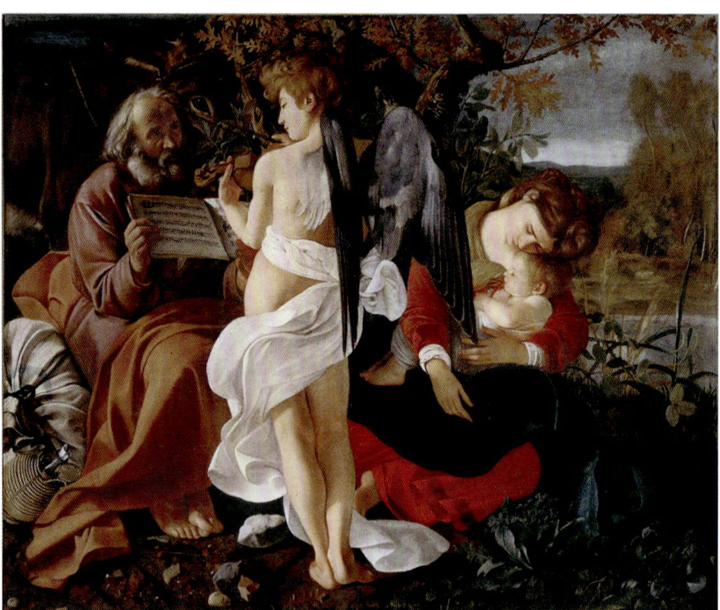

23 Orazio Gentileschi, *The Rest on the Flight into Egypt, c.* 1626–28.
Oil on canvas, 138.5 × 216 cm (54⅝ × 85⅛ in.)

24 Michelangelo Merisi da Caravaggio, *The Rest on the Flight into Egypt,*
c. 1594–95. Oil on canvas, 135.5 × 166.5 cm (53⅜ × 65⅝ in.)

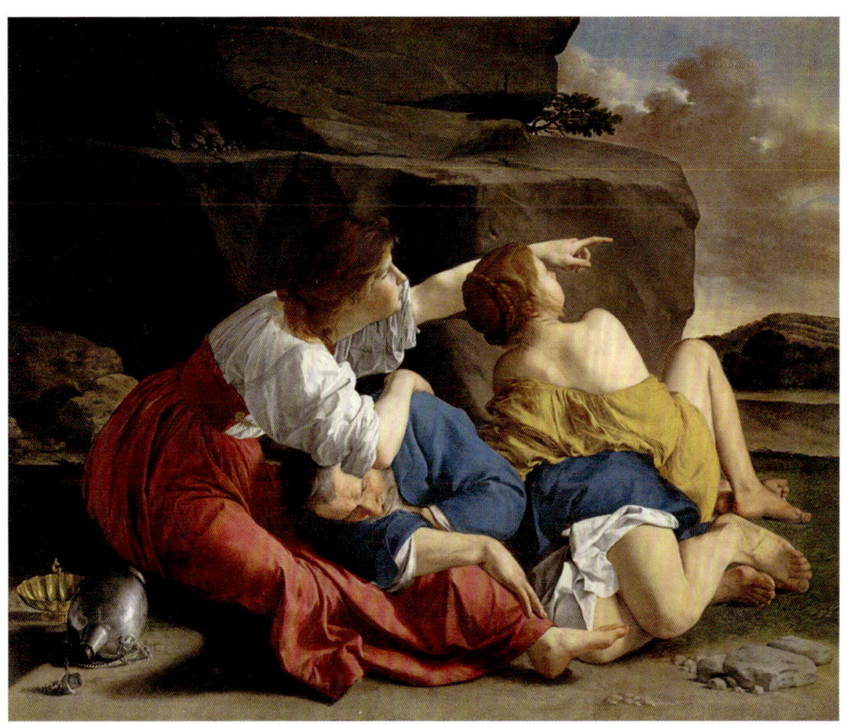

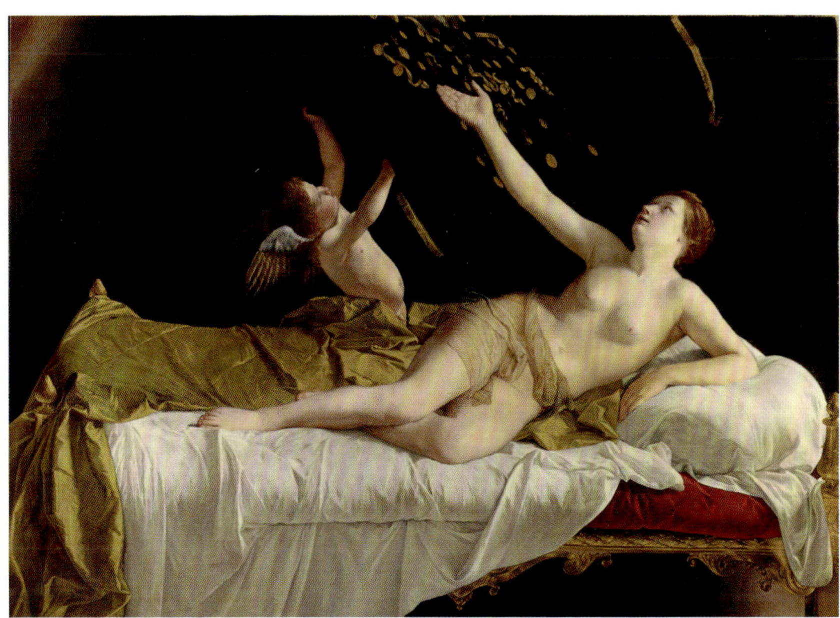

25 Orazio Gentileschi, *Lot and his Daughters*, *c.* 1620.
Oil on canvas, 151.8 × 189.2 cm (59⅞ × 74½ in.)

26 Orazio Gentileschi, *Danaë and the Shower of Gold*, 1621–23.
Oil on canvas, 161.5 × 227.1 cm (63⅝ × 89½ in.)

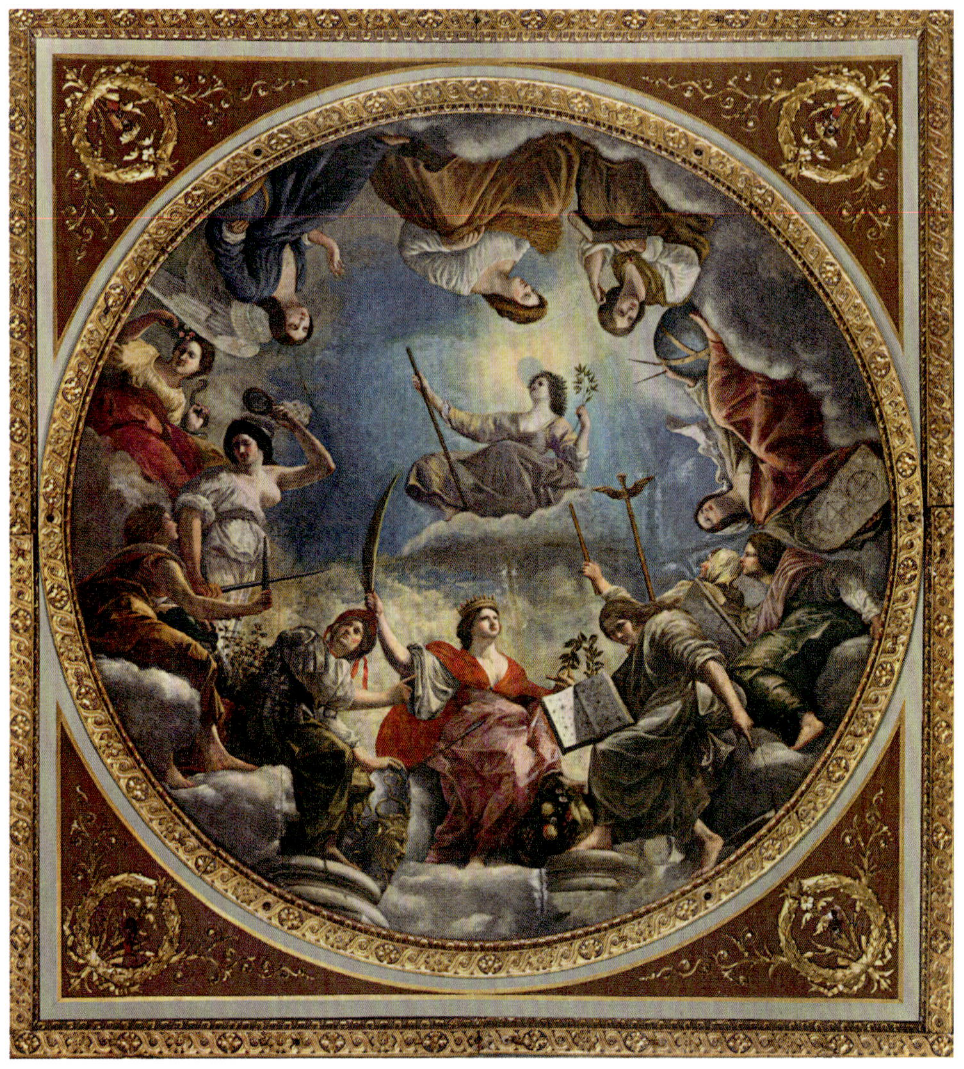

27 Orazio Gentileschi and Artemisia Gentileschi, *An Allegory of Peace and the Arts* (central roundel), *c.* 1635–38. Oil on canvas, mounted on board, diameter 479 cm (188⅝ in.)

28 Artemisia Gentileschi, *Self-Portrait as the Allegory of Painting (La Pittura)*, *c.* 1638–39. Oil on canvas, 98.6 × 75.2 cm (38⅞ × 29⅝ in.)

29 Artemisia Gentileschi, *Susanna and the Elders*, 1652. Oil on canvas, 200.3 × 225.6 cm (78⅞ × 88⅞ in.)

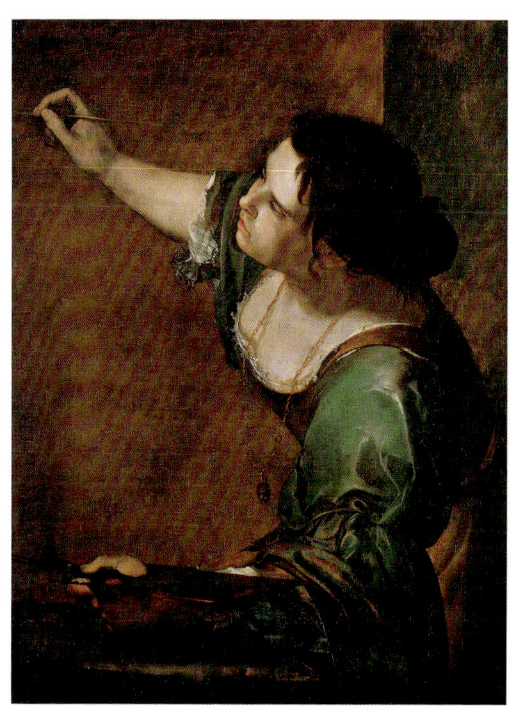

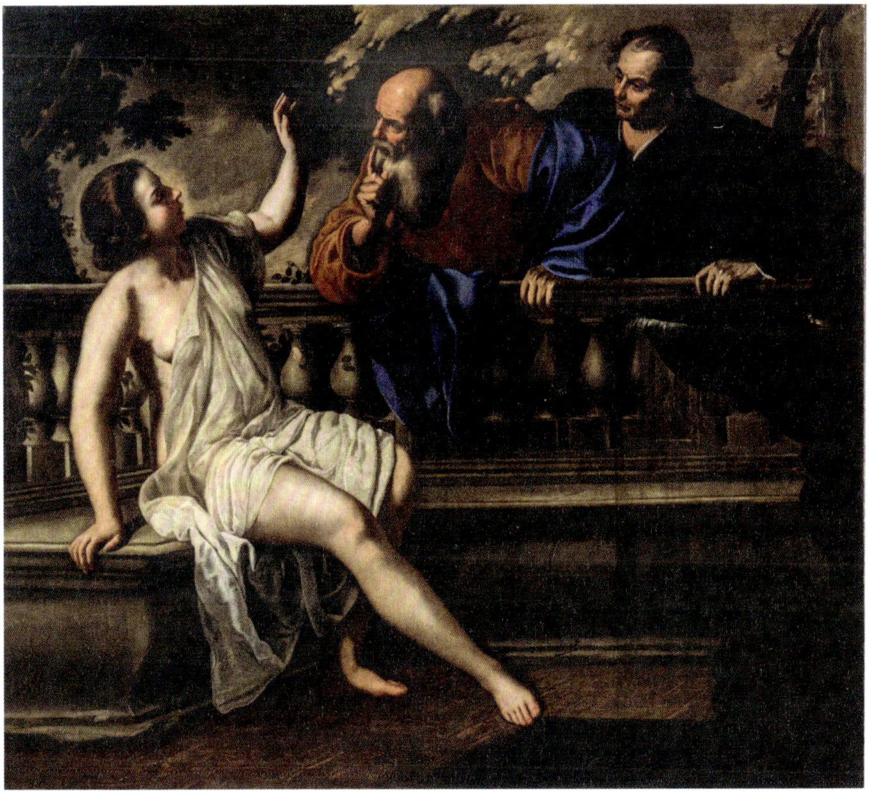

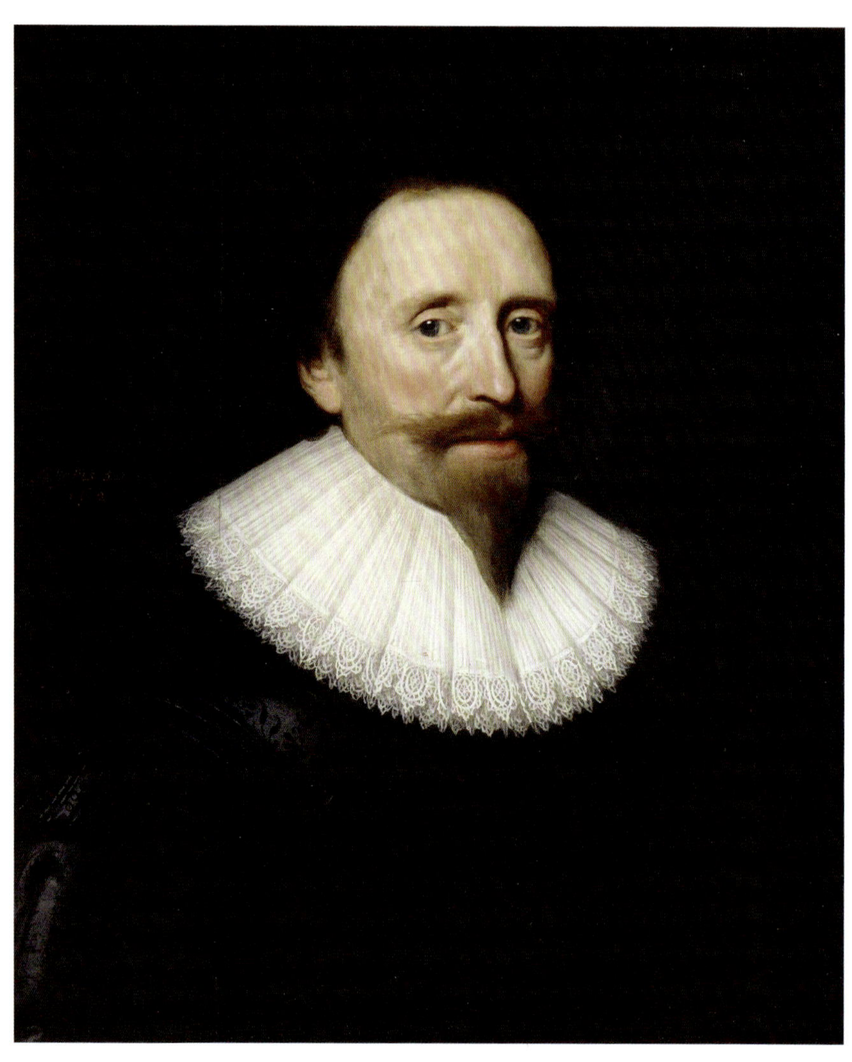

30 Michiel Jansz van Miereveld, *Sir Dudley Carleton*, 1628.
Oil on canvas, 64.5 × 53.6 cm (25½ × 21⅛ in.)

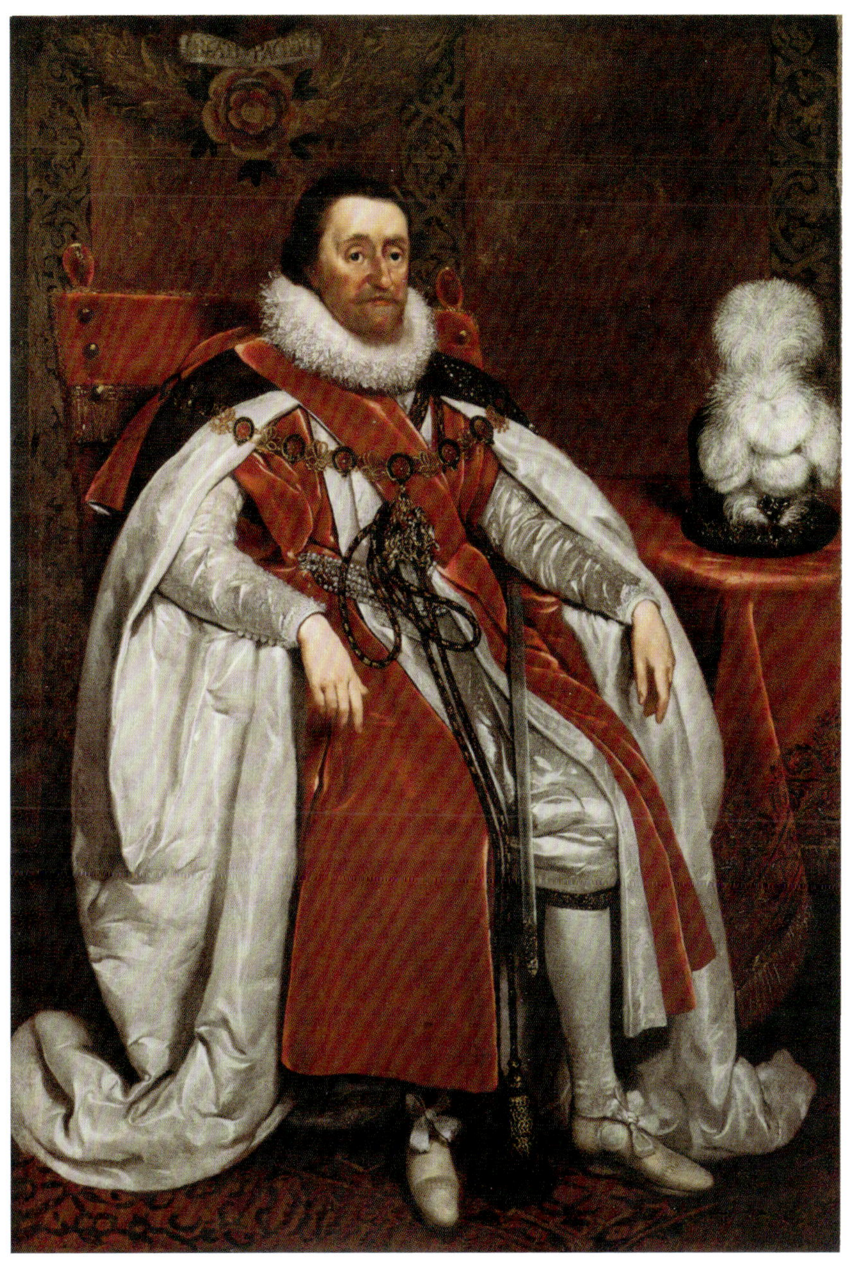

31 Daniel Mytens, *King James I of England and VI of Scotland*, 1621.
Oil on canvas, 148.6 × 100.6 cm (58⅝ × 39⅝ in.)

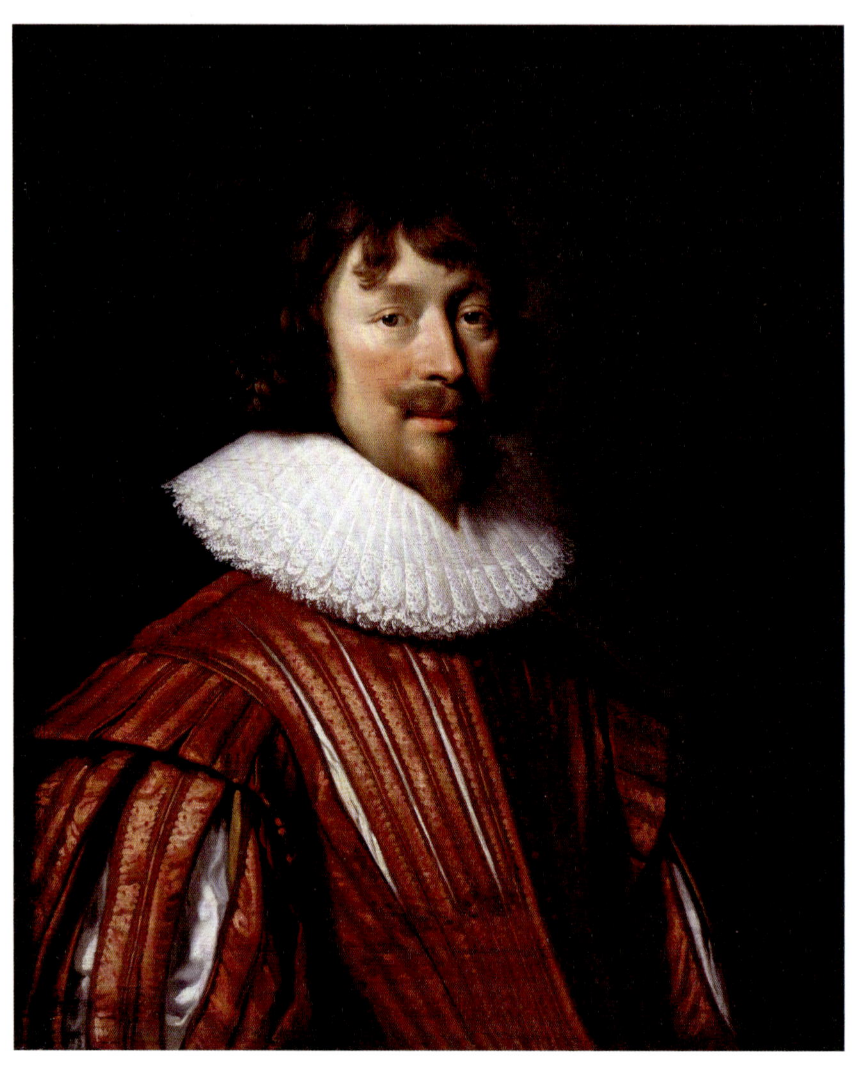

32 Daniel Mytens, *Endymion Porter*, 1627.
Oil on canvas, 76.2 × 63.5 cm (30 × 25 in.)

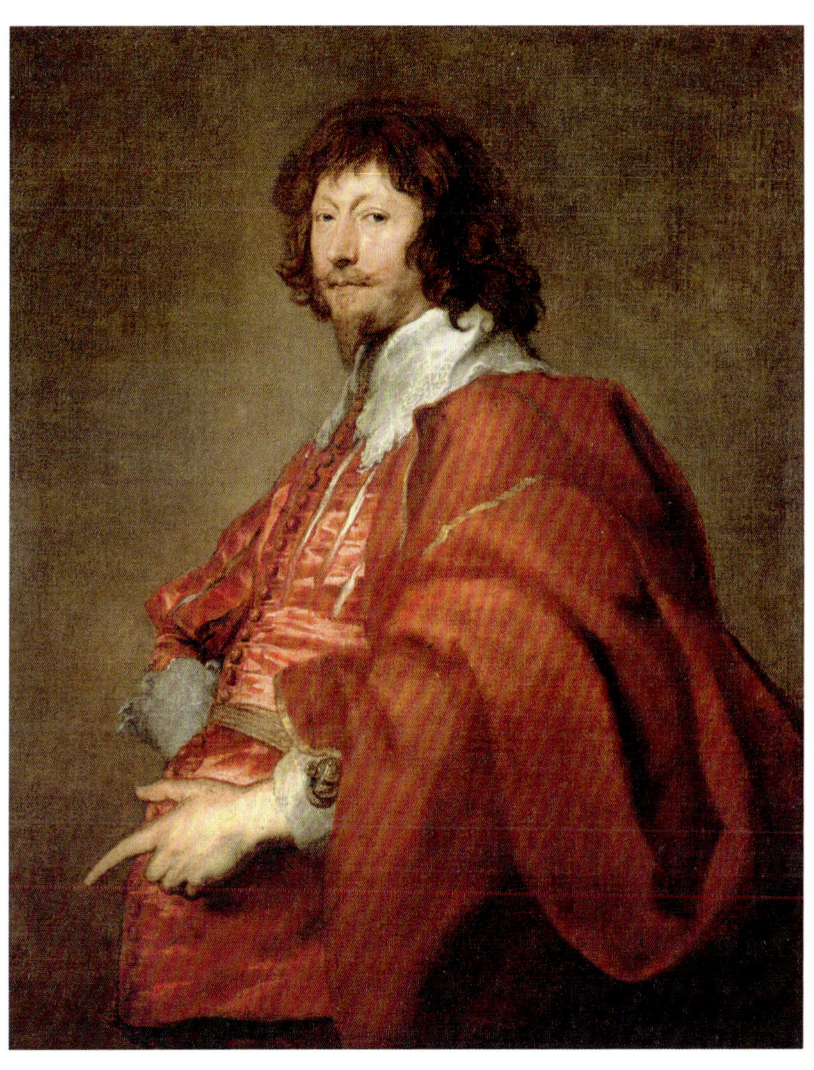

33 Anthony van Dyck, *Endymion Porter*, 1628.
Oil on canvas, 114.5 × 94 cm (45⅛ × 37⅛ in.)

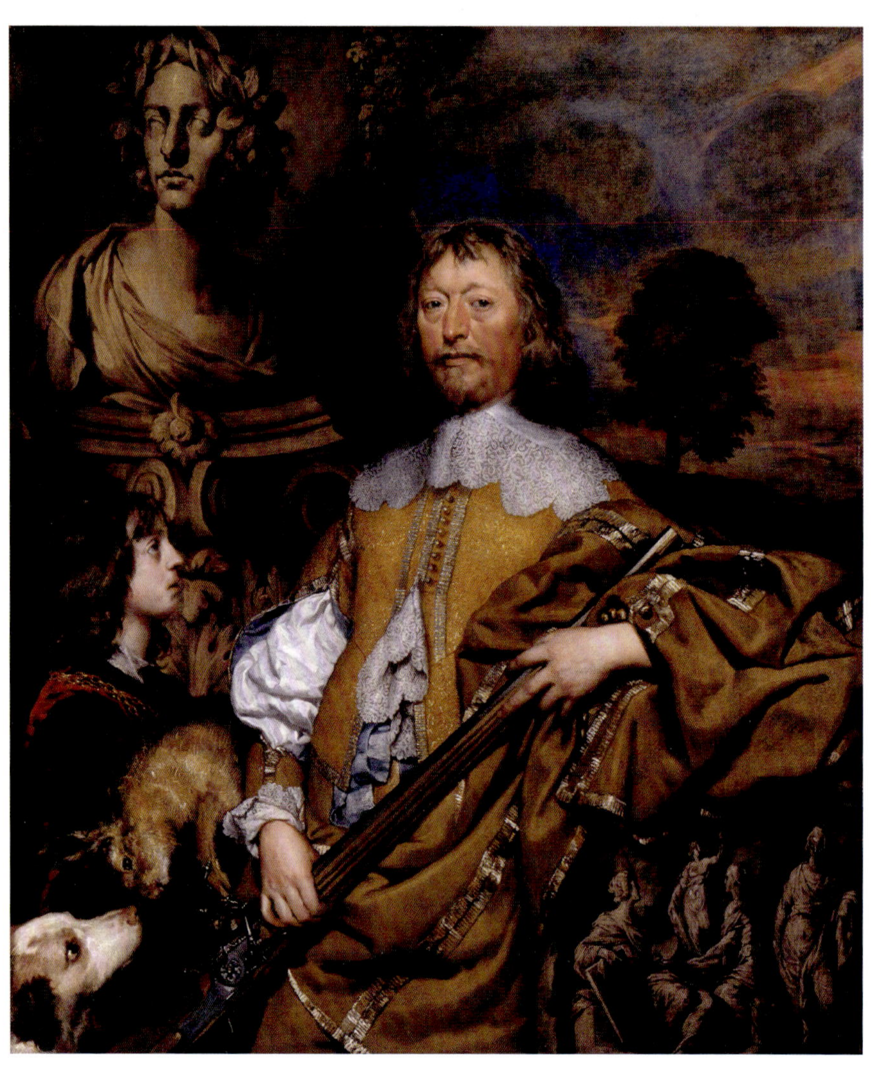

34 William Dobson, *Endymion Porter*, *c*.1642–45.
Oil on canvas, 149.9 × 127 cm (59⅛ × 50 in.)

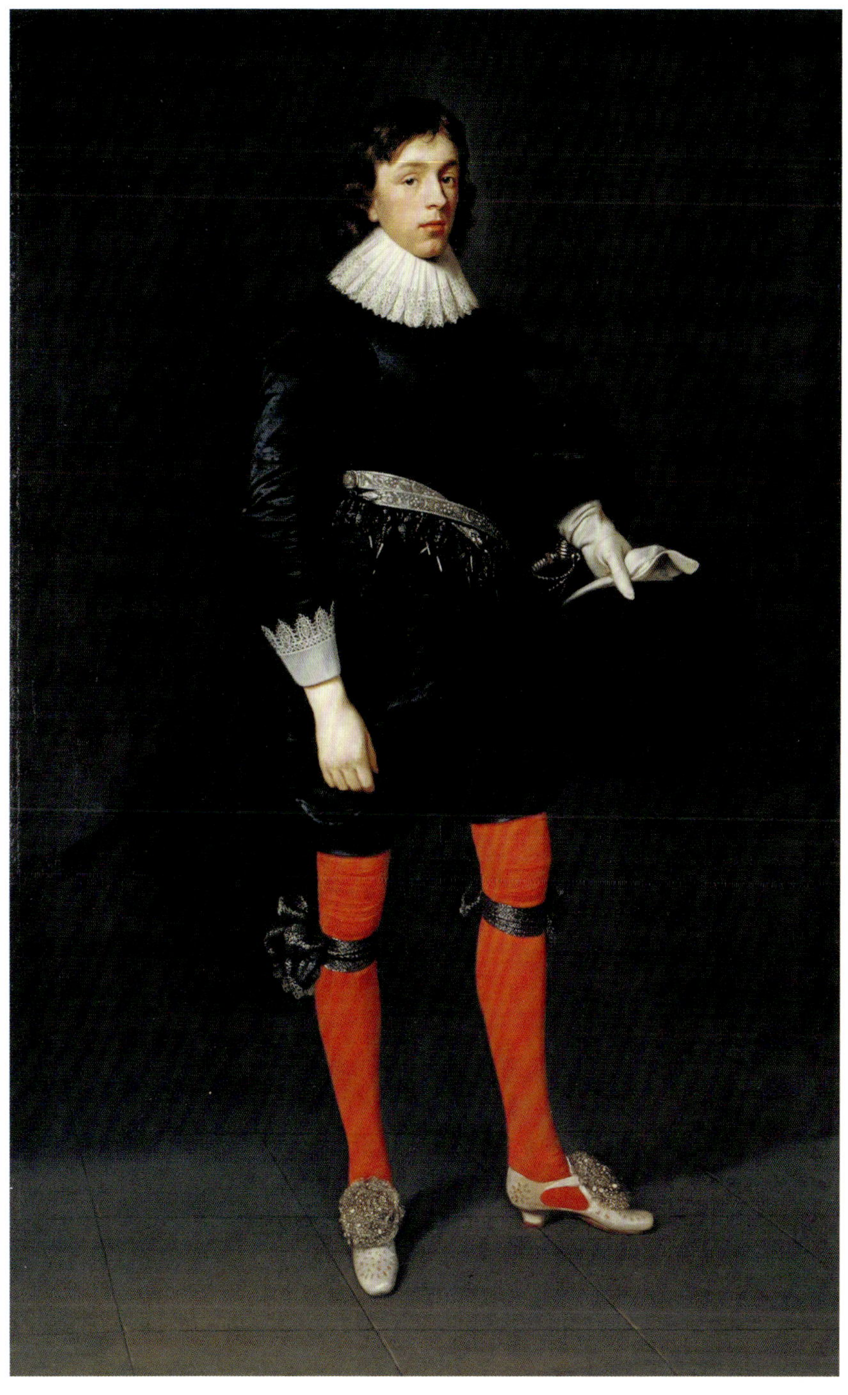

35 Daniel Mytens, *James Hamilton, Earl of Arran, later 3rd Marquis and 1st Duke of Hamilton, aged 17*, 1623. Oil on canvas, 200.7 × 125.1 cm (79 × 49½ in.)

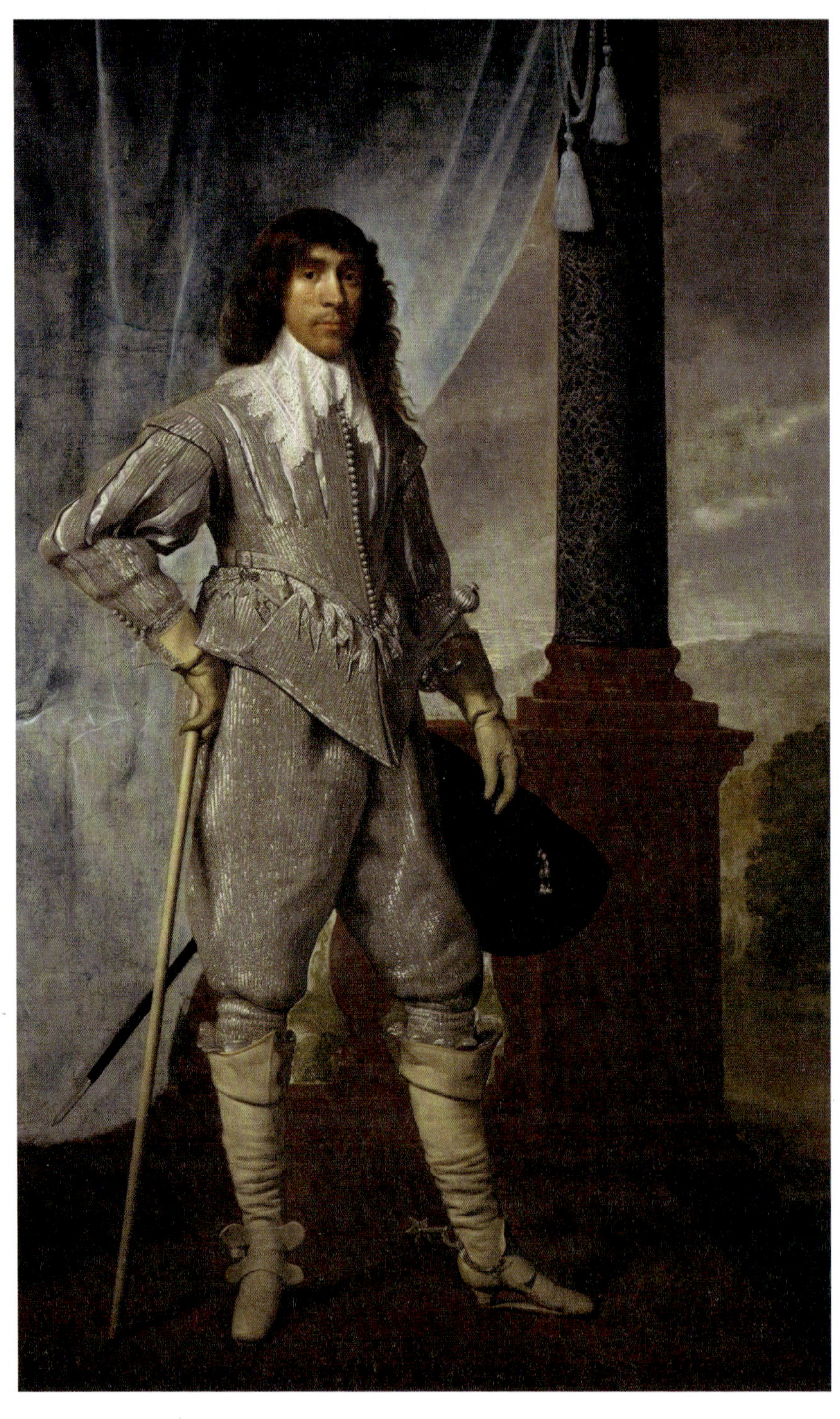

36 Daniel Mytens, *James Hamilton, 1st Duke of Hamilton*, 1629.
Oil on canvas, 221 × 139.7 cm (87⅛ × 55 in.)

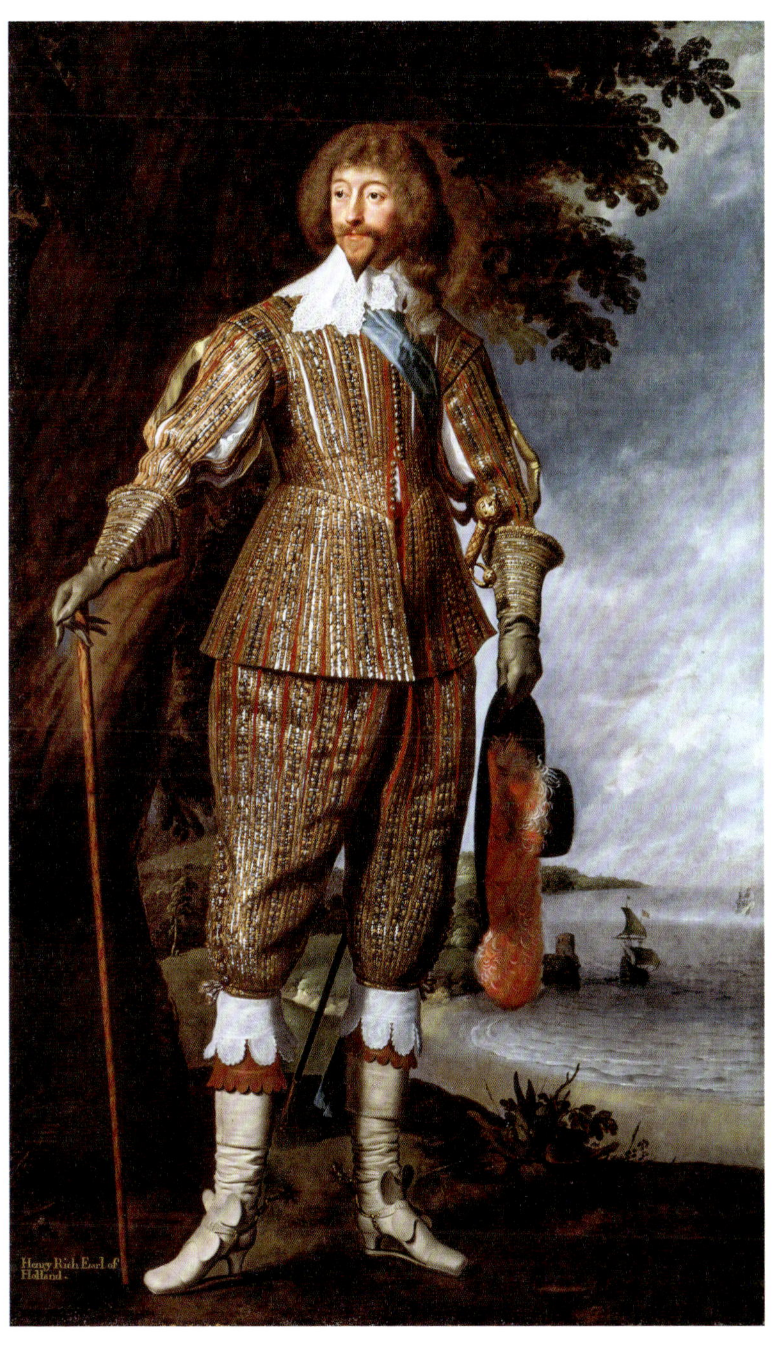

37 Daniel Mytens, *Henry Rich, 1st Earl of Holland*, *c.* 1632–33.
Oil on canvas, 221 × 134.6 cm (87⅛ × 53 in.)

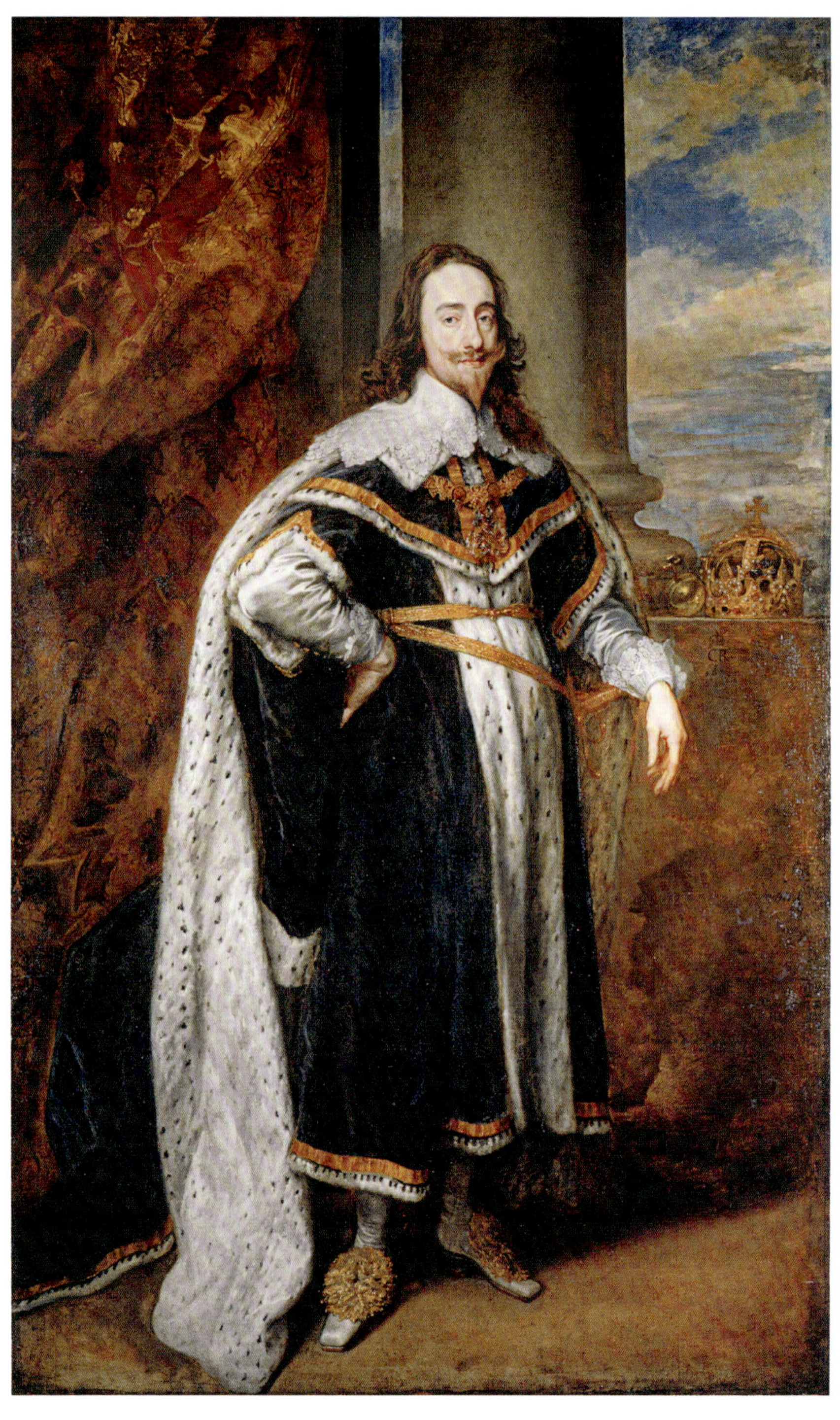

38 Anthony van Dyck, *Charles I in Robes of State, c.* 1636.
Oil on canvas, 248 × 153.6 cm (97¾ × 60½ in.)

that Mytens completed the later Hamilton portrait – Rubens arrived in England. While it cannot be said that Rubens posed an immediate threat to Mytens's position at court at this stage, the new Baroque style of painting that the Flemish artist brought to England in such works as *Peace and War* (see fig. 43) would represent, along with the work of Van Dyck, a slow but inevitable shift in the taste and style preferred by the English court and aristocracy.

Mytens was not unaware of the popularity of Van Dyck's style among English patrons, including his own sponsor, the Earl of Arundel, whom Van Dyck painted in 1620–21 (see p. 147). Indeed, Mytens's own *c.* 1625 portrait of Philip Herbert, 4th Earl of Pembroke (p. 115), consciously uses the compositional style of Van Dyck's portrait of Arundel. But while Van Dyck's seemingly spontaneous application of paint is markedly apparent in the visible brushstrokes in the background landscape over Arundel's left shoulder, the ruff around his neck and the hair in the beard, his style stands in stark contrast to Mytens's clean and less visible brushwork, which produces a much more polished effect. The liveliness of the paint in Van Dyck's portrait gives the work movement and life, whereas Mytens's cool and precise painting seems less lifelike in comparison.

Despite their rivalries, what cannot be underestimated is the extent to which these foreign artists were at the heart of government and power, their paintings used as highly effective tools for propaganda. Those in power learned early on the strength of images in promoting messages of dominance and control, and Mytens produced numerous portraits of the King for these very purposes when needed at the most turbulent moment in his rule. Using the established format of the full-length portrait, Mytens produced images of Charles I that were conceived as official state portraits, and several versions were distributed. These pictures tell a very different story to the reality of Charles's life, since he struggled to hold on to power throughout the period when they were made. In June 1628 he prorogued (paused) Parliament and then suspended it from 1629 to 1640, often known as the Eleven Years' Tyranny. Royalist supporters of the King fuelled a rise in the popularity of full-length portraits in this period, in a demonstration of allegiance and deference to the monarchy. Mytens rode this wave, which witnessed a flourishing of output from his studio.

This increased workload inevitably led to numerous standard compositional portrait types of Charles I, one example being the full-length portrait in the National Portrait Gallery, London, dating from 1631 (p. 116). It is a measure of Mytens's success that variations on this theme appear frequently, and his ability to produce so much work clearly indicates that the artist had established a workshop to meet the demand for his services. But the generic output resulting from such success has led to doubts regarding authenticity in the modern period, including questions about the National Portrait Gallery painting, which is inscribed only with the King's name. Yet a signed and dated version of this work by Mytens does exist, which is almost identical in pose and composition, albeit with a different background and costume (p. 117).

Even as Mytens was consolidating his role as court painter with a series of portraits depicting the most important figures at court, his position was gradually being undermined by the appearance of portraits of those same figures painted by Van Dyck. In particular, Van Dyck's later portrait of Porter, made *c.* 1633 (see p. 156), brings into focus the stark contrast in his relationship with these valuable clients compared to that of Mytens. Van Dyck places himself next to Porter in this portrait, clearly at the request of the patron, signalling in a single image both Van Dyck's ascendance at court and Mytens's waning influence. Mytens had clearly been struggling for some time against the influence of Van Dyck, and his portraits, including those of Robert Rich and his brother Henry Rich, 1st Earl of Holland (fig. 37), though highly competent, were already looking dated, stiff and generic in comparison with Van Dyck's free-flowing style. It cannot be said that Mytens's approach to portraiture was unpopular; the stature of his clientele along with the influence of Arundel led to numerous commissions and even imitators of his style, but such emulation did little to stem the tide of Van Dyck's sway over Mytens's patrons. The popularity of the incoming artist's work marked the beginning of a slow but inevitable erosion of Mytens's position as the King's painter.

The extent to which Mytens would be usurped is epitomized by Van Dyck's full-length portrait of Charles I of *c.* 1636 (fig. 38), which brings the King to life on canvas like never before. The sense of movement evoked by the visible brushstrokes imbues the King's ermine-lined robes with

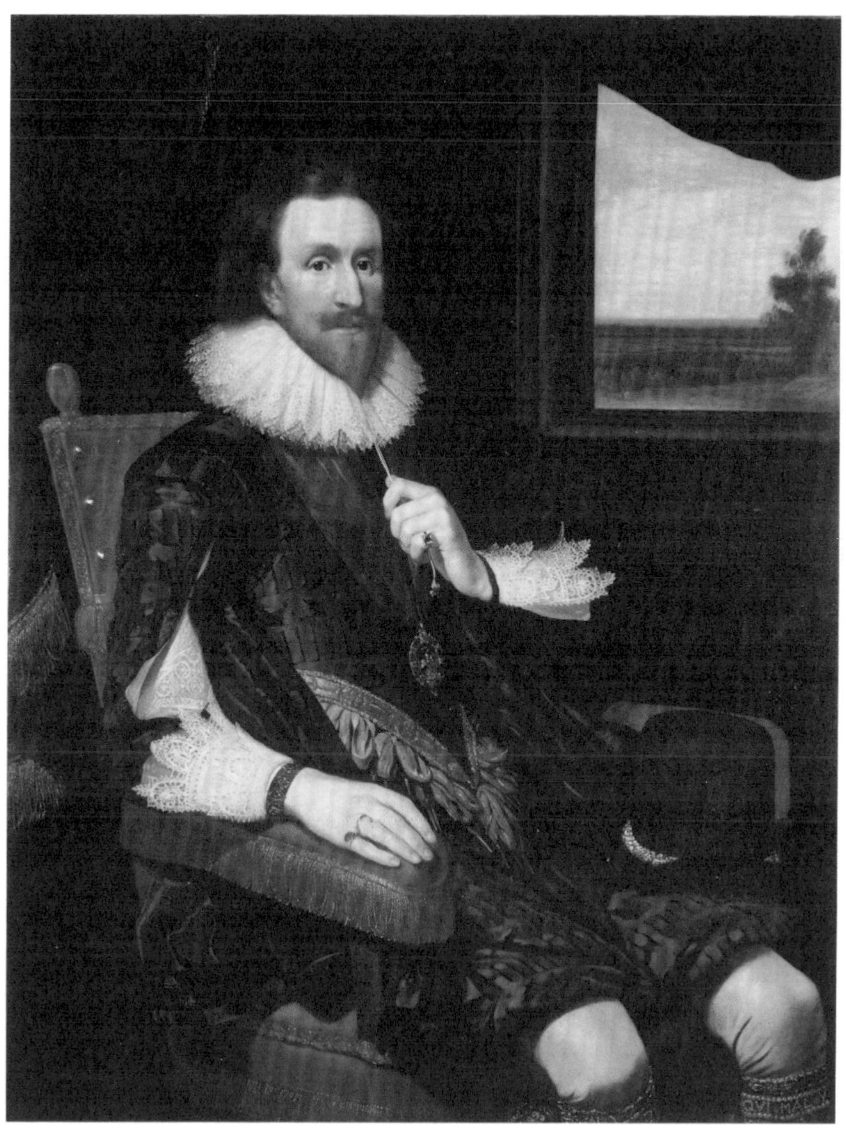

Daniel Mytens, *Philip Herbert (Later 4th Earl of Pembroke)*,
c. 1625. Oil on canvas, 132 × 105 cm (52 × 41¼ in.)

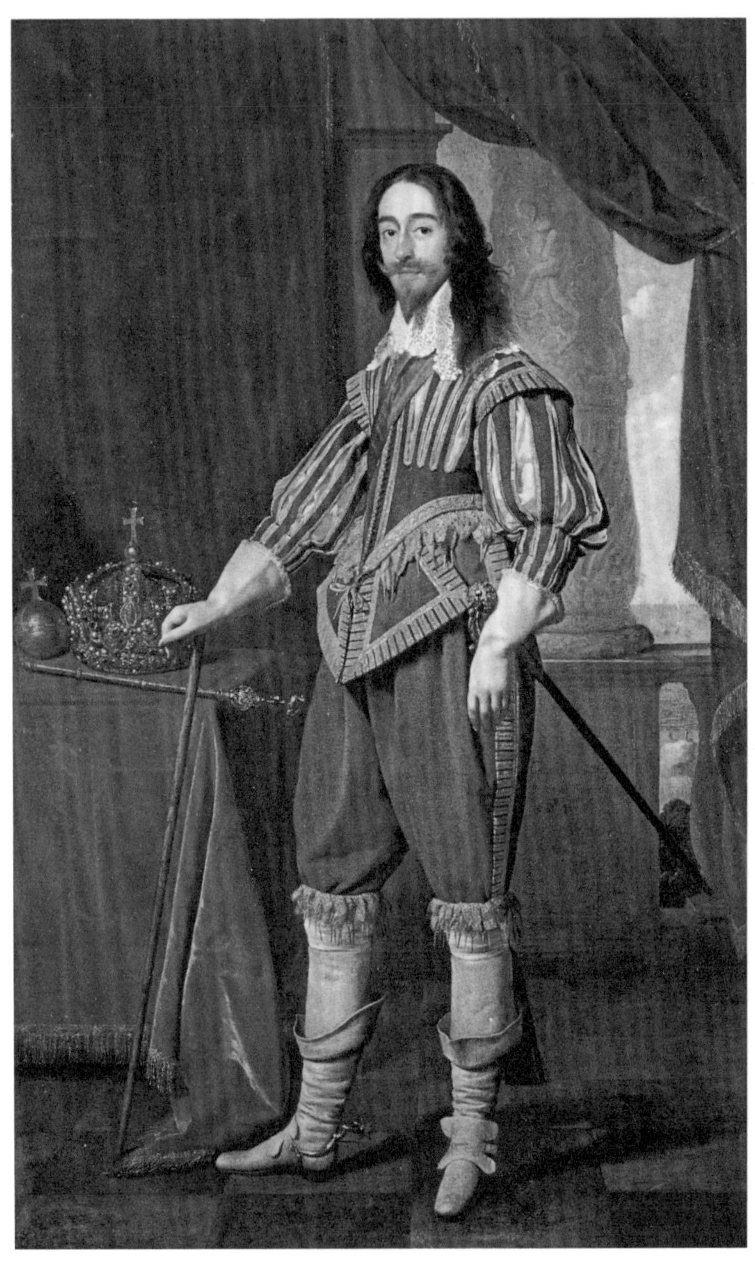

Daniel Mytens, *Charles I*, 1631. Oil on canvas, 215.9 × 134.6 cm (85 × 53 in.)

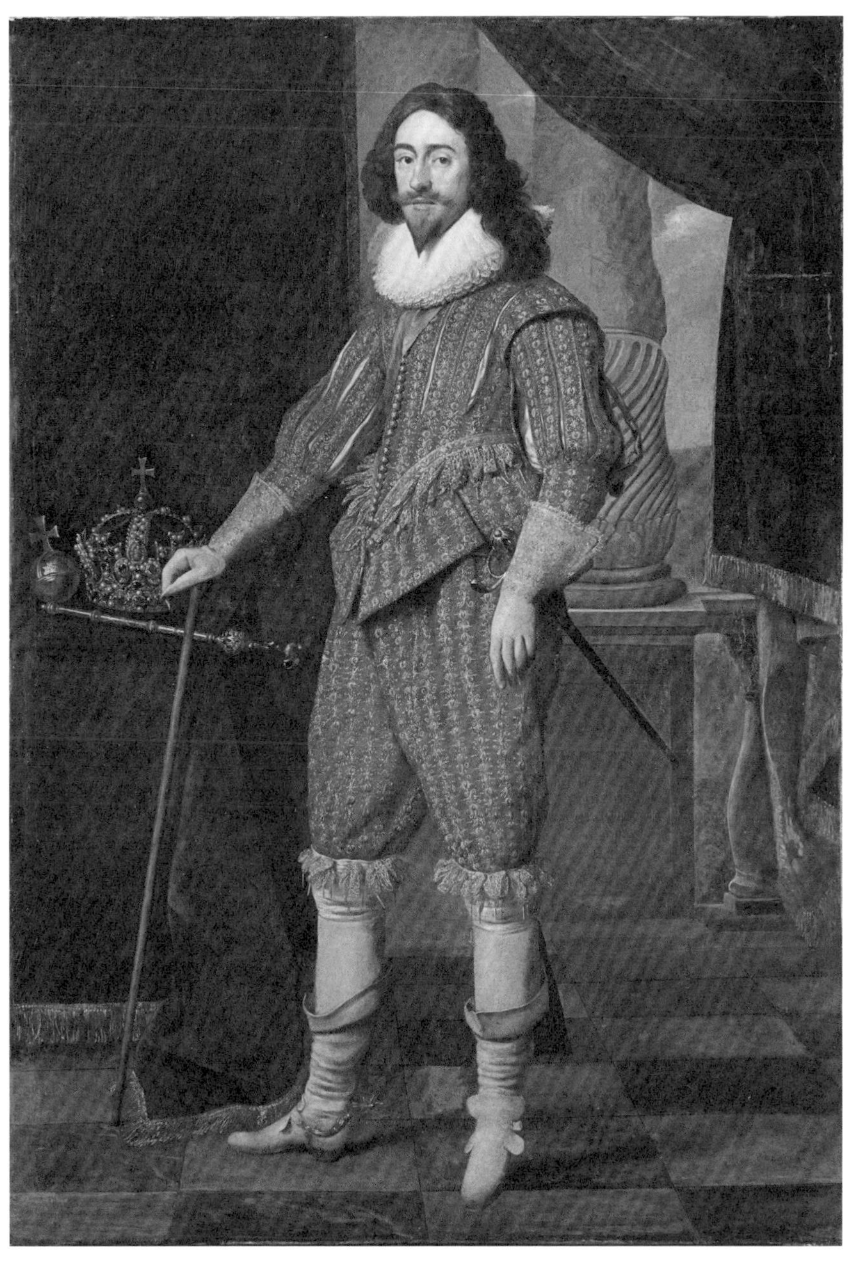

Daniel Mytens, *Charles I, c.* 1629. Oil on canvas, 200.3 × 140.7 cm (78⅞ × 55½ in.)

a tactile quality and the canvas exudes a sense of power, grandeur and relaxed confidence. Such qualities were distinctly lacking in Mytens's own work and would mark the end of his time in England. It is not known precisely when he returned to The Hague for the final time, but the issuing of a 'passe for Daniell Mitten, to goe over into the Low Countries with his truncks' was recorded in September 1630, along with a further pass in May 1631 for his wife, three children and two maids, 'to take with them their trucks apparel &c over into the Low Countries'.[22] The commercial success enjoyed by Mytens is evident from the number of portraits he made, including fifteen of Charles as Prince or King produced by the Mytens studio between 1628 and 1631. But the promise of a pension for life made in earlier documents was not honoured when Mytens returned to The Hague, and it would be a further three years before he received his final royal payment in May 1634 of £100 for two portraits of Charles I.[23]

Despite the relatively short time he spent in England, Daniel Mytens was a commercial success and continued to be one after his return to The Hague, demonstrating that his style of painting and knowledge of the industry was still very much in demand. His departure was not the end of his influence on the British school of painting, because he appears in the records again by 1637, this time in The Hague, where he acted as one of the many agents employed for the collections of the Earl of Arundel. In this position Mytens was able to dictate, or at the very least inform, the taste of Arundel and his fellow English collectors, continuing from abroad the fashion for all things foreign in English painting for perhaps another decade. But Mytens's moment in the British limelight proved to be just that, and although he outlived both Van Dyck and Rubens, these two artists not only eclipsed Mytens in his lifetime but would continue to do so for centuries afterwards in reputation and art historical discourse. For Mytens there would be no public mourning or burial at St Paul's Cathedral as marked the death of Van Dyck; instead the last piece of information we have for him is a perfunctory document of 22 June 1647, which cites him as deceased.[24]

6

Peter Paul Rubens

Painter, Diplomat, Statesman

In British art history, one artist looms particularly large, exerting a huge and far-reaching influence across the British school of painting. The artistic style of this foreigner from Antwerp became so famous in British society that to this day his name is used as an adjective in the English language to describe the fuller-bodied woman: Rubenesque. During his lifetime, the art of Sir Peter Paul Rubens was emulated by a number of English-born artists, including William Dobson, and the Rubens workshop would go on to spawn a host of acolytes, from Anthony van Dyck to Sir Peter Lely, and the legacy of the many collaborations that took place in his workshop led to the transmutation of his aesthetic into a grand Baroque style that was disseminated by his many pupils and followers right across Europe, ensuring that the artist's influence would stretch far beyond his lifetime.

Peter Paul Rubens was born on 28 June 1577, the sixth of seven children, into a wealthy middle-class family in Siegen, a city in Westphalia, Germany. His parents were there having fled Antwerp in the Spanish Netherlands to escape religious persecution. In 1554 the Habsburg Holy Roman Emperor Charles V (r. 1519–56) had ceded control of the Netherlands to his son Philip, soon to be Philip II of Spain (r. 1556–98). As ruler, Philip sought to suppress all non-Roman Catholic worship, in particular Calvinism, a form of Protestantism based on the teachings of the reformer John Calvin in Geneva, which had spread across the Low Countries in the 1550s. Rubens's father, Jan Rubens, a lawyer and alderman, held Calvinist sympathies, leading to the family's escape from the previously prosperous and liberal city of Antwerp.

A reasonably accurate record of the region passed to Philip II is found in *Description of the Low Countries* (1567) by Lodovico Guicciardini, an Italian writer and merchant who lived mostly in Antwerp.[1] It details the state of the Low Countries at the time, noting the presence of two hundred walled cities and twelve thousand villages. Antwerp, which Guicciardini reports as having more artists than butchers or bankers, had become Europe's financial capital, eclipsing the past dominance of Bruges. It was a cosmopolitan city, supporting merchants, wealthy collectors and a well-educated elite, and attracting trade with Portuguese ships carrying spices from what is now Indonesia and English ships carrying linen and wool. Its exchanges dealt in precious metals, including gold and silver from the new Spanish colonies in the Americas. In short, a healthy influx of foreigners had made the city prosperous, a tangible legacy of which was the building and completion in 1566 of a new town hall, which spanned an entire block.

But under the dictatorial and brutal rule of Philip II, within a decade Antwerp's prosperity and liberality came to an end. The city's rich merchant classes and intellectual elite saw the suppression of Calvinism as bad for business, and they were proved correct. When the Duke of Alba, representing Philip II, established the Council of Troubles in 1567, to deal with reformist insurrections by punishing and executing anyone suspected of heresy (see p. 39), those likely to be affected began to leave the Spanish Netherlands in large numbers, along with those who stood against the King's fanatical rule. Philip finally returned to Madrid from the Netherlands in 1559, installing his father's illegitimate daughter Margaret of Parma as Regent. Her approach to ruling the Netherlands was less dictatorial than Philip's, but further crises lay in store, with the severe winter of 1565–66 creating famine conditions, compounded by iconoclastic riots in 1566 and 1567.

Having escaped the turmoil of Antwerp, Jan Rubens took his family to Cologne, arriving in 1568. There, in his capacity as a lawyer, he began work as an advisor to Anna of Saxony, wife of William I, Prince of Orange (r. 1544–84), an opponent of the Spanish who eventually organized revolt against them in the Low Countries. Jan became embroiled in an affair with Anna, the exposure of which led to a two-year spell for him in prison, from 1571 to 1573, having been spared the death penalty thanks to an intervention from his loyal wife, Maria. Following his release, Jan was placed under house arrest in Siegen, a hardship compounded by a spell of poverty, no doubt resulting from losing his work and position at court. He died in 1587, when his son Peter Paul was just ten years old.

After Jan's death, the family returned to Antwerp. Following the accidental destruction by fire of its Stock Exchange and a thirteen-month siege by Spanish forces, the city had fallen in 1585 when, having defeated the Protestant Dutch defenders, the commander of the Spanish forces, Alexander Farnese, Duke of Parma, made a triumphant entry into Antwerp and was handed the keys to the city. With Protestant citizens either exiled or forced to convert, in Antwerp Rubens's family returned to the practice of Catholicism, and for the rest of his life the artist was a devout Catholic and staunch supporter of the Spanish monarchy.[2]

Rubens's father Jan had been fluent in both Latin and Italian, having spent at least five years in Italy studying law at Padua University, possibly the oldest and certainly one of the most prestigious universities in Europe at the time. He passed these skills on to Peter Paul and his older brother Philip. On their return to Antwerp in 1589, the two brothers continued their studies, attending a school run by the Latinist Rombout Verdonk. Here they learned grammar, Latin and Greek rhetoric, so by the time Peter Paul was fourteen years old, he was already familiar with classical authors such as Cicero, Seneca, Horace and Juvenal. Only at this stage did he abandon his education in his father's profession to begin training as a painter, and the abundance of Rubens's surviving correspondence written in Italian, French, Flemish and Latin clearly demonstrates that his classical schooling continued to be integral to his life.

Having trained under various established artists, including Tobias Verhaecht, Adam van Noort and Otto van Veen, Rubens became an independent master in 1598, though very few works painted by him before 1600 survive. Despite abandoning early prospects of a legal career, he remained obsessed with Latin and the classical world and would continue his education for the rest of his life, developing an encyclopaedic knowledge of ancient mythology, philosophy and Catholic doctrine. Such an education was highly unusual for an artist at this time, and

Rubens was significantly more well-read than the average painter, amassing a library of over three hundred books by the time of his death.

To fully appreciate the impact of classical literature on Rubens's art we need look no further than his numerous interpretations of the Greek mythological story of the Judgement of Paris. From his earliest days as a professional artist Rubens was eager to travel and learn from those artists who had come before him, and in May 1600, at the age of twenty-two, he left Antwerp and travelled to Italy to indulge his passion for classical antiquity and to learn from great Renaissance masters of the past such as Titian and Raphael. This marked the beginning of a period of intense interest in the work of these artists, especially the subject of the Judgement of Paris, beginning with one of his earliest paintings of the scene dating from around 1600. His interest in this subject soon became an obsession, and he produced eight paintings of the story between 1600 and 1639, the penultimate year of his life. This obsession is even more extraordinary given that all but one of these works were not commissioned, creating a mystery around why he made them at all. Perhaps the reason lies in the story itself, which depicts the beauty contest between three goddesses, Aphrodite, Hera and Athena, that was the prelude to the abduction of Helen of Troy. The choice faced by Paris, Prince of Troy, between wealth, wisdom and lust would ultimately lead to the disastrous decade-long Trojan War. Perhaps Rubens saw parallels in this story of a supposedly wise, aristocratic prince unable to make the right decision at a crucial moment and the decades-long wars that formed the backdrop to his own life.

In Italy Rubens acquired his first high-profile patron, Vincenzo I Gonzaga, Duke of Mantua, meaning it was now possible for him, perhaps for the first time, to make a living from his work. Some of the artist's earliest extant paintings date from this period and demonstrate the extent of his European ambitions. They include his first equestrian portrait, of the Duke of Lerma (p. 123). Regarded as his first masterpiece, it draws on Renaissance techniques such as foreshortening, which makes the horse seem like it could almost ride directly out of the painting and into our space, along with sculptural modelling effects that reveal the horse's veins and muscles, reminiscent of Roman equestrian monuments.

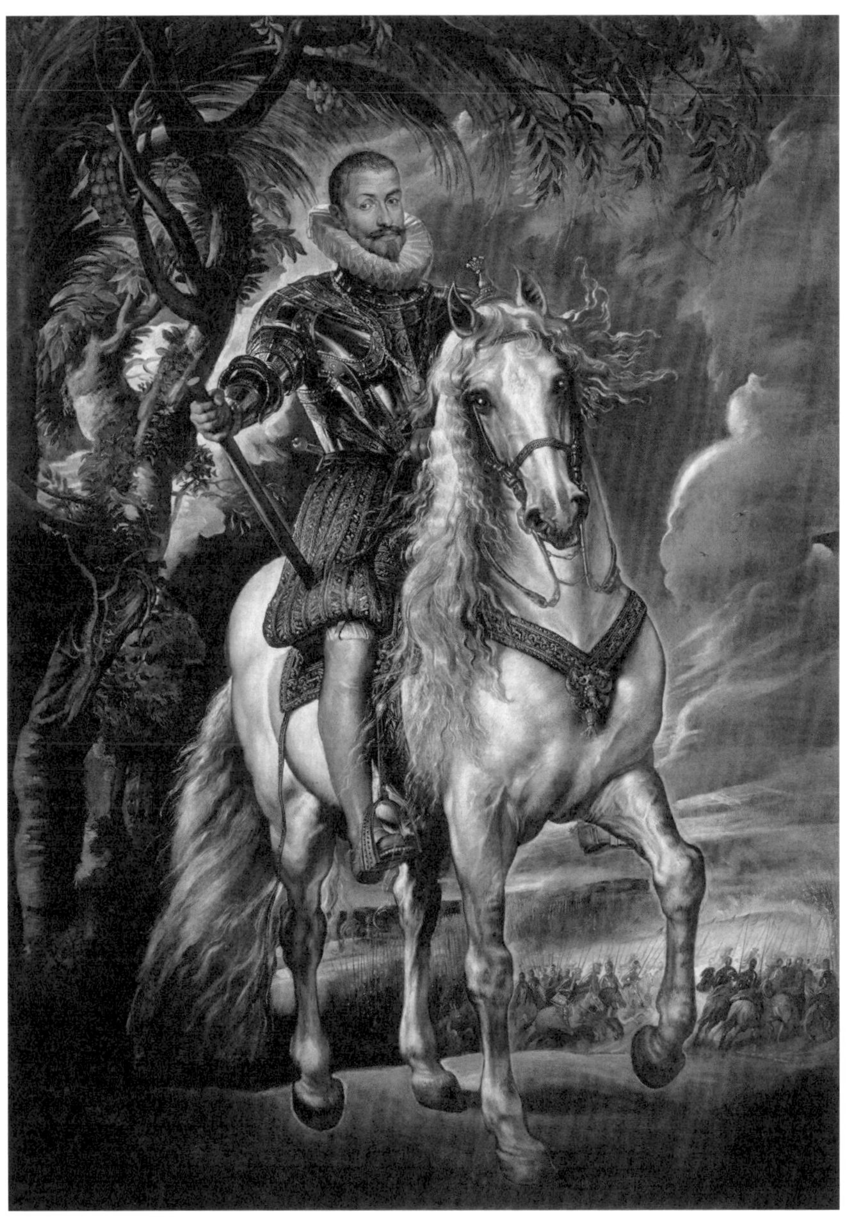

Peter Paul Rubens, *Equestrian Portrait of the Duke of Lerma*, 1603.
Oil on canvas, 290.5 × 207.5 cm (114¼ × 81¾ in.)

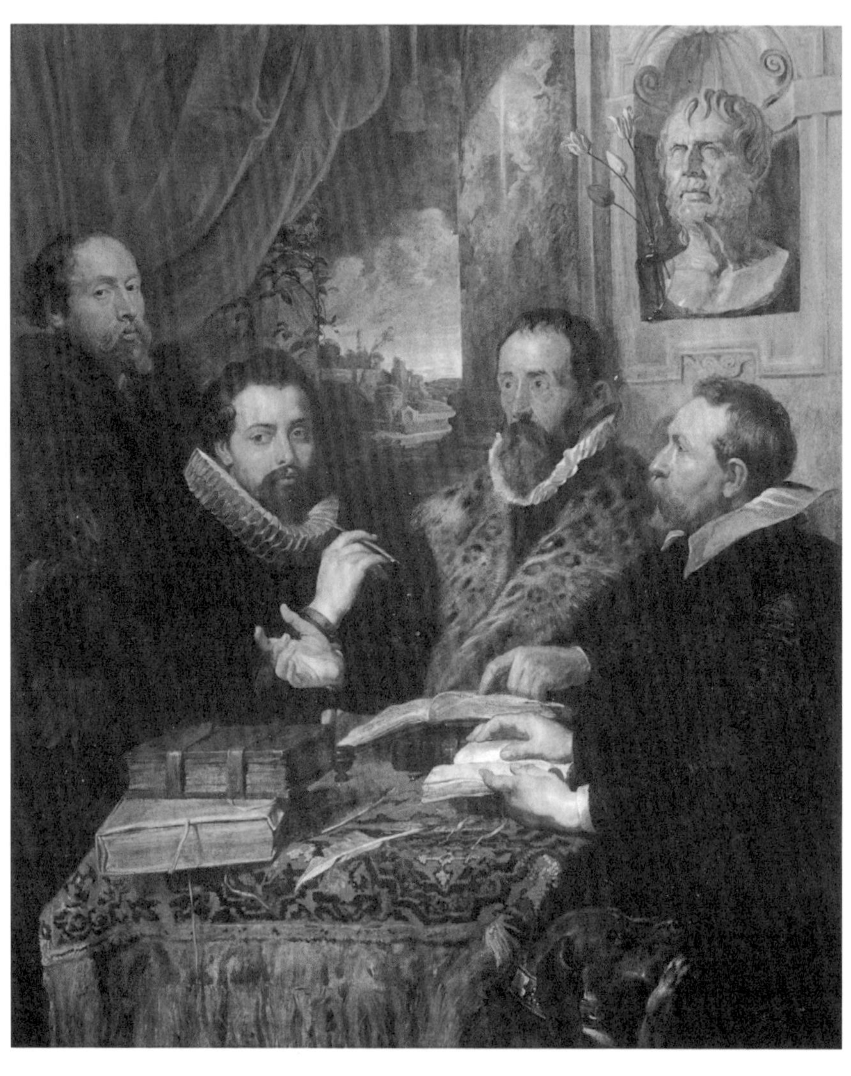

Peter Paul Rubens, *The Four Philosophers – Peter Rubens, Philippus Rubens, Justus Lipsius and Jan van der Wouwer*, 1611–12. Oil on canvas, 167 × 143 cm (65¾ × 56⅜ in.)

Rubens's Italian sojourn lasted for eight years, from 1600 to 1608, punctuated briefly by a visit to Spain around 1603 and 1604. That short trip was an important milestone in his career, marking the beginning of his role as a diplomat, chosen by the Duke of Mantua to act as an ambassadorial envoy to the court of Philip III (r. 1598–1621). In those nine or ten months in Spain, it was the works he saw by Titian in Valladolid and Madrid that made the deepest impression on him, especially the equestrian portrait of Charles V at Mühlberg, painted in 1548 and said to be the closest inspiration for Rubens's Duke of Lerma portrait.[3] A few years later, in 1606, Rubens made another early masterpiece, his portrait of the Marchesa Brigida Spinola Doria (fig. 39). Probably painted about six months after the sitter's marriage to her cousin, the Marchese Giacomo Massimiliano Doria, it is one of the earliest demonstrations of Rubens's deft handling of fabric effects, along with the sheer opulence and sumptuousness he could bring to the art of portraiture.[4] It is not hard to see how such realistic emulation of materials would later inspire other painters in Britain, including the Dutch artist Peter Lely. Indeed, it was spectacular grand-scale paintings like these that eventually brought him to the attention of the English aristocracy.

While in Rome Rubens had the opportunity to sketch works from classical antiquity. One example was a sculpture in the collection of Cardinal Scipione Borghese of a figure then thought to be the ancient Stoic philosopher Seneca, from which he made a black chalk drawing on paper (Hermitage, St Petersburg). The lower part of the sculpture was missing by the time Rubens came to sketch it, and he interpreted the figure as the suicide of the great philosopher. Rubens sketched this sculpture on many occasions, no doubt having unlimited access to the cardinal's collection. In 1611 he produced a somewhat showy self-portrait (p. 124), in which he included his brother Philip along with portraits of the Flemish philologist, philosopher and humanist Justus Lipsius and Jan van der Wouver, a family friend and noted scholar with a number of publications to his name, who went on to be a diplomat appointed as financial advisor to Albert VII, Archduke of Austria, and his wife, the Archduchess Isabella, in 1620. For good measure, Rubens included in the painting a fictive bust of Seneca behind and above all the sitters. The portrait not only tells us something of the circles Rubens was moving in and their interests, but also the important role of the antique in his life and work.

While Rubens's primary interest in visiting Italy lay in furthering his knowledge of classical antiquity, once there he became equally interested in what he could learn from more recent Italian art. He focused in particular on sixteenth-century artists such as Michelangelo, Giulio Romano and Raphael, and produced drawings and retouched works after these artists.[5] His enthusiasm for the classical was especially fired up by the work of Raphael and the circle of painters he influenced, including Perino del Vaga, Baldassare Peruzzi and two assistants from Raphael's workshop, Giovanni da Udine and Polidoro da Caravaggio. As well as a draughtsman, Rubens was also a collector of drawings. His particular interest in Raphael is reflected in his collection, which included some preparatory studies by the Italian artist, known as modelli, that he studied for their technique and retouched and referenced in his own works.[6]

In October 1608 Rubens abruptly returned to Antwerp, prompted by news of his mother being gravely ill, and ten days after his arrival she passed away.[7] But family tragedy was followed by celebration a year later, when in July 1609 Archduke Albert VII and Archduchess Isabella, joint governors of Flanders from 1598 until Albert's death in 1621, appointed Rubens court painter. On first receiving the offer in April 1609, Rubens wrote from Antwerp to his friend in Rome, the doctor, botanist and art collector Johann (also known as Giovanni) Faber: 'I have not yet made up my mind whether to remain in my country or to return forever to Rome, where I am invited on the most favourable terms. Here also they do not fail to make every effort to keep me, by every sort of compliment. The Archduke and the most Serene Infanta have had letters urging me to remain in their service. Their offers are very generous, but I have little desire to become a courtier again. Antwerp would satisfy me, if I could say farewell to Rome. The peace, or rather the truce, for many years will without doubt be ratified, and during this period it is believed that our country will flourish again.'[8]

Four days after this correspondence, on 10 April 1609, the Twelve Years' Truce between Spain and the Northern Netherlands was signed, bringing prosperity back to the Low Countries. Albert and Isabella permitted

Calvinists to practise their faith, though only in private, and artists began to receive commissions for church altarpieces to replace those that had been destroyed in the years of iconoclasm. In October 1609, just three months after his prestigious appointment at the age of thirty-two, Rubens married Isabella Brant. The double portrait of Rubens and his wife is a statement of the artist's success, depicting the newly married couple in rich and flamboyant attire, with Rubens presenting himself not as a painter but instead as a member of Antwerp's wealthy aristocracy, with aspirations to become landed gentry (p. 128).

In the years immediately after the truce, a time that can best be characterized as a Counter-Reformation period in the Northern Netherlands, wealthy benefactors such as the spice merchant Cornelis van der Geest and the former three times mayor of Antwerp, Nicolaas Rockox, would become powerful and influential patrons. Their associations with the region's churches and cathedrals would become the public platform on which Rubens could display his recently acquired knowledge of antiquity from his travels in Italy, and assert his dominance of painting in Antwerp. In June 1610 he gained the chance to do just that when Van der Geest, a church warden at St Walburga, made a significant contribution to the cost of a vast triptych for the church by Rubens, *The Elevation of the Cross* (fig. 40). The muscularity of the figures clearly draws on Rubens's experience of classical sculpture and Renaissance painting, particularly the work of Michelangelo, with the lively movement of the dappled grey horse on the right-hand wing echoing the similar vigour of the horse in the Duke of Lerma portrait, demonstrating Rubens's visual memory and quick economy of working. This was followed in 1611 by *The Entombment* (p. 130), clearly based on Caravaggio's 1602–4 depiction of the same subject and begun just a year after the Italian painter's death. With an almost exact transference of the composition, albeit some calming down of the figures' enthusiastic gesticulations (p. 131), it demonstrates the influence that Caravaggio continued to exert on other painters.

In the midst of these artistic triumphs, Rubens's life was again marked with both sadness and joy; in 1611 his brother Philip died, and his daughter Clara Serena was born (she would die in 1623 at the age of just twelve). The intimate painting he made of his young daughter remains one of

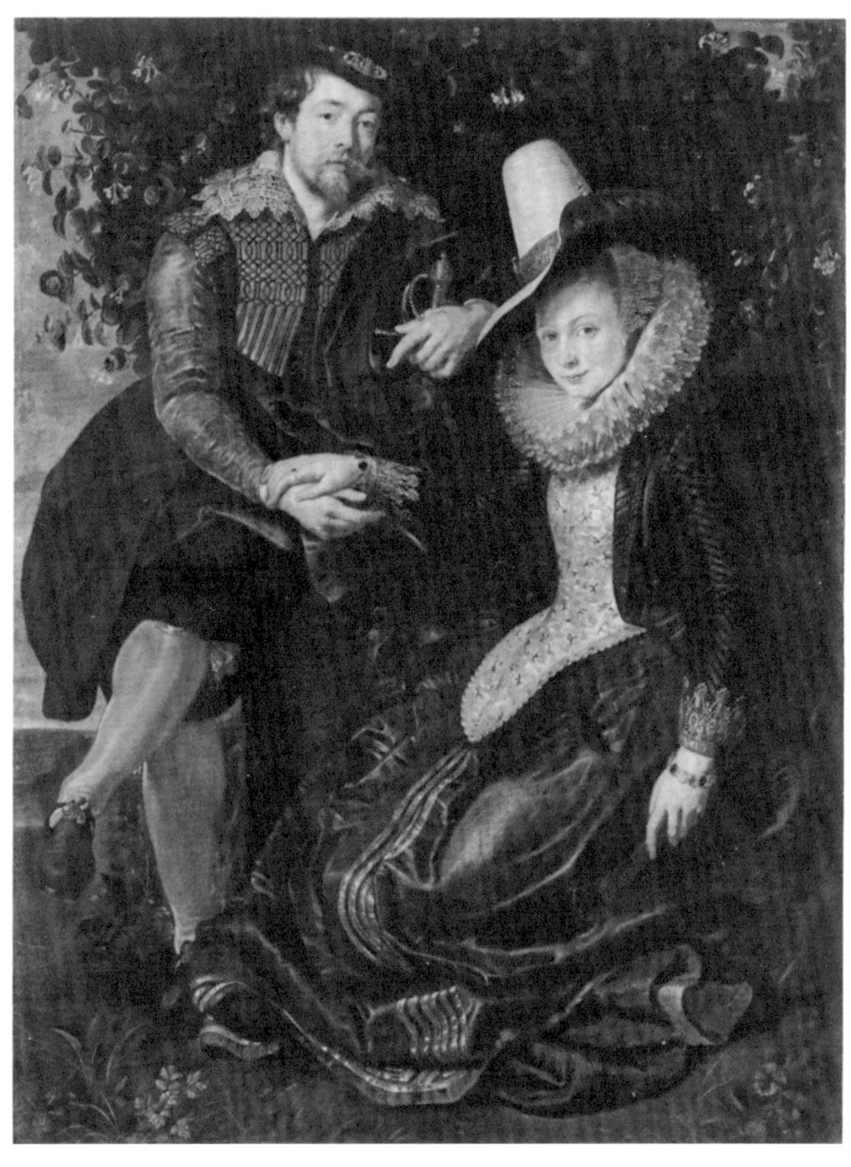

Peter Paul Rubens, *The Artist and his First Wife, Isabella Brant, in the Honeysuckle Bower*, 1609–10. Oil on canvas, 178 × 136.5 cm (70⅛ × 53¾ in.)

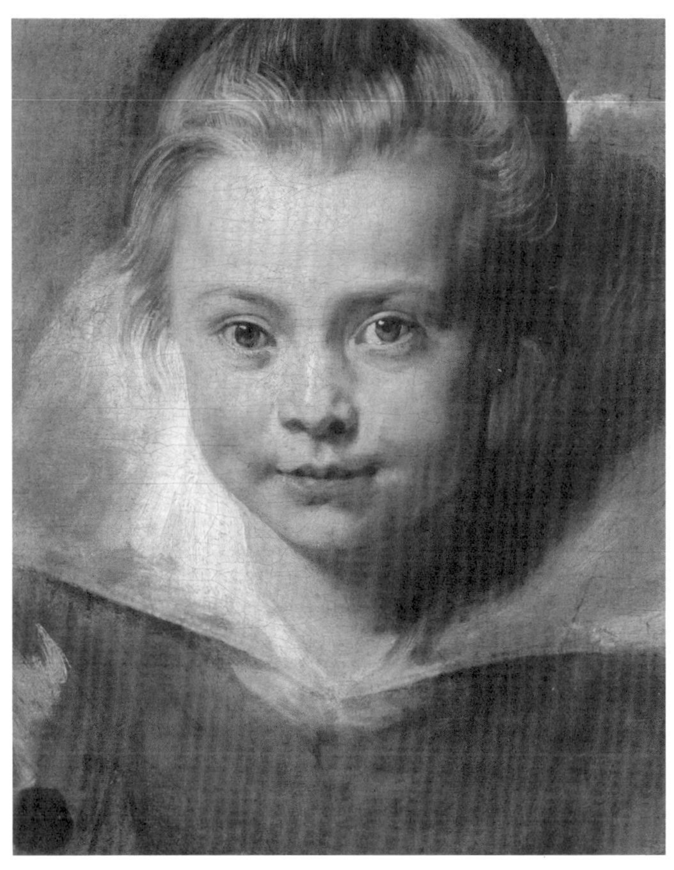

Peter Paul Rubens, *Clara Serena Rubens*, c. 1614.
Oil on canvas, 37.3 × 26.9 cm (14⅝ × 10⅝ in.)

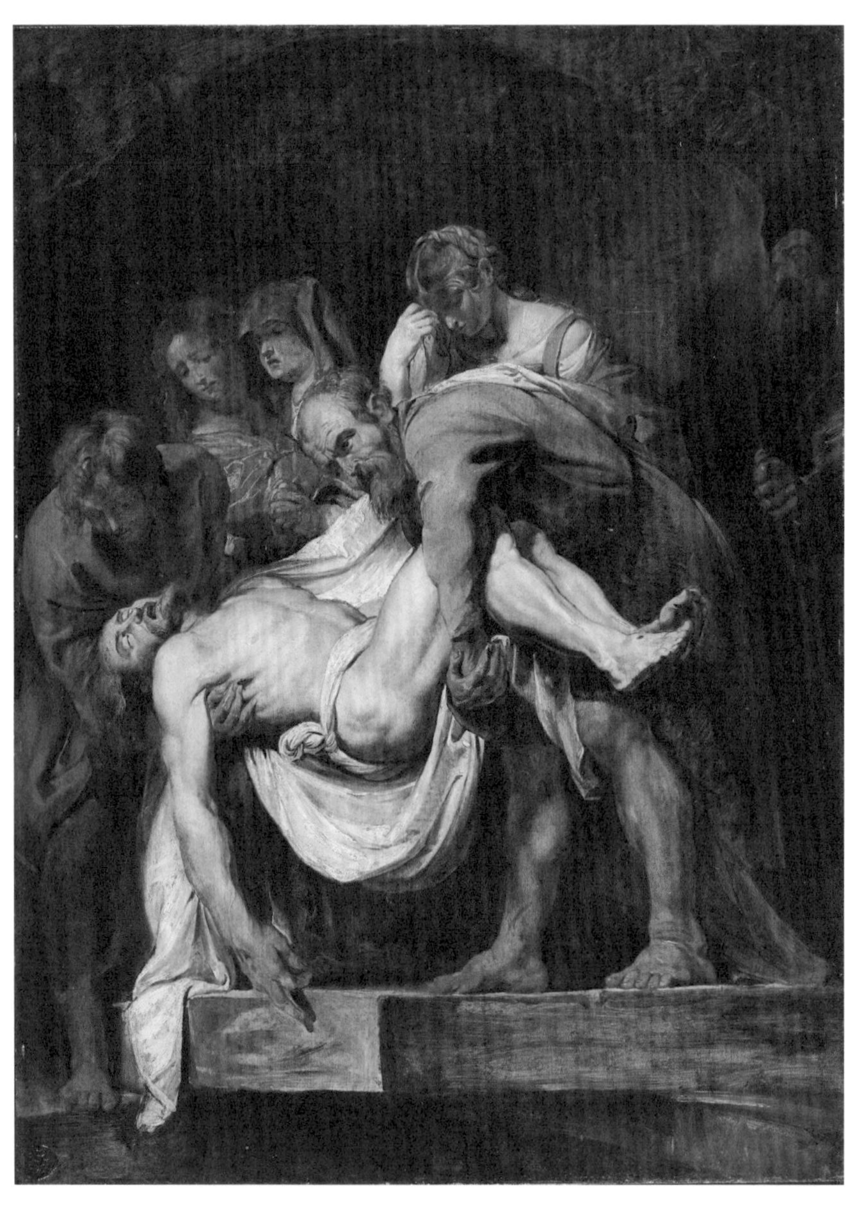

Peter Paul Rubens, *The Entombment*, 1611–12.
Oil on oak, 88.3 × 66.5 cm (34⅞ × 26¼ in.)

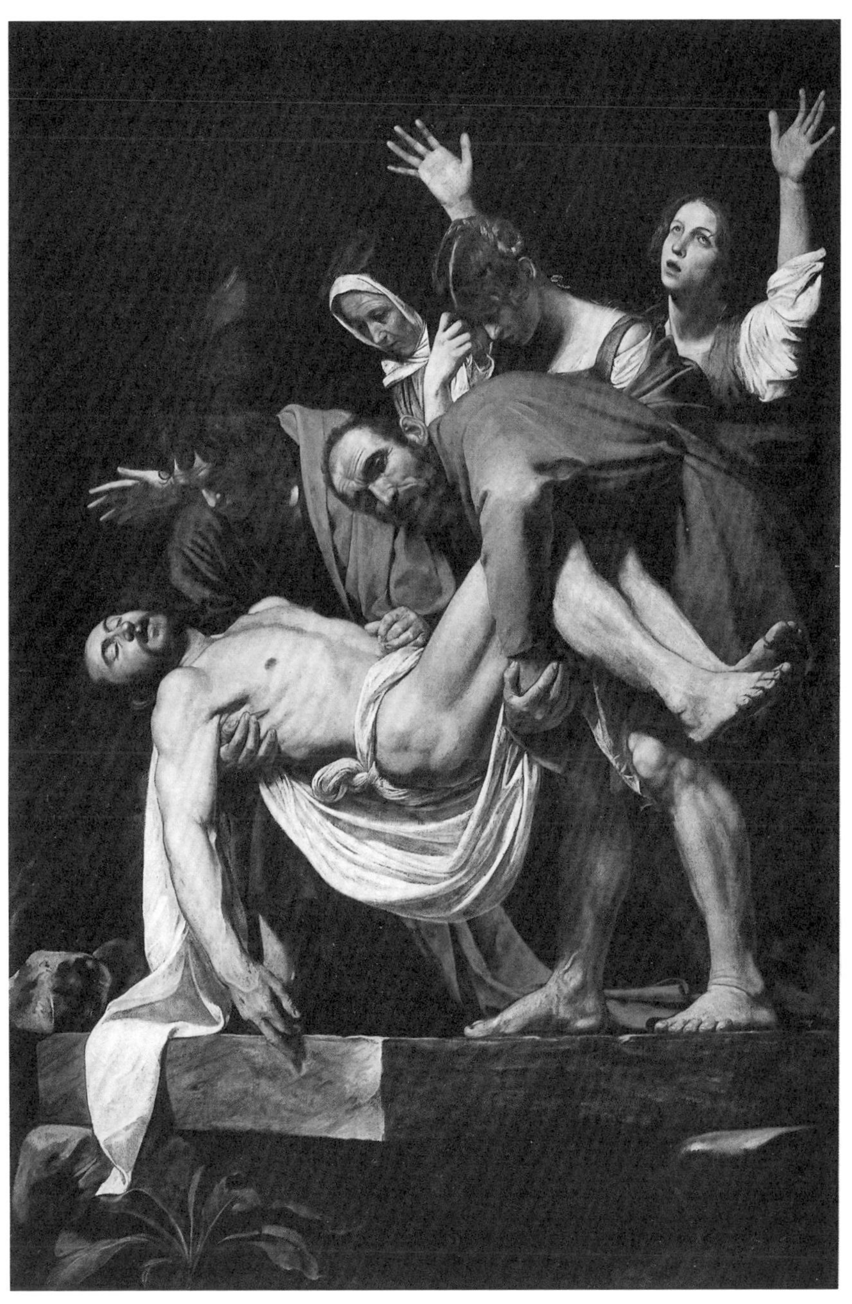

Michelangelo Merisi da Caravaggio, *The Entombment*, 1602–4.
Oil on canvas, 306 × 214 cm (120½ × 84⅜ in.)

the most personal and heartfelt works the artist ever produced (p. 129). Nevertheless, his enthusiasm for travel and education was not dampened, and in 1612 Rubens travelled to the Northern Netherlands, where his first son, Albert, was born in 1614. He returned to Antwerp in 1615, where three years later his second son, Nicolaas, was born. In this period, he painted his celebrated *Assumption of the Virgin* (fig. 42). Taking his lead from Titian's 1516–18 *Assumption*, which Rubens had seen in the Venetian church of Santa Maria Gloriosa dei Frari (fig. 41), he borrows the swirling cloud formation with entwined cherubs, seeking to recreate the weightlessness of the Virgin achieved by Titian. Compositionally, Rubens uses a three-tiered structure to separate the levels between the earthly and heavenly realms, from darkness to light. Further similarities include the upcast eyes of the Virgin and the copious fabrics of her mantle, which both add to the floating effect and contrast with the figures on the ground, who inspect the empty coffin and cast their eyes heavenward.

Works like these made Rubens a highly celebrated artist, and in 1621, the year that saw the end of the Twelve Years' Truce and the resumption of hostilities between Spain and the Northern Netherlands, he was approached to carry out a work in England. The invitation would mark the beginning of more diplomatic work. His intimate position as counsellor to the Archduchess Isabella was consolidated when she took over as ruler of the Spanish Netherlands on the death of her husband in 1621. Rubens was now at the heart of government at a very important diplomatic moment, and by 1622 he was once again involved in the political machinations of the warring European powers.

This time he was sent to France to ascertain the strength of the alliance between France and Spain, and whether the dynastic marriages between these two countries would be sufficient to keep the alliance in place. On his return, Rubens reported that he was reasonably confident in the stability of the situation. Yet only three years later relations between France and Spain deteriorated again, with the French King's new Chief Minister, Cardinal Richelieu, seeking an alliance with Charles I of England, who was at war with Spain. With his own hopes for the reunification of the Netherlands still paramount in Rubens's mind, he sought to influence the situation in Spain's favour through his contact in England, the Duke of Buckingham, favourite of Charles I. When Buckingham sat for a portrait by Rubens, the artist took the opportunity to try and convince the duke of the great part he might play as a peacemaker in any forthcoming negotiations.

In the end those negotiations came to nothing, mainly due to Buckingham's inexperience or possible ineptitude in matters of international politics. In response to this disappointment Rubens made clear his aversion to the horrors of war, commenting on Buckingham's actions: 'When I consider the caprice and arrogance of Buckingham, I pity that young King who, through false council, is needlessly throwing himself and his Kingdom into such an extremity. For anyone can start a war, when he wishes, but he cannot so easily end it.'[9] However, a diplomatic relationship did eventually bear fruit in the form of a commission that would run in parallel with his other activities. In his capacity as envoy of the Duke of Mantua, Rubens had attended in 1600 the marriage of the French King Henry IV to Marie de' Medici, and on Henry's assassination in May 1610, Marie was made Regent. In January 1622 Rubens was summoned to Paris to assess his suitability for the task of decorating the Palais du Luxembourg, which had been constructed for Marie near the Seine, and by February he had been given the commission. It is increasingly clear that Rubens's political activities were an important resource for his artistic activities, the two roles complementing each other in a symbiotic way.

By 1625 Rubens had delivered the complete series of twenty-four paintings for Marie de' Medici, some of which were finished on site at the palace, and once again the artist's works would demonstrate his classical erudition by merging allegorical and historical tableaux with mythological gods and goddesses.[10] He was by this period already the most successful artist in Europe by quite some margin, success that had been made manifest when he moved into a grand house on the Wapper, a prestigious square in Antwerp, in the summer of 1615, and with the construction of a large studio next door, which enabled him to take on assistants. This studio would be the locus for his numerous collaborations with established artists such as Jan Brueghel the Elder, Frans Snyders and the young Anthony van Dyck.

With demand for paintings from his ever-industrious workshop growing across Europe, Rubens's artistic reputation, not to mention his important aristocratic and diplomatic connections, brought him to the attention of English patrons and discussions began involving a specific large-scale project, the creation of a decorative scheme for the Banqueting House in London, then under construction. He responded in ebullient and confident fashion in a 1621 letter to William Trumbull, art agent to King James I, writing in glowing terms of his suitability to take on such a project: 'As for His Majesty and His Royal Highness the Prince of Wales, I shall always be much pleased to receive the honour of their commands; and regarding the hall in the New Palace, I confess that I am, by natural instinct, better fitted to execute very large works than small curiosities. Everyone according to his gifts; my talent is such that no undertaking, however vast in size or diversified in subject, has ever surpassed my courage.'[11] Despite this initial excitement, however, the project lapsed for a while, no doubt owing to more important events in Rubens's life; significantly, they included in 1626 the death of Isabella, his wife of seventeen years, probably from plague.

The opportunity came to revive the project when Rubens was sent in the winter of 1629–30 on yet another diplomatic mission, as an envoy of Philip IV of Spain (r. 1621–65). This time the destination was London, where the artist became involved in preliminary negotiations to establish a peace treaty between Spain and England. Unlike many foreign artists who travelled before him, Rubens was not treated as a mere craftsman on his arrival in London. His education, statesman-like appearance and ambassadorial status afforded him privileges that had not previously been given to any painter of his generation. He is known to have had numerous convivial conversations with Charles I, and his diplomatic efforts were very much appreciated, with Rubens commenting: 'His Majesty was well satisfied because he wishes to know a person of such merit.'[12] In fact, Charles was so taken with Rubens that on 25 June 1630 he knighted him, saying: 'We grant him this title because of his attachment to our person and the services he has rendered to us and to our subjects, his rare devotion to his own sovereign and the skill with which he has worked to restore a good understanding between the crowns of England and Spain.'[13]

That same year Rubens would repay the compliment by delivering to the King a large allegorical canvas, *Minerva Protects Pax from Mars*, often known as *Peace and War* (fig. 43). In this painting Rubens brought to life all his knowledge of mythology and storytelling to depict an allegory representing the ultimate effects of war as inevitably signalling the end of prosperity for all sides in the looming European conflict. In short, it effectively functioned as a manifesto for peace, through which Rubens hoped to express his own desire to soothe relations between the Dutch and the Spanish Netherlands, in his role at the forefront of ongoing diplomatic discussions between the Dutch, the Spanish and the English monarchy. The artist's continued focus on peace was also driven by his own personal interest in the prosperity of his hometown of Antwerp, which was being severely undermined by the blockade of the river Scheldt, its major shipping artery, put in place around 1600 by the independent and largely Calvinist North and United Provinces, headed by Holland. In obvious concern for the fate of the city, Rubens wrote in 1628 to his friend, historian and librarian to King Louis XIV of France, Pierre Dupuy: 'Our city is going step by step to ruin. And lives only upon its savings; there remains not the slightest bit of trade to support it.'[14] As long as the blockade continued, Rubens's own fortunes as a painter in his hometown could not flourish.

Amazingly, the peace talks that were the main purpose of Rubens's visit to England did eventually produce a result. The Treaty of Madrid, which was signed in November 1630, saw England promising to end its support for rebels in the Spanish Netherlands and Protestants in Germany. It also resulted in the artist receiving yet another honour in August 1631, the title of caballero (equivalent to a knighthood), which was conferred on him by Philip IV of Spain in recognition of his years of service and devotion to the Spanish monarchy. The honour had been petitioned for by the Infanta Isabella Clara Eugenia, whose address to the King in July 1631 ('Your Majesty knows him and his good qualities and knows how rare he is in his profession') reveals the high esteem in which Rubens was held and the kind of influence he had within the government.[15]

In 1630 Rubens returned to Antwerp where, at the age of fifty-three, he married the sixteen-year-old Helena Fourment, daughter of his close friend, the tapestry dealer Daniel Fourment, and niece of his first wife, Isabella Brant. Two years later a daughter was born, Clara Johanna, perhaps named in remembrance of his first daughter. By 1633 the couple had another son, Frans. The joy Rubens felt with his new wife and comfortable lifestyle is clearly reflected in a painting he made around this time, which depicts them strolling together with their young son in the artist's Italianate garden in Antwerp (p. 137).[16] Despite what we would now consider a rather uncomfortable age gap, Rubens was enamoured with his new wife, and she makes numerous appearances in portraits, as well as being the model for the goddesses in his 1632–35 *Judgement of Paris* (fig. 44).

In the brief time he spent in London Rubens had achieved a lot, including securing the major commission from Charles I to undertake the decorative scheme for the architect Inigo Jones's Banqueting House on Whitehall, which had been completed in 1622. The project would be the main performance of Rubens's stay in England, eventually consisting of nine large-scale canvases with subjects celebrating the reign of Charles's father, James I (fig. 45). By August 1634 these had been conceived and completed in Rubens's Antwerp workshop but were not sent to London until October 1635. On receipt, Jones and Rubens's assistants unrolled the canvases on to the floor of the Banqueting House, only to discover that they would not fit the designated ceiling spaces of the great hall. The problem seems to have arisen because, although Flanders and England both used feet and inches for measurements, the length of a foot was different in each country. There followed major changes to the canvases, which were made on site to make them fit the ceiling. They were finally installed in the great banqueting hall in 1636, where they remain to this day, the only surviving in situ paintings by Rubens in the United Kingdom and a supreme demonstration of the artist at the height of his powers.

While the ceiling at the Banqueting House was – and is – the most significant work by Rubens in Britain, it is also a late work; by the time it had been completed the artist was already moving towards semi-retirement. In these final years of his life Rubens became increasingly incapacitated by gout, meaning he could not spend long periods of time

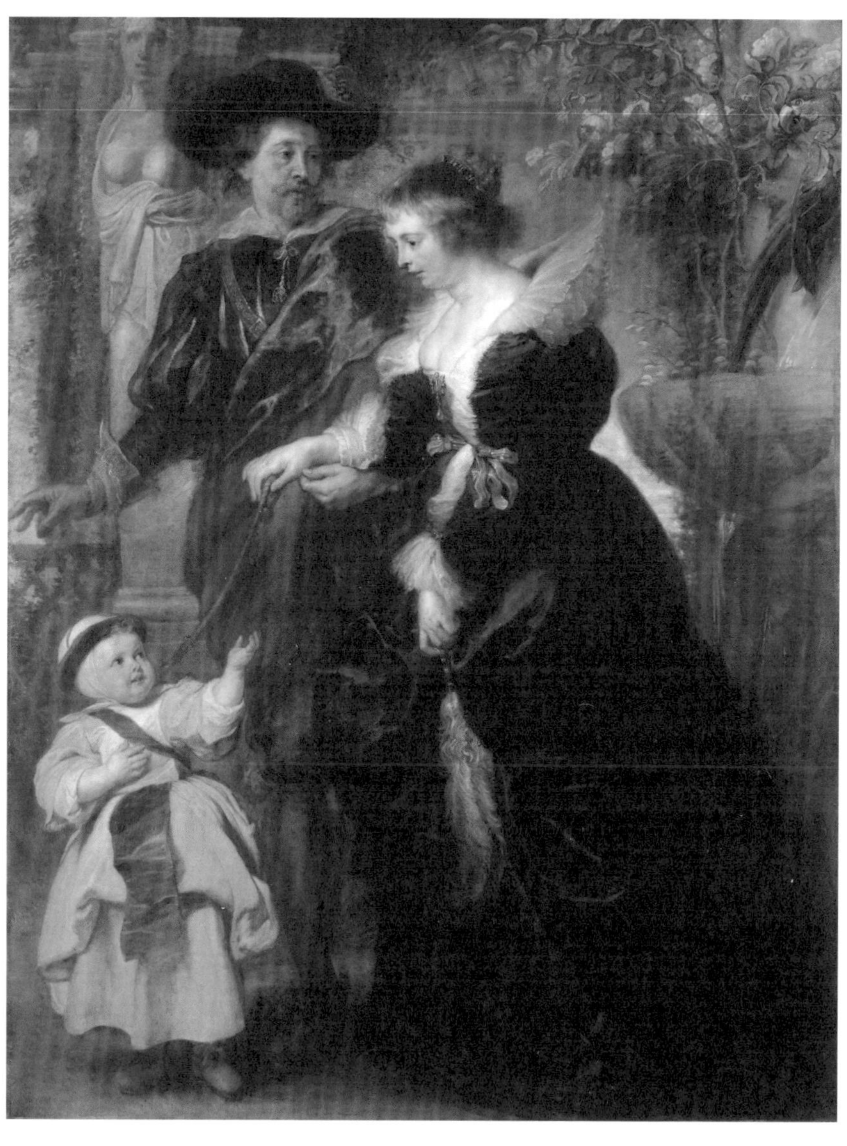

Peter Paul Rubens, *The Artist with his Wife, Helena Fourment and their son Frans*, c. 1635–38. Oil on canvas, 203.8 × 158.1 cm (80 × 62¼ in.)

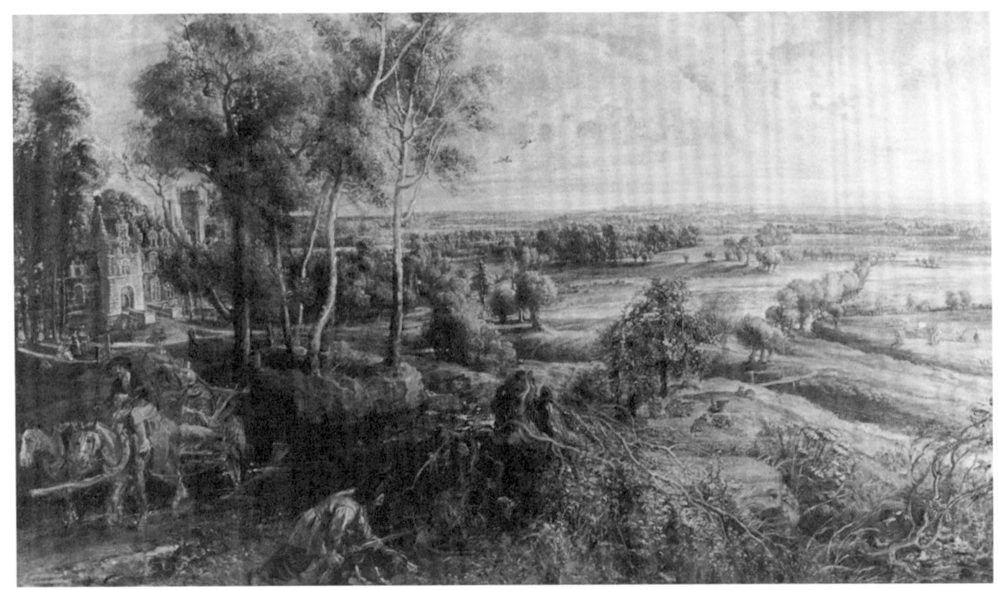

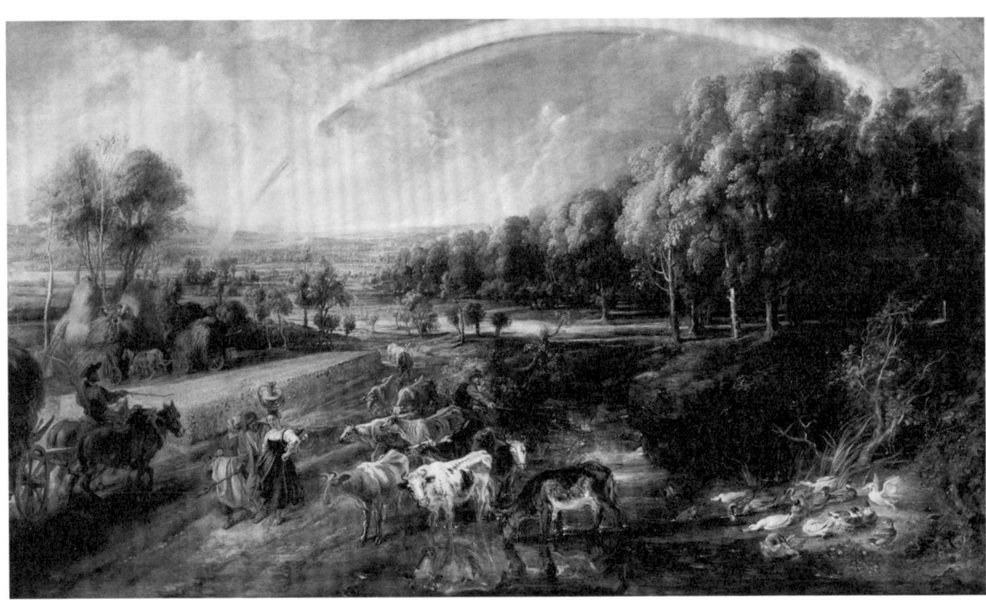

TOP Peter Paul Rubens, *Autumn Landscape with View of Het Steen in the Early Morning, c.* 1636. Oil on oak, 131.2 × 229.2 cm (51¾ × 90¼ in.)

ABOVE Peter Paul Rubens, *The Rainbow Landscape, c.* 1636. Oil on oak, 181 × 285 cm (71⅜ × 112¼ in.)

in his workshop any more, and so he often left work to his assistants. By 1636 he even subcontracted out large-scale commissions, based on his original designs, to other artists' studios.[17]

At this late stage Rubens was now able to devote more time to his previously neglected family life, with his youngest son, Peter Paul – named after himself – being born in 1637. In this period, he worked on the great landscape paintings *Het Steen* and *The Rainbow Landscape* (p. 138), depicting the country estate he had purchased in 1635 near Mechelen in Brabant (which came with the hereditary title of Lord). The estate consisted of a castle with a moat, an orchard, a farm and a lake, roughly three hectares (eight acres) around the house with the remaining purchased land totalling approximately forty-eight hectares (one hundred and twenty acres).[18] By now Rubens had retired from diplomatic duties and was working less often as an artist.[19] These landscapes perfectly reflect his lifelong engagement with the classics, especially some of his favourite texts such as Virgil's *Georgics*, which eulogized the natural world, the land and man's place in the landscape. In a letter written in December 1634 to his close friend Nicolas Claude Fabri de Peiresc, Rubens elucidated the need to extricate himself from his political work, to quit while good fortune was still on his side and enjoy life with his wife and children.[20] The letter revealed not only how lucrative his work was, but also the onerous extent of his diplomatic duties, clearly a burden he was no longer able to bear. His declining health and the pain he was suffering from gout must have made it more difficult to continue to travel in the course of his diplomatic pursuits. But in these later years, Rubens also celebrated the positivity in the diversity of the people he met on his travels and how such interactions might lead to great things in the future.[21]

In freeing himself from diplomatic duties and with no need for further enrichment, Rubens now had time to indulge himself in producing these personal landscapes for his own enjoyment, and their legacy would have a profound effect on English painting. Both works would eventually find their way into British collections, with *The Rainbow Landscape* being bought by James Irvine, agent for the art dealers William Buchanan and Arthur Champernowne, while *Het Steen* was bought by Lady Margaret Beaumont on 25 May 1803 for £1,500. Rubens's landscapes, including

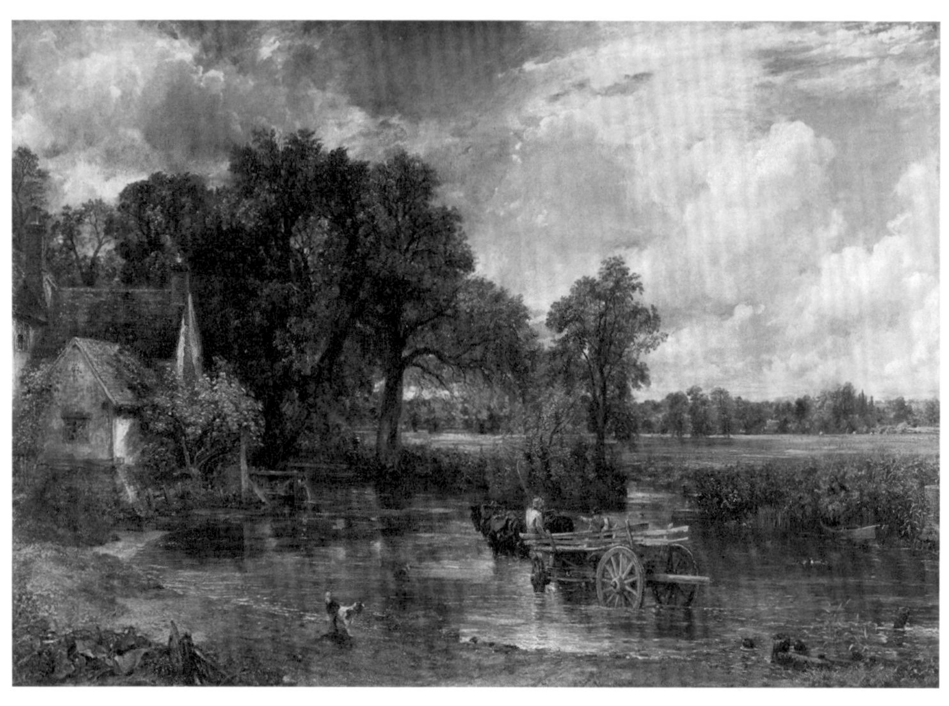

John Constable, *The Hay Wain*, 1821. Oil on canvas, 130.2 × 185.4 cm (51⅜ × 73 in.)

these two, generated intense interest in Britain in the nineteenth century and did much to popularize this once maligned genre. Lady Beaumont eventually presented *Het Steen* to her husband, George, an amateur artist and patron of John Constable, who went on to describe the painting as 'the finest Master' that he had ever seen.[22] It is now widely acknowledged as the inspiration for Constable's large-scale landscapes, including *The Hay Wain* of 1821 (p. 140).

Rubens died in Antwerp on 30 May 1640 at the age of sixty-three. In his lifetime he had achieved fame, fortune and respect for his craft from the most important patrons of his day, among them kings, queens and popes. Like many artists who came to Britain, he brought with him what was considered by his English admirers Continental sophistication, with his extensive experience of travel and knowledge of the ancient world. His classical education was seen by the English court and aristocracy as the very essence of 'good breeding', and to align themselves with such interests reasserted in their own eyes their position in the social hierarchy and confirmed their sophistication and education. It could also be said that Rubens brought to England a slice of the Italian Renaissance, having admired and aspired to emulate the great artists of the past such as Michelangelo, Raphael and Titian throughout his artistic life. By the end of his life, Rubens had arguably surpassed these artists in terms of his international reach, standing among the very few artists who received such numerous accolades and moved in so many exalted circles. According to some, Rubens was the very model of what a gentleman artist should be, ideals that would not be lost on future generations of British artists such as Sir Joshua Reynolds and others who went on to form the Royal Academy in London in 1768.

7

Anthony van Dyck

*The Gentleman Painter
of the English Renaissance*

While Rubens was clearly the dominant force in seventeenth-century European painting, it was his fellow Antwerp master Anthony van Dyck who ultimately had a much more profound impact on English painting, leaving his indelible mark on the nation's art. This was achieved in no small part through his ability to network and promote his own take on the late Renaissance style of Titian, reinvented for the English market. Van Dyck ultimately lived in England longer than Rubens, and as a result was much more embedded in English society; he was also paid more than Rubens, and the status this conferred contributed substantially to the consolidation of his historical reputation in his adopted homeland, where he married, died, and was buried.

Anthony van Dyck was born in Antwerp on 22 March 1599, the seventh of twelve children, to Frans van Dyck, a wealthy silk merchant, and Maria Cuypers, who was already famous for her skills in the art of embroidery. With their encouragement, the young Anthony took up artistic pursuits at an early age, beginning his studies in art at the age of ten. His natural propensity for painting led his parents to seek out a local painter to hone his talents, in 1609 engaging Hendrik van Balen to train him. Principally a painter of small cabinet pictures, Van Balen had become a master of the Antwerp Guild of Saint Luke's around 1592, and was involved in teaching from at least 1602, going on to become dean of the guild.

Van Balen represented Van Dyck's first introduction to just how international the practice of art could be, having trained with Dutch painters who had travelled to Italy and undertaken his own Italian sojourn between 1595 and 1600. Many artists passed through the successful workshop he ran for at least thirty years, several of whom went on to become enormously successful, including Frans Snyders and three of Van Balen's own sons. We do not know how long Van Dyck trained with Van Balen, but artist apprenticeships traditionally lasted between three and four years and so he probably left the workshop around 1614, when he was about fifteen years old.

By 1618 Van Dyck had followed in his master's footsteps by registering with the Antwerp Guild of St Luke, and at some point between 1609 and 1618 he also joined the workshop of Rubens. A portrait of Van Dyck now in the Rubenshuis in Antwerp (fig. 48) was previously thought to have been painted by Rubens around 1615, leading to a belief that he entered Rubens's studio that year.[1] However, recent analysis has revealed that this painting is a self-portrait, so it cannot be relied on for a definitive date.[2] The scarcity of records from this early period of Van Dyck's life means it is not entirely clear whether he joined Rubens's studio as an apprentice or a collaborator. Rubens was known for his many collaborations and, as we have seen, such close working relationships have led to continued misattributions between their works. Nevertheless, it is clear that Van Dyck wanted to emulate Rubens, not only in his successful international art practice but also in his social standing. Van Dyck's self-assured belief in his own gentlemanly status may have resulted from his father's social position in Antwerp; by the time Anthony was born his family was very wealthy from Frans's dealings as a textiles merchant.[3]

Once established in the Antwerp guild and Rubens's studio, Van Dyck made considerable progress in his artistic pursuits across a variety of genres, including portraiture. News of his success reverberated around Europe, eventually reaching Alethea Howard, Countess of Arundel, the wife of Thomas Howard, Earl of Arundel, and a formidable art collector in her own right, who in the summer of 1620 was in Antwerp sitting for Rubens to paint her portrait (now in the Museu Nacional d'Art de Catalunya, Barcelona), bringing her a step closer to Van Dyck. She and other members of the English aristocracy became increasingly eager to procure the talents of this emerging young genius, as reported to the countess's husband by her secretary, Francesco Vercellini, in a letter of July 1620: 'Van Dyck is still with Signor Rubens, and his works are hardly less esteemed than those of his master. He is a young man of twenty-one years; his father and mother are very rich, living in this town, so that it will be difficult to get them to leave these parts, especially since he sees the good fortune that attends Rubens.'[4]

This correspondence contains copious inaccuracies; Van Dyck's mother had died before his eighth birthday and his father's textile business had fallen into steep decline, leaving him in dire financial problems at the time of Vercellini's letter. That said, the acquisition of great artists from abroad required the patron to host at his own expense not just the individual in question but also his immediate family in adequate accommodation. It is quite possible that the hyperbole used in Vercellini's letter was an attempt to convey that Van Dyck and his family already lived in sumptuous circumstances, meaning that a greater financial incentive would be required 'to get them to leave these parts'.[5] This was not the only piece of correspondence to elevate Van Dyck's reputation to that of a gentleman; in 1621–22 Giovanni Pietro Bellori, biographer of the Italian Baroque, described Van Dyck's appearance in a glowing manner: 'He was still young, his beard barely sprouting, yet his youth was accompanied by grave modesty of character and nobility of mien, albeit he was small in stature. His manners were those of a lord rather than a commoner, and he appeared resplendent in rich attire of suits and court dress, because he was accustomed to the society of noble men in the school of Rubens; and being by nature grand and eager to become famous, therefore, in addition to his fine clothes, he adorned his head with plumes and hatbands, wore gold chains crossed on his chest, and kept a retinue of servants.'[6]

In a country that has always subscribed slavishly to ideas of class and so-called breeding, such descriptions of Van Dyck would have significantly piqued the interest of the English aristocracy, and the artist's skill in presenting himself as more than a mere commoner was at least as good as his skill in the art of painting. If he had taken anything from his time with Rubens, it was that this ability was just as important as anything else he learned under the great master. We can gain some appreciation of the circles Rubens was moving in from a 1628 painting by William van Haecht, *The Cabinet of Cornelis van der Geest* (fig. 46). In it, the famous

Antwerp art collector and wealthy spice merchant Cornelis van der Geest (see p. 127) is seen directing the attention of Archduke Albert, in a rather emotional fashion, towards a Quinten Massys painting of the Madonna and Child in his collection, while Rubens, standing immediately behind the Archduke, appears engaged in giving a more precise description of the painting. Although likely a combination of fact and fiction, it has been suggested that the scene marks an actual event when Albert and Isabella, joint governors of Flanders, visited Van der Geest's home along with the Antwerp merchant Nicolaas Rockox, who is seen standing just behind the Archduchess. Featuring in a supporting role is Anthony van Dyck, apparently in conversation with Jan van Montfort, Antwerp's mint master, and behind Van der Geest, whose portrait he had also painted around 1620 (fig. 47). That painting is miraculous in its immediacy and handling, with the visible passage of the brush fibres through the paint becoming the very texture of Van der Geest's hair, especially around the temples, and the treatment of the eyes wholly convincing the viewer of their moistness and vitality. It is scarcely believable that the work was created by a twenty-one-year-old artist.

Van Dyck arrived in England for the first time in the autumn of 1620.[7] His recommendation to royal service apparently came from Rubens, said to have described Van Dyck as 'the best of my pupils', though this can be judged to be hearsay rather than factual reportage.[8] He was awarded a royal pension by James I (r. 1603–25), followed by a payment from the Royal Treasury of £100 in February 1621, the records relating that it was 'by way of reward for speciall service for his Majesty'. Two days later he had a pass to leave England 'to travile [work] for 8 months',[9] at which time he sailed for Antwerp, leaving precious few works executed during this short period in England, save for a portrait of Thomas Howard (p. 147).[10] That single portrait would demonstrate what he was capable of, however, its loose painterly style introducing a new informal realism that set it apart from other painting in England at this time.

Three self-portraits painted between 1620 and 1623 reveal much about the development of Van Dyck's style, though their precise chronology is disputed. The painterly texture of the work now in the Metropolitan Museum of Art, New York, painted around 1620–21 (p. 148), emphasizes the diaphanous material of the shirt emerging around his collar and cuffs. But the proportions of the body are lost beneath the voluminous fabric, and the viewer struggles to imagine where the arm that should be attached to his left hand is; the awkward pose, leaning on the right arm, only serves to highlight these compositional challenges. A self-portrait of 1622–23 (p. 149), now in the Hermitage Museum, St Petersburg, demonstrates just how adept Van Dyck was at resolving these problems in a short period of time. The position of the right arm is less awkwardly arranged, and the left arm is not only clearly visible beneath the clothes but is also elegantly foreshortened to achieve a pose that would soon become standard in English portraiture. Along with the self-portrait at the Alte Pinakothek, Munich, we see in just three paintings the most vivid display of Van Dyck's development as an artist in this period.

Van Dyck shared with his English patrons a passion for Italian Renaissance painting, and this no doubt contributed to his good fortune and success in England. During his brief stay in London between 1620 and 1621, he first saw the Venetian paintings in the collections of the Earl of Arundel and the Duke of Buckingham, and the art of Titian in particular would assume a central role in his life as an artist and change the way he worked. This brief encounter with the artist's works drew him to Italy. Arriving in Genoa in November 1621, Van Dyck travelled on to Venice, hometown of Titian, where he joined the Countess of Arundel. In 1622 he stayed in Rome for eight months, supplemented with brief visits to Florence, Bologna, Padua, Mantua and Milan. Van Dyck would end up spending six years in Italy, and the sketchbook he kept there eventually ran to over two hundred pages, containing copied drawings after Bellini, Giorgione, Tintoretto, Veronese, Raphael, Leonardo, Guercino and the Carracci, with the overwhelming majority being after Titian.[11]

While in Rome Van Dyck made a portrait of Cardinal Guido Bentivoglio (p. 150), one of his most important patrons there, which Bellori describes in glowing terms that highlight its realism and movement: 'Anthony portrayed the cardinal seated, with a letter in his hands looking around as if he has read it; and he conveyed the likeness of that lord's visage and temperate spirit on the canvas, which portrait is to be found today in Florence, in the palace of the grand duke.'[12] He also gained

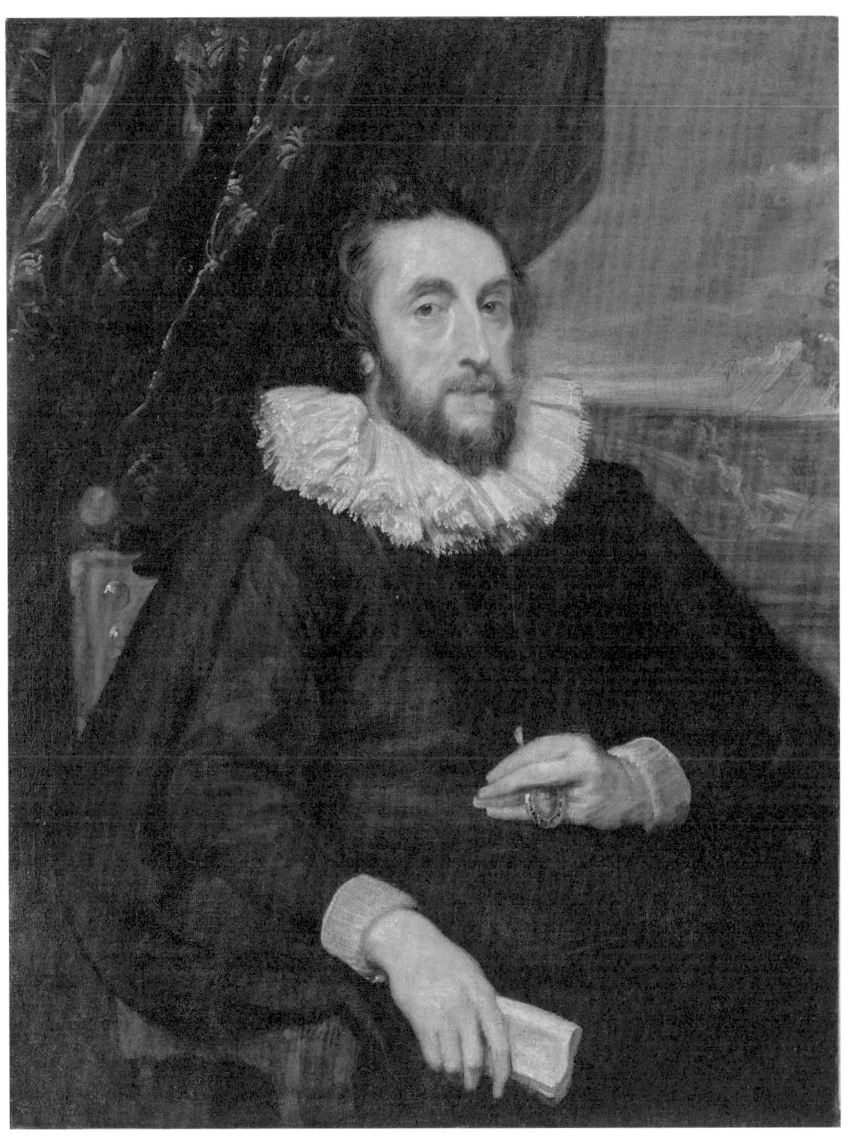

Anthony van Dyck, *Thomas Howard, 2nd Earl of Arundel*, *c.* 1620–21. Oil on canvas, 102.6 × 79.7 cm (40½ × 31½ in.)

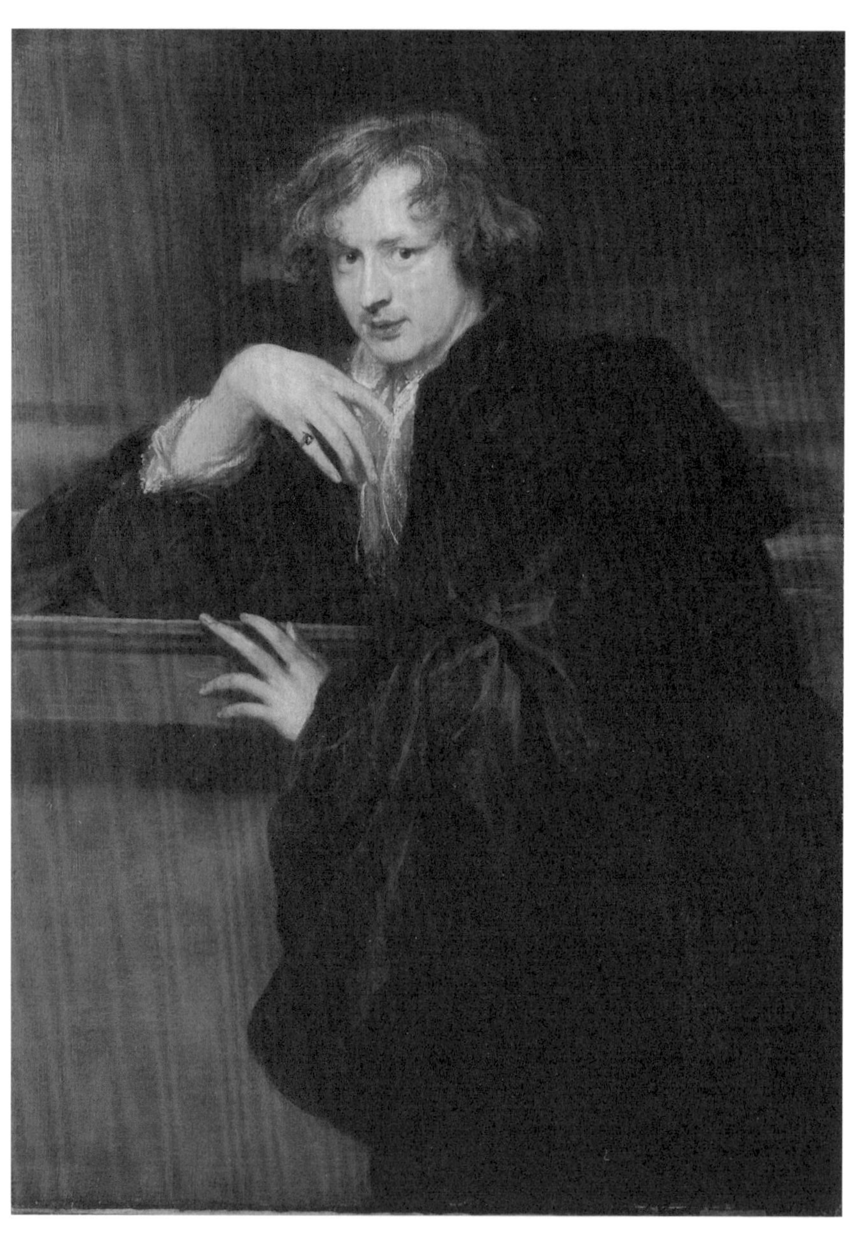

Anthony van Dyck, *Self-Portrait, c.* 1620–21.
Oil on canvas, 119.7 × 87.9 cm (47¼ × 34⅝ in.)

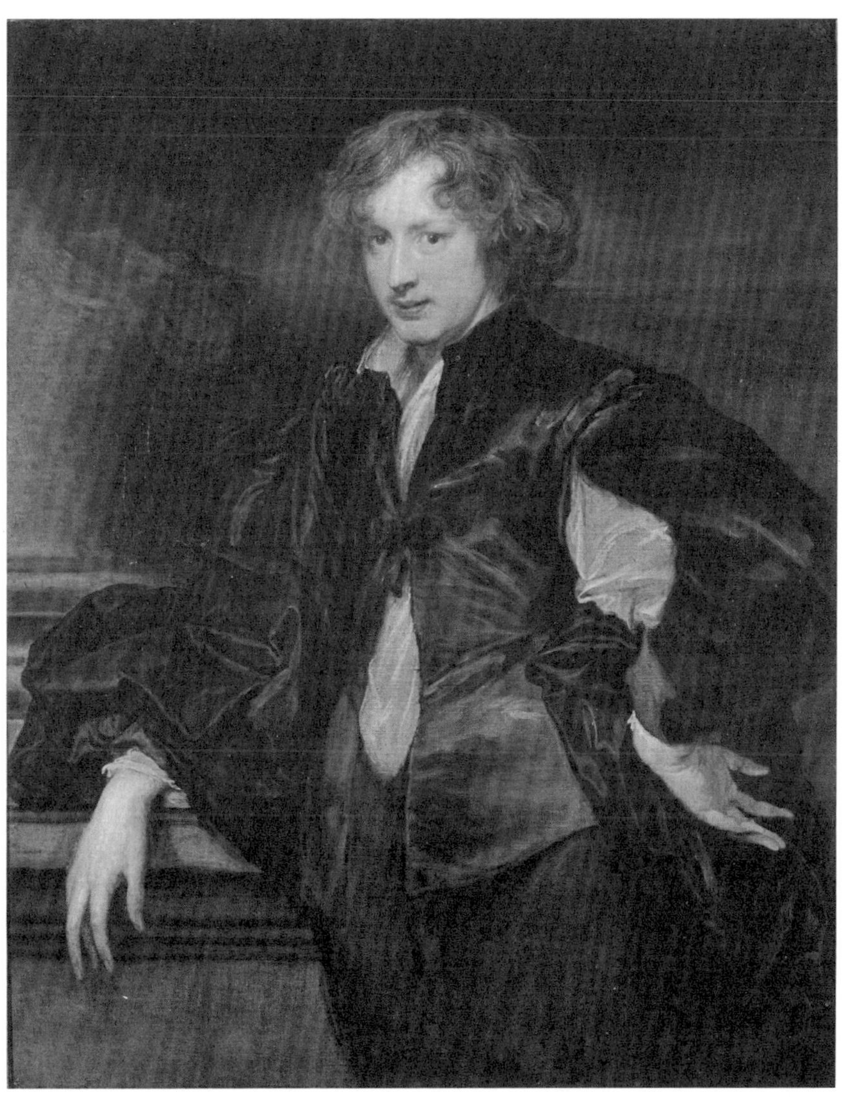

Anthony van Dyck, *Self-Portrait, c.* 1622–23.
Oil on canvas, 116.5 × 93.5 cm (45⅞ × 36⅞ in.)

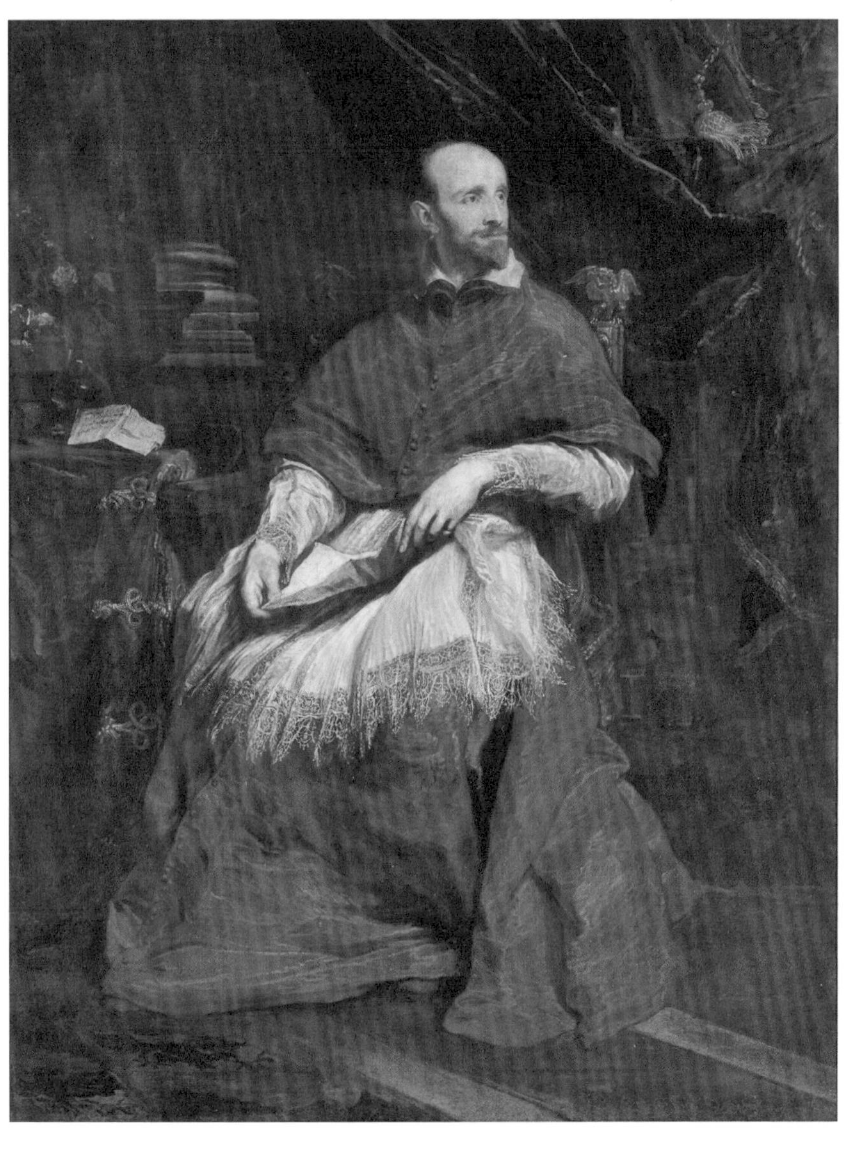

Anthony van Dyck, *Cardinal Guido Bentivoglio*, 1623.
Oil on canvas, 195 × 147 cm (76⅞ × 57⅞ in.)

lucrative commissions from English clients (including Sir Robert Shirley, his wife, Lady Theresa Shirley, and the diplomat and art dealer George Gage) who were on the Grand Tour. This was a rite of passage for members of the aristocracy dating back to the late sixteenth century, which involved embarking on an extensive tour of Europe, especially Italy, with the aim of providing a comprehensive education in European history, in particular the art of antiquity and the Italian Renaissance (see Chapter Eleven). Van Dyck's Grand Tourist portraits would go on to have a profound influence not only on the English aristocracy but also on artists resident in London who, on seeing the effect they were having on clients, sought to emulate his style to further their own progress. First and foremost, it was the foreign painters in London who realized quickly how enamoured their wealthy patrons were with this new style and possessed the skills to emulate it.[13]

Van Dyck may have painted the portrait now identified as George Gage while both men were in Rome. Now in the National Gallery, London, it shows Gage in what seems to be a negotiation with two art dealers, who are perhaps trying to convince him of the value of an antique statue (fig. 49). Today the Gallery attributes the painting to Van Dyck, with the title *Portrait of George Gage with Two Attendants*, but it is interesting to note previous doubts over its attribution. In the Gallery's catalogue of its Flemish school paintings, published in 1970 and reprinted in 1986, it was given the title *Portraits of Three Men* and attributed 'possibly after Van Dyck'. The description has also changed over its lifetime. In the 1970/1986 catalogue, the anonymous Black man in the central background was identified merely as 'the negro', while his companion to the right of the foreground is described as a man, along with the main subject. The distinction is repeated throughout the 1970 description, a reminder of how language was and is often used in a casual manner to dehumanize.[14] With its updated title and attribution, it is interesting to note that the Gallery still seems confident that the unidentified white man is the art dealer, while the Black man is at best perhaps a mere assistant.[15]

While in Italy Van Dyck purchased a number of Italian paintings to add to his growing personal collection, at least nineteen of them works by Titian. They included *Perseus and Andromeda* (p. 153), a stunning large-scale canvas probably acquired by Van Dyck in Milan in 1623, now in the Wallace Collection, London. Titian's late painterly style is especially notable in the handling of the churning waters, while the figure of the Greek hero Perseus displays the artist's mastery of colour balance. A fellow Titian enthusiast was the young Prince Charles, later King Charles I of England and Van Dyck's future patron. Charles was introduced to Titian's work on a 1623 visit to Madrid, where he encountered the numerous paintings by the artist in the Spanish royal collection.[16] The Spanish court had enjoyed a long association with Titian, who began working there in early 1548 after being invited to the Augsburg residence of the Habsburg Holy Roman Emperor Charles V. Titian would effectively be the Habsburgs' official painter for the rest of his life, ending up permanently in the service of Charles V's son and heir, Philip II of Spain. In this capacity he was tasked with providing Philip with about ten paintings a year in return for a regular pension for life, so by the time Titian died in August 1576, his works were well represented in the Habsburg collection.[17] After seeing such works in Madrid, no other artist could come close to rivalling Titian in the young Prince Charles's affections.

Acquiring paintings by the great Renaissance masters was not an easy task, however, let alone works by Titian. The hierarchical model espoused by Giorgio Vasari in *Lives of the Artists* (1550) placed Leonardo da Vinci, Raphael and Michelangelo at the zenith of the Renaissance, and so by Charles's time works by these artists were the most difficult to obtain. Leonardo was notoriously unproductive in his output and Michelangelo annoyingly uninterested in painting; the few of his painted works not executed in fresco were in the hands of the Medici family, who were not likely to part with them, even at the request of a future king.

But although the great artists of the Renaissance had long since passed into historic legend, Prince Charles could call on Anthony van Dyck, who boasted the ability to revive their spirit. Van Dyck would give England the Renaissance it craved, going on to reinvent and set new standards in English art using Titian's flare for colour, precision of application and painterly approach.[18] In this period English society began to particularly value the ability to speak knowledgeably on all aspects of art,

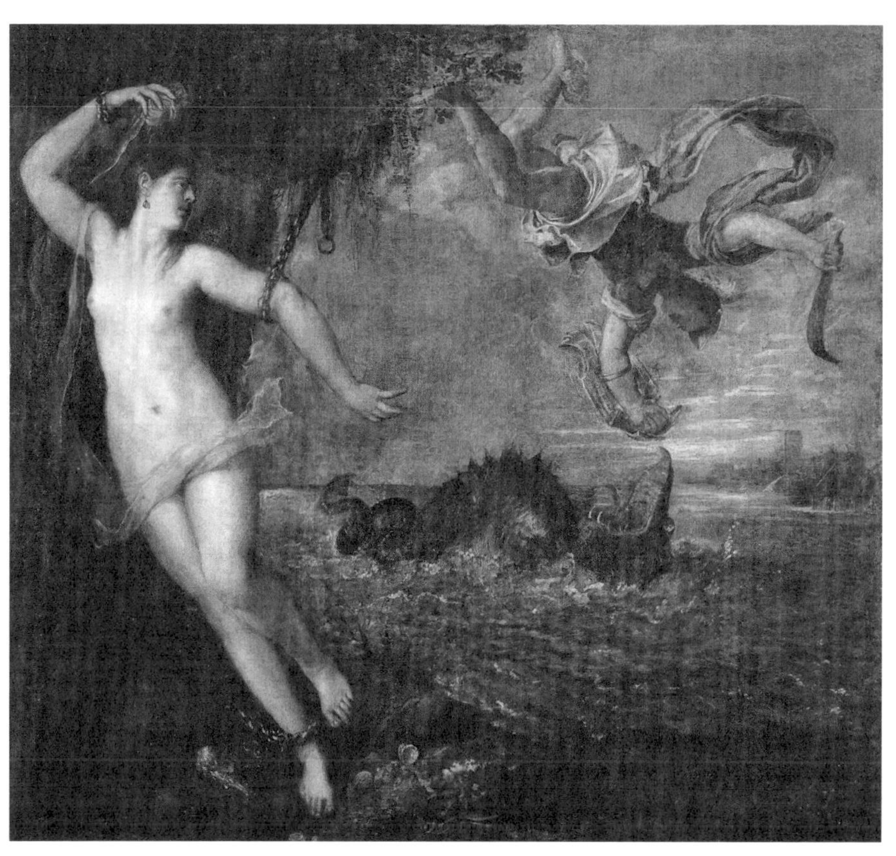

Titian, *Perseus and Andromeda*, c. 1554–56.
Oil on canvas, 230 × 243 cm (90⅝ × 95¾ in.)

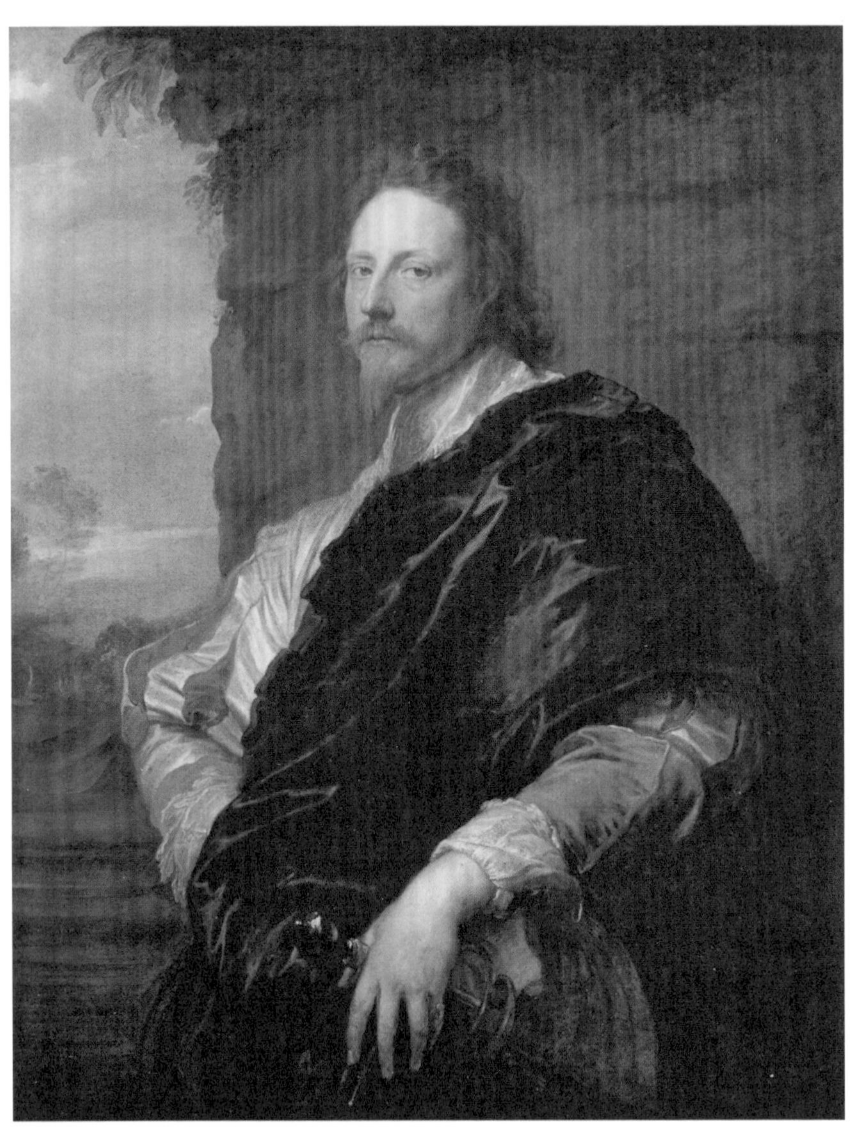

Anthony van Dyck, *Nicholas Lanier*, c. 1632.
Oil on canvas, 111 × 87.6 cm (44¾ × 34¼ in.)

enhancing the perception of one's sophistication and moving people up the social ladder. This led patrons such as the Earl and Countess of Arundel not only to purchase works from the artists they encountered on the Continent but also to encourage foreign artists such as Mytens and Van Dyck to come to England. In the eyes of their peers, such exploits confirmed the collectors' sophistication, under the belief that objects whose origins lay in Continental Europe held particular cultural value, a bias that lingers to this day. The approach effectively began a mania in England for collecting art and *objets*, and ultimately led to the creation of institutions such as the John Soane Museum, the British Museum and the National Gallery.[19]

On the death of his father, James I, in 1625, Charles succeeded to the English throne. The beginning of Charles I's reign was a moment of mounting tension and hostility between the King and his Parliament, not helped by his marriage in 1625 to the Catholic princess Henrietta Maria of France. In 1628, the year Charles prorogued Parliament, his advisor George Villiers, the Duke of Buckingham, was assassinated, and from 1629 to 1640 Charles suspended Parliament, in a period later known as the Personal Rule. Amid these machinations, Charles's collecting activities continued to escalate, with Van Dyck among those who acted as unofficial advisors in the King's ever more ambitious attempts to acquire Italian Renaissance paintings for his growing collection. At this politically vulnerable moment in his reign, Charles may have thought back to his time in Spain and the images that he had seen, particularly those that projected the power and grandeur of the Spanish court. Paintings such as Titian's equestrian portrait of the Holy Roman Emperor Charles V offered huge propagandistic value, which Van Dyck could recreate to bring much needed authority to the King in this troubled period.

Among Charles's advisors painted by Van Dyck was Nicholas Lanier, Master of the King's Music. Born in London, Lanier was, like many artisans in the city, the child of immigrants, in his case court musicians from France and Italy.[20] In a portrait of around 1632 (p. 154), Van Dyck sets Lanier among fashionable Italianate ruins, using an economy of colour and multiple painterly textures to depict his clothes and hair, the architecture and the setting sun to create a romantic, dreamlike effect.

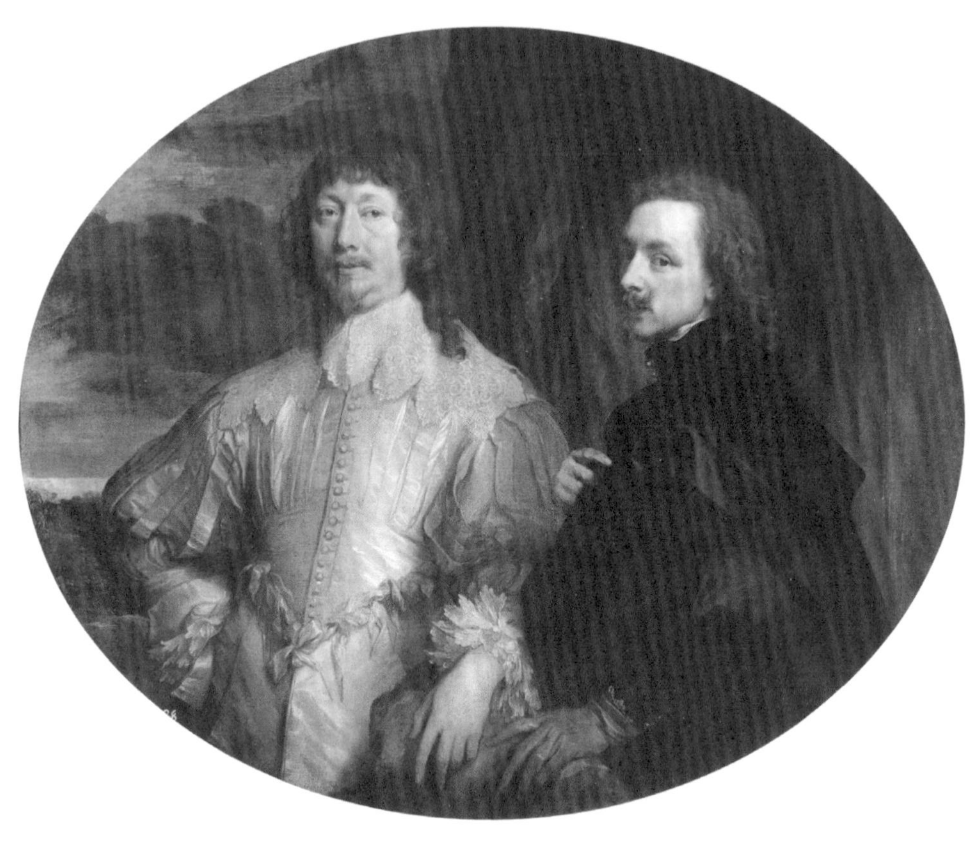

Anthony van Dyck, *Self-Portrait with Endymion Porter*, c. 1633.
Oil on canvas, 119 × 144 cm (46⅞ × 56¾ in.)

Lanier's position demonstrates yet again how important a cosmopolitan world rooted in immigration was in influencing the artistic and cultural life of England. Although his role at court was that of a musician, his Continental credentials were clearly an advantage as a connoisseur of Italian art, a skill he had developed during visits to Italy in the 1610s and 1620s, and in January 1626 an export licence was issued in Rome to allow Lanier to transport from Italy an unspecified number of paintings that he had purchased on the new King's behalf, to be offered via the Earl of Arundel. When Charles's collecting habits reached an all-time high in 1628 with his acquisition of the collection of the dukes of Mantua for the exorbitant sum in two instalments of £28,280 12s 8d, it is likely that both Van Dyck and Lanier were involved in advising the King on the purchase.[21]

Van Dyck returned from Italy in the summer of 1627 to Antwerp, where he remained for five years, and by the summer of 1632 he was back in London at the invitation of Charles I, where he was appointed 'principalle Paynter in Ordinarie to their Majesties'.[22] Documentation of his activities in this period includes a privy warrant seal of 7 May 1633, which notes that Van Dyck was paid £444 for 'Nine pictures of our Royall self and most dearest Consort the Queene', along with a court record from 1637 that suggests he was paid between May and December the vast sum of £1,200 in three instalments by the Crown 'for certeyne pictures by him'.[23] None of the paintings can be identified, but it is entirely possible that they included well-known works from this period such as *The Greate Peece* (Royal Collection), the double portrait of Van Dyck with Endymion Porter (p. 156) and the double portrait of Charles I and Henrietta Maria (fig. 50). The casual flamboyance of the self-portrait with Porter serves as a pictorial statement of Van Dyck's fame and allegiance to the court of Charles I. The artist depicts himself as almost the equal of this high-ranking diplomat and Royalist, while Porter in turn is clearly happy to be portrayed with the superstar artist, who underlines his taste and appreciation of art.

The double portrait of Charles I and Henrietta Maria serves as a useful example of the changes taking place in English painting at this time, fuelled by the rivalry and competition between foreign artists within the employ of Charles I. Van Dyck's painting is in fact the second example of the subject, with Daniel Mytens being the originator of this composition (fig. 52). Perhaps owing to disapproval from the King, Mytens reworked the Queen's likeness in his painting, basing it on a Van Dyck portrait, most likely the one now in the Royal Collection,[24] but even this reworking was eventually supplanted in favour of Van Dyck's version, for reasons that are abundantly clear when the two paintings are compared. Van Dyck's treatment of Charles's hands, for instance, gives a sense of substance below the surface of the skin, while Mytens's attempt looks positively dead in comparison (figs 51 and 53). Van Dyck's introduction of a landscape between the sitters brings an atmospheric realism to the painting, while Charles's ruff is updated to a more modern, fashionable design, and the colour of his clothes is changed to echo the Queen's dress, bow and ribbons, uniting the couple in ways that Mytens failed to realize in his work.

Such bravura in the handling and flattery of Van Dyck's sitters marked the beginning of the end of Mytens's tenure as the King's painter.[25] Correspondence regarding Van Dyck's monetary value reflects the esteem in which he was held by the Crown, which resulted in an unprecedented break with social convention in the summer of 1635, when Charles chose to travel downriver to visit Van Dyck at his home and workshop in Blackfriars 'to see his paintings'.[26] Van Dyck's comfortable and opulent residence with garden, including the new river-access causeway and stairs used by the King on his visit, had been bankrolled entirely by Charles, so one could imagine that he wanted to see how his money was being spent. Unfortunately, little evidence remains of the building and its exact location as it was destroyed in the Great Fire of London of 1666.[27]

Significantly, the strategic location of Blackfriars was designated a 'liberty', placing it beyond the jurisdiction of the city guilds such as the Painter-Stainers' Company of London.[28] The area was swiftly becoming a haven for foreign artists, and home to second-generation foreign artists, many of whom became royal painters, such as the London-born Cornelius Johnson, who was from a Flemish/German Protestant family and known variously in Dutch as Cornelis Janssens van Ceulen, Cornelius Jonson van Ceulen and Cornelis Jansz van Ceulen before settling on his anglicized name. Johnson, who probably trained mainly in the Northern Netherlands, was appointed picture drawer to Charles in 1632. Also in the area was Peter (or Pierre) Oliver, the London-born artist son of the famous miniaturist Isaac Oliver, who himself had arrived in England from France as a Huguenot child refugee. Peter Oliver subsequently became the leading miniaturist at the court of Charles I.

Further development of the nascent English style would come later with the arrival in 1676 of Gottfried Kniller from Lübeck in Germany. By this time England had firmly established itself as a desirable destination for artists seeking fame and fortune, offering fertile ground to fulfil their ambitions. Godfrey Kneller, as he became known, was clearly from a well-to-do background, because his father, the painter Zachary Kniller, was the Chief Surveyor of the city of Lübeck. Gottfried studied mathematics at Leyden University before turning to painting, studying under Ferdinand Bol, himself a pupil of Rembrandt. Kneller clearly had the means to travel and worked in Rome and Venice before arriving in England. He brought to England a portrait style that inspired what would become known as the Grand Manner, an idealized artistic style based on classical theory and usually associated with history painting. This approach to portraiture would later be adopted and championed by the English artist and Royal Academician Joshua Reynolds (see Chapter Ten).

Kneller's transformation into an Englishman was consolidated when he received first a knighthood in 1692, then an honorary Doctorate of Law from the University of Oxford in 1695, and later a baronetcy from George I in 1715. Within just a generation, the boundary between English and foreign painting was becoming blurred beyond recognition through the integration of new styles and the anglicization of artists' names, creating a distinctive style made by English-born painters from immigrant families. Arguably, without these foreign interventions it is hard to see how English painting could have ever achieved the level of sophistication that it did, indicating that immigration and innovation often represent two sides of the same coin. Equally, we can see that time and time again groups that are ostracized come to have much in common with each other and form tight-knit bonds. Foreign communities like those that sprang up in Blackfriars proved yet again that adversity cause by xenophobic business practices brought no advantage to those enforcing such rules, and in many instances engendered the opposite to the intended result, with immigrants forming their own networks through friendship and intermarriage, eventually rivalling the reach and influence of guilds such as the Painter-Stainers' Company.[29]

Like many of these artists, Van Dyck integrated fully into court life in England, yet he evidently retained a great deal of autonomy and freedom because even in a busy period at court he managed to visit the Southern Netherlands between 1633 and 1635, returning to London in the spring of 1635.[30] The last six years of his life would see a prodigious amount of work emerge from his Blackfriars workshop, undoubtedly achieved by his employment of assistants. The workshop system was of course not new – Van Dyck himself came from Rubens's workshop – but his own studio took its lead from the Renaissance bottegas (studios) of the 1470s run by the likes of Verrocchio and Ghirlandaio, which in turn had spawned the next generation of artists such as Leonardo and Michelangelo. Just as we are yet to fully ascertain the internal workings of these fifteenth-century workshops, equally we know little about the specific working practices of Van Dyck's workshop in Blackfriars. One of his sitters, the banker and collector Everhard Jabach, reveals that, 'He would make compositional drawings of the figure and clothing from the life in chalks on coloured paper; he gave this to his assistants, who would enlarge and paint it on canvas', and that he would then 'pass his brush lightly and quickly over what they had done'. Jabach also mentions 'the skilful people he has with him'.[31] Much of this anecdotal evidence, however, does not distinguish between Van Dyck's servants and his assistants, perhaps meaning their jobs were interchangeable.

To make questions of attribution even more complex, it seems that Van Dyck generally adopted the habit of not signing his English paintings.[32] In the latter part of his career he also often repeated some of his own compositions, and numerous copies of his works were made by other artists throughout his time in London. A good case in point is the portrait of Thomas Wentworth, 1st Earl of Strafford, with his servant Sir Philip Mainwaring, which exists in around five versions, all of which seem to

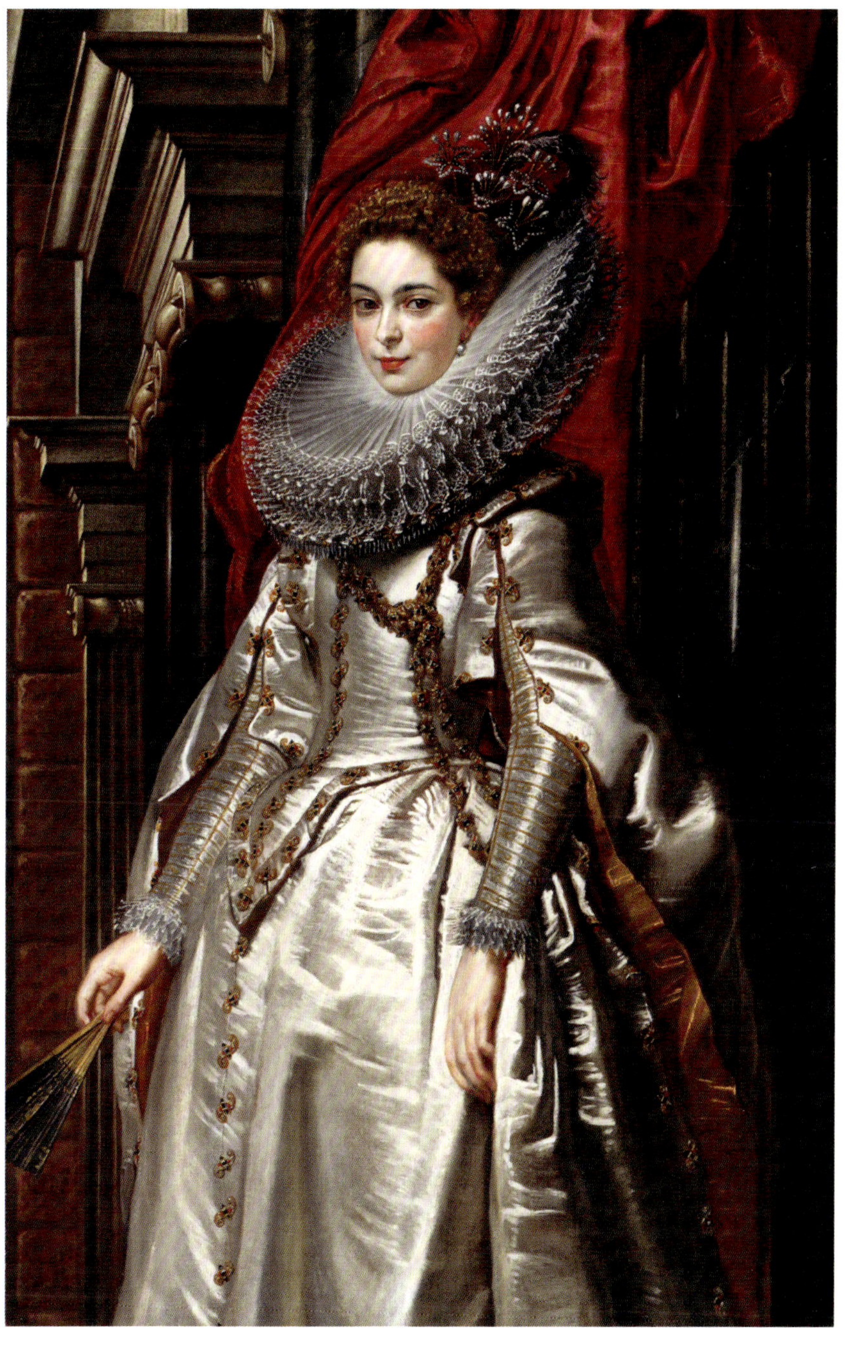

39 Peter Paul Rubens, *Marchesa Brigida Spinola Doria*, 1606.
Oil on canvas, 152 × 99 cm (59⅞ × 39 in.)

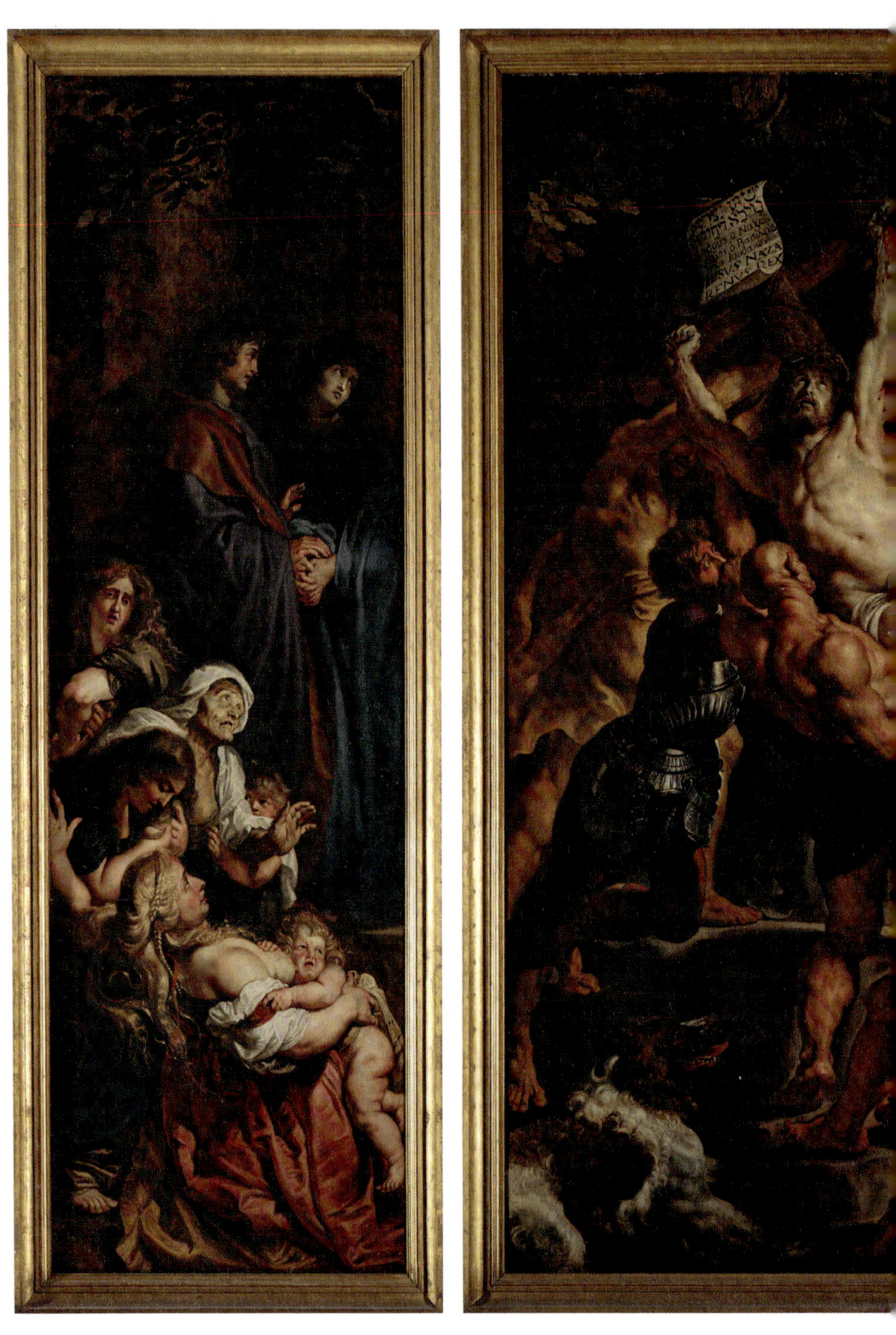

40 Peter Paul Rubens, *The Elevation of the Cross* (triptych), 1610–11.
Oil on panel, 341 × 462 cm (134¼ × 181⅞ in.)

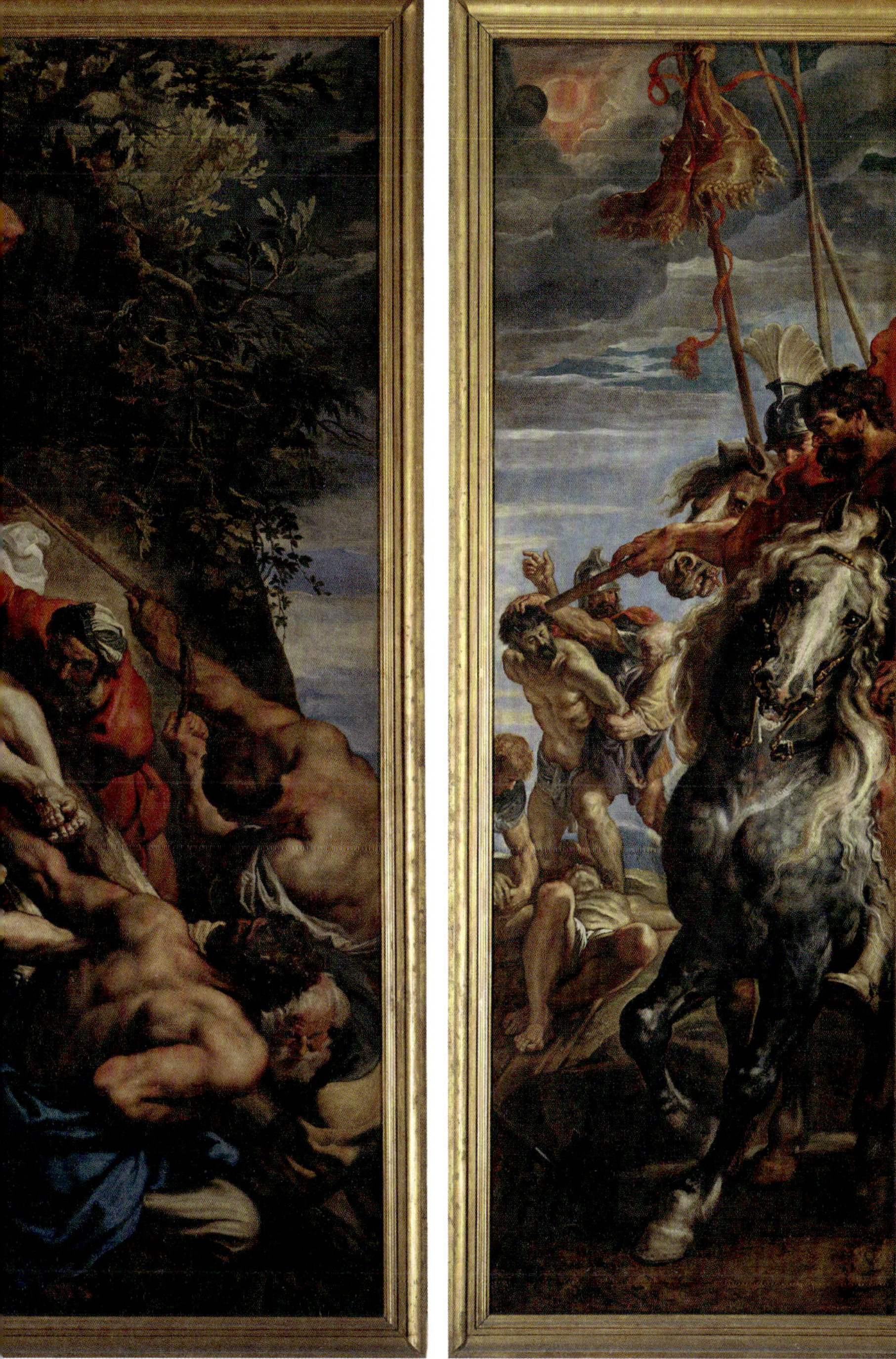

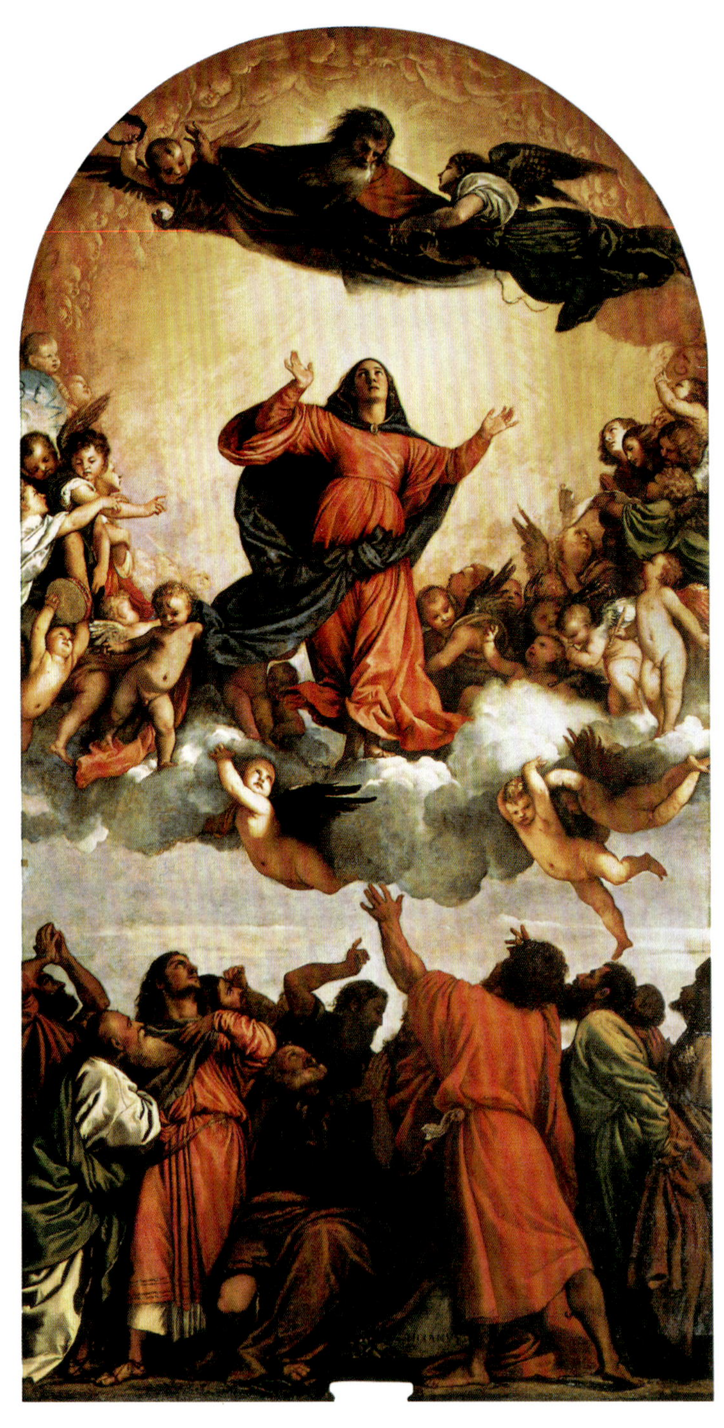

41 Titian, *Assumption of the Virgin*, 1516–18.
Oil on canvas, 6.7 × 3.4 cm (196⅞ × 133⅜ in.)

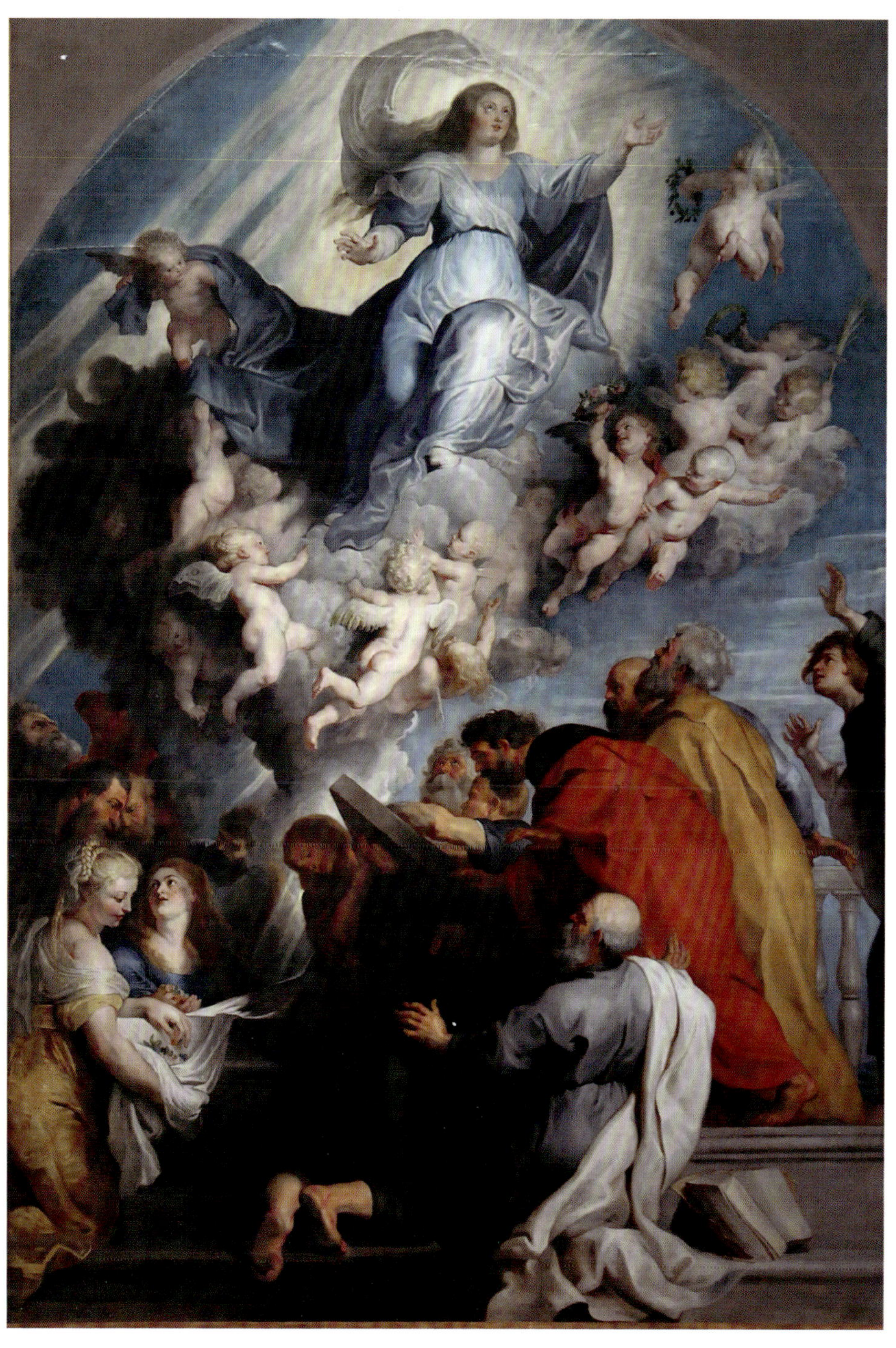

42 Peter Paul Rubens, *Assumption of the Virgin, c.* 1615–29. Oil on canvas (arched), probably transposed from wood to canvas, 500 × 338.5 cm (196⅞ × 133⅜ in.)

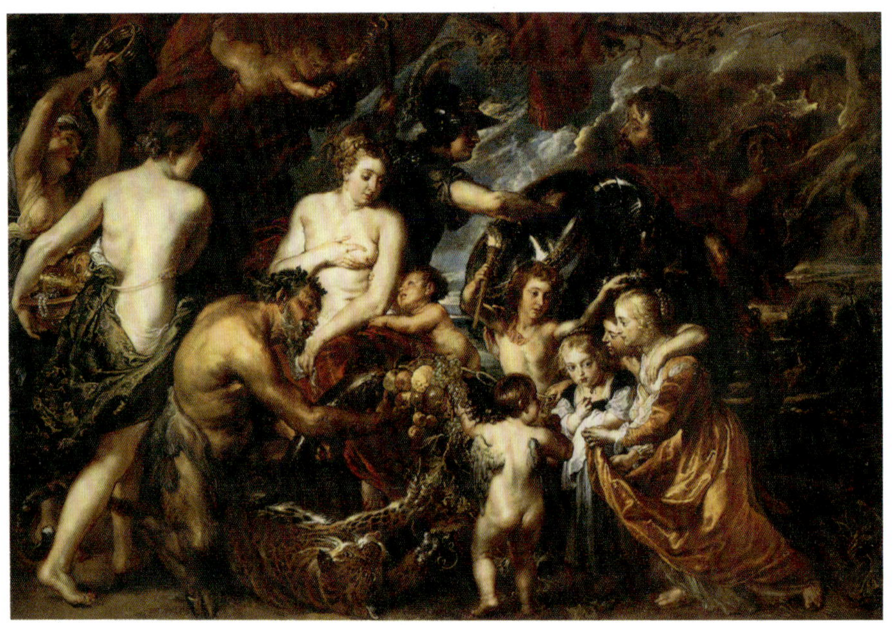

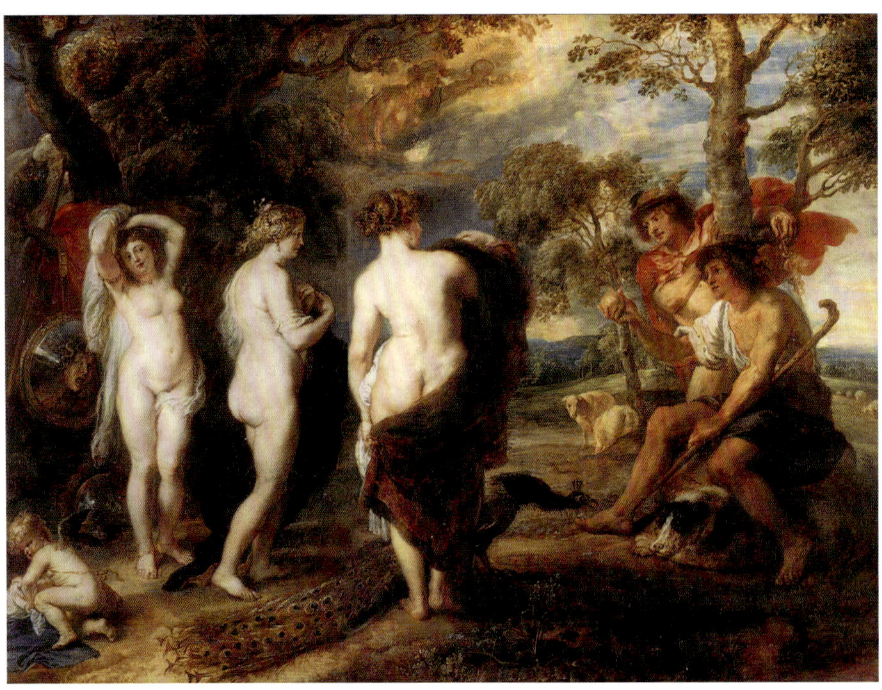

43 Peter Paul Rubens, *Minerva Protects Pax from Mars (Peace and War)*, 1629–30. Oil on canvas, 203 × 298 cm (80 × 117⅜ in.)

44 Peter Paul Rubens, *Judgement of Paris*, 1632–35. Oil on oak, 144.8 × 193.7 cm (57⅛ × 76⅜ in.)

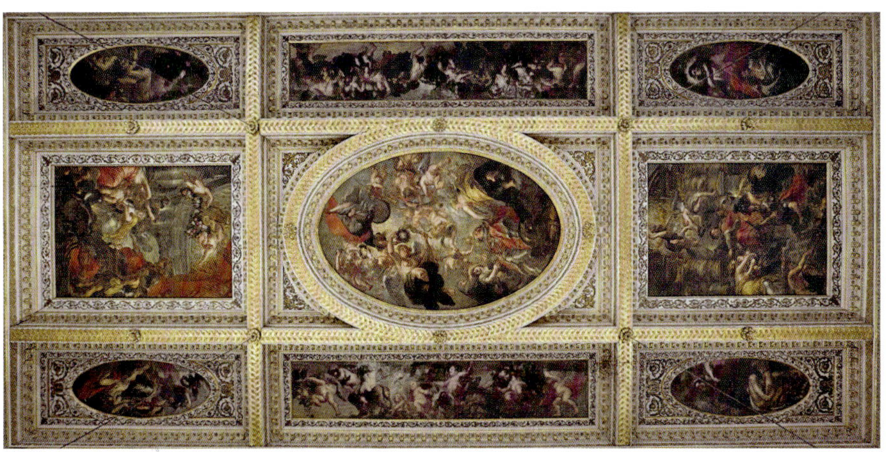

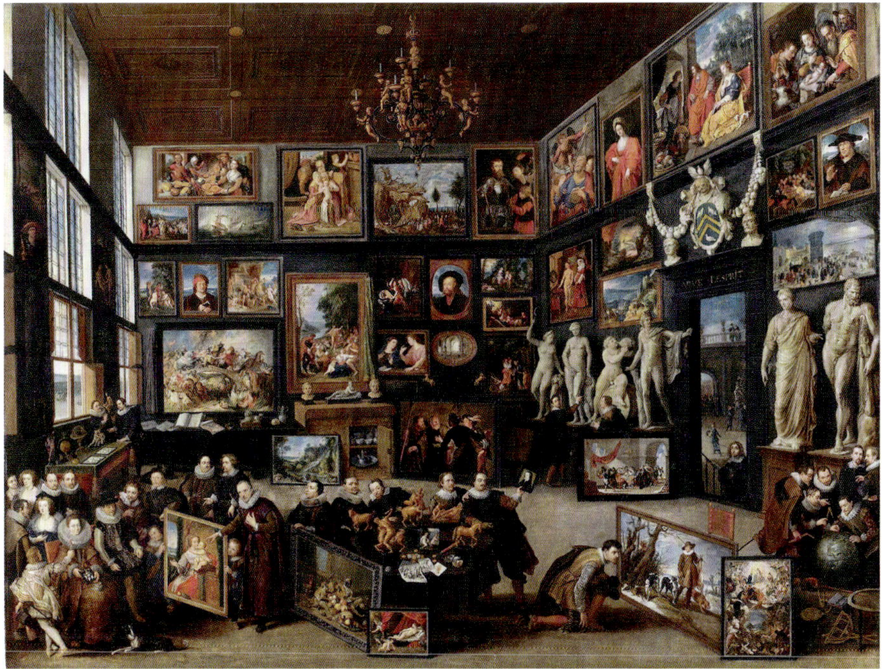

45 Peter Paul Rubens, Banqueting House (built 1619), ceiling views, 1633–36. Oil on canvas, 225 sq. m (2,420 sq. ft)

46 Willem van Haecht, *The Cabinet of Cornelis van der Geest*, 1628. Oil on canvas, 99.9 × 136 cm (39⅜ × 53½ in.)

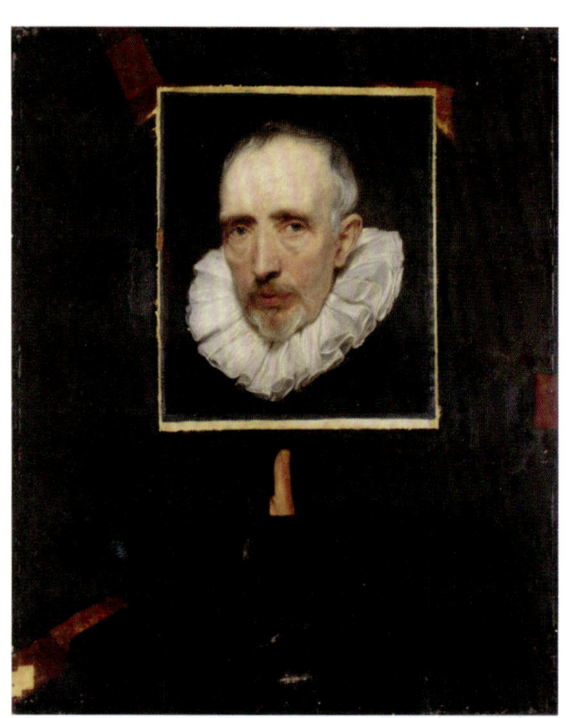

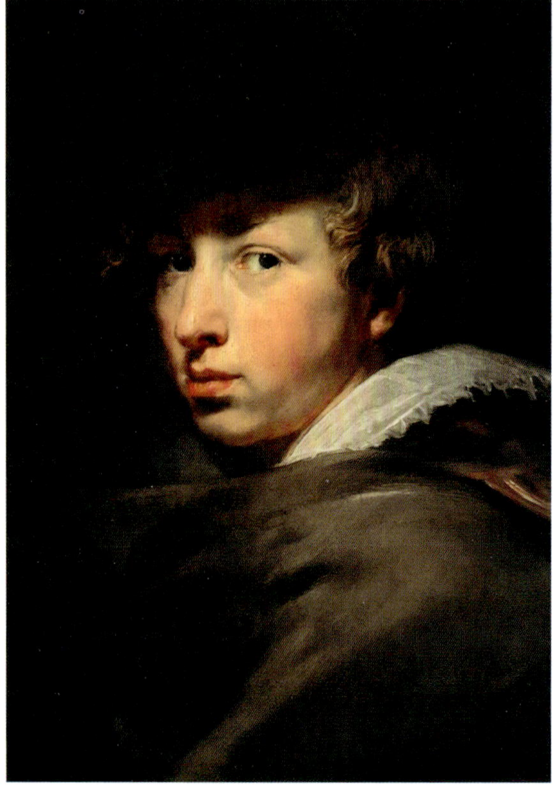

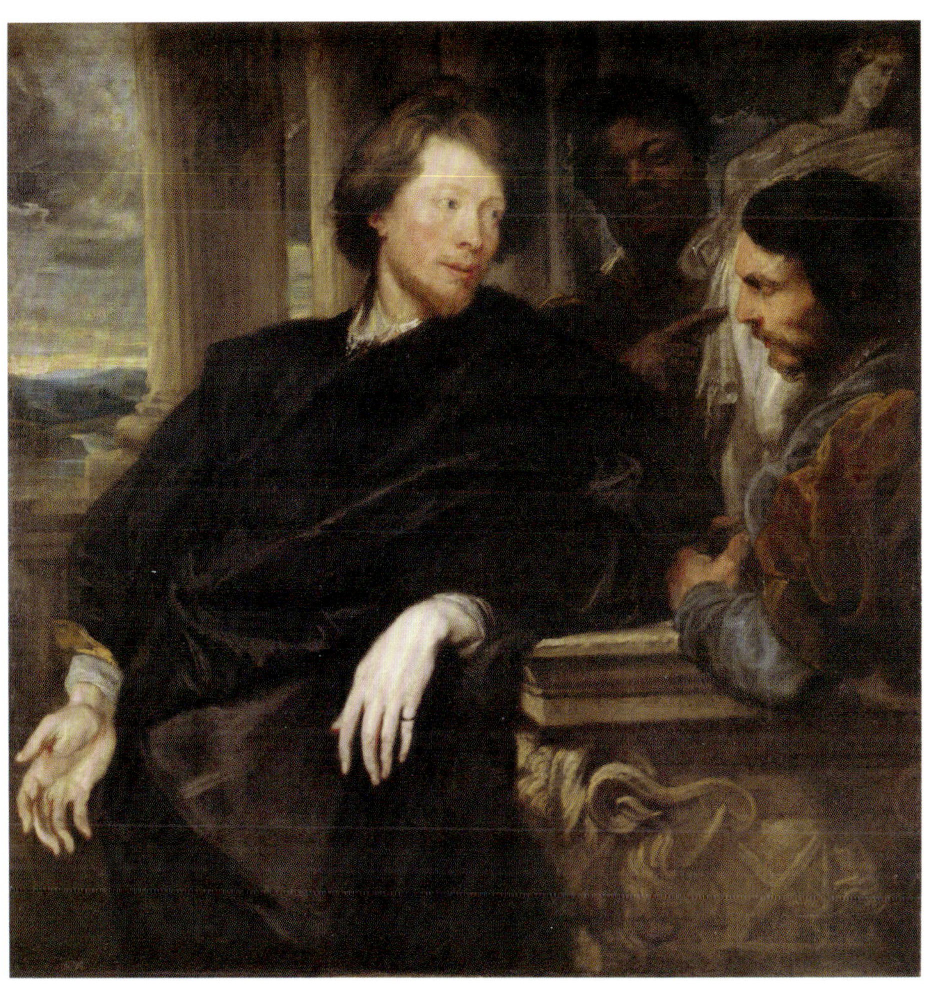

47 Anthony van Dyck, *Cornelis van der Geest*, c. 1620.
Oil on oak, 37.5 × 32.5 cm (14⅞ × 12⅞ in.)

48 Anthony van Dyck (formerly attrib. Peter Paul Rubens), *Self-Portrait*, 1615.
Oil on panel, 36.5 × 25.8 cm (14⅜ × 10¼ in.)

49 Anthony van Dyck, *Portrait of George Gage with Two Attendants*, 1622–23.
Oil on canvas, 115 × 113.5 cm (45⅜ × 44¾ in.)

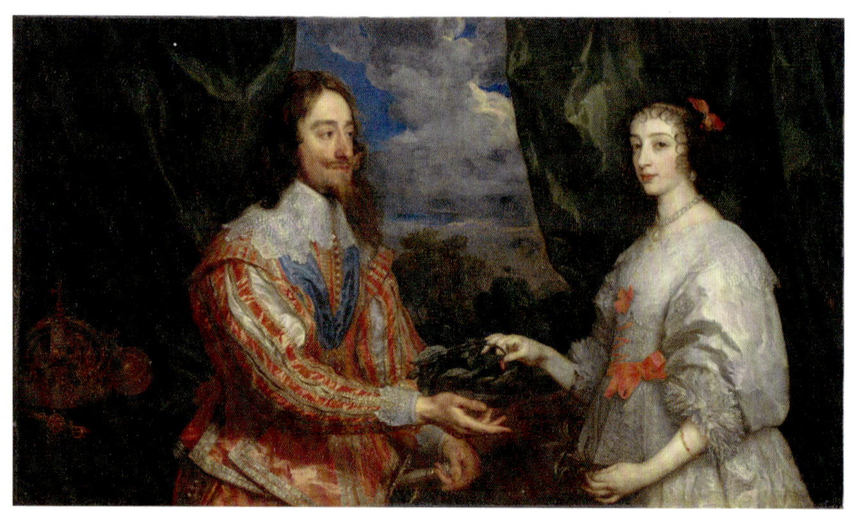

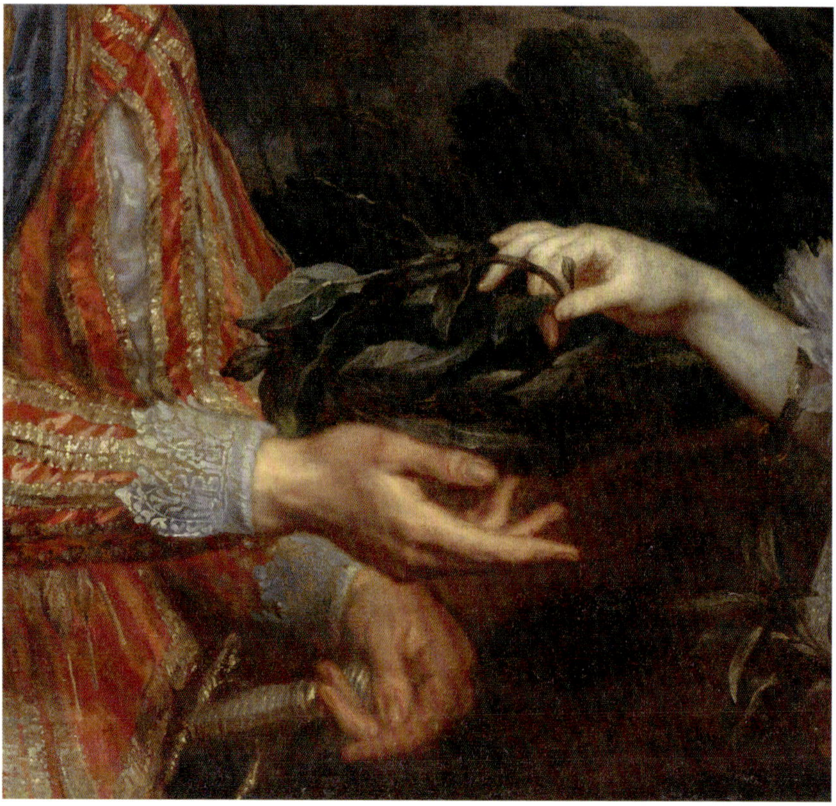

50 Anthony van Dyck, *Charles I and Henrietta Maria*, 1632.
Oil on canvas, 113.5 × 163 cm (44¾ × 64¼ in.)

51 Anthony van Dyck, *Charles I and Henrietta Maria*, 1632 (detail).

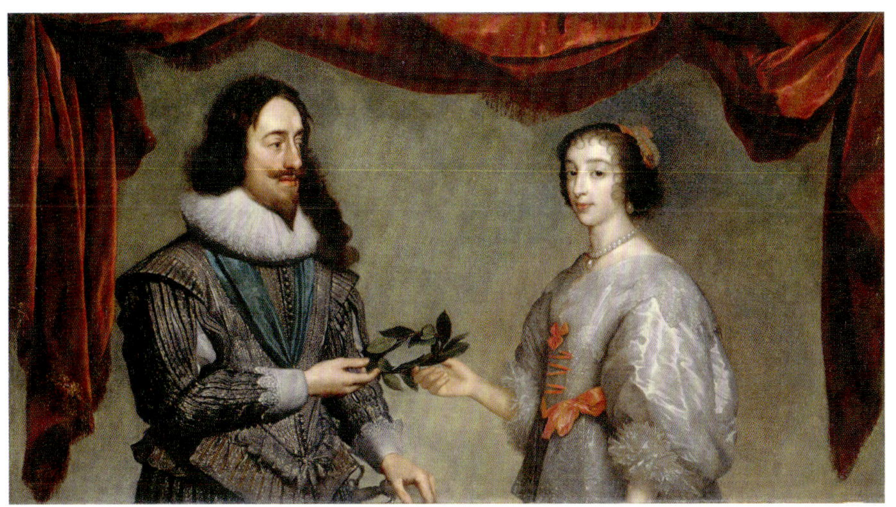

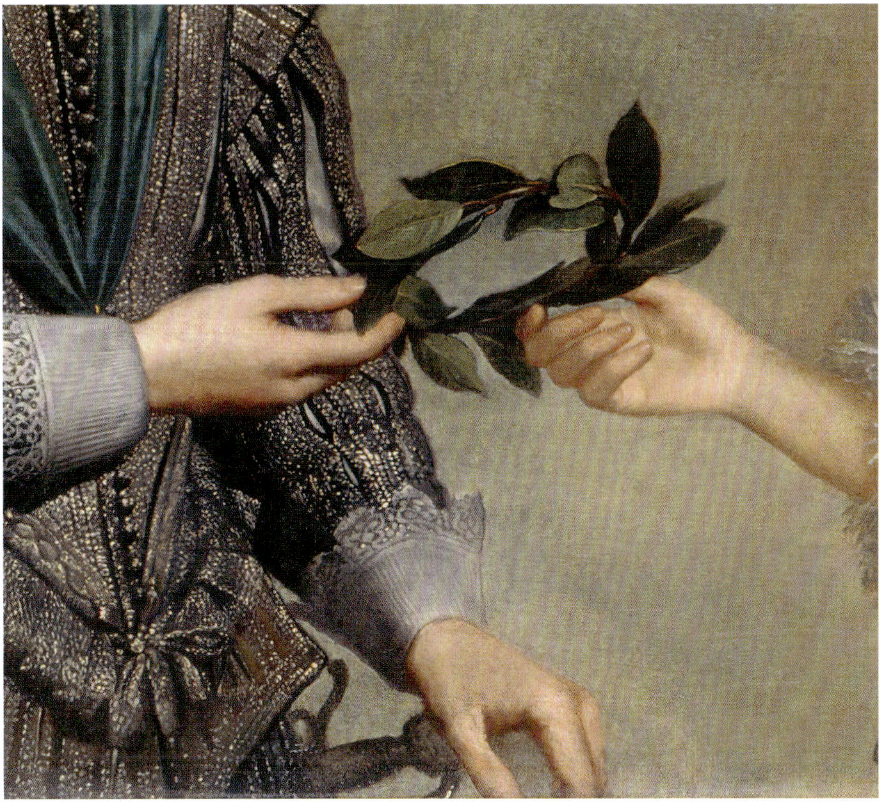

52 Daniel Mytens, *Charles I and Henrietta Maria*, *c*. 1630–32.
Oil on canvas, 95.6 × 175.3 cm (37¾ × 69⅛ in.)

53 Daniel Mytens, *Charles I and Henrietta Maria*, *c*. 1630–32 (detail).

54 Anthony van Dyck, *Self-Portrait*, *c*. 1640.
Oil on canvas, 56 × 46 cm (22⅛ × 18⅛ in.)

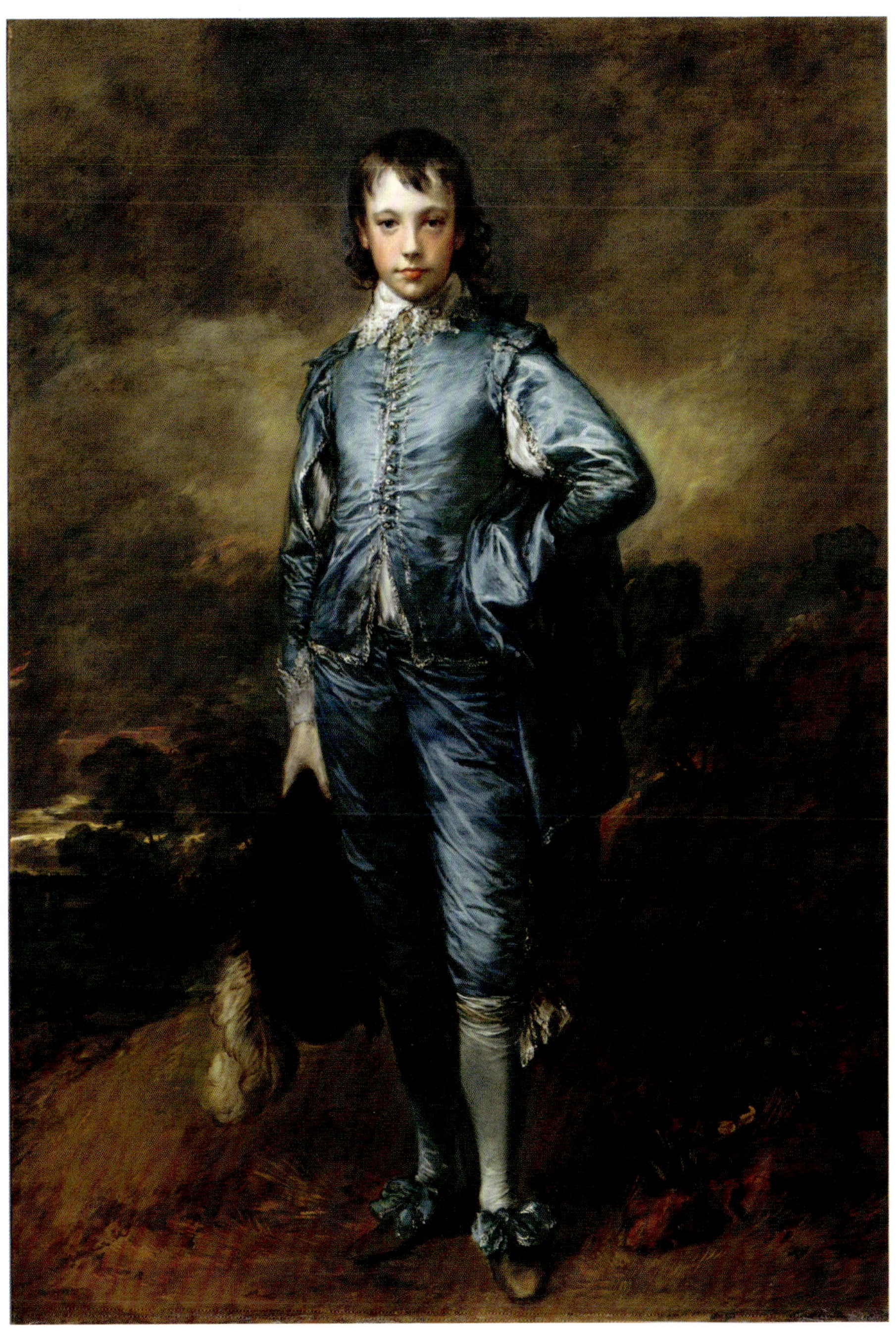

55 Thomas Gainsborough, *The Blue Boy*, *c.* 1770.
Oil on canvas, 179.4 × 123.8 cm (70¾ × 48¾ in.)

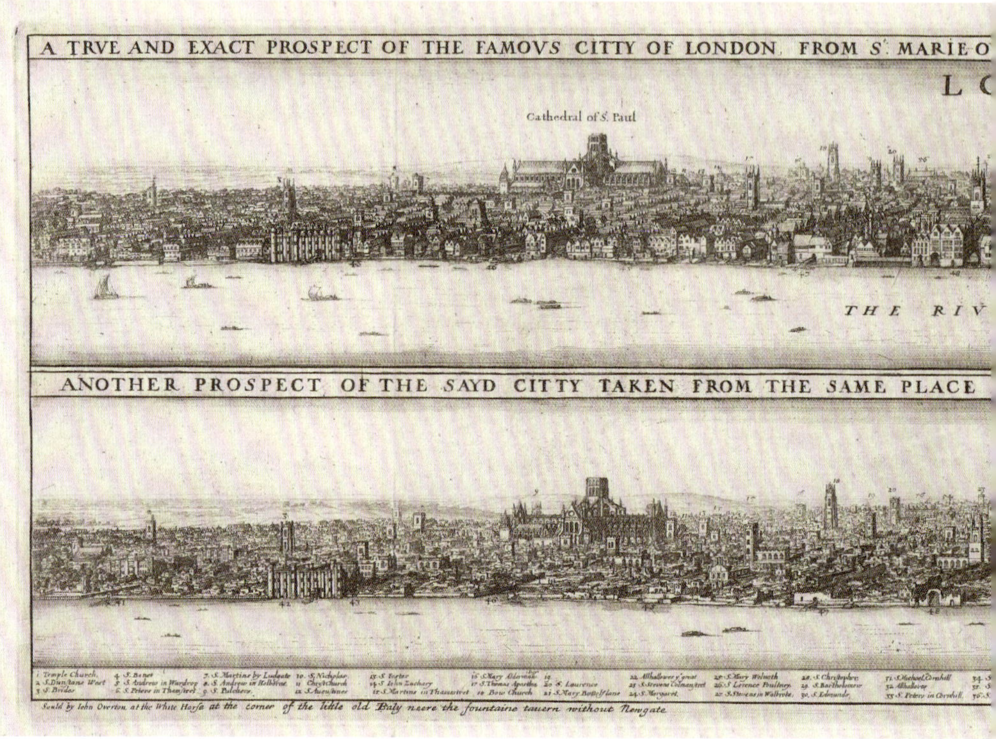

A TRVE AND EXACT PROSPECT OF THE FAMOVS CITTY OF LONDON, FROM S. MARIE O
LO
Cathedral of S. Paul
THE RIV
ANOTHER PROSPECT OF THE SAYD CITTY TAKEN FROM THE SAME PLACE
1 Temple Church.   4 S. Benet   7 S. Martins by Ludgate   10 S. Nicholas.   13 S. Foster   16 S. Mary Aldarmak   19   22 Alhallower y great
2 S. Dunstans West   5 S. Andrew in Wardrop   8 S. Andrew in Holborne   11 Christchurch   14 S. Iohn Zachary   17 S. Thomas Apostles   20 S. Laurence   23 S. Stevens Colman tret
3 S. Brides   6 S. Peters in Thamstret   9 S. Pulchers.   12 S. Austines   15 S. Martins in Thamesstret   18 Bow Church   21 S. Mary Bottolf lane   24 S. Margaret
Sould by Iohn Overton, at the White Horse at the corner of the little old Baly neere the fountaine tauern without Newgate

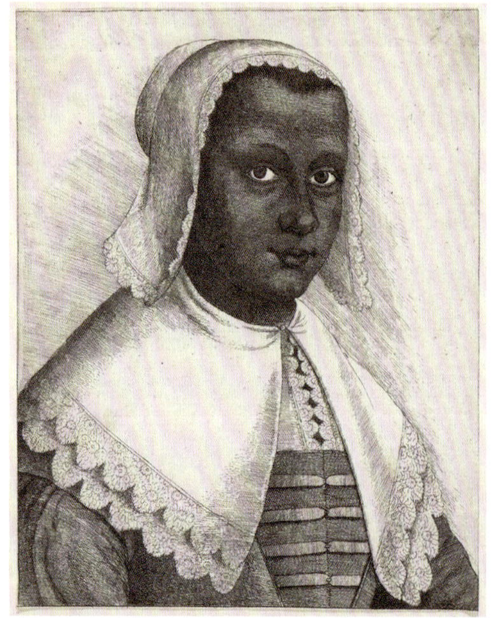

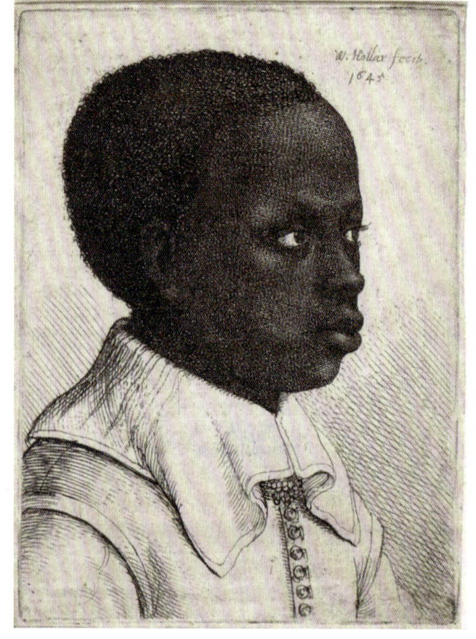
W. Hollar fecit
1645

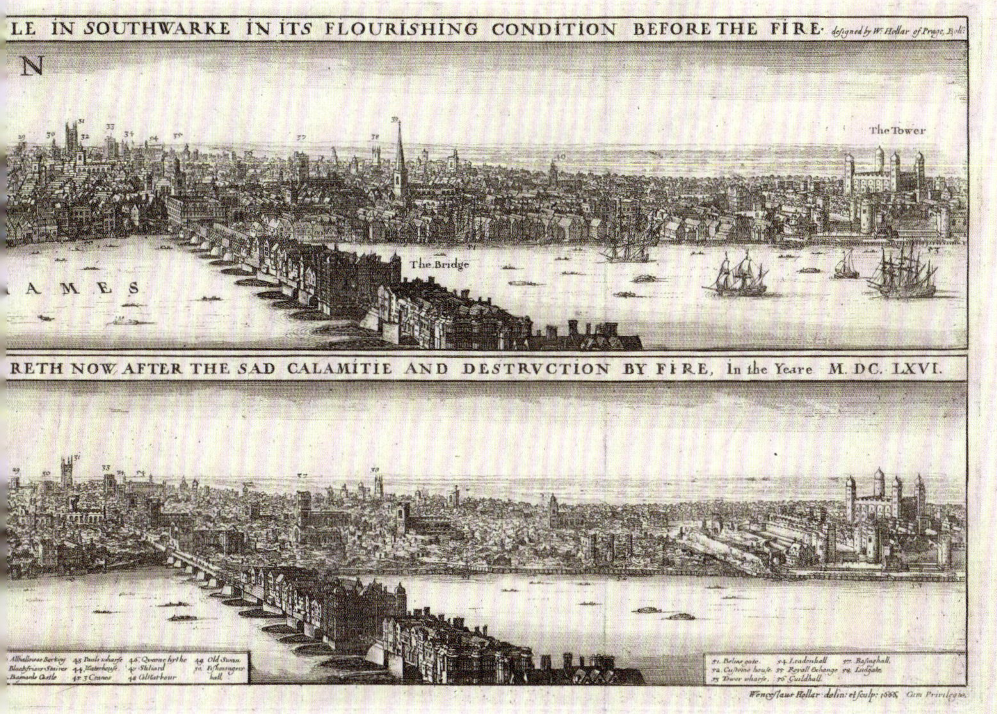

56 Wenceslaus Hollar, *A true and exact propect of the famous citty of London ... before the fire [and] ... after the sad calamitie and destruction by Fire in the yeare MDCLXVI*, 1666. Etching, 22.4 × 67.8 cm (8⅞ × 26¾ in.)

57 Wenceslaus Hollar, *Head of a Young Black Woman in Three-Quarter Profile to the Right*, c. 1640–50. Etching, 20.1 × 16 cm (8 × 6⅜ in.)

58 Wenceslaus Hollar, *Portrait of a Young Black Boy*, 1645. Etching, 8 × 5.9 cm (3⅛ × 2⅜ in.)

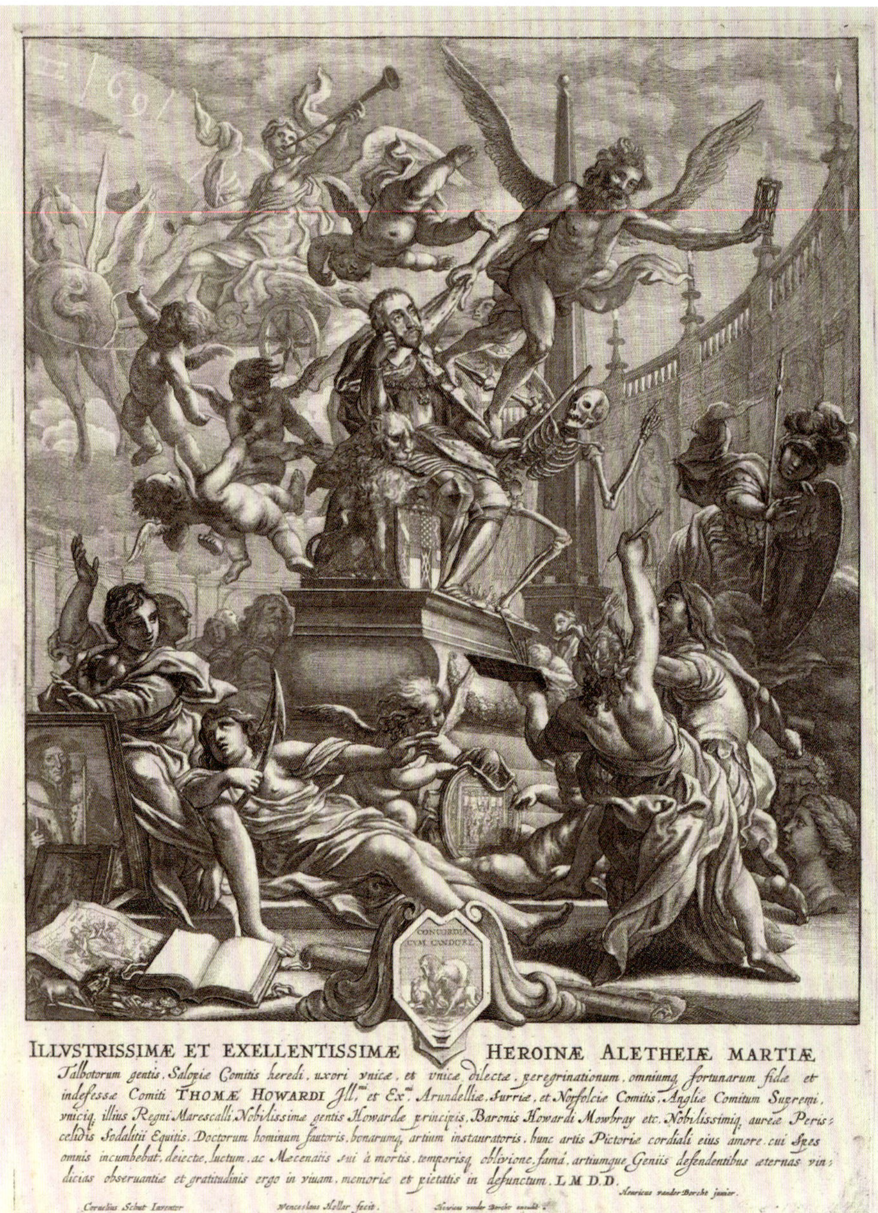

59 Wenceslaus Hollar, *Allegory of Death and of the Earl of Arundel*, c. 1646.
Etching, 43.7 × 32 cm (17¼ × 12⅝ in.)

be derived from a painting now in a private collection. The others are of dubious quality, except for a version currently at Blenheim Palace, which is perhaps the most convincing rendition and comes closest in quality to the original. It is likely that many such copies were commissioned by those who were already in possession of original works by the artist: one might be able to afford a single Van Dyck, but several might be beyond one's means. The artist's death in 1641 if anything increased demand for his work, and judging by the number of paintings now attributed 'after Van Dyck' it is apparent that an entire industry sprang up in imitation of his style. Both within his lifetime and beyond, we see Van Dyck's style being co-opted as a quintessentially English one. Works by the English-born artist Robert Walker, for example, were so Van Dyckian that for many years it was assumed he had worked in the artist's studio (need-less to say, no evidence has been found to support this hypothesis). This aping of Van Dyck's style would continue in the eighteenth century with portraits such as *Brownlow, 9th Earl of Exeter* by the Devon-born painter Thomas Hudson and *Letitia Townshend, Countess of Exeter* by John Powell (both at Burghley House, Lincolnshire).[33]

By 1635 Van Dyck had moved permanently to London with his entire art collection; it is thought that he bought another large-scale Titian, *The Vendramin Family*, to add to it sometime after 1636. He clearly had the funds to continue indulging his lifelong admiration for the Renaissance master, but it seems that such purchases were predicated on the assump-tion of a forthcoming, supposedly regular income.[34] But as we have seen already, monarchs could not always be relied on to pay their bills, and towards the end of 1638 Van Dyck sent Charles I a reminder requesting outstanding payment for twenty-five paintings, for some of which the King, quite amazingly, still insisted on price cuts.[35] In the same docu-ment, Van Dyck drew attention to the backlog in his pension payments of £200 a year, which had not been paid for the previous five years. These major discrepancies were only partially resolved when the King some-what reluctantly agreed to pay Van Dyck £603 for the pictures, to be received in stages between February and May 1639.

In early 1640 Van Dyck married the Scottish noblewoman Mary Ruthven, daughter of the self-titled Lord Ruthven, though the title had been forfeited and the family was impoverished by the time of the marriage. The couple had been introduced at the wedding of Charles I and Henrietta Maria and it seems to have been the King who insisted they should marry. Such a request from his patron was also a clear instruction to Van Dyck that he should end his relationship with Margaret Lemon, who he painted several times up to the year before his marriage. Characterized variously as a muse, a model, and even a courtesan, Margaret was not deemed an appropriate match for Sir Anthony van Dyck, though such language was used in this period to describe any woman who did not conform to societal norms. In the year of their marriage Van Dyck produced a stunning portrait of his new wife (p. 163). It is an image laden with status, with deft handling of the paint to create the sumptuous blue dress and copious amounts of pearl jewellery set against Mary's pale white skin, demonstrating the supposedly pure beauty of both. In its formality the painting confirms Van Dyck's allegiance to a social structure that had no place for women like Margaret Lemon, described by the artist Wenceslaus Hollar as violently jealous to the point of having once attempted to bite Van Dyck's thumb off, though such statements say more about the widespread misogyny that women endured in everyday life than about the individual.[36] Van Dyck's portrait of his new wife could be seen as a repudiation of his previous lifestyle, while also proving that his ability to produce high-quality portraiture had not waned despite his workload, peripatetic lifestyle and the burden of outstanding payments.

On news of the death of Rubens in May 1640, Van Dyck was invited to Antwerp to supervise the master's workshop for a limited period. When he returned to England, it seems that the constant travelling and overwork had taken its toll, with contemporary commentators remarking on his poor health. Eventually the King sent his own physician, offering him £300 if he could save Van Dyck. Amid all this Van Dyck's wife gave birth to their daughter, Justiniana; three days after her birth Van Dyck made his will, dying just five days later on 9 December 1641, one year after his master Rubens, though considerably younger at just forty-two years old.

The self-portrait Van Dyck made in the last year of his life (fig. 54) exemplifies the painterly approach to art that had been pioneered in the

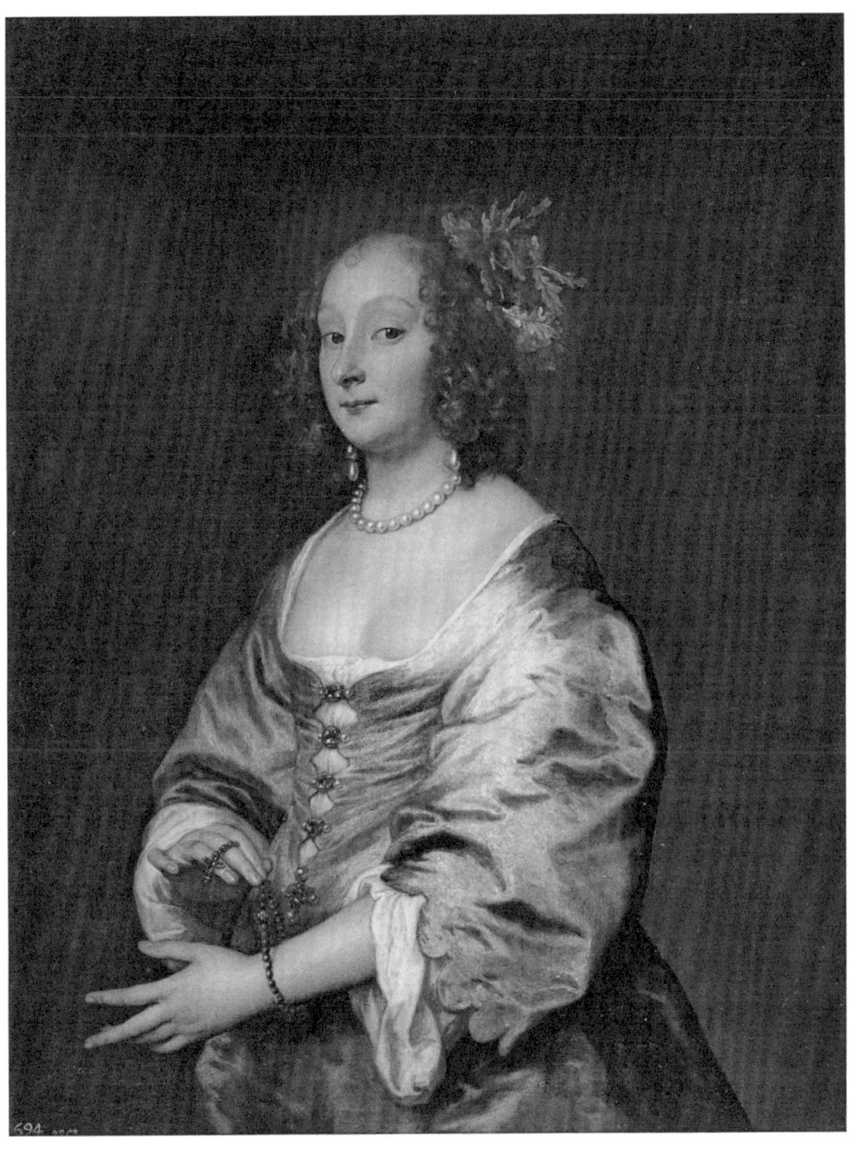

Anthony van Dyck, *The Artist's Wife, Mary Ruthven, Lady van Dyck,*
c. 1640. Oil on canvas, 104 × 81 cm (41 × 32 in.)

sixteenth century by Venetian painters such as Veronese, Tintoretto and Titian but was new to England. The deliberate roughness of the broad, visible brushstrokes delineating the texture of his clothes and collar contrasts with the smoother, finished textures that he applies to his hair and face. The casual glance over his shoulder towards the viewer implies an effortlessness in the execution of this work. This could not be further from the truth, however: like all great geniuses Van Dyck conceals how difficult this quality of work is to achieve.

Van Dyck left an enormous artistic legacy that grew exponentially and impacted the work of virtually all British artists who followed. They included the Dutch artist Pieter van der Faes, who was born in Westphalia, Germany, in 1618 and arrived in England around 1641, the year of Van Dyck's death. On his arrival he seems to have almost immediately adopted the surname Lely, now thought to be an unusual anglicization of *lis*, the French word for lily, perhaps chosen because as a child this symbol had adorned the gable end of his father's house. It cannot have escaped his attention that a French-sounding name would be infinitely more fashionable and easier to pronounce in England than his Dutch name, while lending him an air of supposed sophistication.

The timing of Peter Lely's arrival in England so soon after the death of Van Dyck placed him in the perfect position to ease himself into the void left by the great master. He arrived at a turbulent moment in the nation's history, as the English Civil War was being fought between Royalists (supporters of the King) and Parliamentarians (supporters of the Parliament), yet Lely managed to steer a careful path between the two factions. During the period between the execution of Charles I in 1649 and the restoration of his son Charles II in 1660, known as the Interregnum, Lely was careful to stay in contact with the exiled future king and those associated with him, allowing him on the Restoration to return to Charles II the pictures he had bought at the sale of the late Charles I's possessions.

In London he encountered Italian Renaissance paintings and the work of Anthony van Dyck, both of which had a long-lasting impact on his own work, and throughout his time in England Lely seems to have adopted Van Dyck's style, evident in his society and royal portraits such as *Elizabeth Murray, Lady Tollemache, Later Countess of Dysart and Duchess of Lauderdale, with a Black Servant* (*c.* 1651; Ham House, Surrey) and *The Three Younger Children of Charles I* (1647; Petworth House, West Sussex). Yet in many respects Lely did not represent a mere continuation of Van Dyck's style, but arguably presented a more luxuriously polished version of his portraiture in England, as seen in works such as *Lady Mary Fane* (*c.* 1662; James Stunt Collection).

In October 1661 Lely was appointed Principal Painter to Charles II. His naturalization as an Englishman followed in 1662, and in 1679, the year before his death on 30 November 1680, he was awarded a knighthood. A combination of the styles of Van Dyck and Lely would endure in the work of English-born painters such as William Dobson and beyond, with Thomas Gainsborough's *Blue Boy* of *c.* 1770 (fig. 55) demonstrating a clear debt to Van Dyck's portraiture in the Grand Manner.[37] It was the emulation of Van Dyck that became the de facto style of what art historians now call the British school of painting.

8

Wenceslaus Hollar

*The Bohemian Chronicler
of London*

Somehow we know him without knowing him, because etched into the minds of all who imagine London before the Great Fire of 1666 are his topographical views (fig. 56), images that take us back to a gritty, unsanitary city of narrow lanes, back streets and wooden houses that populated even the bridges that crossed the Thames (though it must be said that on close examination these scenes represent a sanitized, utopian view of the city, probably the reason they evoke such nostalgia).[1] His name is not as familiar in the public imagination as those of other seventeenth-century artists like Rubens or Van Dyck, but his work has nevertheless given us a rich and indispensable source of information, offering a fascinating window on to London's past. Because he is not so well known, we often fail to acknowledge the rich legacy bequeathed to us by one we would without hesitation call our own, a true Londoner and inventor of original scenes in British art. This great artist was another of those immigrants who made and embraced London as their second home, an itinerant artist who would always regard Prague as his first home, as evidenced by his works, which more often than not are signed 'Wenceslaus Hollar of Bohemia'.

He was born Václav Hollar on 23 July 1607 in the Neustadt, Prague, in the country then known as Bohemia (now the Czech Republic). His father, Jan Hollar, was a lawyer by profession who had been knighted in 1600 by the Holy Roman Emperor Rudolf II (r. 1576–1612) and held high office in the Bohemian land registry. Hollar's mother, Margaret, who died when Wenceslaus was just six years old, came from an equally privileged

166

background; her father had been the town burgher and may well have been knighted too. Her family was originally from the Upper Palatinate (now in Bavaria, Germany), which had a rich tradition of Calvinism.[2]

Hollar's ability to pursue his chosen profession was no doubt helped by the established status and wealth of his family.[3] Jan probably intended his son to follow him into the law, but it seems that from an early age his passion was instead for art. A short biographical text added by Hollar to a self-portrait etching made in London in 1649 (p. 168) confirms this interest, and mentions his father's displeasure at his chosen path: 'Wenceslaus Hollar – Gentleman, born at Prague in the year 1607, was by nature much inclined to the art of the miniature, especially to illumination, but was much held back by his father.' It is clear from this self-portrait that Hollar aspired to make the profession of etcher a respectable one, displaying as it does his comfortable middle-class clothes, a buttoned-down doublet and his family's coat of arms over his right shoulder, which served to align his Bohemian nobility with that of his trade, represented by his etching tools.[4] Significantly, he signed his name on this and later works in the anglicized form Wenceslaus, rather than his native birth spelling, Václav, making a clear declaration of the duality of his life as an immigrant and a Londoner. He most definitely became a Londoner, steeped in the history and traditions of the great city, but he was also a proud son of Bohemia. Although in our contemporary period some may find this duality problematic, it has never been so for most immigrants or those of dual heritage.

Like many of the foreign artists who came to the British Isles before him, Hollar had travelled extensively in Continental Europe, in his case for at least ten years before his arrival, so he was not unaware of their legacy. His etched portraits bear witness to such familiarity, with a roll-call of these past heroes of English art immortalized in his work. They include Hans Holbein the Younger, made in 1647, just over a century after the artist's death; Marcus Gheeraerts the Younger, made in 1644; Peter Paul Rubens, made perhaps a decade after his death in the mid-seventeenth century; and Anthony van Dyck, also made in 1644, only three years after his death. Hollar produced not only portraits of these artists for the cabinets and collections of the growing merchant classes, but also extensive

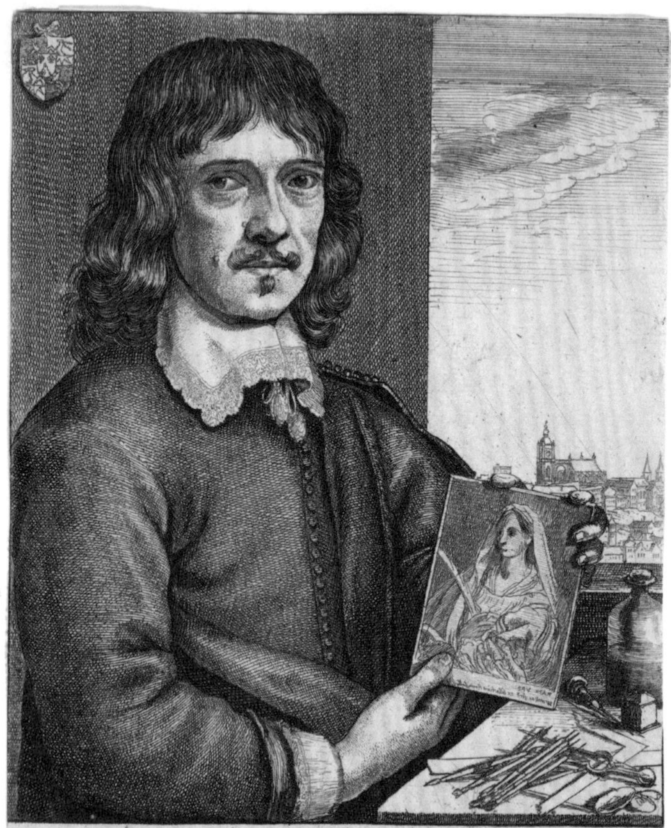

Wenceslaus Hollar, *Self-Portrait* (from *Image de divers Hommes: The True Effigies of the Most Eminent Painters*), 1649. Etching, 16.6 × 11.9 cm (6⅝ × 4¾ in.)

etched reproductions of their works, especially those of Van Dyck and Holbein. These artists had reached the highest echelons of the arts in their lifetimes and Hollar no doubt sought to align himself with their achievements. The sheer volume of these works points towards an affinity, or a posthumous camaraderie, between Hollar and his fellow foreign artists. Hollar understood these artists; he spoke their language both literally and figuratively, and now he was travelling on the same path they had taken so many decades – even centuries – before him.

From a young age Hollar had embraced the life of the journeyman artist (*Wandergeselle*). His early wanderings may have been precipitated first by the uprising of the Bohemian nationalist burghers of Prague against the German Catholics, triggered by the death in 1619 of Matthias, Holy Roman Emperor, and then by the tumultuous Battle of White Mountain in November 1620.[5] This would mark the beginning of the Thirty Years' War, which resulted in the sack of Prague and the ruin of Hollar's family when he was just thirteen years old. While the English engraver and antiquarian George Vertue claimed in 1759 that the Hollar family's ruin resulted from their close allegiance to those in power,[6] Hollar's eventual departure from Prague in 1627 was not necessarily because of the conflict, even though it was still in progress at the time. As we have seen throughout this book, the reasons why immigrants leave their native countries, at least from a European perspective, to take up residence in Britain have been many and varied across the centuries and tend to fall broadly into categories such as war, famine, religious persecution and economic destitution, or a combination of all these factors.

In the case of Hollar, we are hampered by inconclusive evidence. The seventeenth-century English writers John Evelyn and John Aubrey suggest that, as Protestants, Hollar and his family found themselves in danger when Catholics prevailed in the Bohemian conflicts and so were forced to flee.[7] Another theory suggests Hollar departed for artistic reasons, though the idea that no craftsmen of any substantial aptitude were present in his native Prague leads to the argument that if that were true Hollar would have found much work there; yet he returned only once in his lifetime.[8] While we are unable to fathom why Hollar chose to spend most of his productive years in exile from Prague, we can speculate that the ongoing wars in the region cannot have been conducive to supporting artistic production.[9] The artist's subsequent association with the Earl of Arundel certainly gave him a financial incentive to eventually settle in England.[10]

Hollar's itinerant lifestyle after he left Prague in 1627 can be charted through his many dated topographical etchings of places on his journey, such as his views of Stuttgart (1627–28) and Strasbourg (1629–30). Vertue's publication *A Description of the Works of the Ingenious Delineator and Engraver Wenceslaus Hollar* (1759) is an invaluable source for this early period, containing an extensive catalogue of Hollar's work; Vertue also notes that '[Hollar] made several little Essays before he left his native Country'.[11] From this period and considered among the artist's earliest extant works are six prints of a portrait of Dürer dated 1625, after an original woodcut of *c.* 1527 by the Nuremberg-born Erhard Schön, and three prints after Dürer woodcuts, *Christ Taking Leave of his Mother*, *Christ in Majesty* (both dated 1625) and *Virgin and Child Seated by a Tree* (dated 1626), all now at the Fitzwilliam Museum, Cambridge.[12]

It has been suggested that Hollar's early training may have begun under a local artist in Prague, Gilles Sadeler, aka Aegidius (indicating that there *were* in fact competent craftsmen in the city at this time). Born in Antwerp, Sadeler settled in Prague in 1597, where he became court engraver to Rudolf II. However, his death in 1629 would have presented Hollar with a rather narrow window of opportunity for training. In addition, Sadeler's fame was firmly attributed to his skill as an engraver, and so far we have no known works by Hollar in this medium.

Engraving is different from Hollar's preferred medium of etching in a few ways. The former uses a sharp, pencil-shaped metal tool known as a burin to physically cut lines into the surface of plates made of materials such as copper, tin, pewter and – the hardest – brass. These materials were chosen for their pliability and ease of cutting, but plates (especially tin) wore away rapidly under the pressure of printing and were swiftly rendered unusable after multiple prints. In contrast, the etching process involves coating an iron or steel plate with a varnish or wax substance, through which the design is cut with a stylus. The entire plate is immersed in an acid bath, usually containing mordant (a caustic liquid) or vinegar prepared in a paste or liquid solution; the acid flows across the smooth surface of the varnish or wax, only biting into the exposed surface of the hand-cut design, creating an etching once the varnish or wax has been removed.[13] While engravings were being made in the 1470s by artists such as Andrea Mantegna and Antonio del Pollaiuolo, the earliest uses of etching in printmaking started to appear around 1500, perhaps for the first time in the Augsburg workshop of Daniel Hopfer, a now largely under-appreciated master of the medium. Notable artists who took up the practice include Albrecht Altdorfer and Albrecht Dürer, who produced landscapes in the 1520s, and Lucas van Leyden, whose biblical works *Susanna and the Elders* and *Adam and Eve Mourning the Death of Abel* were made around 1529–30.

Although we may not know exactly who trained Hollar, we do know that in 1631–32 he collaborated with the prominent and well-known Swiss-born engraver Matthäus Merian the Elder in Frankfurt. Merian had worked for most of his career in that city, where he also ran a publishing house and practised prodigiously in the medium of etching. From 1634 to 1636 Hollar was active in Cologne, producing a number of views of his journeys up the Rhine. The artist's travels were instrumental in allowing him to observe and absorb new influences, while his copious output helped him to hone and perfect his etching technique. In Amsterdam he was given the opportunity to demonstrate the sophistication of his technique by observing and making images of Black people (fig. 57), whose presence in the city resulting from the Dutch slave trade offered a new artistic challenge for Hollar. The nation's involvement in transatlantic slavery via the Dutch West India Company intensified in this period, largely as a result of unseemly squabbling between the European powers over money, land and assets. These assets were, of course, people, who had been turned into commodities by Western nations. From 1630 to 1654 the Dutch West India Company ruled over a colony in northeastern Brazil that relied on slave labour, and in 1637 it seized the fortress of Elmina on the west coast of Africa from the Portuguese, pioneers of European involvement in African slave trading. The result of all this prodigious activity can be measured by the estimated 164 slave voyages that were launched by the Dutch between 1640 and 1660. However, in 1644 a city law in Amsterdam decreed that 'within the city of Amsterdam and its jurisdiction, all men are free, and none are slaves'. The law went on to clarify that anyone entering the city became 'free beyond the control and authority of their masters and [master's] wives' and that, should there be any doubt, 'the persons concerned can arraign said masters and mistresses in the court of law of this city, where they then shall formally and legally declare them to be free'.[14]

The provenance of the Black people Hollar depicted has been linked to Amsterdam because of the simple mode of dress typically associated with servants in that city at the time, casting the sitters as slaves before the decree and servants after it.[15] However, these people, whose names, religion and lives were stripped from them to the extent that these aspects are lost to a modern audience, were still slaves in all but name. It is worth observing that the white collars and headdresses in these etchings allowed the artist to highlight the black skin of his sitters, enhancing and emphasizing their difference and novelty to the white audiences who would have been likely viewers of the etchings. These people of colour depicted by Hollar were only free as long as they remained in Amsterdam. If they left or were taken out of the city by their masters, they faced the immediate danger of being re-enslaved.

Given that Hollar made at least five etched portraits of Black people between 1634 and 1645, probably beginning with an etching of the head of a young Black boy in 1635, from which he later made another version around 1645 (fig. 58), it is clear that he benefited from the opportunity to depict them, because it was a technical challenge that would prove his mastery of the medium. As noted in the 2020 Rembrandt House Museum exhibition catalogue *Black in Rembrandt's Time*, black skin was extremely difficult to reproduce in an etching as 'there was a high risk that the close hatching grooves meant to hold the ink would break down'; this would leave shallow pits in the engraving plate that could not hold ink, resulting in white spots appearing on the finished print.[16] The catalogue notes that these works by Hollar are unlikely to have been commissioned portraits or indeed intended as portraits at all, owing to the lack of detail in the backgrounds and the absence of names; it is doubtful the sitters themselves would have been able to afford such expensive items.

Such consolidation of Hollar's skills was already in place before the artist had his first encounter with the English. That happened in May 1636, when he met Thomas Howard, Earl of Arundel, in Cologne. Arundel's embassy was passing through the German city on its way to Regensburg, Vienna and Prague, before finally returning to London by the end of the year. For most of his working life Hollar would enjoy the patronage of the earl, who represented the artist's gateway to the British Isles. Such an association ensured that the work of Wenceslaus Hollar became inextricably bound up with English society, politics and aesthetics, making it an essential component of what we now call the British school of painting. But the artistic qualities that Hollar brought to England, now seen to define an English style, in fact derived from a Northern European tradition steeped in the practice of Renaissance and Baroque artists such as Albrecht Dürer, Lucas van Leyden, Jan and Pieter Brueghel the Elder and Adam Elsheimer. In Prague, Hollar's privileged position as Jan's son meant he would have certainly been able to gain access to Prague Castle, which held many works by these artists.

While in Regensburg, Arundel managed to persuade the Holy Roman Emperor Ferdinand II to grant Hollar a patent of nobility. This was a lower division of nobility, and while it did not initially carry a title, it did raise an individual to the peerage, meaning that once he was in England, Hollar could expect to receive less discrimination resulting from xenophobia and would be allowed to seek out the most lucrative commissions among this rank in society. He was now part of the exclusive coterie – with the English monarchs at the forefront – who could discriminate against other, less fortunate members of society. The implicit taste and sophistication suggested by such elevation of rank was reiterated in 1980 by art historian Graham Parry, who described Arundel as 'a fine example of a complete Renaissance man', reminding us of the British propensity to identify with the Italian Renaissance and import artists who had imbibed its spirit.[17] But at what cost? Parry's tone almost seems to revel in Arundel's often nefarious means of acquiring artworks, describing how 'his celebrated collection of classical marbles had been purchased, bribed and stolen from Greece and the Levant by his enterprising minions who had ransacked the ancient sites with a mixture of guile and gusto that was typical of the early enthusiasts for the antique.'[18] If this approach to the acquisition of antiquities was indeed typical, and by implication acceptable, one wonders whether Parry would have employed similarly celebratory language regarding, say, the acquisition of the Parthenon marbles by Lord Elgin. While Arundel was indisputably the catalyst behind the introduction of many foreign artists to Britain, Parry's text reminds us that our capitulation to such shallow concepts of sophistication paradoxically relies on a belief that foreigners are better at all things creative than our own home-grown talent, which becomes a self-fulfilling prophecy with the importation of artists from the Continent. Nevertheless, Parry does rightly acknowledge that Hollar's work in the development of the landscape genre 'marks a significant point in the history of English aesthetics'.[19]

On his return to England in December 1636 (the year Marcus Gheeraerts the Younger died), the Earl of Arundel brought with him an extensive retinue, which included Wenceslaus Hollar ('I have one Hollarse with me, who draws and eches printes in strong water quickley, and with a pretty spiritte').[20] Hollar married Margaret Tracy, a member of Lady Arundel's entourage, in 1641,[21] and the couple had a son and a daughter (his son, whom he had diligently trained in the art of etching, died in the Great Plague of 1665).[22] The artist's first period in England under the sponsorship and patronage of the Earl of Arundel is copiously documented, not least by his views of Arundel House. Although these were printed in 1646 and 1649 by Hollar's Antwerp publisher, Adam Alexius Bierling, they clearly hark back to his time in England and probably constitute his earliest etchings made there. Situated on the Strand, Arundel House overlooked the Thames and was probably Hollar's principal residence at this time, hence the multi-directional views, including prospects of London from its roof. As detailed in Chapter Five, Arundel had acquired an unprecedented collection of sculpture, paintings and all manner of *objets d'art*, all housed at Arundel House. Hollar was employed by Arundel to make etched copies of the paintings, but it seems that the rather flexible terms of his contract also allowed him to make work unconnected with the collection. This included his now famous topographies of London and of other towns such as Hull, where he produced one

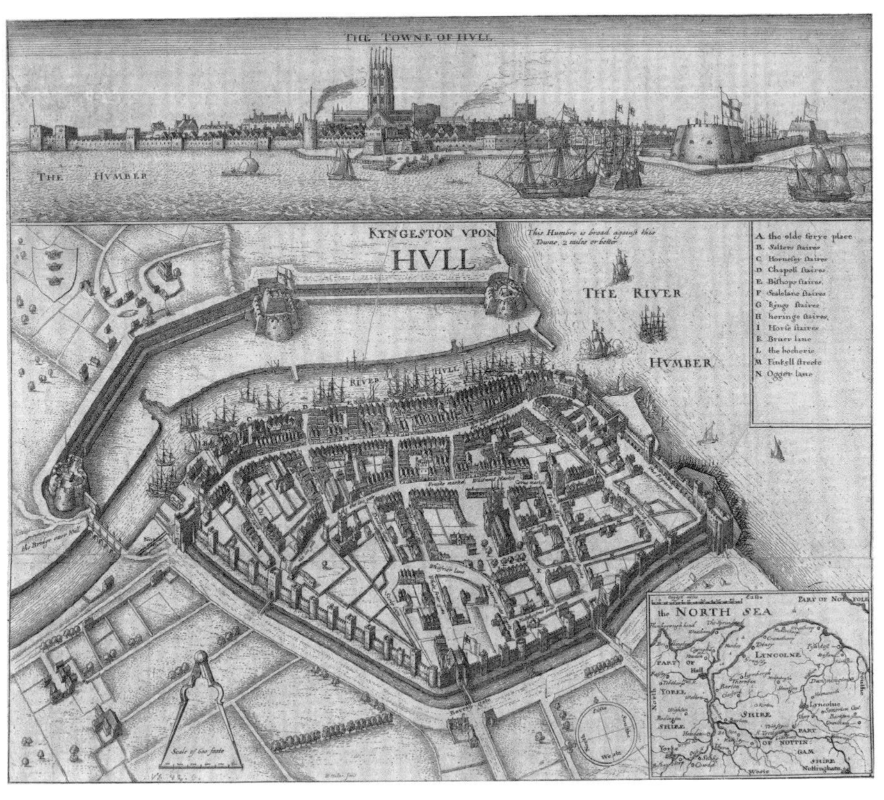

Wenceslaus Hollar, *Kyngeston upon Hull*, 1639, published London, *c.* 1642.
Engraving with pen and ink, 31 × 30 cm (12⅛ × 11⅞ in.)

of his earliest English map views (p. 175). These works form an invaluable source of architectural and topographical information on England's past.

Two of Hollar's earliest topographies of London are his 1636 view of Greenwich and his 1638 view of Richmond Palace. The Greenwich view, in its first state, is dedicated to Queen Henrietta Maria. At the centre is the Queen's House, completed just a year earlier by the English-born architect Inigo Jones, whose architectural ideas were firmly based on those of Andrea Palladio, a famous architect of the Italian Renaissance. This small detail provides a modern viewer familiar with the surrounding area as it is now with an immediate visual contrast of the past with the present. Print historian Richard T. Godfrey wrote of the Greenwich print, 'it is a high point of Hollar's art, and it stands with Van Dyck's watercolour landscapes as one of the foundation stones of the English landscape tradition', again readily co-opting foreign artists into an English tradition.[23]

Hollar's lodgings at Arundel House afforded him some of the best views of London, especially over the Thames, teeming as it was with all the trade and activities that made the city such a hive of industry. This aspect of urban life inspired Hollar to produce some of his most memorable topographical views, like his pen and ink *View of Westminster and the Thames from Lambeth House* and his watercolour *London, Whitehall Palace*, which featured Britain's first Palladian building, Inigo Jones's Banqueting House (pp. 178–79). Only recently completed in 1622, the Banqueting House dwarfs all the buildings around it, reminding us just how significant a structure it was at the time and how it has been subsumed today by subsequent building developments. Other London vistas that continue to fascinate include the etched group of views across the Thames, such as *Westminster from the River* and *Lambeth Palace from the River* (pp. 178, 179).

While Hollar's European travels were documented by the artist via his prodigious output of etchings, especially those with topographical views and published dates, such is the ubiquity and portability of his prints that it has now become all but impossible to determine a precise date for Hollar's departure from England. A series of etchings dated 1643, depicting European women's fashions, including those in Antwerp, suggest that he was perhaps in the city by then; he also produced three sets of a series, *Half-Length Women as Allegories of the Four Seasons*, dating from 1644, which he is known to have published shortly before his departure.[24] Another series of etchings, *Aula Veneris*, was published in London in 1644, and one would expect that *Westminster from the River* was published in London, even though it is dated 1647 (p. 178). It is clear that there was no impediment to Hollar taking his plates with him abroad or leaving some with the commercial printseller and publisher Peter Stent to publish after his departure, especially as some plates from this period carry the name of the Antwerp publisher Johannes Meyssens.

While the date of Hollar's departure is unclear, the reasons are not, as the artist found himself embroiled in the maelstrom of the English Civil War, circumstances that cannot have been conducive to accurate record-keeping or artistic production. Already familiar with such a situation, Hollar clearly believed there was an affinity between his actual and adopted homelands, for instance producing an etched map of England, dated between 1642 and 1649, that draws a comparison between the English and Bohemian Civil Wars (p. 181). Like his family before him, Hollar was very much embedded in the milieu of the aristocracy and the monarchy, on whom he relied for his income, meaning that he found himself in immediate danger when war broke out between the Parliamentarians and the Royalists. With a Parliamentarian victory looming, it was clear that Hollar and his fellow Royalists could no longer remain in England. His patron the Earl of Arundel had already fled in 1642 to Antwerp (or, more accurately, had chosen to remain there having accompanied Mary, the eldest daughter of Charles I and Henrietta Maria, for her marriage to William II of Orange). The earl's departure left his household impoverished and deprived Hollar of his chief source of income. He was left with little choice but to rely on Stent, whose name would begin to appear on the artist's work from this period onwards. Writing over a century later, Vertue suggests that Hollar joined Royalists including John Paulet, 5th Marquess of Winchester, and the printseller Robert Peake (grandson of the painter Robert Peake the Elder) in defending Paulet's property Basing House in Hampshire. The narrative goes on to claim that with the Parliamentarian victory at Basing House, Hollar was taken prisoner before escaping and joining the Earl of Arundel in Antwerp.[25]

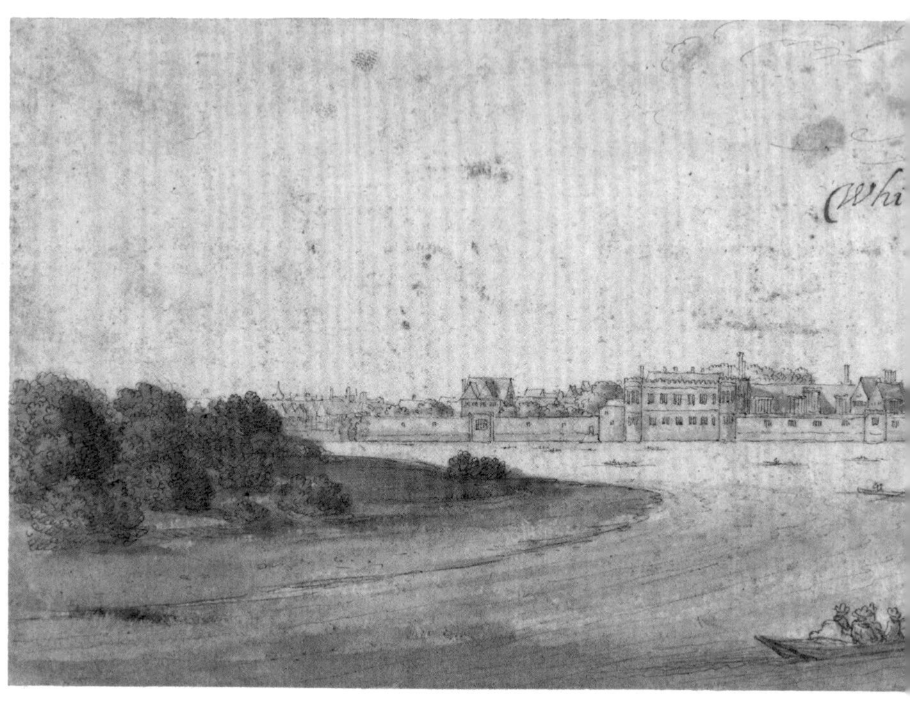

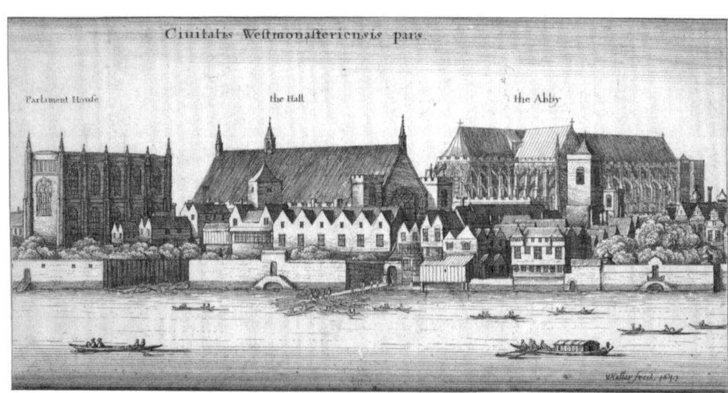

TOP Wenceslaus Hollar, *London, Whitehall Palace*, 1637–43. Watercolour on paper, 9.8 × 29.3 cm (3⅞ × 11⅝ in.)

ABOVE Wenceslaus Hollar, *Westminster from the River*, 1647. Etching, 15 × 28.5 cm (6 × 11¼ in.)

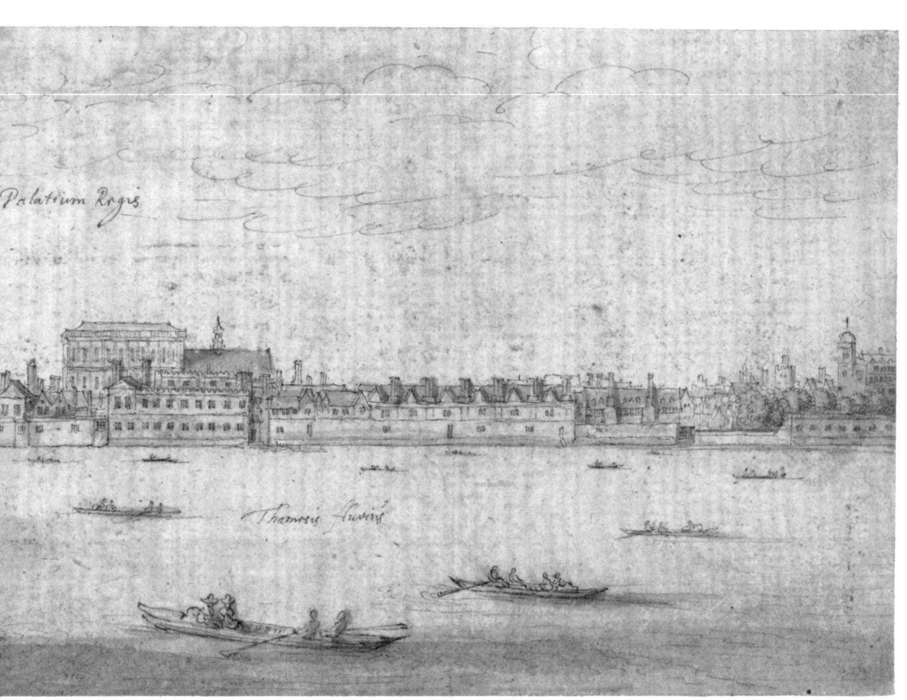

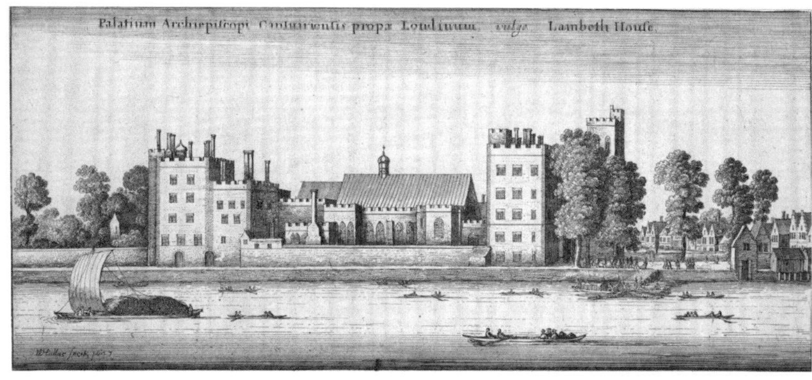

ABOVE Wenceslaus Hollar, *Lambeth Palace from the River*, 1647.
Etching, 14.3 × 31.9 cm (5⅝ × 12⅝ in.)

In 1652 Hollar returned to London, perhaps encouraged by the newly passed Act of Pardon and Oblivion, which gave amnesty to former Royalists. The antiquarian and natural philosopher John Aubrey, famed for his publication *Brief Lives*, described Hollar's first impressions of the newly Puritan England on his return: 'I remember he told me that when he first came into England, (which was a serene time of peace) that the people, both poore, and rich, did looke cheerfully, but at his returne, he found the countenances of the people all changed, melancholy, spightfull, as if bewitched.'[26] Hollar could not have been in a very good position at this time. His illustrious patron the Earl of Arundel had by now died, leaving his family desperately squabbling over his estate. In 1646, the year of Arundel's death, Hollar produced an allegorical etching commemorating the earl's life and his dedication to the arts (fig. 59). He took care to include in it reproductions of a portrait of Arundel's great-great-grandfather, Thomas Howard, Duke of Norfolk, originally painted by Hans Holbein around 1539, and a miniature by Holbein, *Solomon and the Queen of Sheba*, a watercolour version of which exists in the Royal Collection. Both may have been in Arundel's collection and demonstrate that both artist and patron were clearly enamoured with the work of Holbein.[27]

Hollar's other Royalist patrons remained either impoverished or in exile, and it is unclear why Hollar did not stay in Antwerp, where he had many established contacts with local dealers. It is possible he left the city because the closure of the river Scheldt, initiated by the Treaty of Münster and signed in 1648, had ended Antwerp's golden age of prosperity. It is also more than likely he received lucrative offers that tempted him back to London, though there is no documentation to back this up. Following Margaret's death in 1654, Hollar married Honora Roberts in 1656 at the church of St Giles in the Fields in London. They had several children, but unfortunately there are no further records of this second marriage.

Judging by the work Hollar executed in this period, at least two influential patrons must have been at hand. The first was William Dugdale, who held the court position of Chester Herald and was said to be the greatest living English antiquary (in 1677, the year Hollar died, Dugdale was knighted and appointed Garter King of Arms).[28] Hollar

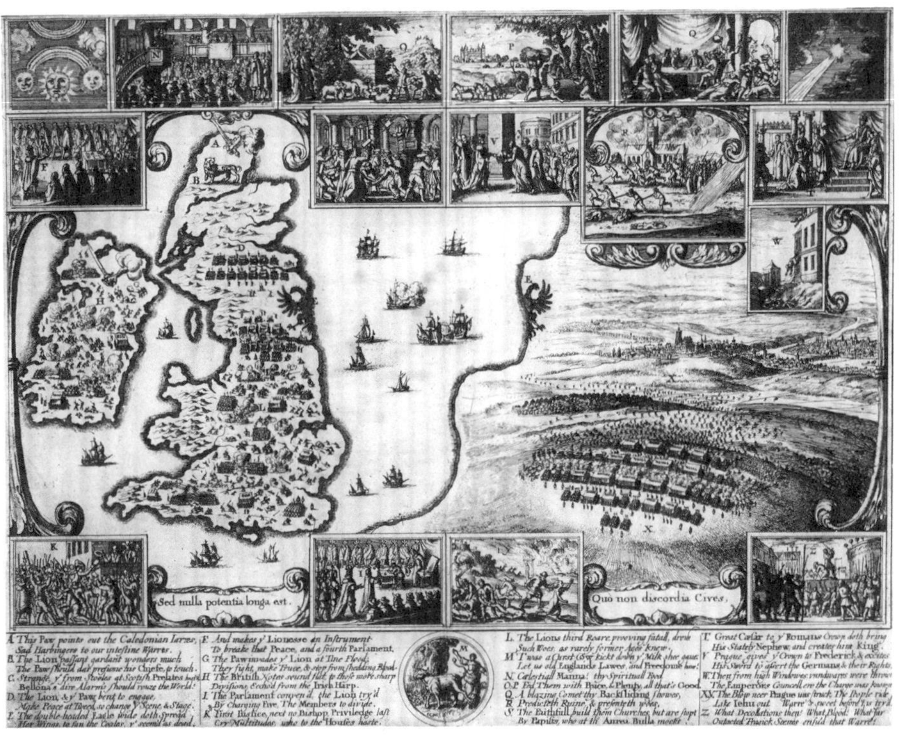

Wenceslaus Hollar, *Map of England and View of Prague with Scenes of the Beginning of the Civil War*, c. 1642–49. Etching, 29.5 × 37.5 cm (11⅝ × 14¾ in.)

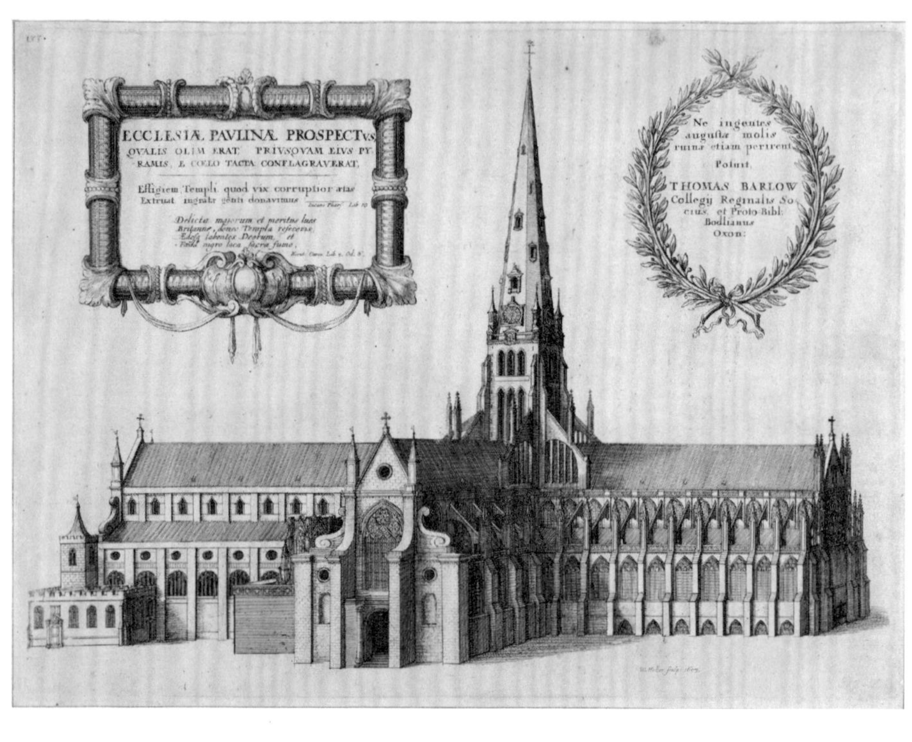

Wenceslaus Hollar, *St Paul's Cathedral from the South Showing the Spire* (from William Dugdale's *The History of St Paul's Cathedral in London*, 1658), 1657. Etching, 26.3 × 35.2 cm (10⅜ × 13⅞ in.)

provided illustrations for many of Dugdale's major publications, including *Monasticon Anglicanum* (vol. I, 1655), *The Antiquities of Warwickshire* (1656) and *The History of St Paul's Cathedral in London* (1658). Looking at the prefaces of these publications along with the surviving correspondence between Hollar and Dugdale certainly provides corroboration of their work together.

With Hollar's engraving expertise, Dugdale was determined to record for posterity religious relics of the past, because he could see from past iconoclasms – for instance during the reign of Henry VIII – how rapidly such artefacts could be lost. In fact, iconoclasms by Puritans were even more pronounced in Dugdale's lifetime than in the past. Such worries led Dugdale to suspect there would be more vandalism in the future, so in 1641 he asked Hollar to make drawings of monuments in the major London churches. This record-making was the forerunner of the contemporary practice of church recording, which nowadays is carried out by volunteer groups representing the Arts Society. What Dugdale could not have predicted, however, was how precious the Great Fire in 1666 would make Hollar's prints, which would be the only surviving evidence of the appearance of old London, along with major landmarks such as the old St Paul's Cathedral, shown with its original spire that was struck by lightning and destroyed in 1561 (p. 182). The undertaking was made possible by a seventeenth-century version of crowdfunding, which saw Dugdale's friends effectively sponsoring the project by paying £5 for a plate to which their name was added.

Hollar's other employers included John Ogilby, dancing master and tutor to the children of the Earl of Strafford and a self-made autodidact. Ogilby taught himself Latin and Greek in order to make translations of the classics, which he self-published.[29] In 1654 he published the works of the Roman author Virgil, in a volume that would initiate new standards in luxury book production in England, containing forty-four full-page illustrations by Hollar. Although etching had been practised in Britain before Hollar's arrival, it was seldom used for anything beyond portraiture or book frontispieces. Ogilby's translation of Virgil was followed in 1662 by a luxuriously illustrated edition of Aesop's fables, to mark the coronation of Charles II, and then by two geographical books, *Africa* of

1670 and *Britannia* of 1675.[30] The wide variety of subjects exhibited in Hollar's work was unknown in Britain before 1640, and so we must look to him as a catalyst behind the subsequent flourishing of the English print industry, demonstrating the true potential of etchings for the first time in Britain.[31]

Hollar's greatest project was one that never fully came to fruition and can only be reconstructed from remaining fragmentary texts. One of these, dated 1660, contains a proposal to produce a map of London and Westminster and begins: 'This map is to contain 10 foot in bredth and 5 foot upwards wherein shall be expressed, not only the streets and lanes, alleys etc. proportionally measured; but also, the buildings (especially of the principall Houses, Churches, Courts, Halls etc) as much resembling the likeness of them as the convenience of the roome will permit. Example whereof is in considerable part to be seen.'[32] Hollar sought subscribers for his map at £3, payable in three instalments, with 'the charge thereof being found by experience to be wery great and too heavy to be borne by the author himself alone'. The only surviving work that best fits this description is the print map plan of the west central district of London, an unfinished impression of which is in the British Museum (p. 186). If we are to take Hollar at his word (and there seems no reason to do otherwise), going by the scale of this surviving sheet the entire plan measuring ten by five feet would consist of approximately twenty-eight sheets, combining the grid of a map with a perspectival delineation of the buildings. Sadly, it was never completed, probably owing to a lack of support for the project.

In the immediate aftermath of the Great Fire in October 1666, Hollar sought official recognition from Charles II (r. 1660–85) of his position as His Majesty's Scenographer, mentioning that such a title would serve as encouragement towards finishing his map of London, parts of which the King had seen, and insisting 'the work, when perfected, will be a very remarkable monument and record to all posterity'. He eventually obtained his title, but was given little encouragement by the Crown, because in August 1667 he once again petitioned the King to help him perfect his map of London, on which he had spent seven years and run up a debt of £100. He pointed out in his petition that no man living other than himself could leave such a record of the old city for posterity. He received £50 the following year, but this is the last we hear of the project. What really finished it off, ironically, was the fact that the Great Fire had rendered most of Hollar's surveys and drawings obsolete; no one was interested in views of a city that no longer matched how it looked, like the street map of the City he made in his final years (p. 186).

Hollar's last great expedition would be yet another attempt to stave off impending financial disaster. In 1669 Lord Henry Howard, grandson of the late Thomas Howard, Earl of Arundel, was sent with an embassy to the English territory of Tangier in Morocco. The sorry state of the outpost at the time is described by Richard T. Godfrey as 'one of the less glorious episodes in England's imperial history' (though one might wonder if there were *any* glorious episodes in English imperialism).[33] The territory had been given to the English Crown by Portugal as part of a dowry payment on the marriage of Charles II to Catherine of Braganza in 1662. The English occupation began in earnest in 1662 and – typically for the two European countries involved in this transaction – there is no mention of the native Moroccan population and their right to live in their own country without their land being bought and sold by European powers. Constant attacks by the Moroccans trying to drive out their oppressors, led by Moulay Ismail Ibn Sharif, Sultan of Morocco (r. 1672–1727), gradually eroded the financial viability of the colony for the English and they were finally driven out in 1684.

The embassy of 1669 represented a chance for Hollar to gain lucrative employment, and he petitioned Charles II to join the embassy as the official Scenographer to His Majesty. To carry out this task he asked of the King, 'one hundred pounds towards the fitting of my selve and leaving my House and Family in good condition in my absence'.[34] On his return to England Hollar was paid the sum he had asked for, but this covered only necessities and not the cost of either his time or the etchings and drawings he had produced on the embassy.[35] John Aubrey's account of Hollar, written between 1669 and 1696, is complimentary of the artist's character but suggests that he was lazy or lacked ambition, saying, 'He was a very friendly good-natured man as could be, but shiftless to the World and died not rich.'[36] But Vertue, in his much later account *A Description*

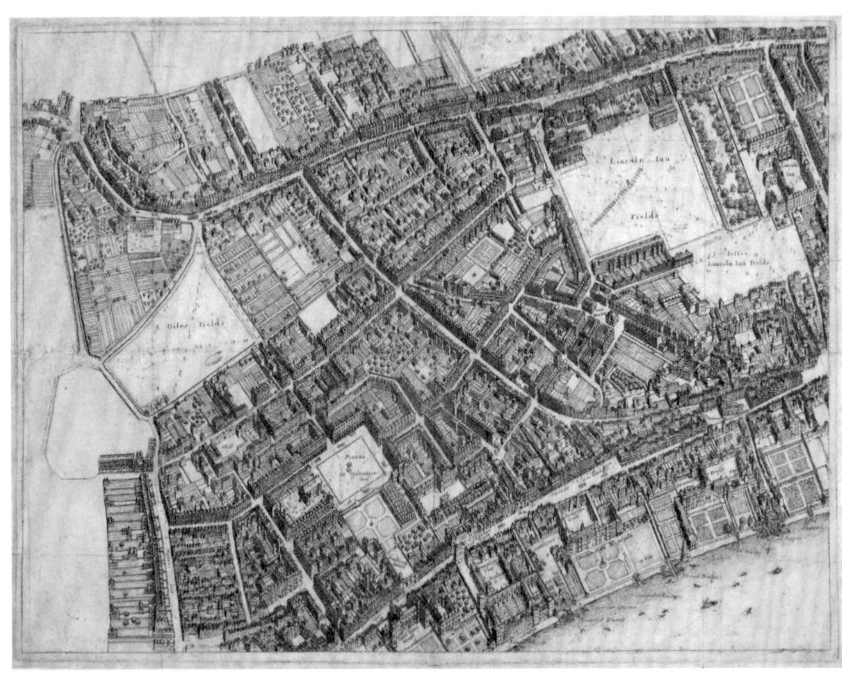

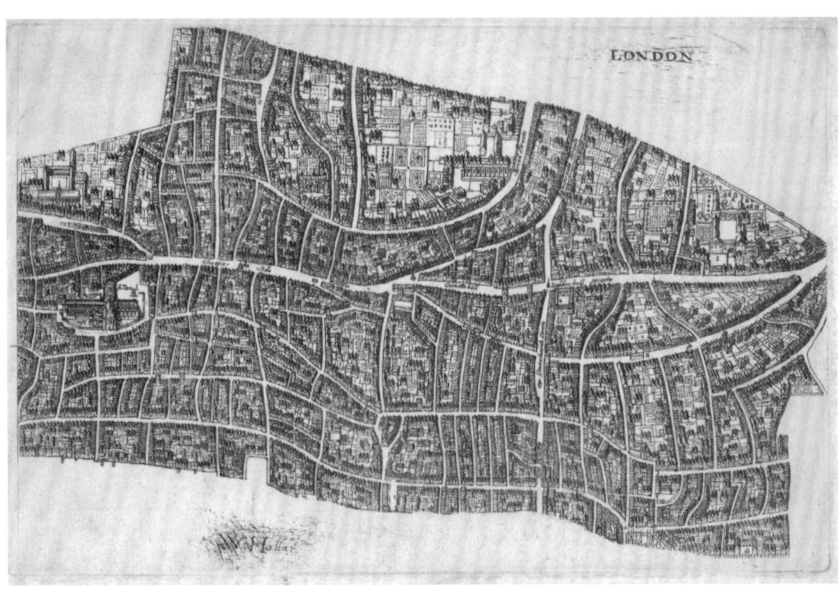

TOP Wenceslaus Hollar, *A bird's-eye plan of London: From St Giles on the left to Chancery Lane on the right, Holborn at top, the Thames from Savoy Stairs to Essex Stairs at the bottom*, 1660–66. Etching, 34.4 × 45.5 cm (13⅝ × 18 in.)

ABOVE Wenceslaus Hollar, *Street Map of the City of London Before the Great Fire*, 1666–67. Etching, 10.8 × 17 cm (4⅜ × 6¾ in.)

of the Works of Wenceslaus Hollar of 1759, attested to Hollar's substantial production while also confirming his poor financial situation.

As we have seen, throughout his life Hollar clearly did not make much money and does not seem to have had the best sense of the value of his own time and work. The lack of recompense by the English monarchy, the aristocracy and seemingly rapacious printsellers was indicative of their failure to recognize Hollar's true historical worth to English culture. He died on 25 March 1677, penniless and far from his homeland. Yet with the benefit of hindsight we can see the key role he played in the making of London, bequeathing to us a rich legacy in the historical record. Hollar was buried at St Margaret's Church in London; as we recognize his contribution to that city it is hard to conceive that he could have been buried anywhere else.

9

William Hogarth

Impolite Society and British Identity

The elusive 'British identity' has long been a mass of contradictions, encompassing opposing notions: support for the underdog, versus the exploitation of non-European countries through the force of superior arms; a sense of 'fair play', versus a sense of superiority over the working classes, women and people of colour; enlightenment, versus a sense of entitlement; and humanitarianism, versus treating those who are not white as subhuman. Some combination of, if not all these facets play a part in the make-up of the British psyche to this day, and were certainly present in the society in which William Hogarth grew up. In fact, the very term 'British', though used since medieval times, only gained official significance in 1707, when Hogarth was just ten years old, after Scotland formally joined England and Wales to form the United Kingdom of Great Britain. Hogarth himself was a mass of contradictions, an English-born painter whose contemporary standing rests squarely on the shoulders of those foreign artists who came before him, many of whom he sought to emulate in one way or another while proudly proclaiming his identity as a British artist. Yet he also represents an anomaly that the British art establishment would subsequently struggle to get to grips with, meaning an institutional ambivalence towards Hogarth has endured, quite at odds with his mass appeal to the general public.

Hogarth's father, Richard, was a teacher and classical scholar, versed in Latin and Greek, who clearly expected his education to serve him well in business and elevate him up the social ranks. In 1689 he published a textbook, *Thesaurarium trilingue publicum: Being an Introduction to English,*

188

Latin and Greek, in which he laid out a series of anecdotal moral lessons that would not be lost on his future son.[1] By 1701 Richard had opened a coffee house in St John's Gate, close to the Smithfield Bars, which marked the northern boundary of the City of London. He encouraged his clientele there to speak Latin, a venture that seemed to Richard an ideal way to attract an educated elite and provide him with networking opportunities. But unfortunately, the business failed catastrophically, leading to Richard's arrest in the winter of 1707–8 for debts incurred.

Following his arrest, Richard and his family – wife Anne, daughters Ann and Mary and young son William (born in 1697) – had to endure the indignity of spending four years in lodgings just outside the notorious Fleet debtors' prison, in an area known as the 'Liberty of the Fleet'.[2] At a time when prisons were commercial profit-making businesses, with all manner of ancillary charges such as fees to release iron chains and handcuffs and payment for food and lodgings, Richard had to use the little money he had to pay for the prison keeper's loss of earnings while he worked in the lodgings, lest he receive a custodial sentence in the prison proper. The daily atrocities that went on within the prison walls, where many inmates were forced to beg assistance from passers-by through open grilled windows that faced on to the street, were a constant reminder to Richard and his family of the hardship that was being endured nearby by those who could not afford even his miserable means.

The circumstances of William Hogarth's early life led to him leaving school around the age of thirteen or fourteen, clearly in order to earn a living and support his family. Around 1713 or 1714, the family managed to leave the debtors' prison lodgings, moving to Long Lane in Smithfield, and this period also marked the beginning of Hogarth's apprenticeship in the arts, as recorded in the Registry of Apprentices of the Merchant Taylors' Company.[3] At about sixteen or seventeen years old, Hogarth was in fact quite past the usual age to begin an apprenticeship, with such positions traditionally commencing around the age of thirteen or fourteen. He started his apprenticeship as a silversmith (or as the artist himself said, a silver-plate engraver), but according to his own testimony, he soon found this profession too limiting and by the age of twenty his ambition was to become an engraver on copper, though he probably did not achieve this until around 1720.[4]

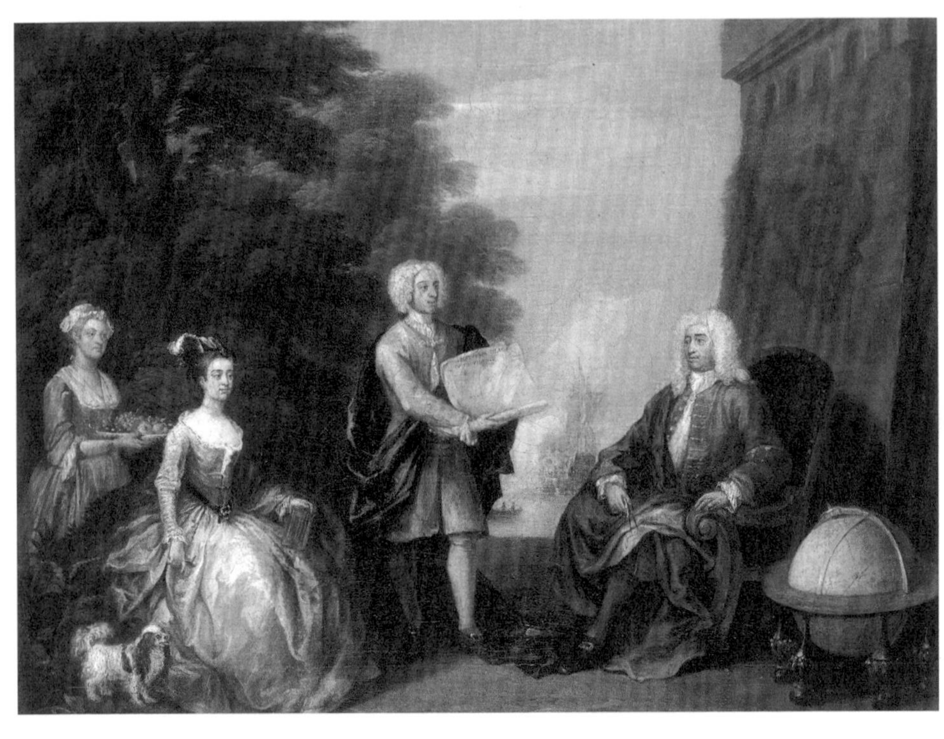

William Hogarth, *Woodes Rogers and his Family*, 1729.
Oil on canvas, 35.5 × 45.5 cm (14 × 18 in.)

By 1718 his poverty-stricken father had died without a penny to his name, but by then the twenty-one-year-old Hogarth was already self-sufficient, and by 1720 he had enrolled in the newly formed St Martin's Lane Academy of painting in London.[5] Established by the Paris-born artist Louis Chéron, a Huguenot émigré, and the London-born John Vanderbank, the son of a naturalized Huguenot immigrant from Paris, the Academy gave Hogarth an early introduction to a foreign artistic aesthetic. His early attempts at studying draughtsmanship there seem to have had disappointing results, but by 1729 the largely self-taught Hogarth had begun to paint small groups and conversation pieces (small-scale informal group portraits, often set in gardens or domestic interiors), such as *Woodes Rogers and his Family* (p. 190). What would ultimately prove more successful, however, was Hogarth's affinity with and insight into the so-called lowlife stories he depicted in his 'modern moral subjects', which drew on aspects of his early childhood and upbringing.

Although several recent exhibitions have rightly elevated Hogarth's prominence in the story of British art, despite an impressive output his work is rarely granted the grand status given to earlier incoming artists who achieved international fame in their lifetimes, like Rubens or Van Dyck. Even artists who did not come to Britain, such as the French painter Claude Lorrain, arguably enjoy a more elevated status there than Hogarth. What sets Hogarth apart from all these artists is his subject matter. His work represents a critical transition from the artistic sensibilities of the seventeenth-century Grand Manner to an eighteenth-century coming of age for British art. Although a precursor to the great age of revered native-born British artists such as Reynolds, Gainsborough and Stubbs, Hogarth's art nevertheless seems to break with convention against more traditional subjects such as mythological or religious scenes. Historically, many images produced were of those in power and of great means, representative of the so-called high genre of history painting.

Hogarth initially avoided such subjects, instead depicting ordinary people, perhaps for the first time in English painting. This included representations of Black people, and there seems to have been no shortage of people of colour available as models for Hogarth to include in his works. By Hogarth's time it is estimated that more than ten thousand Black people were living in the larger cities of Britain, especially those associated with the slave trade, such as Liverpool, Bristol and London.[6] These enslaved people were largely children and young adults, for the most part fulfilling the role of domestic servants. The numerous sales advertisements in newspapers in England and Scotland along with notices of runaway slaves in this period attest to the age demographic of the Black population, who were often dressed in fine livery and metal collars as a way of advertising their owners' wealth and prosperity.[7] The proliferation of these people elicited racist vilification, with many blaming them for any woes afflicting the country at that time, while the media and those in power would stoke this prejudice throughout the centuries. By Hogarth's period it is clear such irrational fears, leading to hatred, were still very much part of the British psyche, as revealed in an anecdotal *Daily Journal* report of April 1723: ''Tis said there is a great number of Blacks come daily into this City, so that 'tis thought in a short Time, if they be not surpress'd, the City will swarm with them.'[8]

Hogarth's break with the subjects of the past did not necessarily mean he lacked reverence for the foreign aesthetic in British art, and his work is suffused with influences of antique and Italian Renaissance art. A plethora of European artists including Jean-Antoine Watteau and Nicolas Lancret also emerged out of this legacy, producing works throughout the 1700s that embodied a narrative of storytelling. Interest in such works brought some of these European artists to Britain; they included Hubert-François Gravelot, who was born in Paris in 1699 and emigrated to London in 1732, and Philippe Mercier, an artist of French Huguenot descent born in Berlin in 1689, who spent most of his active years in England.

Hogarth also brought to his practice a knowledge of French prints and printmaking, going on to transform the pastoral conversation pieces of the contemporary French artist Jean-Antoine Watteau into interior set pieces, in the process reinventing the genre for an English market. But despite his apparent admiration for French art, the painting *O the Roast Beef of Old England* (*The Gate of Calais*, fig. 60) illustrates perfectly how Hogarth used xenophobia, in this case largely towards the French, to connect with populist English antipathy towards all things foreign. In the painting, a fat French monk is depicted drooling over a sirloin of imported English beef, playing to a myopic, egotistical belief that other nations gaze upon Britain with envious eyes. The skinny, underfed French soldiers with their meagre bowls of soup reinforce this narrative of envy, while the xenophobic attitudes on display are ramped up by the starving, somewhat mangy-looking Jacobite Scotsman in the foreground, dressed head to toe in tartan. Misogyny and anti-Catholic sentiment are added into the mix as two women wearing crucifixes huddle around a large skate, in which they believe they see the face of Christ, both intimating superstitious Catholic beliefs and derogatorily characterizing the women as 'fishwives'.

This painting serves as a record of Hogarth's second visit to Paris, in the summer of 1748 (the first was in 1743). The artist includes himself at the far left of the picture in a scene that recalls his arrest, while sketching, at the old city gate of Calais on suspicion of being an English spy. According to the diarist George Vertue, writing in August 1748, Hogarth was thrown into the Bastille, but returned to England soon after his release.[9] In the painting Hogarth depicts a hand grasping his shoulder, about to apprehend him, conferring heroic status on himself. The title of the work, taken from a well-known English popular tune, further ingratiated him to his audience, using roast beef as a symbol of England's power, wealth and supposed superiority.

Very early on, Hogarth expressed frustration with the print medium and reluctance to learn the skill: 'This I thought my only chance for eminence, as I found that the beauty and delicacy of the stroke in engraving was not to be learnt without much practise and demanded a larger portion of patience than I felt myself disposed to exercise. Added to this, I saw little probability of acquiring the full command of the engraver, in a sufficient degree to distinguish myself in that walk; nor was I, at twenty years of age, much disposed to enter on so barren and unprofitable a study, as that of merely making fine lines.'[10] That said, he also ridiculed the atmosphere of reverence surrounding old master paintings, especially those of the Italian Renaissance, which the art establishment considered the apogee of great art, meaning no student of art could progress without being exposed to them. To this attitude, Hogarth retorted: 'The Italian students avail themselves of the works of antiquity as a coward do of putting on the armour of an heroe.'[11] The distinction at the heart of this statement effectively allowed Hogarth to continue to indulge his interest in the old masters without any philosophical contradiction; he was effectively saying that to uncritically absorb such works en masse in dogmatic fashion, as advocated by the establishment of the day, taught one nothing about art, whereas the study and development of a personal relationship with specific historical artists would bring greater insight and appreciation of their work.

Such semantics could not hide the fact that Hogarth valued the kudos he hoped was brought to his work with the inclusion of numerous obvious references to Italian art of the past, like those in his series *Marriage A-la-Mode* (1743–45). By demonstrating his deep knowledge of Renaissance and Baroque art he aimed to silence his detractors and elevate his work. The series's faux French title, taken from John Dryden's play of the same name first performed in 1672, gave the work foreign legitimacy while also allowing Hogarth to ridicule the French. Hogarth's obvious borrowing of ideas from European art of the previous centuries seems to contradict those who suggest Hogarth made strenuous efforts to achieve his artistic goals without recourse to his knowledge of the Italian masters.[12] What is clear, however, is that he employs such references to criticize and ridicule his bourgeois subjects, with every detail laden with meaning. For example, in *The Toilette*, the fourth work of the series (fig. 61), the paintings on the walls depict multiple scenes of lascivious activities, including the rape of Ganymede behind the flautist's head; the rape of Io (a near exact copy of an extant work by Correggio); and the incest between Lot and his daughters (based on an engraving by Louis Du Guernier the Younger, said to be based in turn on a lost Caravaggio). As well as highlighting the poor taste shown in choosing to hang a secular subject next to a religious one, these last two paintings are hung directly above the heads of the adulterous countess and her lover to allude to the inappropriate sexual activities on which they are about to embark.

One of the great levellers in Hogarth's 'modern moral subjects' is that everyone is caricatured in one way or another, with no one spared. In

The Toilette, for example, the hairdresser attending to the countess is given an oversized nose to indicate his French origins, while the vulgarly dressed castrato opera singer (too much jewellery, too much gold brocading) at the extreme left foreground is given a porky countenance to reflect his overindulgence and the riches gained from his rare and specialist profession. The two Black figures in the scene have been treated in a particular way though, with the figure in the foreground dressed in so-called Eastern garb, complete with turban. The process of setting people of colour apart using signifiers such as dress, in the process making them exceptions to a perceived normality, is now known as 'othering'. But paradoxically, their 'otherness' frees the Black people in these scenes from complicity with the absurdity of the European foibles on display. In fact, they are privy to intimate and seemingly ridiculous interactions within the home, because the European society they inhabit treats them much like domestic pets, arrogantly assuming that they have little understanding of the complex lives and supposed superiority of their masters. Hogarth's Black subjects, as stereotypical caricatures cast in the role of outsiders, are seen to ridicule the customs of those around them as they quietly laugh to themselves.

In the years before the formation of the Royal Academy in 1768, many painting academies sprung up, all of them operating within a strict hierarchical top-down management structure. Hogarth rejected such establishments, arguing that they were synonymous with foreign (in particular French) institutions, and clearly foolish: 'I propose that every member should contribute an equal sum to the establishment and have an equal right to vote in every question relative to the society. As to electing Presidents, Directors, Professors, etc., I considered it was a ridiculous imitation of the foolish parade of the French Academy'.[13] By associating folly and frippery with foreigners, Hogarth suggests in time-honoured fashion that denigrating foreigners – in this case the French – by implication emphasizes one's own patriotism. This lack of understanding of the difference between patriotism and xenophobia is one that many nations, including the British, continually fail to grasp. In fact, Hogarth's nationalism and xenophobia represented two sides of the same coin, ideas mirrored in much the same way in today's divided Britain, where some who voted in 2016 for the United Kingdom to leave the European Union exhibited a similar false sense of patriotism, resulting in xenophobia towards Europeans, and especially the French.

Although Hogarth railed against convention, and had nothing but contempt for the prejudicial British class system that successfully kept the so-called lower orders in their place while being propped up by slavery, like many British people he longed to be admitted into these supposed upper echelons. In the art world this hierarchy was soon represented by the painting academies, the first one set up in London in 1711 and run by Godfrey Kneller (see Chapter Seven). Hogarth had been a member of this academy since its inception, and his future father-in-law, Sir James Thornhill, would become its next governor in 1716.[14] Thornhill's rise up the ranks would continue, being made court painter to George I in June 1718 and Serjeant Painter in March 1720. In May 1720 he broke an artistic glass ceiling, becoming the first native-born British painter to be awarded a knighthood for his services to art. He became master of the Painters' Company and was elected an MP in 1722 and a fellow of the Royal Society the following year.

Thornhill's trajectory was precisely the one Hogarth desired for himself, and he would spend the rest of his life trying to achieve this exalted, socially sanctioned status. Yet it speaks volumes of Thornhill's opinion of Hogarth's social status compared to his own that, having fallen in love with Thornhill's daughter, Jane, Hogarth had to elope with her, the couple marrying in 1729 clearly without her father's approval. This was perhaps not the ideal way for Hogarth to fulfil his ambitions of ascending to a more favourable position in society, but he did eventually receive Thornhill's approval of the marriage. When Thornhill died in 1734, Hogarth was in the perfect position to inherit the equipment of his father-in-law's old Covent Garden academy and set up his own painting academy at St Martin's Lane in 1735.[15] The apparent contradictions in Hogarth's psyche and his rapacious need for social validation perfectly illustrate the British obsession and love/hate relationship with class. British art historian Sir Ellis Waterhouse later wrote of him: '[Hogarth] pursued his ends with something of the engaging *naïveté* of a (quite imaginary) African native who would eat a white missionary on the assumption that he would thus become possessed of the white man's knowledge and powers, and it never occurred to him that Thornhill's position was largely due to the aptness of the times in which he lived to support a history painter of his class, and that the times had changed.'[16] In true British fashion, Waterhouse hides behind a false veneer of respectability by concocting an imaginary characterization to make his point. But his comments only serve to support the British class system, validating racist ideas that persist to this day. Having gained a knighthood himself, Waterhouse pours scorn on Hogarth for desperately seeking to achieve the same. Both Waterhouse's derision and Hogarth's attempts at social climbing are characteristics embedded in the British class system, transmitted across the centuries and into our own period, where they remain hidden in plain sight.

Soon after his marriage came one of Hogarth's early successes, *A Scene from The Beggar's Opera*, originally conceived as part a series of paintings made between 1728 and 1731 (p. 199). The artist had produced earlier group portraits that could be considered conversation pieces, but this project marked a transition towards the genre that would become known as morality pieces, echoing the tone set by his father's publication. This approach used portraiture of real people – actors from the play and even recognizable members of the audience – within a fictional scene, creating a now successful formula of combining fact with fiction. The tableau Hogarth created purposely resembled a stage set, complete with painted backdrop. He even included as a framing device the stage curtain, which looks like it has just been raised to reveal the scene, the mouths of the players animated as though mid-dialogue.

With his inclusion of a small Black slave/servant at the lower right of the picture, Hogarth perhaps voices his disdain or judgement of the boy's wealthy upper-class owners who surround him. Written only a few years earlier in 1728, John Gay's *The Beggar's Opera*, about London's lowlife criminals and prostitutes, was devised to demonstrate that there was little difference between the wealthy landowners portrayed and the politicians who ran the country, except the latter were caught and punished for their crimes while the former were celebrated. The satire of *The Beggar's Opera* was directly aimed at the corrupt administration of then

Prime Minister Robert Walpole. With this painting (one of many versions), Hogarth would capitalize on the success of Gay's opera, which chimed with his own abhorrence of those in power. In his diaries Hogarth would later describe how original he thought his new approach to painting was, and what he wanted to achieve with this fresh take on the conversation piece.[17]

In 1732 Hogarth consolidated the genre of the 'modern moral subject' with the series *A Harlot's Progress*, featuring the fictional story of country girl turned prostitute Mary (Moll) Hackabout. The contrast drawn between the seemingly pure and innocent beginnings of Moll's life and the overtones of her future demise made it a compelling story for audiences. We still recognize this trope in movies today, when an idyllic opening scene almost inevitably prefigures an impending disaster. The seeds are sown in the opening scene of the series (p. 200). Moll arrives in the big city on a stagecoach; in the corner, a note around a dead goose's neck explains that she should have been met by her indolent cousin, but instead she is greeted by brothel owner Mother Needham, who will tempt her into a life of prostitution. Further young victims arrive on the stagecoach, while Moll's first client, the odious and nightmarish Colonel Francis Charteris, waits in the doorway pleasuring himself; this will not end well for Moll, and the viewer knows it.[18]

A Harlot's Progress almost immediately made Hogarth a celebrity both in England and throughout Europe. The original set of canvases was bought by William Beckford, a politician and plantation owner. Beckford made a fortune from slavery, enabling him to build the Gothic Revival folly Fonthill Abbey in Wiltshire. He was able to pass his Jamaican plantation, political position and fortune on to his son William Thomas Beckford, but in 1755 Fonthill Abbey was unfortunately destroyed in a fire, taking with it Hogarth's original canvases. This did not put an end to the success of the series, however, because the engraved copies, published in 1733, proved so popular that 1,240 sets were eventually sold by subscription. The ability to make successful reproductions inevitably led to issues of piracy, and Hogarth campaigned for a law to prevent such fraudulent activities. The Engravers' Copyright Act was passed in June 1735, benefiting not just Hogarth but the entire engraving profession; the

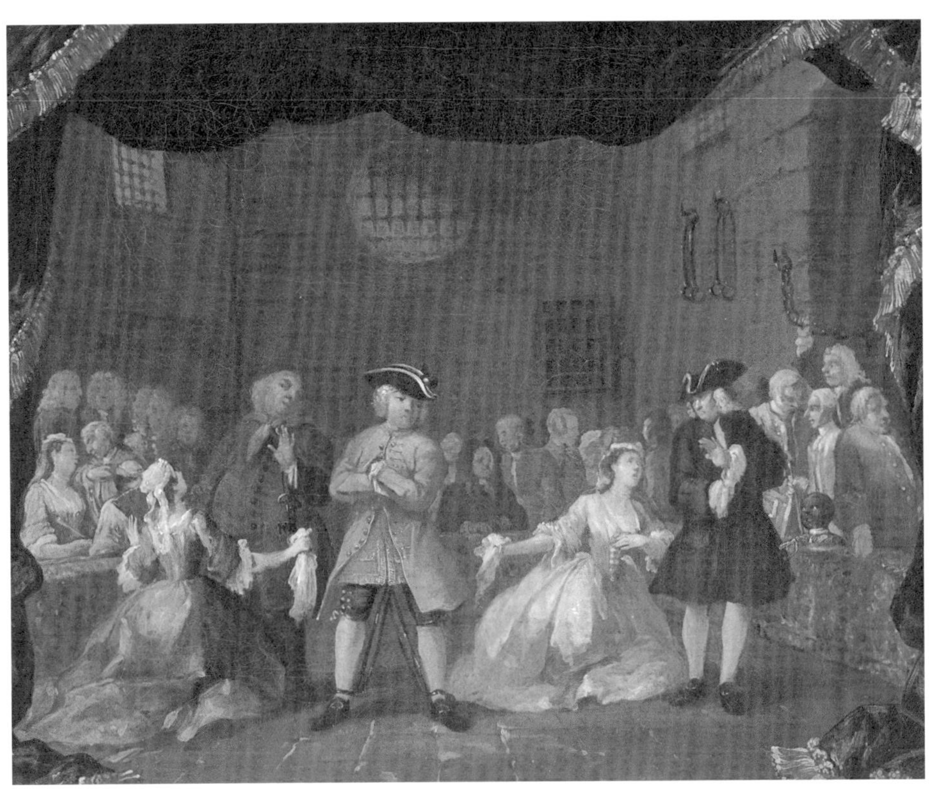

William Hogarth, *A Scene from The Beggar's Opera*, 1728–29.
Oil on canvas, 51.1 × 61.2 cm (20⅛ × 24⅛ in.)

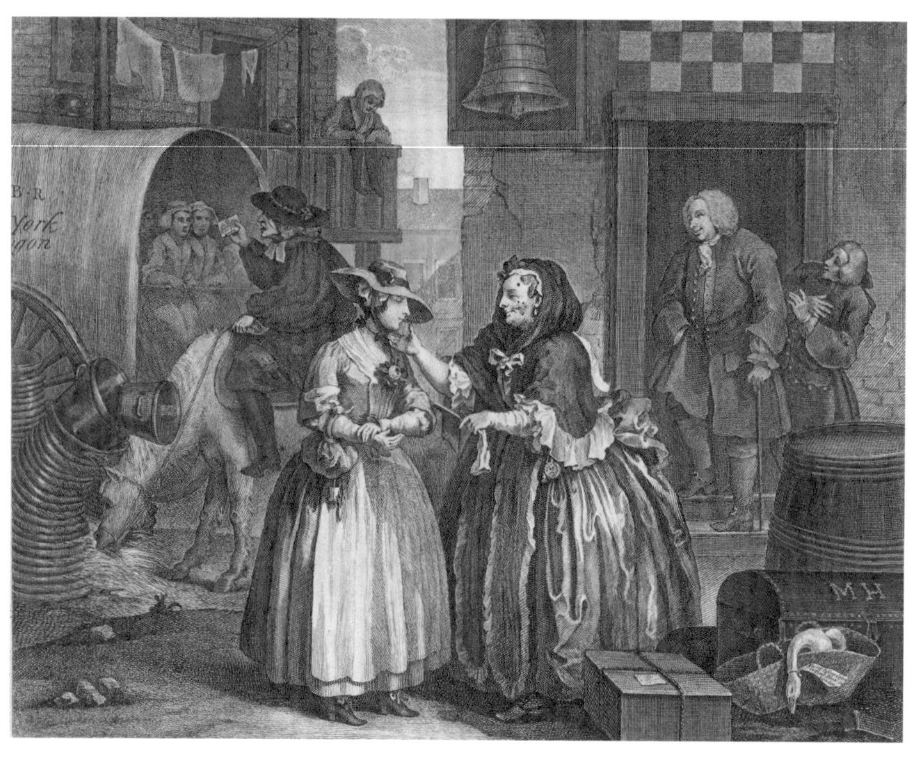

William Hogarth, *A Harlot's Progress, I, Moll Hackabout Arrives at Bell Inn*, 1732. Etching and engraving, 33.9 × 40.7 cm (13⅜ × 16 in.)

legislation came to be known colloquially as Hogarth's Act. Hogarth was not the first artist to find himself in this position of course. More than two centuries earlier, Albrecht Dürer had found himself in a similar situation, leading him in 1511 to issue a dire warning to plagiarists. This was followed in 1512 by a council decree ordering fraudsters to cease using the artist's famous 'AD' device on their works.[19]

Following a strategic delay in publication until the Engravers' Copyright Act was passed, in 1735 Hogarth released the follow-up series, *A Rake's Progress*.[20] In each of his series, Hogarth presented fully formed lowlife personalities, both real and fictional, who were immediately recognizable to his audience. Like an accomplished modern drama, however low and depraved his characters were, they were sufficiently developed that the viewer could not be entirely ambivalent to their plight as they progressed along their fateful journeys to self-destruction. The artist tapped into a rich seam in British society that cut across all social classes, taking a secret pleasure in voyeurism, titillation, sleaze and perversion. These morality tales gave Hogarth a platform to satirize the hypocrisy of 'polite' society, which he exposed as little more than a veneer covering a seedy underbelly.

The conversation piece was not a new genre, and Hogarth was drawing on a rich tradition created by seventeenth-century Dutch painters such as Gerard ter Borch, Jan Vermeer and Pieter de Hooch. However, Hogarth brought a particularly English satirical element to the genre rooted in recognizable social mores and political activities of the day, imbuing his works with a uniquely British character. In the fictional narrative *March of the Guards to Finchley* of 1749–50 (fig. 62), for example, Hogarth encompasses a quintessentially English mass of contradictions and paradoxes. Its patriotic subject of soldiers defending their capital city echoes Rembrandt's *Night Watch*, painted a century earlier in 1642. But compared with the orderly arrangement of Rembrandt's part-time soldiers, Hogarth shows his English ones as indecisive. The grenadier guard at the centre of the composition appears uncouth and unable to make the right decision. He stands with a gormless expression on his face, torn between a debauched life (here represented by the soldier groping the milkmaid on his left and the procuress who tugs on his left arm) and his pregnant wife who hangs on his right arm, representing the supposedly correct path.

The guard's difficult choice is further complicated as Hogarth makes clear he has a third option: visible on a leaflet hanging from his wife's basket are the words 'Duke of Cumberland'. The third son of King George II, as a general the duke was known for his harsh suppression of the Jacobite rebellion in Scotland of 1745 (an attempt by the Stuarts to regain the British throne) and his triumph at the Battle of Culloden in April 1746, at which 1,250 Scots died. After that battle he remained in Scotland for a further three months, rounding up 3,500 men and summarily executing 120 of them in cold blood, earning him the nickname 'Butcher Cumberland'. Does the appearance of his name on this leaflet mean the guard's wife would prefer him to go to war than stay with her and end up like the drunken soldiers seen at the far lower right of the painting? In the image the soldiers range from drunken, undisciplined men in the foreground to regimented soldiers in the far background, before finally reverting to their brutish nature, with bare-knuckle fighting in the mid-background on the right, perhaps alluding to the bloody nature of war.

The detail of the leaflet not only links this imaginary scene with actual events, but also references the painting's final location. In true entrepreneurial style Hogarth had organized a lottery around the painting, offering subscribers a chance to win it by purchasing lottery tickets at three shillings each. When the offer closed, the artist found himself with 167 unsold tickets, which he donated to the Foundling Hospital, a children's home in London of which he was a governor. Among them was the winning ticket, and Hogarth personally delivered the painting to the hospital governors, who also included the Duke of Cumberland.[21]

In true English fashion, by showing many facets of being a soldier Hogarth sits on the fence regarding his own views, to the extent that George II was said to have remarked, 'does the fellow mean to laugh at my guards?' However, his role as a hospital governor means Hogarth must have been aware of the duke's similar connection, and so the artist is presumably signalling his patriotic support of Cumberland and his brutality in Scotland. If so, this further consolidates Hogarth's support of brutal English nationalism, despite the Union flag displayed at the heart of the picture. His overriding stance seems to be one of toxic nostalgia: that the social order must be maintained for fear of the collapse of civilization. He makes it clear in *A Harlot's Progress*, *A Rake's Progress* and *Marriage A-la-Mode* that to entertain ideas above one's station will only end in tragedy. Yet he clearly believed in his own potential for social mobility while denying it to his characters, and in 1757 he did indeed ascend to the position he craved, as royal painter.

The hypocrisy inherent in Hogarth's attitude to class can be characterized as a quintessentially British state of mind, famously lampooned in what is known as the 'class sketch', broadcast on the satirical television show *The Frost Report* in 1966. Throughout his life the artist seems to have wrestled with these contradictory impulses, and the fact that he had as many detractors as admirers indicates that a large segment of the British public shared his ambiguity towards issues of class and social mobility, an attitude clearly not unique to Hogarth's times. The main critique of his detractors was what they saw as Hogarth's willingness to depict 'lowlife' subjects in his biting observations of contemporary life, in their view dragging art from its supposedly highbrow position into what they considered the gutter. This kind of negative attitude towards Hogarth continued throughout his lifetime and into the nineteenth and twentieth centuries, with the painter and art critic Roger Fry using the French word *primaire* – meaning small-minded bigot – to describe the artist.

The lack of flattery in Hogarth's work, along with his forensic observations of ordinary urban life and his penchant for satirical irony, ran contrary to but parallel with the popularity of representations of romanticized poverty and rustic idylls. In his third discourse to students at the Royal Academy of 14 December 1770, Sir Joshua Reynolds recommended that only limited praise should be given to the works of Hogarth because, like the Dutch genre painters of the past, he had confined himself merely to low subjects.[22] Yet despite attempts by contemporary critics such as Reynolds to damn Hogarth with faint praise, in the process imposing notions of acceptable taste both on his work and art in general, it was essentially out of their hands. The burgeoning commercial art market, ironically boosted by the annual summer show at the Royal Academy, of which Reynolds was president, ensured plenty of interest in Hogarth's work, despite his critics' objections.

The world in which Hogarth operated was one on the brink of an explosion of mass media, propelling art into the homes of those who could not previously afford such luxuries. The rise of auction houses at this time, with Sotheby's newly established in 1744 and Christie's established in 1766, just two years after Hogarth's death in 1764, could only have happened in the febrile atmosphere of demand for printed matter that Hogarth was instrumental in popularizing. Nevertheless, it is hard to escape the sense of an innate inferiority complex on the part of the British public, stemming from an inability to define precisely what it is that constitutes their own culture. Hogarth's legacy seems to counter these perceived inadequacies, and his conversation pieces continue to occupy a unique position in the history of British art, painting a vivid impression of British society during Hogarth's lifetime. The artist finally allows us a glimpse into the lives of ordinary people, as in the painting of his servants from *c.* 1750–55 (Tate) or *The Shrimp Girl* of *c.* 1740–45 (National Gallery, London). He also reminds us that life in Britain was divided, with the poor getting poorer while a small minority got richer. In chaotic scenes such as *An Election Entertainment* of 1754, Hogarth shows us this breakdown in order and social cohesion.

In his own inimitable way Hogarth himself would help to alter government policy, in an attempt to steer society in the right moral direction and away from the path of self-destruction. In two engravings from 1751 (pp. 206–7), he presents a typical polemic of England versus Europe. In *Gin Lane*, the cursed spirit of European origin threatens the very fabric of society, while in *Beer Street* the home-grown brew offering strength and vitality rides to England's rescue. The text that accompanies *Gin Lane* takes a very English approach of condemning all things foreign without expressing this explicitly. It is only when one reads the accompanying text for *Beer Street*, which speaks of the 'happy produce of our Isle' and 'water leave to France', that this xenophobia disguised as patriotism is made clear.

The foreign origins of gin would have been well known in the British Isles in this period. The juniper berry (in Italian, *ginevra*) was used by Italian monks in the eleventh century to flavour distilled spirits. Its metamorphosis into the alcoholic beverage called genever seems to have happened in the 1550s in Holland where, ironically, it was intended as a medicinal drink. It spread first to Flanders and then to southern France before finding its way in the late 1680s to Britain, where its name was abbreviated to gin.

In Britain gin quickly became the narcotic of its day, temporarily relieving the poor of their miserable circumstances, but ultimately wreaking havoc among those sections of society. This dire situation was created by a 1689 Act of Parliament that banned the import of French wines and spirits, meaning gin was now the cheapest readily available intoxicant for the masses. Rather conveniently, English gin was distilled from local crops grown by wealthy landowners, which in turn increased state revenue – a cycle that benefited the landowning Members of Parliament while compounding the deprivation and suffering of the lower classes, all under the guise of patriotism. With gin drinking spiralling out of control, the government had no choice but to pass the 1736 Gin Act to curb the greed of landowners, because the drink was now considered responsible for a rise in crime and infant mortality. This act proved unpopular and unsuccessful, however, leading to a second one in 1751, this time utilizing the talents of Hogarth.[23] Both *Gin Lane* and *Beer Street* proudly carry the inscription 'Publish'd according to Act of Parliament Feb 1, 1751'.

With this evil foreign intoxicant being held responsible for all society's ills, the propaganda battle waged by Hogarth in these two engravings cannot be underestimated. *Gin Lane* is set in the real and very poor London district of St Giles, where one in five houses sold gin. In his image Hogarth includes self-explanatory details: in front of the 'Kilman' distillery, mothers neglect children, men hang themselves and pawnbrokers prosper. In *Beer Street*, by contrast, the pawnbrokers have fallen into ruin while the population are content drinking beer. The power of British beer is shown to be the only way to counter the foreign invasion of gin, a point hammered home further in Hogarth's didactic accompanying text.

The British have a tendency to paint public figures who have achieved the status of 'national treasure' as being whiter than white, including Hogarth. But no one can measure up to such an ideal, no matter how great their achievements. The conundrum is often dealt with by not mentioning at all what is seen as out of character – or at best a temporary

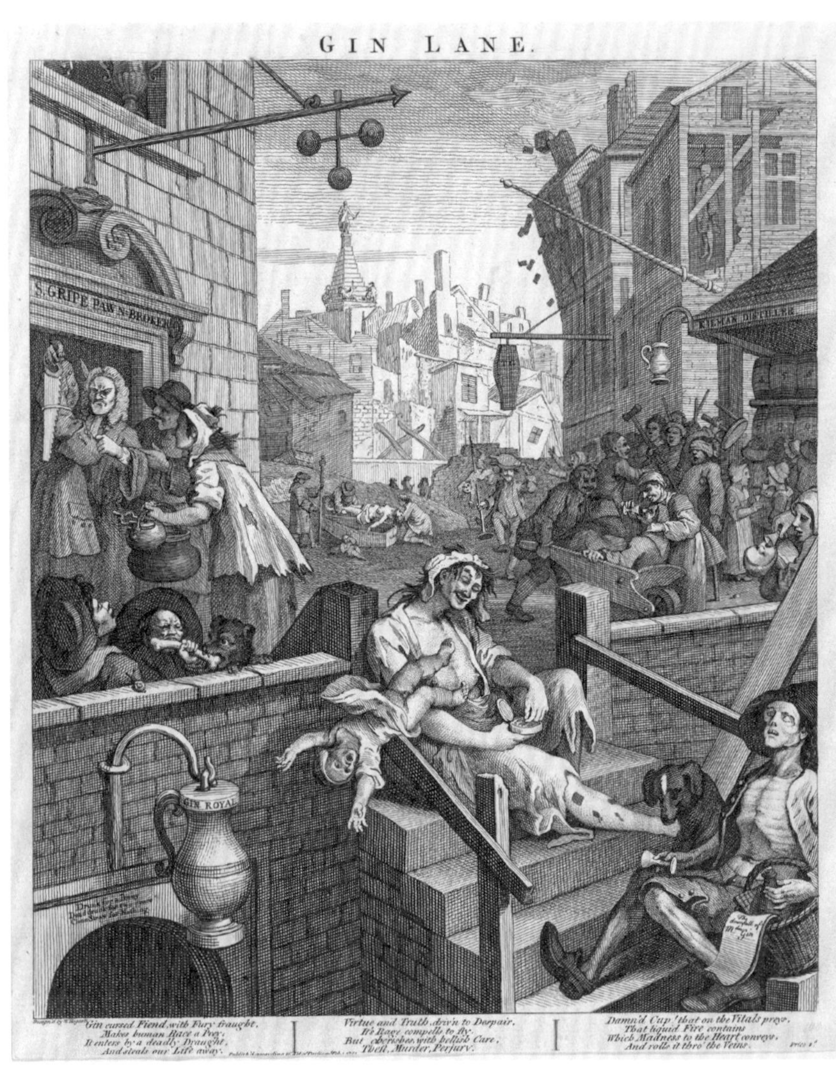

William Hogarth, *Gin Lane*, 1751.
Etching and engraving, 40.6 × 33.7 cm (16 × 13⅜ in.)

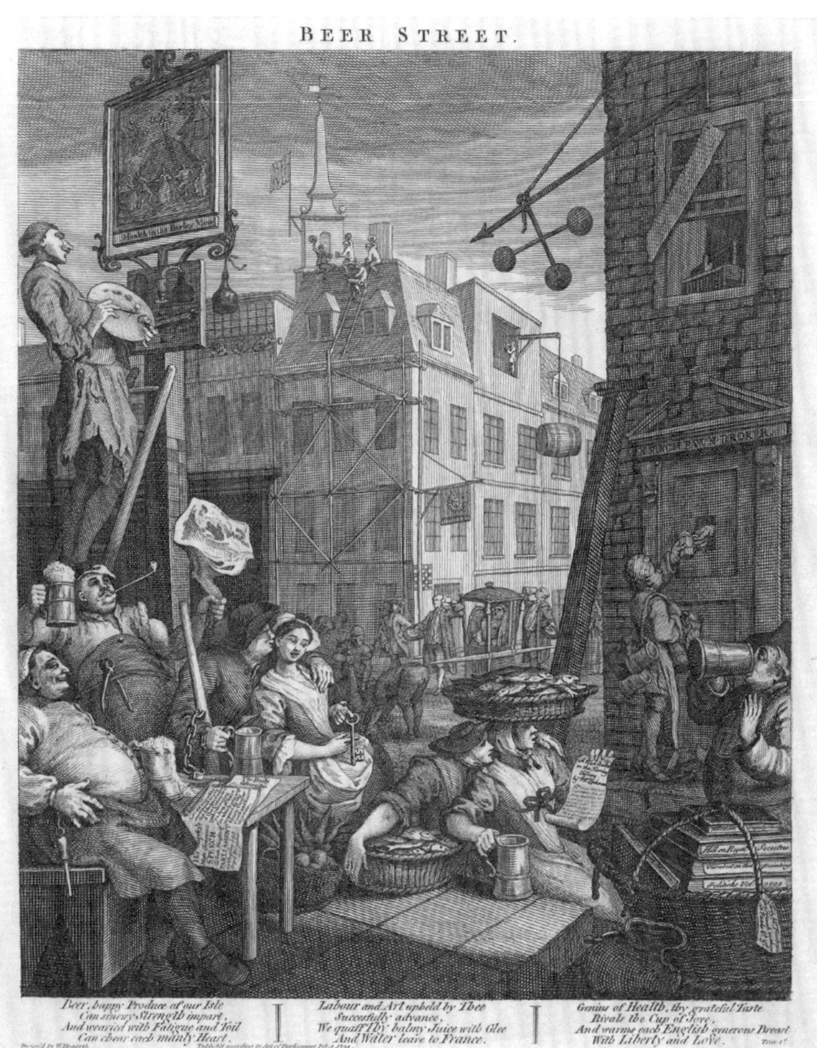

William Hogarth, *Beer Street*, 1751.
Etching and engraving, 40.6 × 33.7 cm (16 × 13⅜ in.)

anomaly – when appraising a life. Such reluctance to view history with an unflinching eye, which can also be characterized as a lack of bravery, is further compounded by condemning anyone who dares mention the flaws of a figure now placed on a pedestal of moral virtue. But Hogarth's own 'modern moral subjects' suggest that no one is above reproach, a rule he perhaps did not apply to himself.

Nevertheless, omitting to mention the uncomfortable areas of someone's life simply because they represent a small fraction of the whole cannot help us build a fully rounded account of an individual and brings us no closer to revealing the truth of Hogarth's personality or his motivations in producing art. This approach presents a sanitized and nationalistic view that chimes with some sectors of British society, who mistakenly believe they are under attack or held responsible for Britain's past atrocities around the world. This leads to echo chambers of their own making that function in an atmosphere of wilful ignorance and naivety, stoked by politicians and media figures who stand to gain from the situation. The idea that the achievements of someone who exhibits both good and questionable characteristics cannot be fully celebrated is flawed and simplistic.

Hogarth's acerbic criticism of the French in *O the Roast Beef of Old England* and ridicule of Italian fashion in *Taste in High Life* (c. 1742) contrast notably with his love of French engravings by artists such as Chardin and Italian masters such as Correggio, Titian and Caravaggio. But in creating these *tableaux vivants* the artist manages to make manifest in his pictures contrary aspects of the British psyche that until Hogarth's time had no representation in the nation's visual culture. In doing so Hogarth paved the way for a unique expression of British satirical humour that would be taken up in the late eighteenth and nineteenth centuries by British illustrators such as James Gillray, Thomas Rowlandson and George Cruikshank. One could even say that the British character and temperament itself can be summed up in the two words: William Hogarth.

10

Joshua Reynolds

*Grand Manner Portraiture
and the Legacy of Mai*

In July 1774 a visitor from Polynesia, a man in his early twenties by the name of Mai, arrived in Britain on board the ship HMS *Adventure* and swiftly became a celebrity in London society, known to the British as Omai. The events surrounding his arrival now represent a famous moment in British history when two worlds collided and brought into focus the key players in Mai's story, his time in Britain, how he was perceived and his interactions. Several artists made images of Mai, the most well-known of which is the grand full-length portrait of *c.* 1775 by the British-born painter Sir Joshua Reynolds (fig. 63), then president of the Royal Academy. In this portrait, Reynolds 'ennobles' his subject in the Grand Manner style, bringing to it everything he had learned in his time in Italy studying the art of ancient Greece and Rome and the Renaissance. The result is an iconic image representing Britain at the height of its imperial powers, which tells us much about eighteenth-century British society and its preconceptions of the non-white European, infused with the artist's Continental aesthetic, but nothing about Mai's life or what happened when he returned to the South Seas.

This was a period that imposed on people outside of the European experience the Western invention of exoticization. This othering cemented the way in which the people and land of the South Sea Islands were perceived through the invention of a European version of paradise, ideas that became crystallized in the work of the landscape artists who travelled with Captain Cook, including John Webber, Johann Reinhold Forster and his son Johann Georg Adam Forster, and Sydney Parkinson.

209

The legacy of Reynolds's painting has become emblematic of Britain's colonial culture and its general unwillingness to come to terms with the more unsavoury elements of its past, perhaps because it does not fit a more recently invented narrative of a benevolent United Kingdom. To understand how and why Reynolds came to paint his portrait, and what it meant both to audiences in its day and to the public now, one has to ask how its subject, a person from halfway round the world, became such an important celebrity in Britain in so short a period of time. This was a period full of contradictions, with a person of colour being readily accepted into the slave-owning society of eighteenth-century Britain, but not treated as a slave himself.

The pioneering sea voyages that spawned a plethora of artistic interactions with the South Pacific islands began in Tahiti with the first British ship to visit the region, HMS *Dolphin*, which made landfall in June 1767 under the command of Captain Samuel Wallis. A few images from this first voyage have come down to us in the form of engravings by now unknown artists. They paint a picture of conflict, resistance, and eventual subjugation of the Tahitian population at the hands of the British using what were then weapons of mass destruction. Works like *The Natives of Otaheite Attacking Captain Wallis, the First Discover of that Island* and *Captain Samuel Wallis of HMS Dolphin being received by the Queen of Otaheite, July 1767* (p. 211) – in which the Tahitian people literally bow and scrape before Wallis and his crew members – clearly set the tone for the supposed superiority of the British. This initial voyage was swiftly followed between 1768 and 1771 by a mission in which HMS *Endeavour*, commanded by Lieutenant James Cook, sailed to the southern hemisphere, primarily on a secret mission to try to discover whether a great continental land-mass – Terra Australis Incognita or 'unknown land of the south' – existed in the vicinity. Alongside territorial expansion and colonialism, the purpose of these missions was described as scientific, with Cook and his crew going there to find and categorize new species of flora and fauna and to witness a solar phenomenon known as the transit of Venus, which the British thought might help them in matters of global navigation and so domination and colonization of more lands and people. Cook and his crew set sail in August 1768, with information

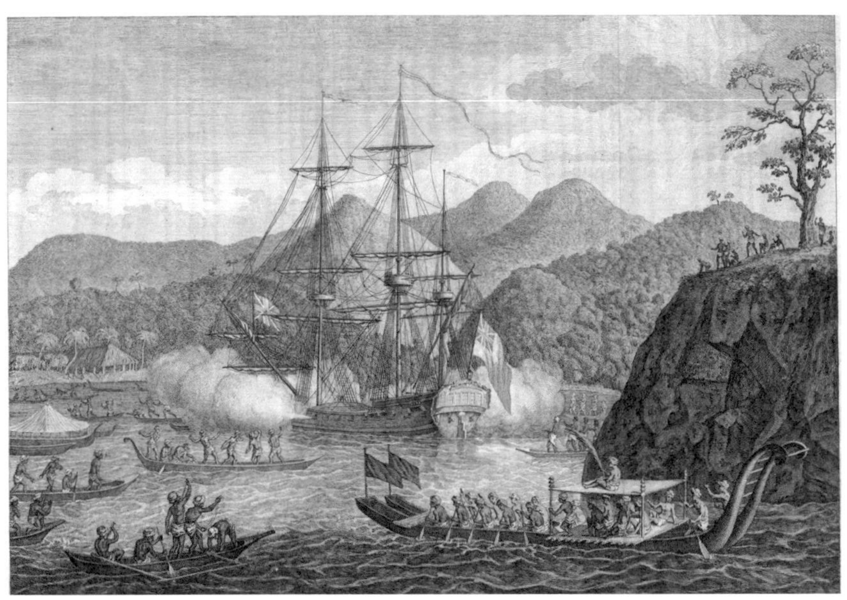

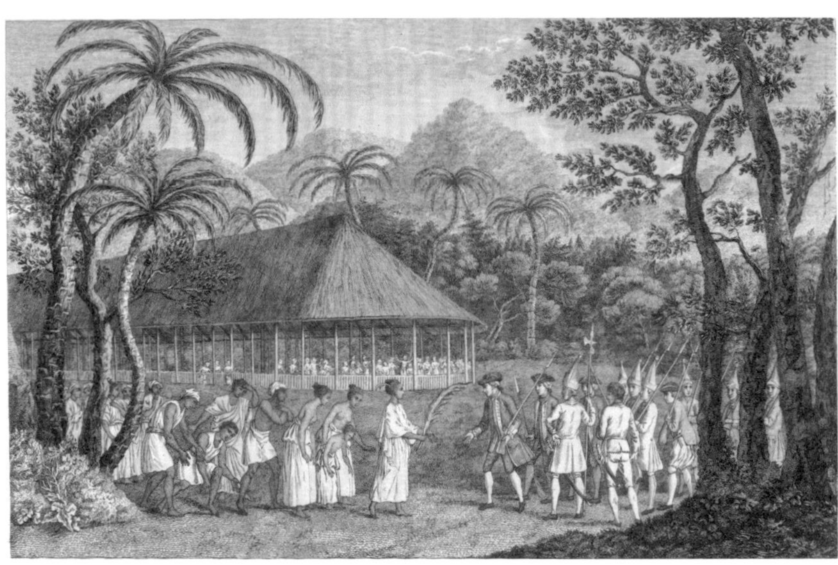

TOP Unknown Artist, *The Natives of Otaheite Attacking Captain Wallis, the First Discoverer of that Island*. Engraving, 23 × 31.2 cm (9⅛ × 12⅜ in.)

ABOVE Unknown Artist, *Captain Samuel Wallis of HMS Dolphin being received by the Queen of Otaheite, July 1767*, 1773. Engraving, 23.8 × 33 cm (9⅜ × 13 in.)

gleaned from the writings of the Astronomer Royal Edmond Halley, who had reasoned before his death in 1742 that a transit of Venus would take place in June 1769. This natural solar phenomenon involved Venus crossing the face of the sun, but such transits occur only in pairs eight years apart and separated from each other by approximately one hundred and twenty years. The explorers would have to arrive before this date to witness the transit within their lifetimes, since the next occurrence would be in 1874. In an extraordinary feat of navigation, they arrived mostly intact and two months ahead of schedule in April 1769, meaning when the transit happened in June, they were in place to make their observations.

Other scientific observations were to be conducted on this mission by the Lincolnshire-born naturalist, scientist, botanist and wealthy landowner Joseph Banks and his colleague, the Swedish naturalist and botanist Daniel Charles Solander. It was on this first expedition that the idea of bringing back what would have been described at the time as a live native specimen (a Polynesian person) was first mooted by Banks. The specimen they brought on board was not Mai but an individual called Tupaia. No ordinary man, Tupaia was a high priest, artist, linguist, scholar, navigator and all-round intellectual, described by the artist Johann Georg Adam Forster as a genius. Cook would mention him in his writings, saying, 'I have before hinted that these people have an extensive knowledge of the Islands situated in these seas – Tupia as well as several others hath given us an account of upwards of seventy'.[1] In his journal entry of 12 July 1769 Banks details not only the occasion of meeting Tupaia but also his value in matters of chart-making and navigation, making it worth bringing such a person to Britain.[2] Tupaia was indeed a desirable asset aboard the *Endeavour*, becoming the main navigator of the South Pacific area, as evidenced by a chart of seventy-four islands he made with Cook (which survive only as Cook's copies).

Inexplicably, Cook left no account of Tupaia's navigational skills in his journals. With his abilities as a linguist, Tupaia also acted as a diplomatic link between Cook's crew and the indigenous peoples of the South Pacific, though the downgrading of Tupaia's navigational skills to 'novice cartographer' indicates the erasure of his intellectual capacity by the Europeans, as noted by the scholar Harriet Parsons.[3] It is clear from

Banks's commentary that the value he placed on Tupaia was also that of a curiosity, comparable to an animal, which surely gives a good indication of his future perception of Mai. Such attitudes towards people of colour were not uncommon at this time and would persist throughout the eighteenth century and beyond; in 1774 Philip Stanhope, 4th Earl of Chesterfield, a supposedly enlightened man, instructed his son in the ways of the world by informing him that Africans were 'the most ignorant and unpolished people in the world, little better than lions, tigers, leopards, and other wild beasts'.[4] Unfortunately, on the return journey, as the *Endeavour* reached Java, an unknown sickness broke out on board, which resulted in the death of Tupaia along with several crew members, bringing to an end not only that particular attempt at scientific observation, but more importantly the life of a true intellect.

Cook's second mission to the South Seas would see him promoted to captain and in overall charge of two ships, HMS *Resolution*, under his own command, and HMS *Adventure*, commanded by Captain Tobias Furneaux. On board the *Adventure* this time, embarking from the Polynesian island of Huahine, was Mai. He struck up a friendship with Lieutenant James Burney, brother of the novelist Fanny Burney, which led to Mai's enrolment on the ship as an able seaman or supernumerary by Furneaux (this was in order to circumvent Cook, who described Mai as 'dark, ugly and a downright blackguard', objecting in no uncertain terms to bringing him to England).[5] Given the name Tetuby Homey, he was commonly referred to by his shipmates as Jack, soon becoming known as Omai. When the *Adventure* returned to England on 14 July 1774, Mai was placed in the care of Banks and Solander.

This was the beginning of the legend of Omai, propagated by multiple images that assigned him various personalities and identities, culminating in Reynolds's iconic Grand Manner portrait. While Banks had played no part in this second voyage, owing to a disagreement with Cook regarding the extensive entourage Banks had requested to accompany him on it, his absence freed up room to give a thirty-year-old English landscape painter, William Hodges, an opportunity to be part of the historic mission. Along with some of the most iconic images of the island paradise, Hodges also made a portrait of Mai. Unlike Reynolds, Hodges depicts Mai directly engaging with the viewer, arguably imbuing him with a degree of humanity (p. 215). An engraving by James Caldwell after Hodges's original bust-length painting shows Mai in similar robes to those he wears in the Reynolds painting, though significantly the turban is absent from Hodges's work, and we can see the subject's long flowing curly hair; the engraving is inscribed 'drawn from nature by W. Hodges, engraved by J. Caldwell', perhaps suggesting a degree of accuracy. The facial features are very different, however, for reasons that will become clear: his chin is noticeably shallower and less pronounced, and his eyes are much further apart, giving him a wider face than the narrower, finer features seen in Reynolds's full-length portrait. So different are the facial features in these two portraits in fact that one would not take them for the same person.

William Hodges was of humble origins. The son of a London blacksmith, he joined the studio of the landscape painter Richard Wilson as an apprentice shortly after Wilson returned from his tour of Italy in 1757. With his working-class background, Hodges could not join as a paying pupil, a distinction that meant he was much more involved in the everyday tasks of assisting Wilson in his works rather than receiving instruction. This direct method of learning ensured that Hodges was likely to absorb Wilson's style of painting, which had shifted from portraiture to landscape painting, probably under the influence in Rome of the French painter Claude-Joseph Vernet.

Hodges's 1776 oil painting *HMS Resolution and Adventure in Matavai Bay, Tahiti* (fig. 64) is still held in high regard in Britain today. He most likely sketched the image on Cook's second voyage and eventually worked it up into a full-scale painting in his London studio. It conjures up an idyllic scene in which we can observe in the middle distance the British ships at anchor in the bay. A near perfect grasp of aerial perspective captures a convincing view of mountainous terrain receding far into the distance. In the close foreground is a liberal scattering of Tahitian people, in boats or just lying around, including a traditionally topless Tahitian woman. When scenes like this appeared in Britain, they brought home to Europeans the idea of an earthly paradise, with the inclusion of naked natives enhancing such a perception among European

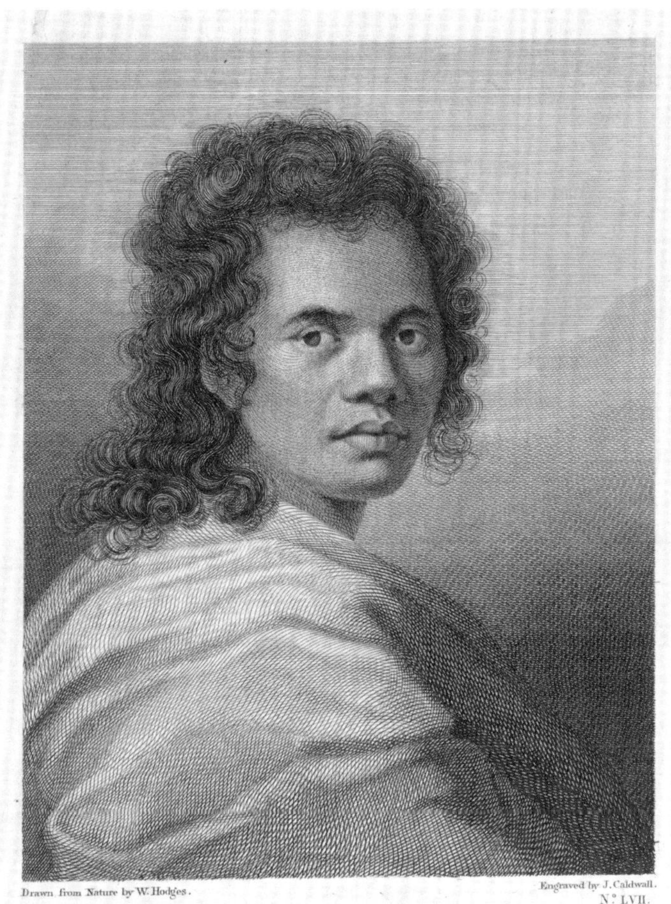

James Caldwell after William Hodges, *Portrait of Omai*, 1777.
Engraving, 30 × 25 cm (11⅞ × 9⅞ in.)

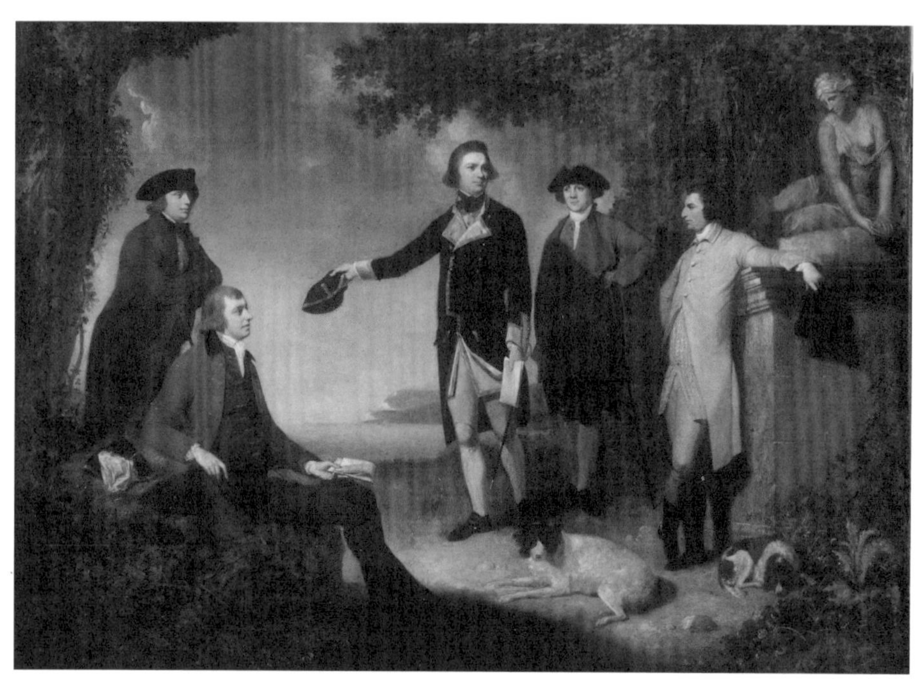

John Hamilton Mortimer, *Captain James Cook, Sir Joseph Banks,
Lord Sandwich, Dr Daniel Solander and Dr John Hawkesworth*, c. 1771.
Oil on canvas, 120 × 166 cm (47¼ × 65⅜ in.)

men while also providing titillation. This effect was probably not unintentional on Hodges's part as similar scenes appear in other works by him, such as *Tahiti Revisited* of *c.* 1776, also in the National Maritime Museum, London, which even features elaborate native tattoos on the naked Tahitian women that further add to their exoticism for European viewers.

This aspect of life in Tahiti was not lost on Banks and his European contemporaries either. Even before they had set foot on the island, they believed they would discover a fabled paradise or arcadia, populated by simple, uneducated, idle natives, over whom they would rule like kings.[6] It is clear from Banks's observations that his thoughts about the native Tahitians, especially the women, were anything but scientific. Delighting in their fuller figures, he nevertheless feels the need to qualify his attraction to them by extolling the virtues of a white complexion over that of the Tahitian women: 'Except in the article of Complexion in which our European Ladies certainly excell all inhabitants of the Torrid Zone I have no where seen such Elegant women as those of Otaheite. Such the Grecians were from whose model the Venus of the Medici's was copied. Undistorted by bandages, nature has full liberty [of] the growing form in whatever direction she pleases and amply does she repay this indulgence in producing such forms as exist here only in marble or canvas nay, such as might even defy the imitation of the Chizzel of a Phidias or the Pencil of an Apelles.'[7]

The imposition of a classicizing aesthetic on the Tahitians had the effect of removing any agency they had in how they were perceived and was typical of the mindset of most white Europeans in this period, with an inability to see the world through any lens other than a classical one, placing themselves at the pinnacle of human civilization. A similar attitude is demonstrated, for instance, in John Hamilton Mortimer's conversation piece of *c.* 1771, *Captain James Cook, Sir Joseph Banks, Lord Sandwich, Dr Daniel Solander and Dr John Hawkesworth*, where the subjects present themselves in poses suggesting self-aggrandizement and male dominance (p. 216). On the right, Lord Sandwich rests his arm on a (possibly faux) classical statue of a semi-nude woman, as if demonstrating an implied ownership of women's bodies, while the statue's presence proclaims their intellectual superiority. It must be said that such a limited world-view could be ascribed to most nations without experience of other peoples and cultures, and perhaps the British are not dissimilar to many others in this respect. Such views must surely have been the impetus, for instance, behind the many inter-island battles that had taken place between various Tahitian communities long before the British arrived. But while it could be argued that the language used by Banks is entirely characteristic of the period, the underlying belief of white-skinned (and by implication European) superiority continues to be promulgated to this day.

Another of the many artists who ventured to the South Pacific islands on Cook's three voyages to the region was the Scot, Sydney Parkinson, an illustrator and amateur botanist. Parkinson produced botanical and zoological drawings alongside landscapes and numerous studies of Māori people, drawing particular attention to their tattoos. It is clear from archival correspondence that the traditional scientific taxonomical approach these artists used to illustrate the flora and fauna of foreign lands was also applied to depictions of the Māori as an indigenous population. In fact, it seems European explorers largely considered such peoples to be no more than animals (perhaps an unsurprising attitude given that the Aboriginal populations of Australia were not granted any rights as human beings until 1967), and while in the care of Banks and Solander for supposedly scientific purposes, Mai was evaluated according to his reaction to 'polite society' and the Western idea of civilization.

Another artist inspired by the spectacle of Mai was William Parry, a pupil of Reynolds. His image, possibly made in the same year as Reynolds's painting, depicts Mai in the presence of Banks and Solander. Like many British painters of this period, Parry had embarked on a Grand Tour of Italy and had just returned from Rome, where he had resided from 1770 to 1775, imbibing its classical influences. Parry's painting, made between 1775 and 1776, soon after his return from Rome, shows Mai in what seem to be comfortable, opulent surroundings. The composition of figures in an interior of sumptuous drapes, with an expensive (possibly imported) rug placed on a table and a window opening on to a landscape, follows very closely a style that was a popular mainstay of portraiture in Britain throughout the preceding century, seen in the works of artists including Gheeraerts the Younger and Mytens. It could also be said to closely follow the format of 'friendship portraits', like those produced by Titian in the 1530s and popularized by Rubens and Van Dyck in the first half of the seventeenth century. Parry's portrait of Mai shows him wearing almost the same outfit as in Reynolds's painting, further indicating close proximity in date for the two works, but the differences in this portrayal lie in the absence of three details: the turban, the sash across his waist and his tattoos.

Unlike Reynolds, Parry overtly emphasizes the supposed superiority of the white Europeans by placing Mai in the position of a specimen in the process of being examined, with Solander at a desk taking notes and Banks pointing at an area of interest (fig. 65). It has been suggested that Banks was pointing to tattoos on Mai's hands and that these may have been inadvertently removed from the painting in a later restoration.[8] However, the idea that Mai is 'not quite being portrayed as an ethnographic specimen' and that he is certainly 'seen very much as Banks's protégé', as suggested by art historian Caroline Turner, seems at odds with the body language of the painting's subjects.[9] While Mai probably did undertake some study under Banks, the idea of his position as a protégé is somewhat tenuous, given he became neither a botanist nor a fully fledged member of the Royal Society (the national academy of sciences founded in 1660). Turner goes on to say that the turning of Mai's head towards the viewer indicates him 'emphasizing his individuality and humanity', yet one might also interpret this faraway gaze as a longing to be anywhere other than in this position.

The description of this painting on the National Portrait Gallery's website suggests that it 'seems to celebrate the eighteenth-century principle of equality and collaboration in the pursuit of knowledge'.[10] But whose knowledge, and who will benefit from it? Surely not those whose lands have been claimed by Britain. There is a spirit of collaboration in both this and the Reynolds painting, if somewhat unwittingly on the part of both artist and sitter, for it can certainly be said that Mai participated – even colluded – in the construction of the image of himself he wanted to convey. But to suggest there was a principle of equality in the eighteenth century seems to be convenient revisionism, which seeks to continue the promotion of a supposedly enlightened European mindset while dismissing or erasing the reality of attitudes towards people of colour in Britain in this period. Mai's position in the painting cannot be said to be of equal standing with the white Europeans pictured, because there is a clear hierarchical composition, whether imposed consciously or unconsciously by the white European artist. In fact, one might alternatively argue that this is an insensitive portrayal that clearly demonstrates taxonomy at work, with Banks pointing out areas of interest on Mai to Solander and the viewers and Solander taking notes on him as a specimen of exotic animal life. In my view, the idea that eighteenth-century observers of this painting would have seen Mai as an equal rather than as an object of curiosity is unsupported given the number of images produced of him in the period, most of which verge on caricature, suggesting that he was barely seen as human.[11] The tropes perpetuated by the picture and the contemporary reading of it promote a sense of white Europeans being incapable of empathizing with or seeing Mai through any other prism than that of their own, mostly unconscious sense of exceptionalism, giving rise to an ill-judged and misplaced sense of superiority.[12]

Mai's passage to Britain was just one of a few successful attempts to bring members of indigenous societies to Europe for the purposes of entertainment as well as 'science'.[13] The French captain Louis-Antoine de Bougainville, for example, introduced the first Tahitian, Ahutoru or Aoutourou, to Europe in 1769. Ahutoru, who was said to enjoy opera, was presented to the French King Louis XV and paraded around like a trophy or curiosity; like Mai, he was also described as a protégé, this time of Bougainville. He eventually embarked on the journey back to Tahiti but made it only as far as Madagascar before succumbing to smallpox in 1771.

As Mai's fame began to spread throughout English society, reproduction images in the form of engravings helped to propagate his celebrity status. Any chance of an individual character emerging from these many reproductions seems to be very unlikely though, as each artist imposed their own ideas of exoticism on him, as can be seen in the full-length portrait engraving by Francesco Bartolozzi after a painting by Royal Academician Nathaniel Dance (p. 221). In this engraving Mai is dressed

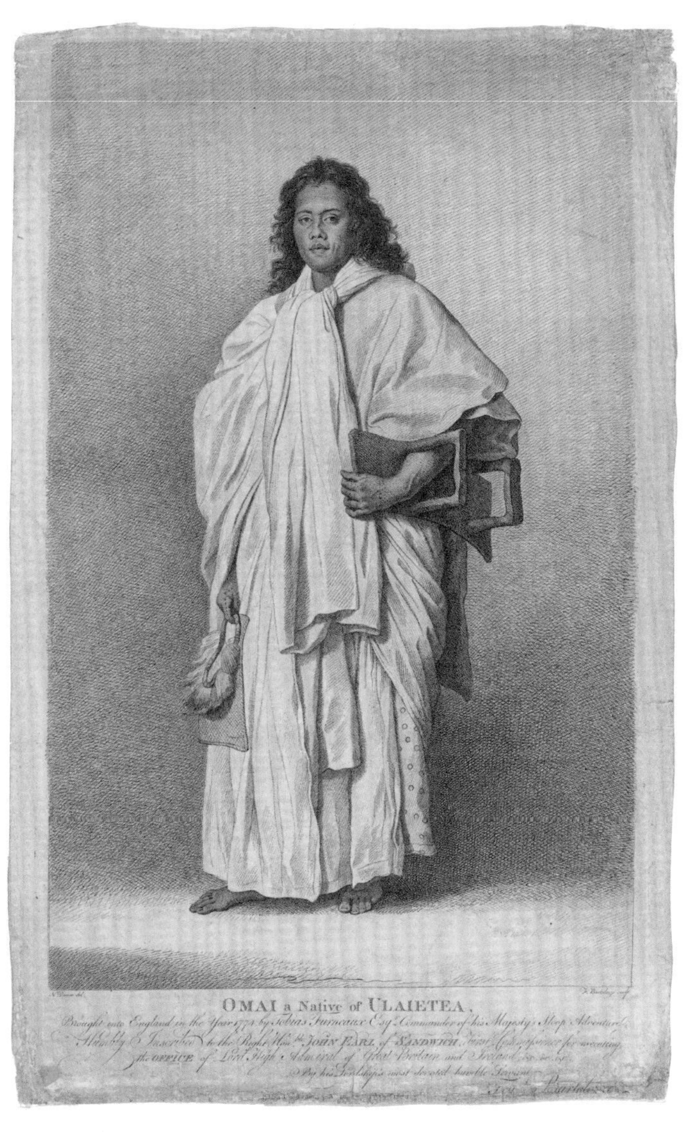

Francesco Bartolozzi after Nathaniel Dance, *Omai, a Native of Ulaietea*, 1774. Engraving and etching, printed in black ink, from one copper plate, 46.5 × 29.1 cm (18⅜ × 11½ in.)

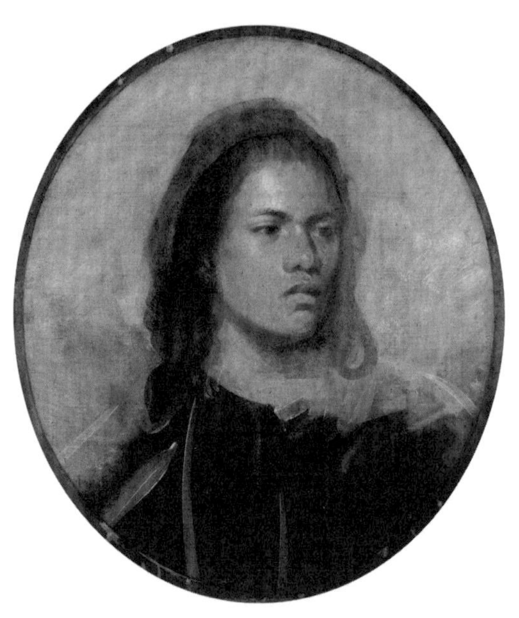

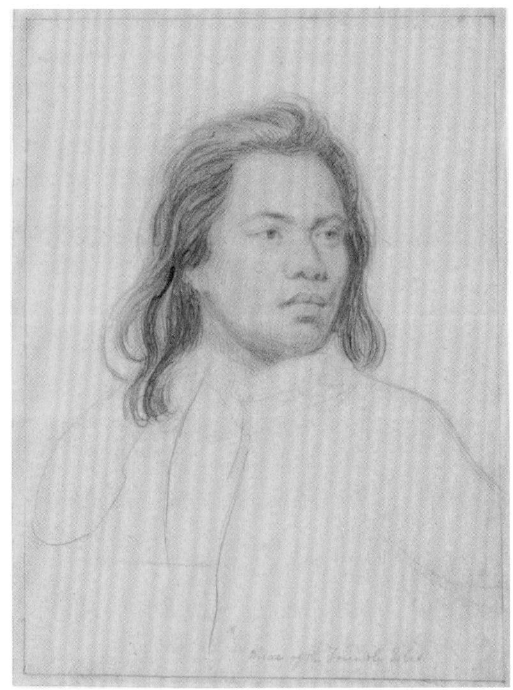

TOP Joshua Reynolds, *Sketch for Omai, c.* 1774.
Oil on canvas, 63.8 × 55.9 cm (25⅛ × 22⅛ in.)

ABOVE Joshua Reynolds, *Omai of the Friendly Isles, c.* 1774.
Pencil, 26.5 × 20 cm (10½ × 7⅞ in.)

in robes similar to those he wears in the Reynolds painting but, as in the Hodges engraving, there is no turban and no sash across his waist. Like Reynolds, Dance makes a point of featuring Mai's tattoos, and a Tahitian headrest completes his exoticization. His facial features are given a much more robust treatment though. Gone are the fine features of the Reynolds portrait; instead, Mai's eyes are closer together, he has a slight dimple on his left cheek and his lips are no longer wide from cheek to cheek but compact, presenting us yet again with an entirely different character.

Reynolds's portrait of Mai clearly did not arrive fully formed: like all classically trained artists, he followed a process that led to the image we see today. Two sketches made around 1774 are the only other representations of Mai by Reynolds known to exist, and perhaps offer an insight into the making of the finished painting. In these preliminary artworks we might at last glimpse a more accurate representation of Mai's physiognomy, and when we compare the oil sketch and the pencil drawing there does seem to be a similarity between them (p. 222). The pencil drawing is reputedly the best physical likeness of Mai.[14] However, when compared to the engraving after Hodges in particular, and to a certain extent the Reynolds oil sketch, it seems that we are looking at two different individuals, who bear little relation to Reynolds's own experience of Mai. So, who should we believe has the most authentic experience of Mai, and how can we be sure which of these renditions is closest to an accurate depiction of him? If we take into account the inconsistencies in an individual artist's work, as seen in the two Reynolds sketches, what is clear from all these images is that they are either of two or three completely different sets of people or that all these artists are adjusting Mai's physiognomy according to their own conscious or unconscious prejudice relating to the amorphous European notion of exoticism.

Notably, in terms of his attire, contemporary descriptions of Mai do not match any of the multiple extant images of him. Sightings of Mai were very public; he was guest of honour at the Royal Society, had his own apartment, attended the Handel oratorio *Jephtha* at Covent Garden and was introduced to members of Reynolds's circle, including the lexicographer Samuel Johnson, the literary critic Giuseppe Baretti and the writer Fanny Burney (she thought him 'by no means handsome' but with a 'pleasing countenance').[15] But a cleric who had a brief encounter with Mai gives perhaps the best description we have, describing Mai's complexion as 'that of a European, accustomed to hot climates: His features are regular – his eyebrows large & dark – His countenance is often illuminated by a most unaffected smile – His hair black & dressed in the English fashion.'[16] When Mai met Burney he was described as wearing a satin-lined velvet suit, a bag wig, lace ruffles and a very handsome sword given to him by the King.[17]

Mai's celebrity status was clearly not gained because of the novelty of his skin colour; by the eighteenth century there was a population of at least ten thousand Black people in Britain, many of them domestic servants whose circumstances were a far cry from the fame and finery that characterized Mai's life.[18] The majority of people of African descent living in Britain were never more than one sale away from being returned to the nightmare that was plantation life, and so had ceased to carry any of the exotic appeal projected on to Mai by Reynolds and his contemporaries. But, interestingly, since the first arrival in Britain of three Beothuk from Newfoundland in 1501, indigenous people from the Americas had been treated in a similar fashion to Mai. More than a decade before Mai's arrival, in 1762, Reynolds had painted a newly arrived Cherokee chief, Ostenaco, in his *Portrait of Syacust Ukah*, now in the Gilcrease Museum, Tulsa (fig. 66).[19] Painted in the style of military portraits of the previous century, Reynolds's subject bears the regalia of a gorget, baton and King George III peace medal, along with a wampum belt, an object of great significance to the Cherokee people. Such trappings demonstrate this earlier visitor's importance in the eyes of the British, displaying an elevated status that Mai arguably sought to achieve for himself, but never did.

We now know that Mai himself was complicit in the presentation of his exotic transformation by supplying his own robes. Although the fabric (tapa) of his sash and turban do originate from Tahiti and relate to Tahitian dress, the overall costume was clearly invented by Mai in an attempt to aggrandize himself. His reasons were quite different to Reynolds's though. Mai was born on the island of Raiatea around 1751 into a society with a strict hierarchical structure; he belonged to a landowning class, above which was the ruling *ari'i* class. When Mai was about

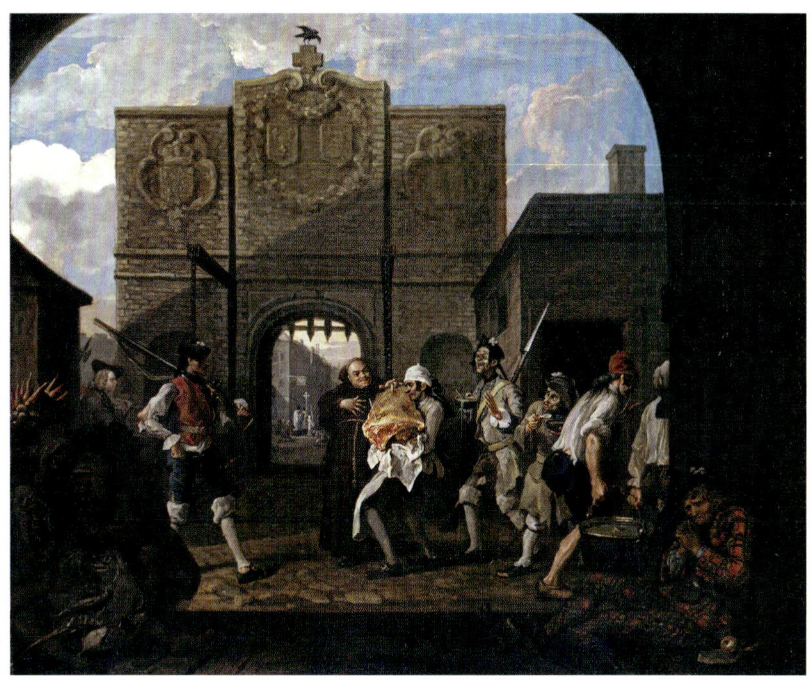

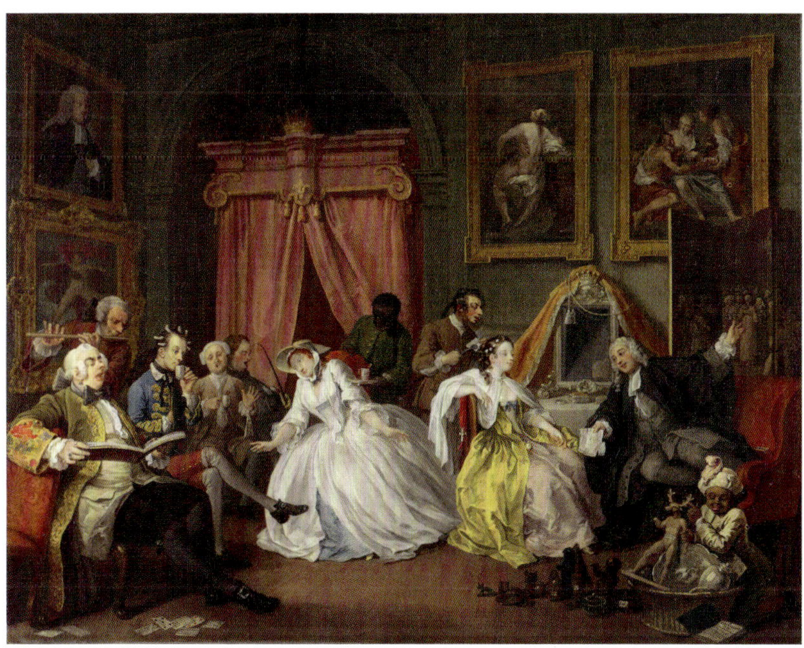

60 William Hogarth, *O the Roast Beef of Old England (The Gates of Calais)*, 1748. Oil on canvas, 78.8 × 94.5 cm (31⅛ × 37¼ in.)

61 William Hogarth, *Marriage A-la-Mode, 4, The Toilette*, c. 1743. Oil on canvas, 70.5 × 90.8 cm (27⅞ × 35¾ in.)

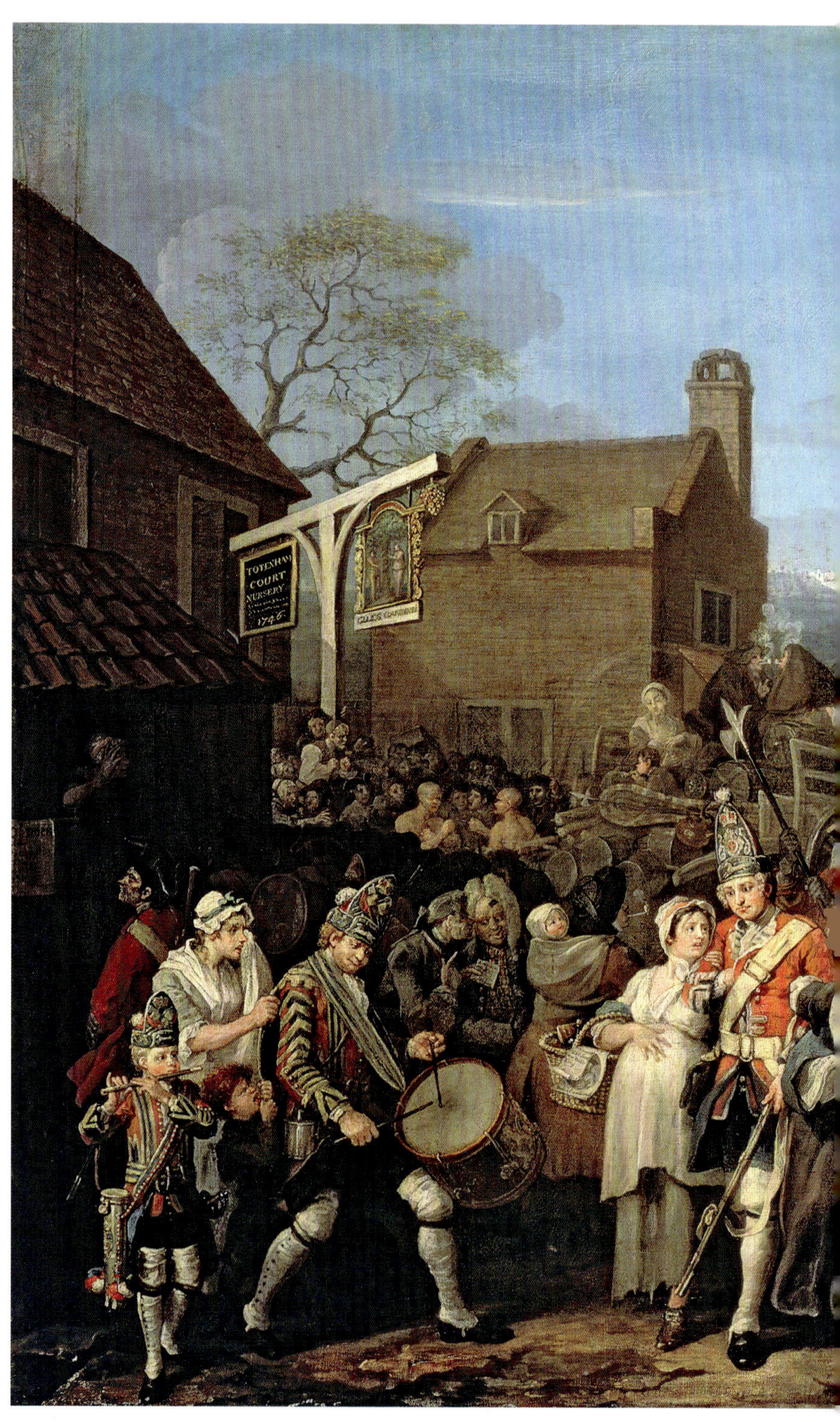

62 William Hogarth, *The March of the Guards to Finchley*, 1749–50.
Oil on canvas, 100.3 × 133.3 cm (39½ × 52½ in.)

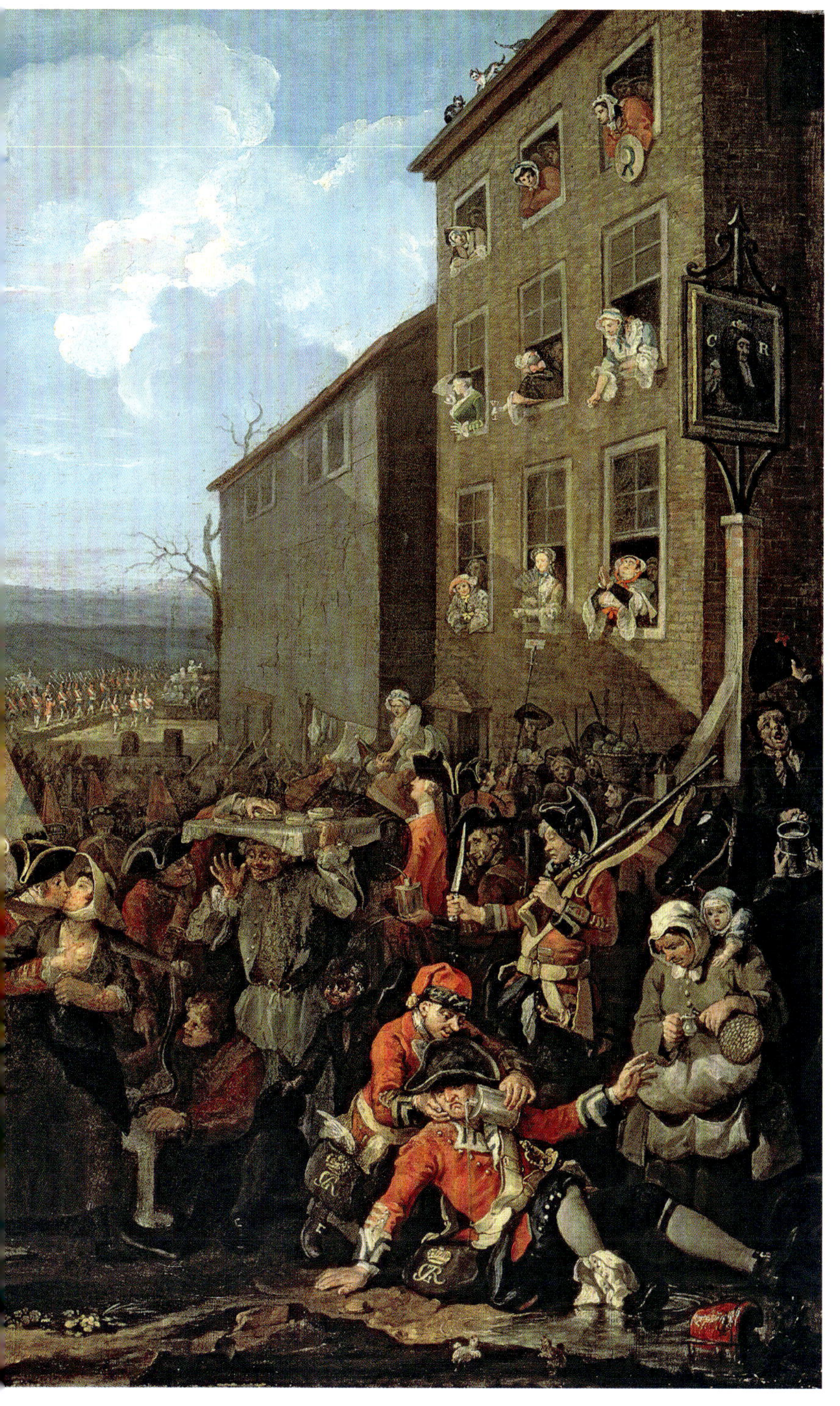

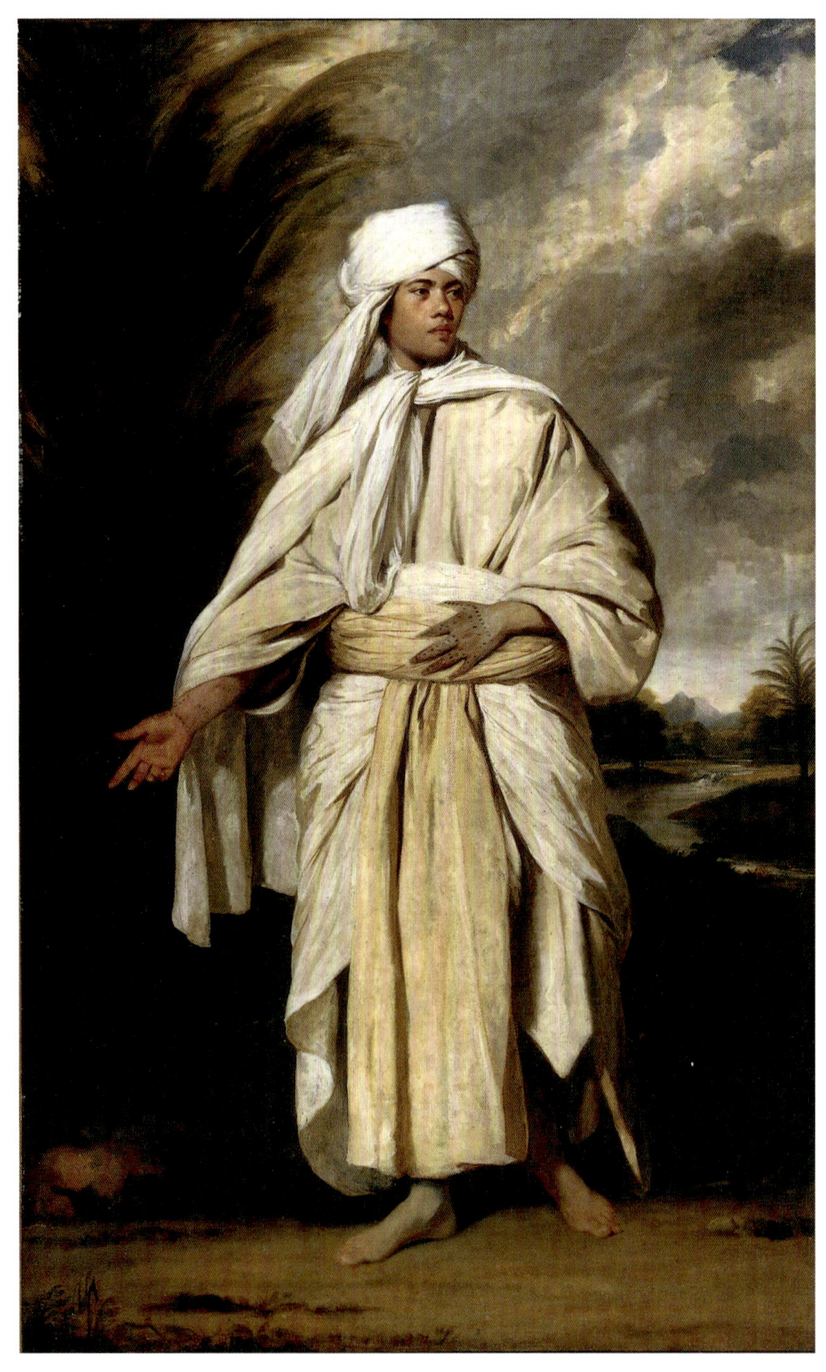

63 Joshua Reynolds, *Portrait of Omai*, *c*. 1775.
Oil on canvas, 236 × 145.5 cm (93 × 57⅜ in.)

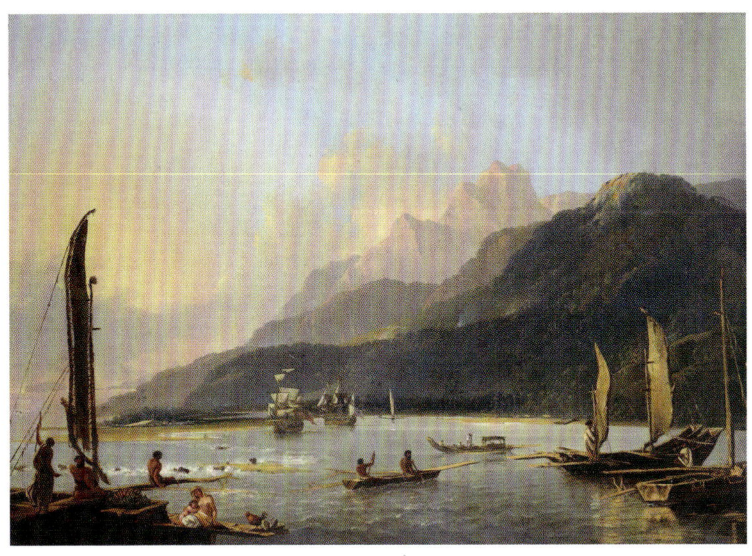

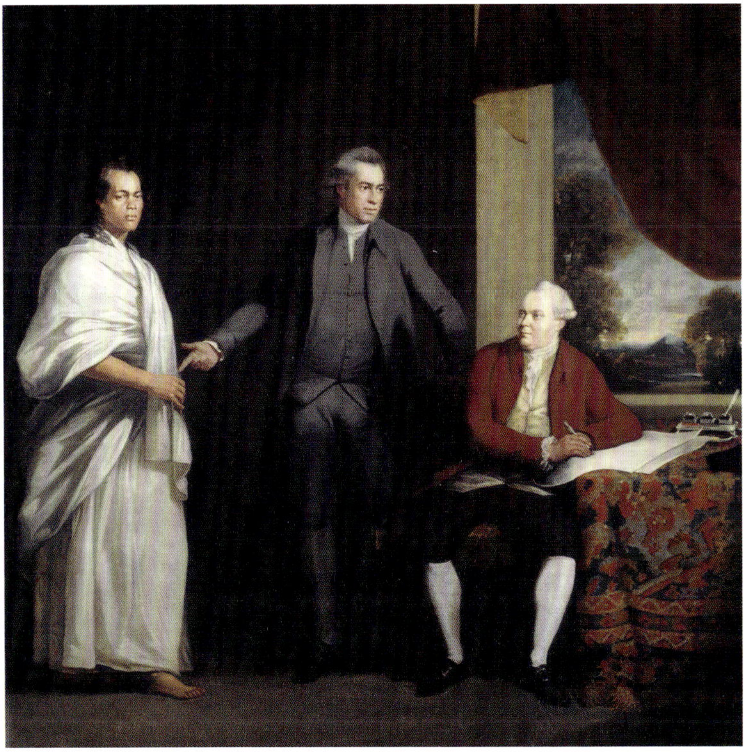

64 William Hodges, *HMS Resolution and Adventure in Matavai Bay, Tahiti*, 1776. Oil on canvas, 137.2 × 193.2 cm (54⅛ × 76⅛ in.)

65 William Parry, *Omai, Sir Joseph Banks and Daniel Charles Solander*, *c.* 1775–76. Oil on canvas, 152.5 × 152.5 cm (60⅛ × 60⅛ in.)

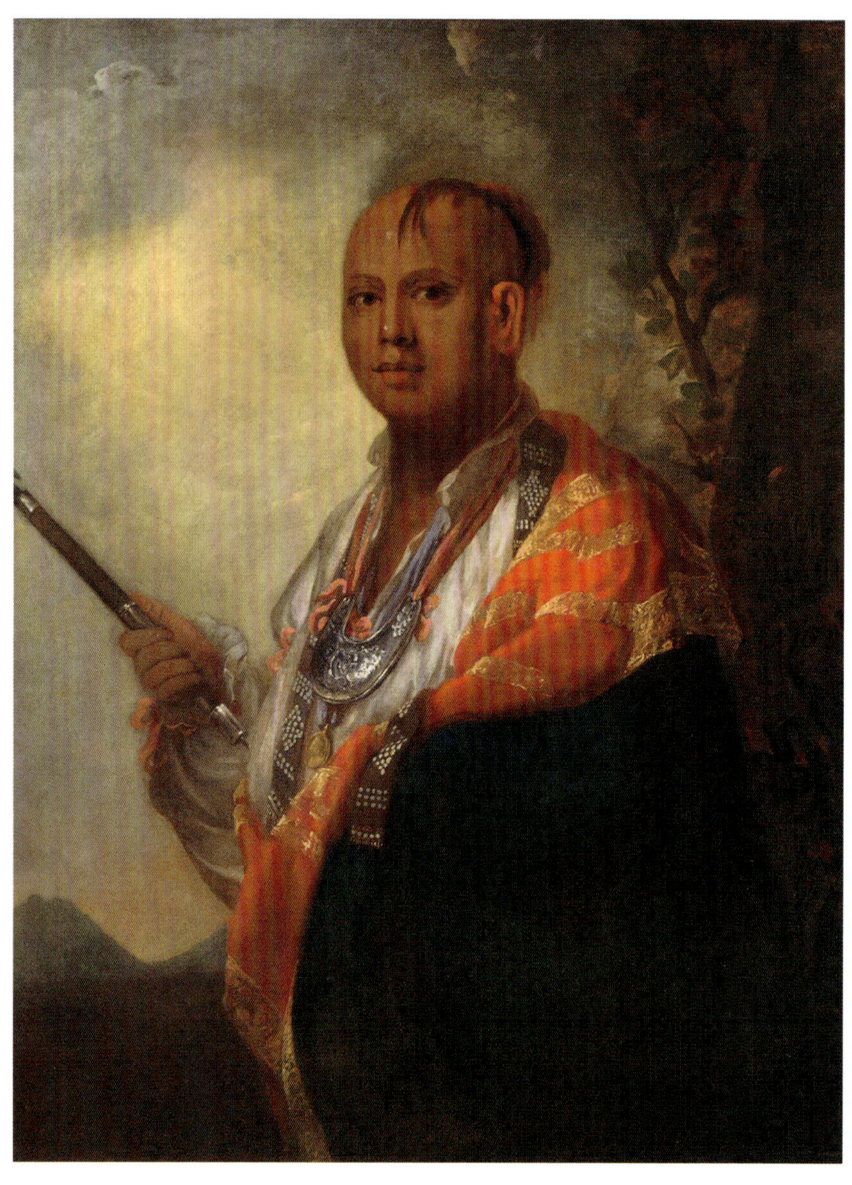

66 Joshua Reynolds, *Portrait of Syacust Ukah*, 1762.
Oil on canvas, 140 × 109.5 cm (55⅛ × 43⅛ in.)

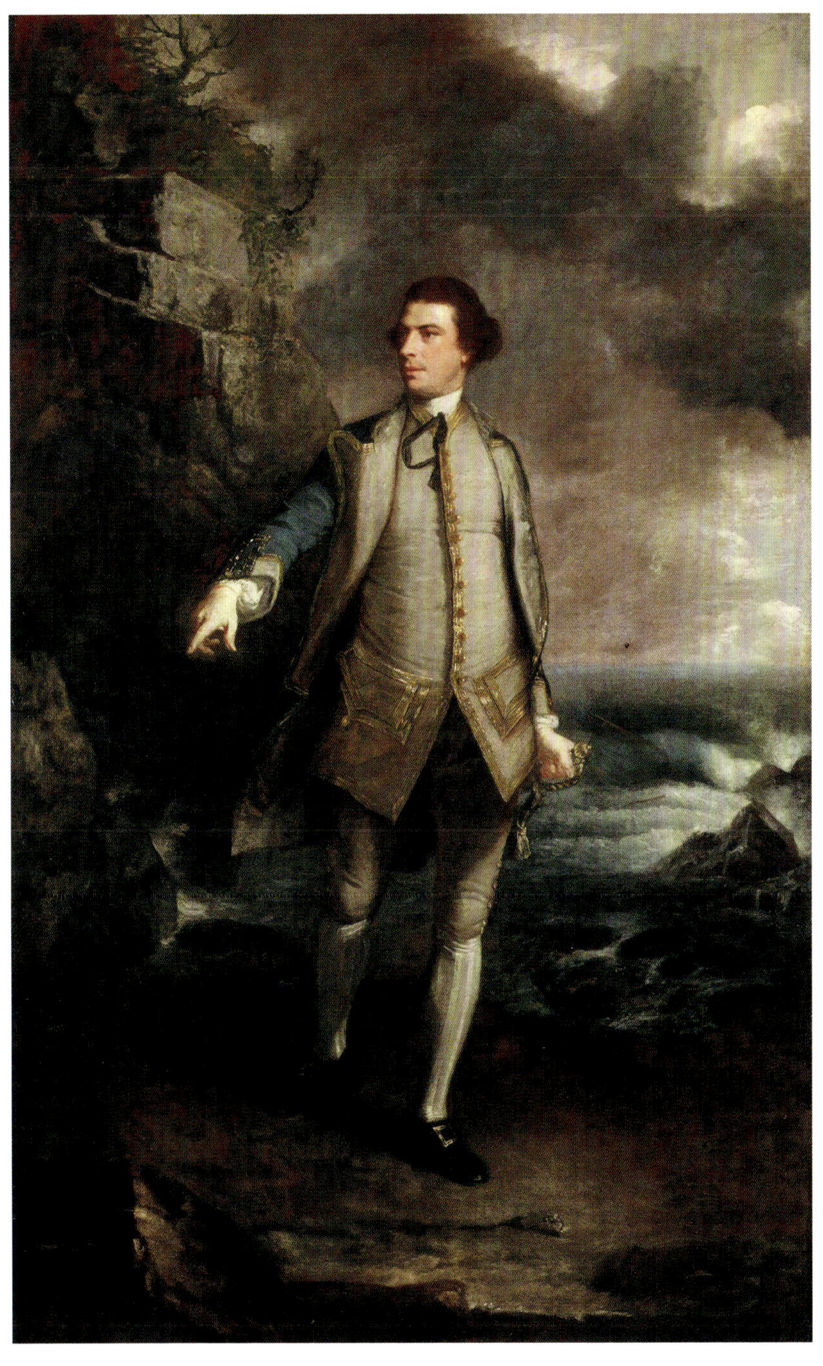

67 Joshua Reynolds, *Portrait of Augustus, 1st Viscount Keppel*, 1752–53.
Oil on canvas, 239 × 147.5 cm (94⅛ × 58⅛ in.)

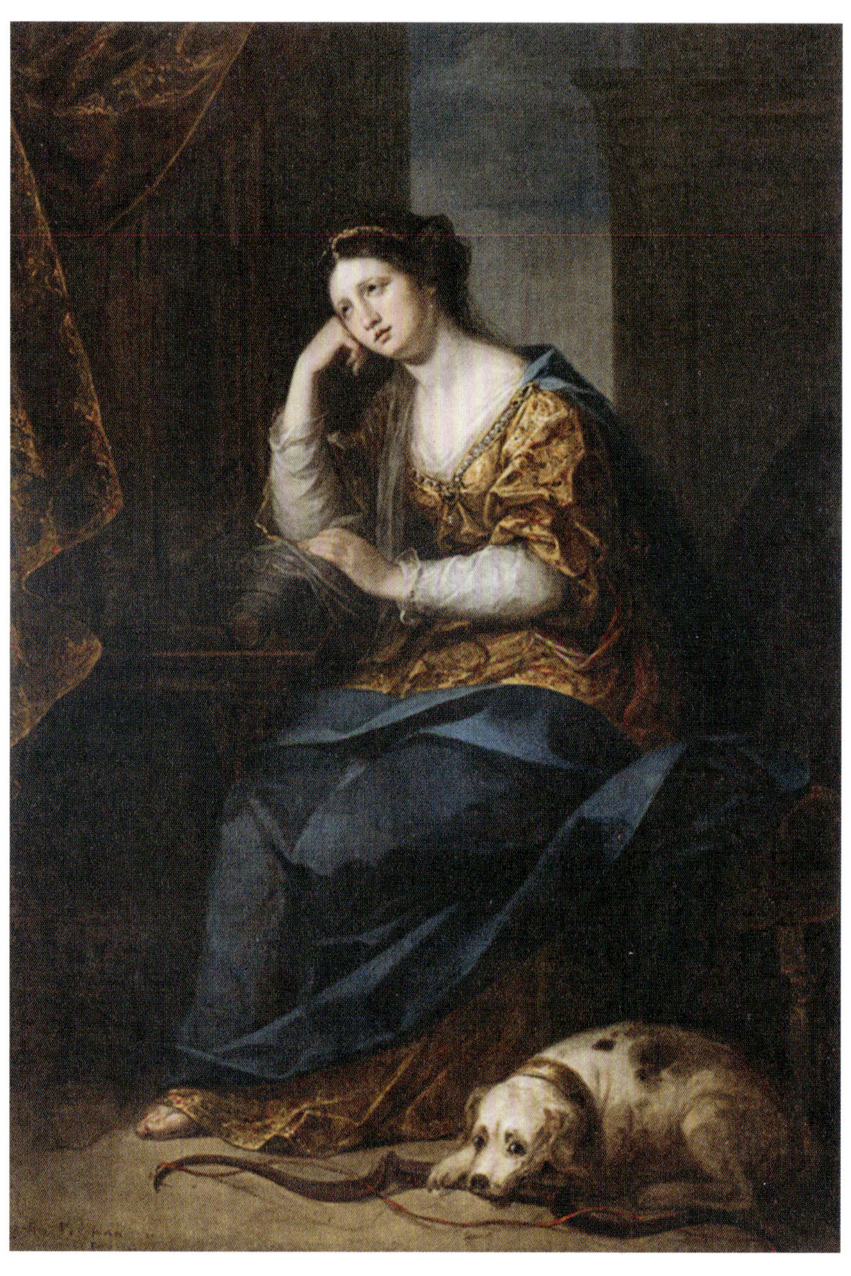

68 Angelica Kauffman, *Penelope at her Loom*, 1764.
Oil on canvas, 169 × 118 cm (66⅝ × 46½ in.)

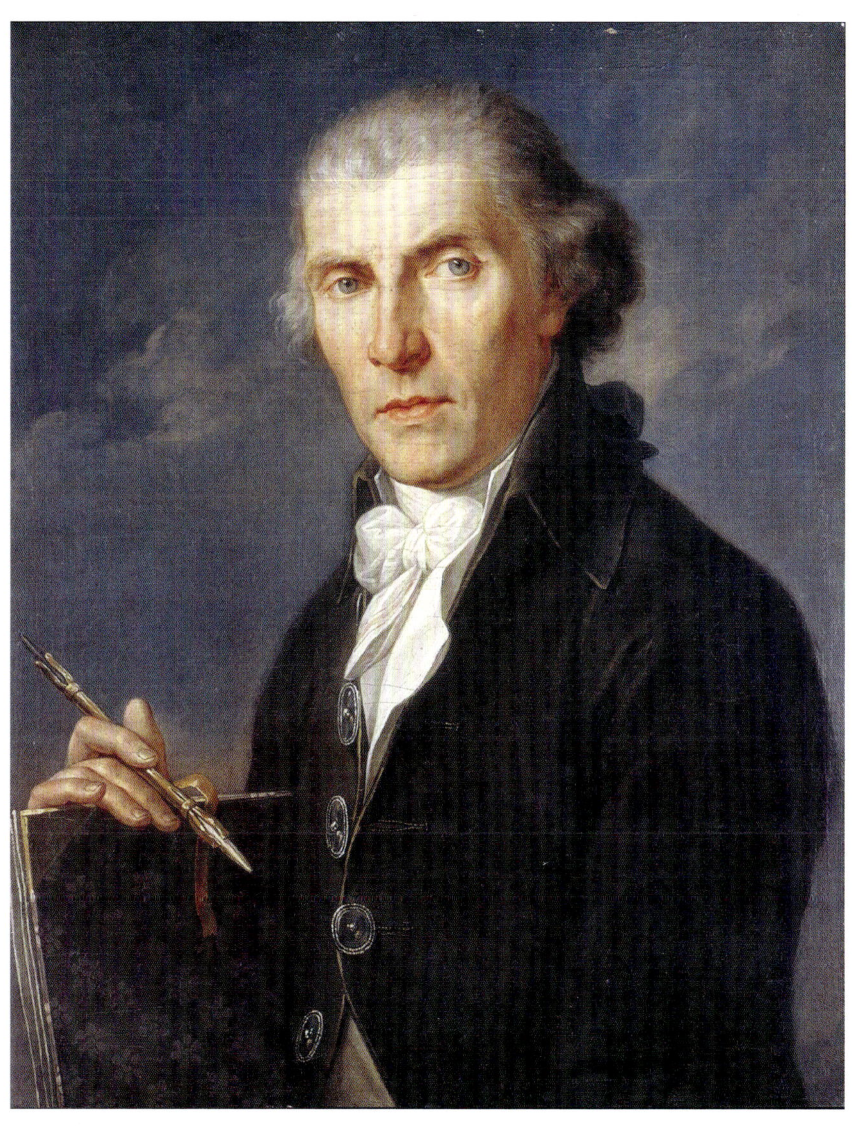

69 Angelica Kauffman, *Portrait of her Father, Johann Joseph Kauffman*, after 1763. Oil on canvas, 63.2 × 50.9 cm (24⅞ × 20 in.)

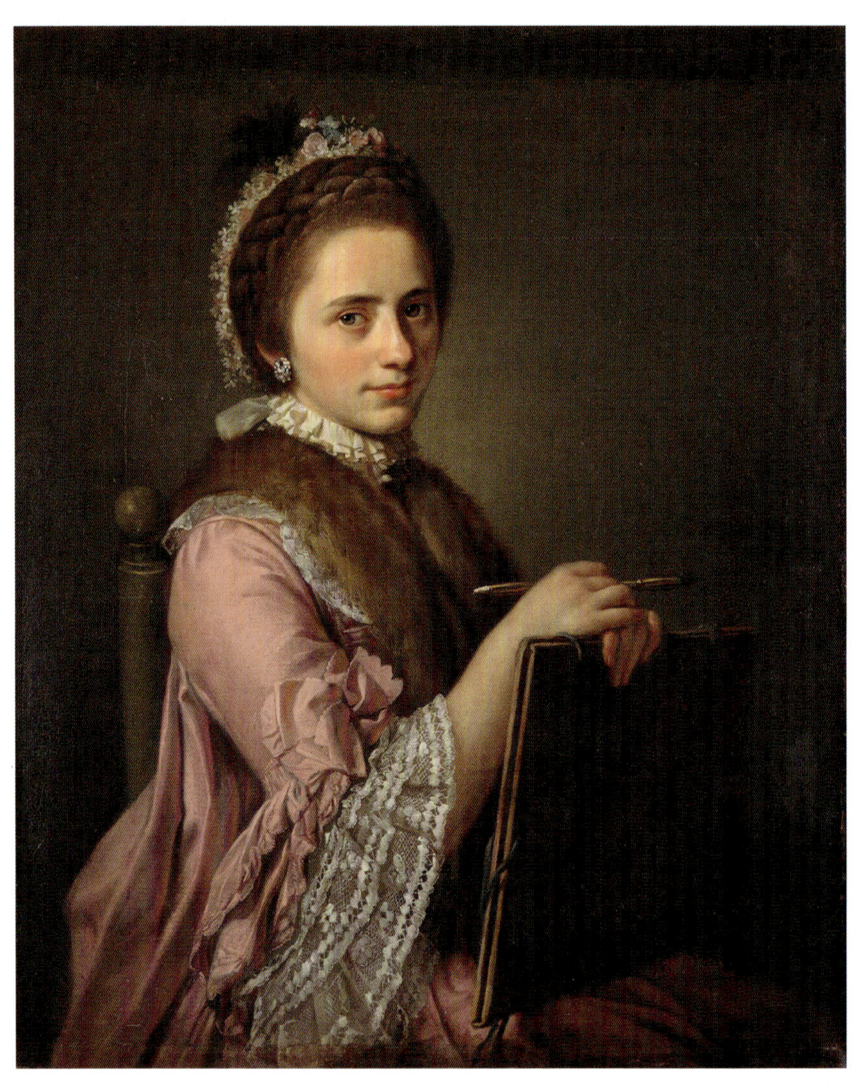

70 Nathaniel Dance, *Angelica Kauffman*, c. 1765.
Oil on canvas, 83 × 69 cm (32¾ × 27¼ in.)

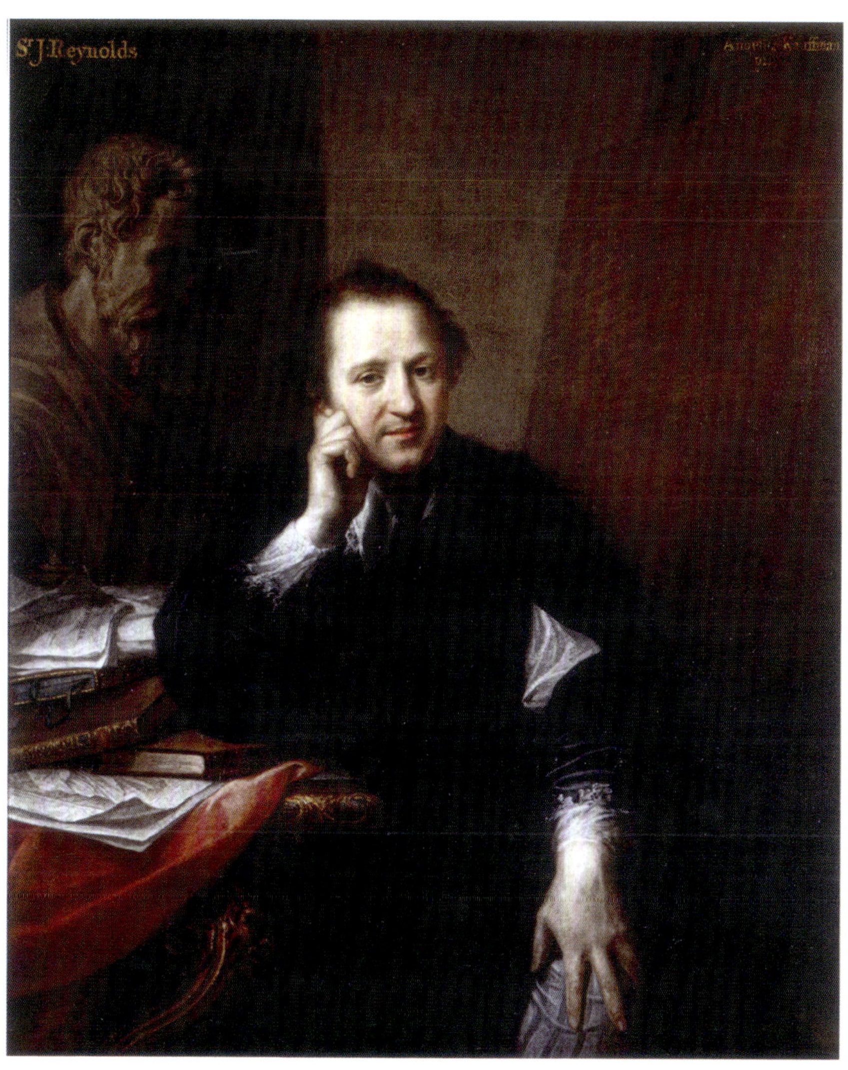

71 Angelica Kauffman, *Joshua Reynolds*, 1767.
Oil on canvas, 127 × 91.5 cm (50 × 36⅛ in.)

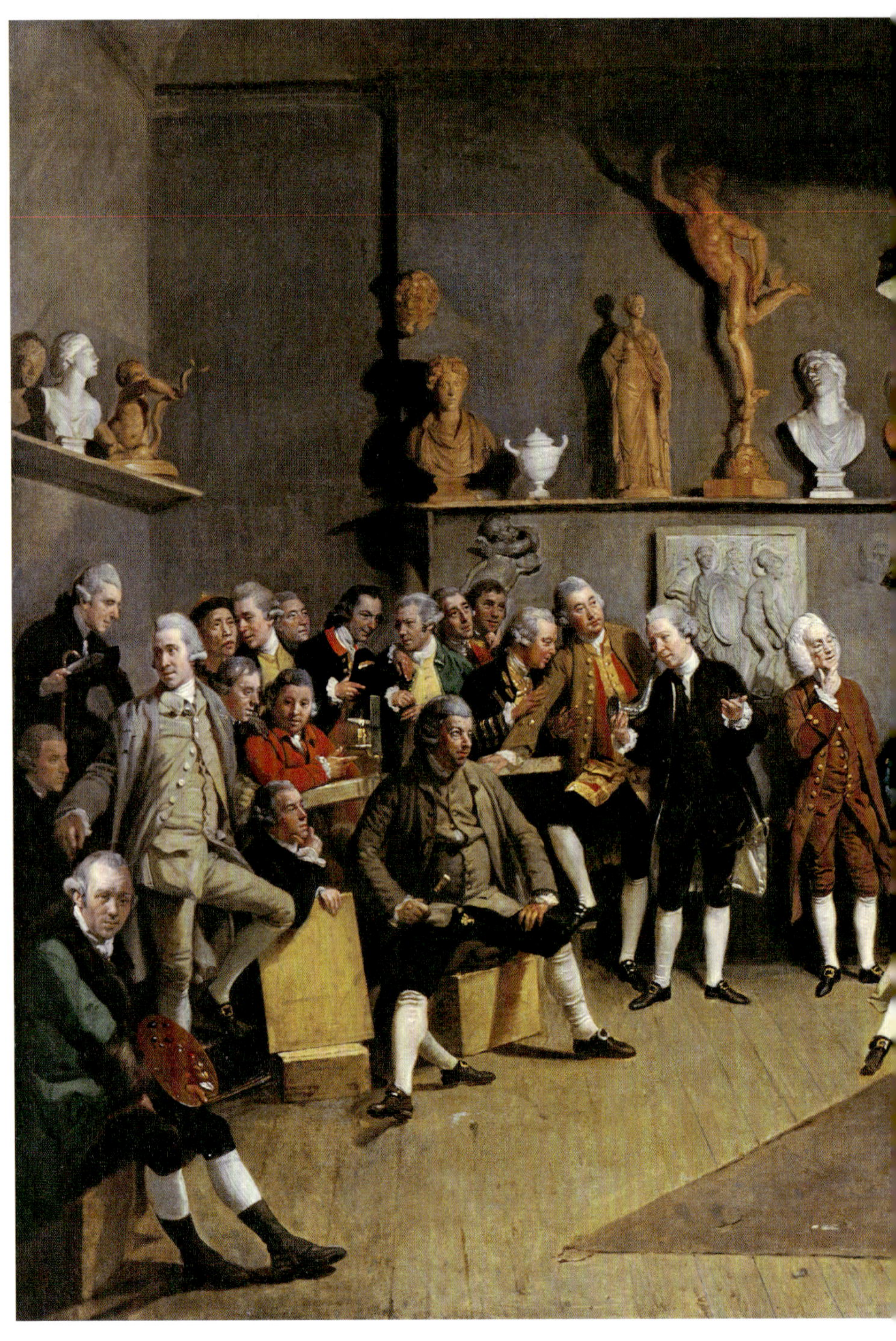

72 Johann Zoffany, *The Academicians of the Royal Academy*, 1771–72. Oil on canvas, 101.1 × 147.5 cm (39¾ × 58⅛ in.)

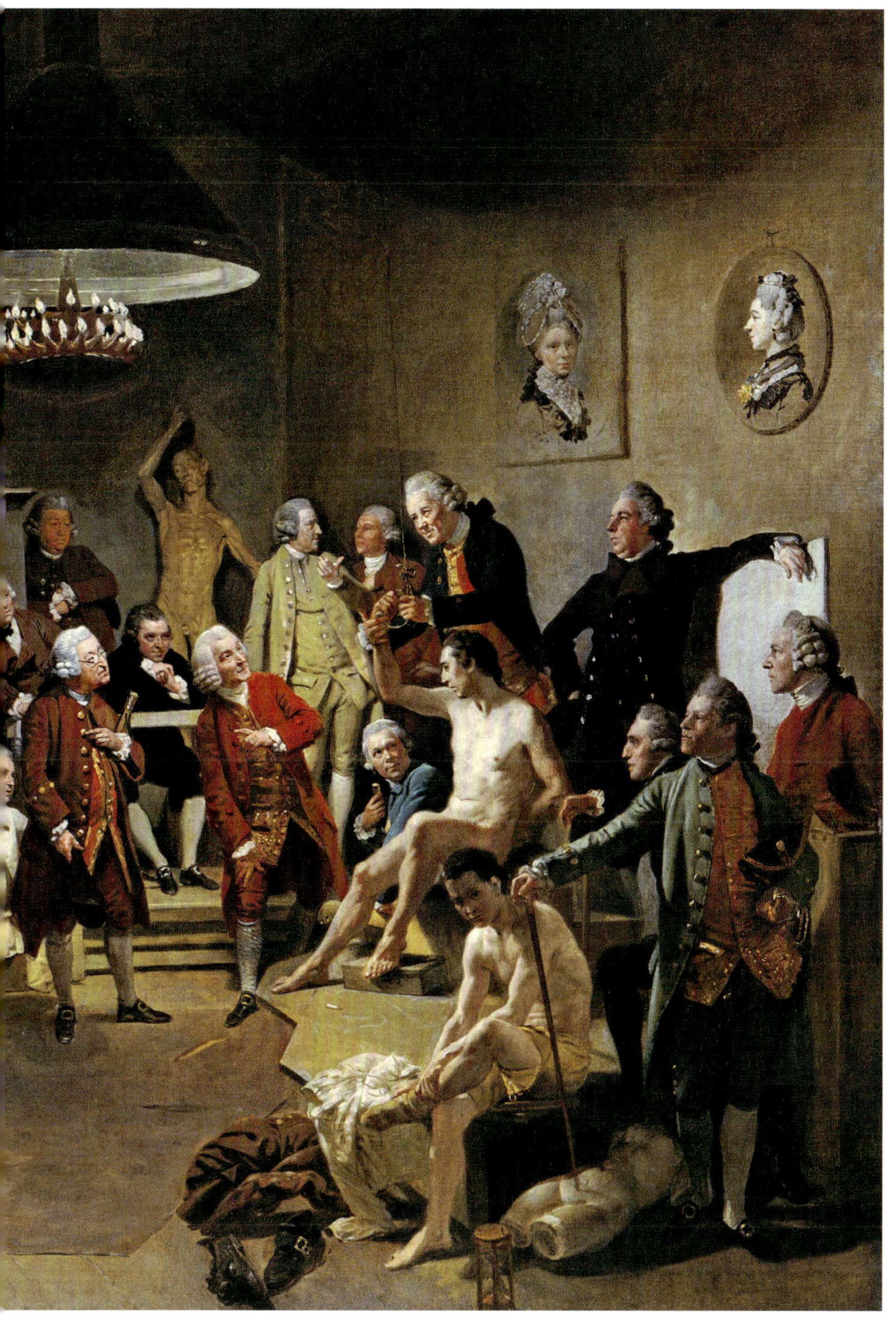

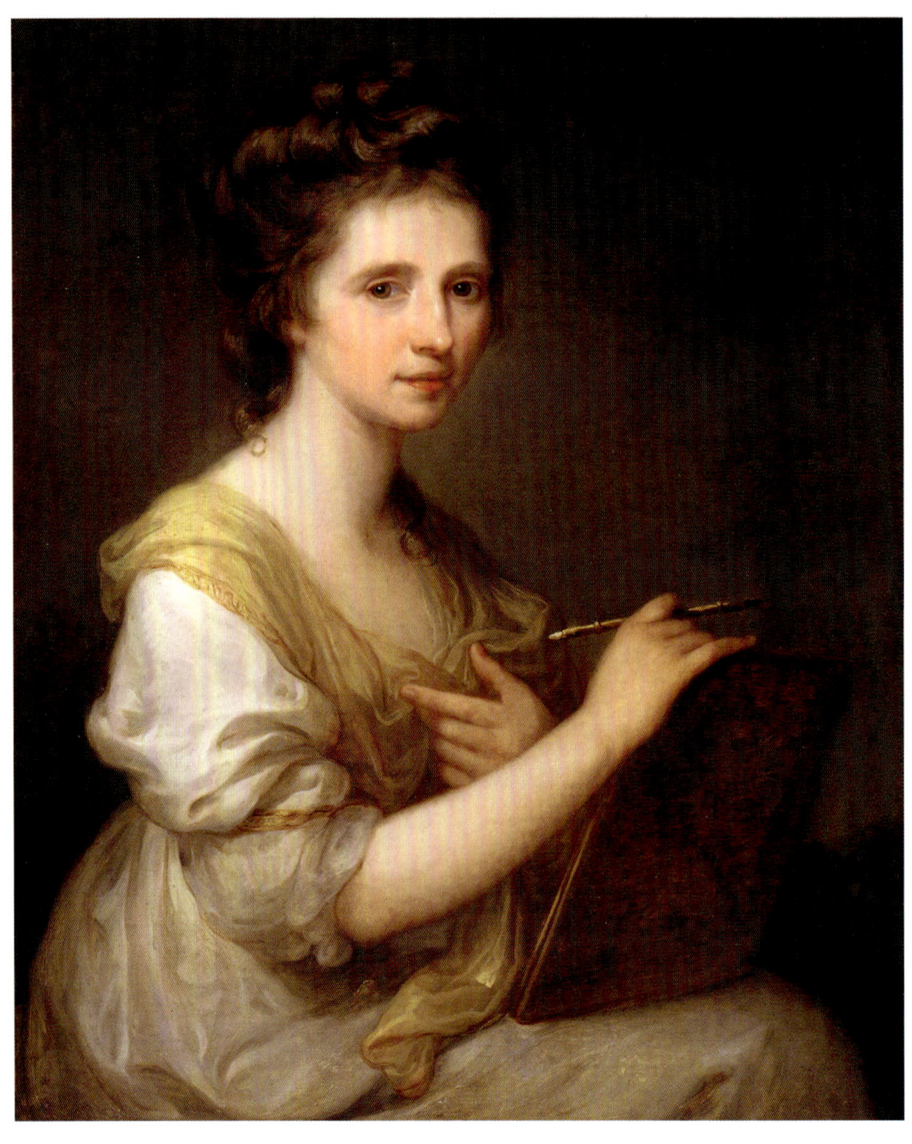

73 Angelica Kauffman, *Self-Portrait*, *c.* 1770–75.
Oil on canvas, 73.7 × 69 cm (29⅛ × 27¼ in.)

74 Henry Singleton, *The Royal Academicians in General Assembly*, 1795.
Oil on canvas, 198.1 × 259 cm (78 × 102 in.)

75 Angelica Kauffman, *Zeuxis Selecting Models for Helen of Troy*, *c.* 1778.
Oil on canvas, 71.8 × 109.2 cm (30¾ × 43 in.)

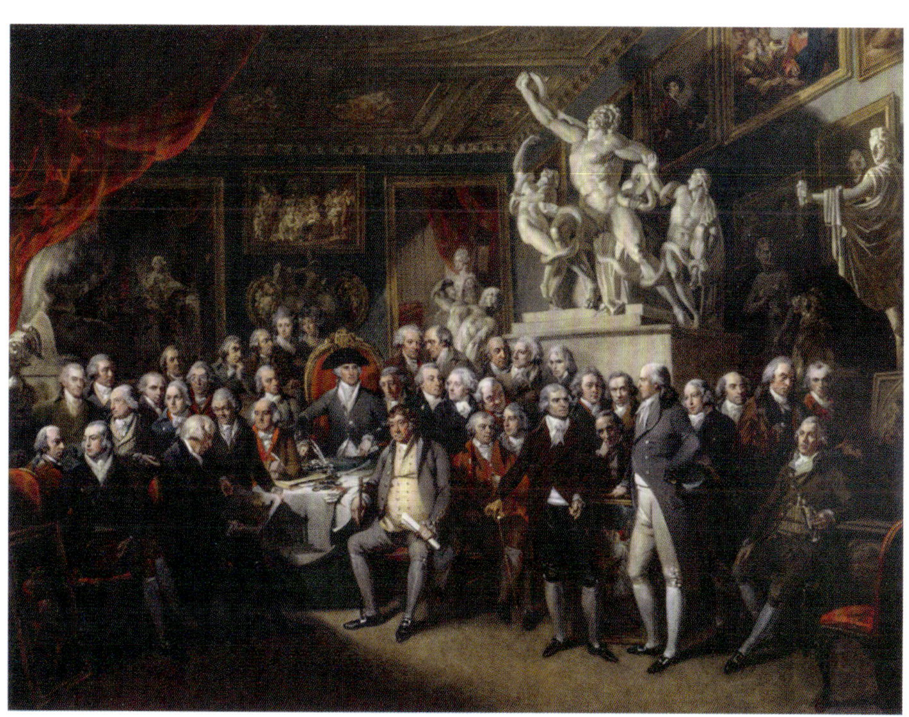

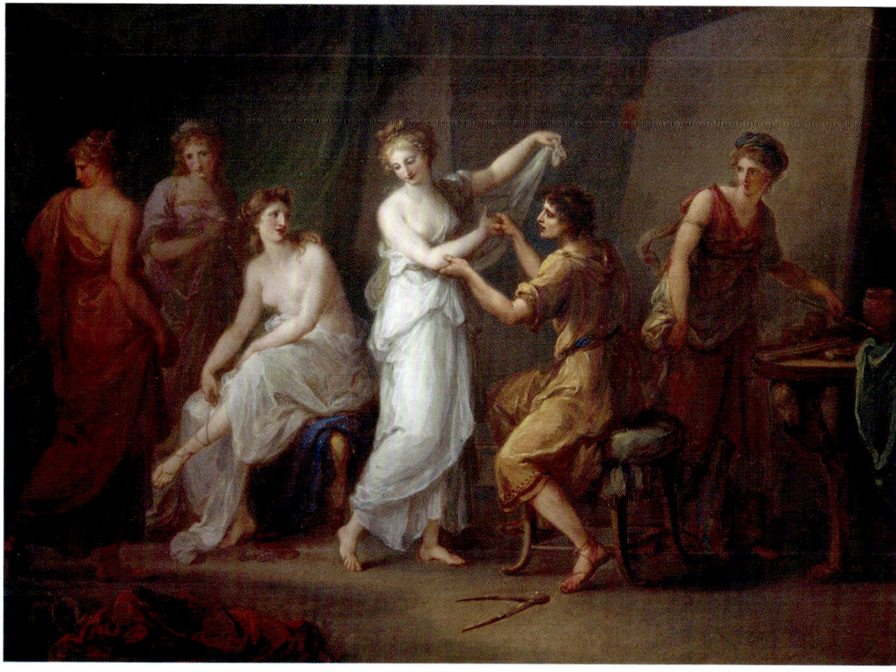

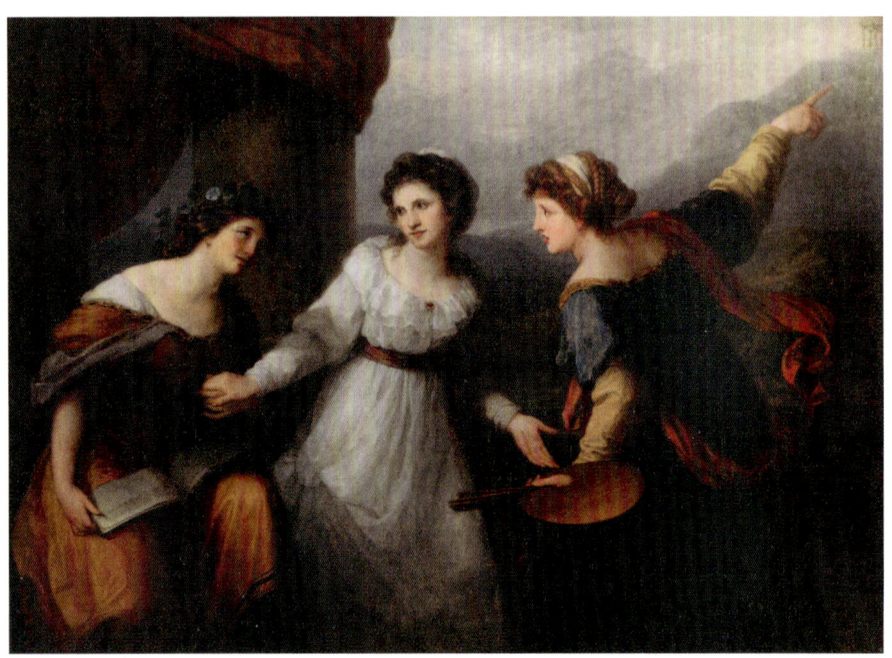

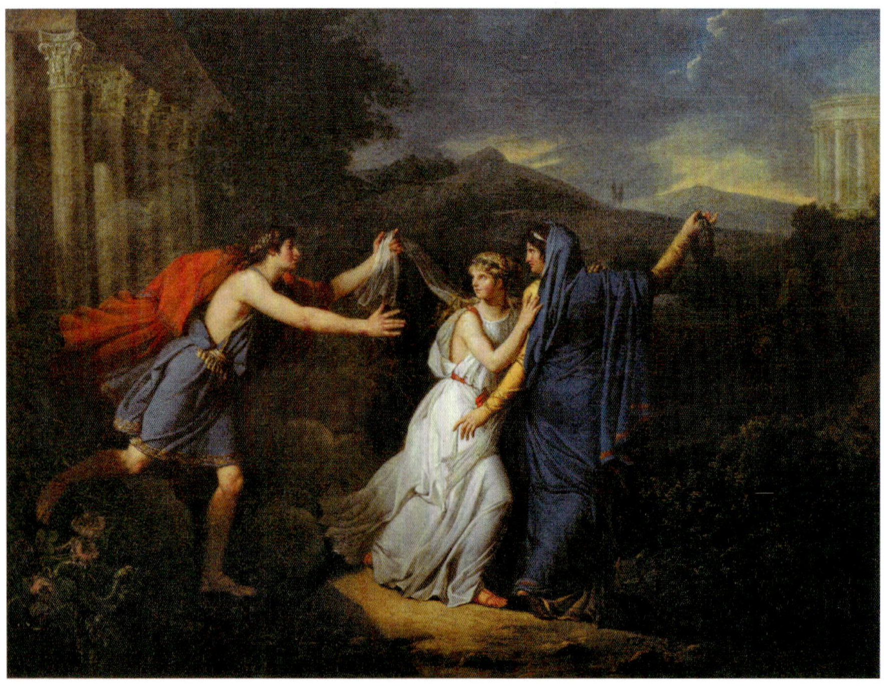

76 Angelica Kauffman, *Self-Portrait of the Artist hesitating between the Arts of Music and Painting*, 1794. Oil on canvas, 147.3 × 215.9 cm (58 × 85 in.)

77 Marie-Guillemine Laville-Leroux, *Innocence between Virtue and Vice*, 1791. Oil on canvas, 87 × 115 cm (34⅜ × 45⅜ in.)

ten, Raiatea was invaded by the men of the neighbouring island Bora Bora, resulting in Mai's father being killed and Mai himself becoming an exile on the next neighbouring island of Tahiti. These personal circumstances lay behind Mai's reasons for coming to England, as he saw the British as potential allies and suppliers of arms to fight against the men of Bora Bora to reclaim his family's land. White tapa was an indication of high rank in Polynesian society, and in Mai's eyes these robes would display to his British supporters the status he held among his people. No reference to a Western classical tradition was ever intended by Mai.

Nevertheless, Reynolds's own beliefs regarding portraiture would inevitably influence the countenance and character of the subject who came to be known as Omai. The flourishing of artistic production witnessed in Britain in the eighteenth century was underpinned both by knowledge of the Italian Renaissance brought by foreign artists such as Rubens and Van Dyck in the preceding centuries, and by what artists had seen and learned themselves on their Grand Tours of Europe. Classicism and academic theory were at the heart of what was believed to constitute great art, and as president of the newly founded Royal Academy, Reynolds argued that these lessons could be applied not only to history painting but also to portraiture. He championed these theories in his *Discourses on Art*, a series of fifteen lectures given to students at the Royal Academy between 1769 and 1790, in which he advocated a style of portraiture that would eventually become known as the Grand Manner, characterized by the idealization of the subject in a classical mode. In his fourth Discourse, Reynolds noted: 'if an exact resemblance of an individual be considered as the sole object to be aimed at, the portrait-painter will be apt to lose more than he gains by the acquired dignity taken from general nature. It is very difficult to ennoble the character of a countenance but at the expense of the likeness, which is what is most generally required by such as sit to the painter.'[20] He reveals it was not just antiquity at the forefront of his mind when it came to portraiture, and demonstrates how his primary aim to 'ennoble the character' would govern his creative process when it came to the image of Mai.[21]

In taking this approach when painting Mai, Reynolds reveals that he did not consider the subject in his natural state to be noble and that the painter needed to transform him in order to portray a higher state of being: 'But it is not enough in Invention that the Artist should restrain and keep under all the inferior parts of his subject; he must sometimes deviate from vulgar and strict historical truth, in pursuing the grandeur of his design.'[22] Reynolds's contemporaries noted that the artist was quite indifferent to likeness and conceded that he often combined truth with fiction and realism with imagination when depicting a subject.[23] However, Reynolds contradicts himself elsewhere when describing the making of the earlier portrait of Ostenaco: '[if one] meets a Cherokee Indian, who has bestowed as much time at his toilet, and laid on with equal care and attention his yellow and red oker on particular parts of his forehead or cheeks, as he judges most becoming; whoever...feels himself provoked to laugh, is the barbarian. All these fashions are very innocent; neither worth disquisition, nor any endeavour to alter them; as the change would, in all probability, be equally distant from nature.'[24] This suggests that he cannot have been entirely indifferent to likeness, which is echoed in his placement and positioning of Mai's hands, where Reynolds makes a point of emphasizing the subject's tattoos, in his words for the sake of accuracy.

The problems Reynolds faced in his depiction of Mai seem to have resulted from the fact that his subject's facial features did not exactly conform to European ideals of beauty and nobility: the noble savage needed to be improved. In his fifth Discourse, Reynolds outlined why he thought it necessary for contemporary subjects to be depicted in the style and costume of the antique: 'The simplicity of the antique air and attitude, however much to be admired, is ridiculous when joined to a figure in a modern dress.'[25] Although he makes clear in his seventh Discourse that his comments primarily relate to female dress, one cannot imagine that he would have missed the opportunity to apply such a rule to his showpiece painting of Mai.[26]

The painting's composition seems to have been based on the picture that launched Reynolds's career, his portrait of the sea captain Augustus Keppel (fig. 67), painted in 1752–53. At the time it was made, this portrait was revolutionary in British art as it moved away from the traditional static pose usually found in formal portraiture to instead depict its subject as active and dynamic. This was achieved through the use of a classical device known as the contrapposto pose, in which a figure stands with one leg taking their full weight while the other leg is relaxed, which originated in ancient sculptures such as the *Apollo Belvedere* and had already been widely used in European Renaissance portraiture.

When artists like Reynolds ennobled European individuals in the Grand Manner style, they did so with their subjects' approval, the classical allusions employed serving to aggrandize both sitter and artist. Historically, the ruling families of Italy considered themselves to be descended from ancient Roman nobility, and in the Renaissance commissioned works of art to reinforce such claims. These notions echoed down the centuries via European royal and aristocratic families and were absorbed into eighteenth-century Britain, especially the upper classes, who had undertaken a Grand Tour and wanted to reinvent their own past and present as grand and noble. To meet this demand, Reynolds envisioned a grand style of British art that would raise the nation's taste and culture through exposure to Continental and Renaissance ideals, which to him marked the pinnacle of civilization.[27]

When non-white subjects were similarly ennobled at the hands of European painters, however, such impositions take on a wholly different connotation, because these people were ennobled as 'other', rather than as individuals with personalities and inner lives. In this respect the writings of the eighteenth-century French philosopher Jean-Jacques Rousseau cannot be discounted for the impact they had on Reynolds and his wider circle of those who saw themselves as intellectuals in the eighteenth century. In works such as *Discourse on the Arts and Sciences* (1750) and *Emile, or On Education* (1762), Rousseau postulated that man is essentially good, a 'noble savage' when in the 'state of nature' (the state of all the other animals, and the condition man was in before the creation of civilization and society), and that good people are made unhappy and corrupted by their experiences in society. Although Rousseau did not invent the phrase 'noble savage' (that accolade goes to the seventeenth-century poet and playwright John Dryden), he certainly popularized it in the eighteenth century, when the term became shorthand to describe anyone seen as 'other'.

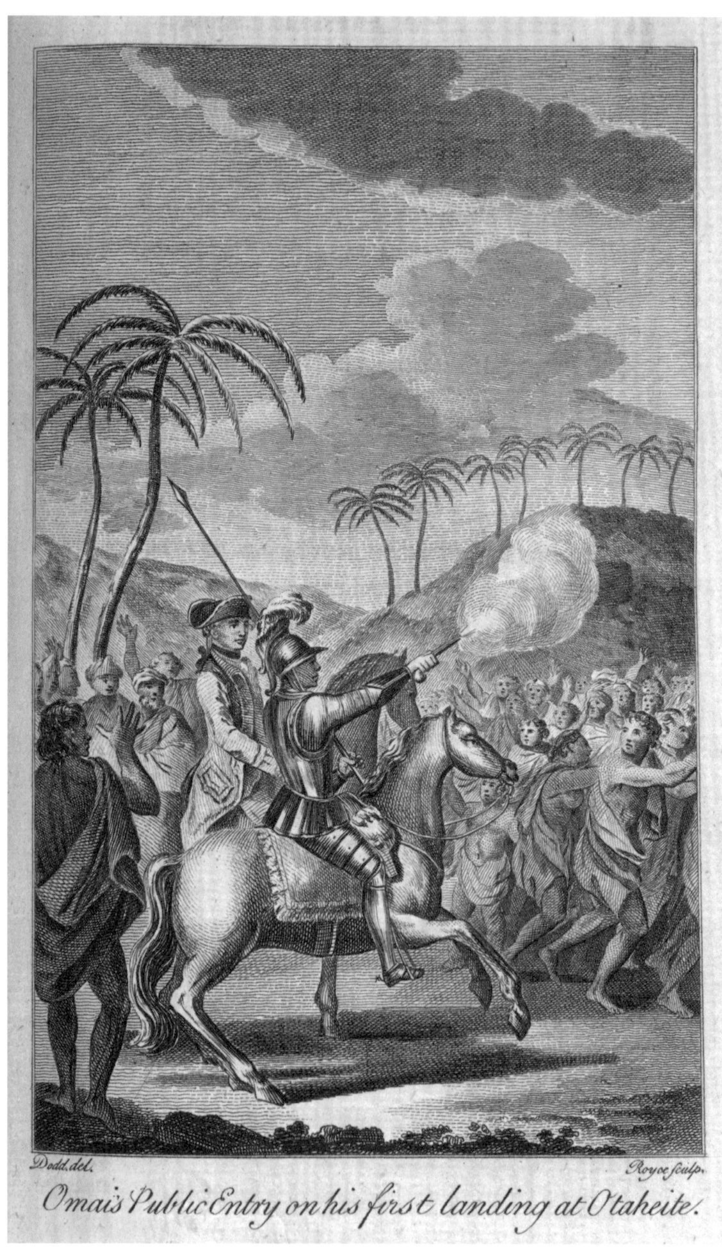

Unknown Artist, *Omai's Public Entry on his First Landing at Otaheite*, *c.* 1776. Engraving, dimensions unknown

Renaissance writings also played a part in the way non-white physiognomies could be altered to ennoble the sitter, including Giovanni Battista Alberti's 1435 publication *Della Pittura* (On Painting). With four English translations produced by the Venetian architect Giacomo Leoni between 1726 and 1755, the work would have a profound effect on Reynolds and the Royal Academy. Alberti claimed that, in depicting the human form, 'Everything should…conform to a certain dignity',[28] and the impact such teaching had on Reynolds is clear in his painting of Mai. Reynolds's own writings, along with those from the Renaissance up to the Enlightenment, fired the imaginations of the literary intelligentsia of the day, to which Reynolds and his contemporaries certainly considered themselves to belong. The timing and confluence of these ideas must have had an important influence on the public's perception of Mai as being the very embodiment of the 'noble savage'.

In the final analysis it is clear that something of Mai's personality has been lost in the many depictions of him, consumed by the fickle celebrity culture of eighteenth-century Britain and leaving us with mere avatars. It is Mai as a person that I believe has been neglected by most art historians to this day; instead, we speak of the painting and the artist. In these fragments represented by the images of him, it seems something of the original man was left behind in England, and it is unlikely that the Mai who left Tahiti was the same person who returned there two years later in 1777.

His return seems to have been precipitated by the unfortunate fact that English society had become bored with this latest novelty; Mai's brief moment of fame was over because he was now indelibly tainted by European ways and English society, becoming the antithesis of the philosophies propounded by Rousseau. Commentators remarked that Joseph Banks and his entourage 'have made him more of the fine Gentlemen than anything else' and taught him 'nothing…but to play cards, at which he is very expert'.[29] Unfortunately, Mai's plans to use his British allies to defeat those who had killed his father and taken his land did not come to fruition. The British returned him not to his home island of Raiatea but instead to Tahiti. The Mai who returned to the South Pacific was a new Europeanized man who felt himself to be thoroughly

British; he rode ashore on a stallion, wearing a suit of armour given to him by the Earl of Sandwich, First Lord of the Admiralty.

His return was depicted by an unknown engraver, possibly in the same year, but it is not possible to discern whether this image presents a realistic portrayal of the event (p. 228). Believing himself now to be better than his fellow South Pacific islanders, he even managed to insult the King of Tahiti by rejecting his daughter on the grounds that she was too plain. Apparently fearing for his safety, Cook removed Mai to the neighbouring island of Huahine, hoping to avoid bloodshed and territorial battles between Mai and the Tahitian islanders. Mai was set up with a house of European design, built by ships' carpenters, and given some guns and gunpowder, livestock, a Bible, a barrel organ and a collection of miniature soldiers. But even here he did not fit in; the islanders grew intensely jealous of him, and he soon became isolated. Back in Britain, some commentators said that Omai had been returned home without knowledge, skills 'or articles of real use' to his people or himself.[30]

Reynolds painted the image of Mai without a specific commission or buyer for the work. Nevertheless, it debuted to great acclaim when it was exhibited at the eighth Royal Academy exhibition in 1776. Although the artist never went to Tahiti, the invented tropical location in which he placed Mai, with palm trees and mountainous terrain in the distance, conforms to the European fashion for paradise and the exotic, and certainly benefits from Reynolds's knowledge of the landscape paintings by William Hodges, John Webber, and the many other artists who did travel to the South Pacific islands. Sadly, Mai was not present for the grand unveiling, and he died perhaps four years later in his house in Huahine, probably before his thirtieth birthday. According to a later missionary, William Ellis, 'The spot where Mai's house stood is still called Beritani, or Britain' by the local inhabitants, echoing the name of the place that irreversibly changed Mai's life forever.

11

Angelica Kauffman

The Grand Tour and the Europeanization
of British Art

By the mid-eighteenth century, a Grand Tour of Europe was firmly established as a rite of passage for male British artists and aristocrats, underwritten
by the wealth Britain had accumulated through industry and centuries of
global trade including, of course, the continued trade in enslaved people.[1]
The legacy of these Grand Tours was tangible back home as they enabled
rich patrons to embellish their town and country houses with art collections,
while artists returned from Italy enthused by their exposure to classical and
Renaissance art. The legacy of this increased learning led to the foundation
of the Royal Academy of Arts in London in 1768, with Sir Joshua Reynolds
appointed as its first president. Educational theories were firmly based on
the premise that foreign artistic ideas were the very pinnacle of creativity, rooted in a belief in the supremacy of the male form and the supposed
intellectual superiority of men. Nevertheless, among the thirty-six founder
members of the Royal Academy were two women: Mary Moser, an English
painter and daughter of the Swiss-born artist George Michael Moser, and
the Swiss artist Angelica Kauffman.

Kauffman was born on 30 October 1741 in the large Swiss town of
Chur, and as a child travelled with her parents between Switzerland,
Austria and northern Italy for her father's work. Her father, Joseph
Johann Kauffman, a painter of religious scenes and imagined classical
architectural vistas, seems to have been responsible for her early artistic
training,[2] while her mother, Cleophea Lutz, gave Angelica instruction in
music and languages.[3] This would have been an unusually rounded education for a woman at the time, and Angelica was clearly something of a

child prodigy in both music and art. Her earliest known painting, a reasonably accomplished self-portrait holding a sheet of music, was made in *c.* 1753, when she was just twelve (p. 234). She had an excellent soprano singing voice, played the clavichord for aristocratic families throughout northern Italy, and went on to master four languages (German, Italian, French and English) while still in her teens.

The death of her mother in 1757 likely put to rest any further ambitions Angelica held to pursue a musical career. However, she had been accepting painting commissions since the age of fifteen, and around 1757–59 she produced a *Self-Portrait in Bregenzerwald Costume with Brush and Palette* (Uffizi, Florence), in which her intention to be seen as an artist is made clear by the painter's tools she confidently holds. Her international ambitions are suggested by the traditional costume she wears, which hails from the mountainous, forested Bregenzerwald region in Austria, just on the border with her native Switzerland. It would not be long before she would head across the border in the other direction, to Italy, arriving in 1760, shortly before her twentieth birthday.

Kauffman travelled widely in Italy throughout the 1760s with her father (who had quickly realized that his daughter's skill and ambitions had surpassed his own) in pursuit of her aim to become a professional artist. At this time Rome was a hotbed of artistic and antiquarian activity. The celebrated antiquarian Johann Joachim Winckelmann was living in the city from about 1758, giving guided tours of Roman antiquities to German (and occasionally English) Grand Tourists,[4] and in 1764 his book *History of the Art of Antiquity* was published to critical acclaim. Winckelmann's interest in classical antiquity was further fuelled and informed by the discoveries at Herculaneum and Pompeii, which had started to be systematically excavated in 1738 and 1748 respectively, and he visited the sites in the late 1760s with his friend, the German painter Anton Raphael Mengs, one of the most famous artists in Europe at this time. Mengs was among the artists influenced by Winckelmann's writings whose style began to move in the 1760s from the dominant Rococo style, characterized by excess and exuberance, towards a more sober aesthetic that consciously took formal elements and subjects from classical art, a style that would come to be known as neo-classicism.

Winckelmann and Mengs were among the many prominent figures Kauffman met and befriended during her travels in Italy. In 1764 she produced a portrait of Winckelmann, along with her earliest single-figured history painting, *Penelope at her Loom* (fig. 68). This early mythological work, which concentrates solely on the leading female protagonist in *The Odyssey*, demonstrates that Kauffman shared an interest in the ancient world with the renowned antiquarian, and signals her intention to venture into the male-dominated art world on her own terms. Her close friendship with Winckelmann would set her on the path towards changing her own artistic style towards a neo-classical direction.

It is clear that Kauffman learned a lot quickly during her time in Italy: a portrait she painted of her father during this period is one by a mature artist, distinct from her works of only a few years earlier (fig. 69). She copied works by Correggio in Parma and Annibale Carracci in Bologna, and in 1762 she obtained special permission to copy in the Uffizi in Florence, later producing a copy of a Rembrandt self-portrait in pencil on paper. That year she was accepted into Florence's prestigious Accademia del Disegno, and the equivalent institutions in Bologna and Rome in 1765.[5] In Italy Kauffman became an integral part of an international group of intellectuals, going on to form close friendships with figures including the German writer Johann Wolfgang von Goethe, the French revolutionary Jean-Paul Marat and the English poet George Keate.

With a glittering European career under her belt, in 1766 Kauffman arrived in England. Already there was her friend, the Philadelphia-born artist Benjamin West, who had spent three years in Italy studying Renaissance art before arriving in London in 1763. Between them, Kauffman and West can be said to have introduced the neo-classical style to Britain, with works such as Kauffman's *Venus Appearing to Aeneas, Penelope with the Bow of Ulysses* and *Hector Taking Leave of Andromache*, and West's *Farewell of Regulus and Venus* and *Venus Mourning the Death of Adonis*.[6] A founder member of the Royal Academy and its second president, succeeding Joshua Reynolds in 1792, West became one of the most celebrated American painters in Britain, so much so that when he died in 1820 his acceptance into the pantheon of British art was effectively endorsed by his burial in St Paul's Cathedral, in the company of such luminaries as Horatio Nelson, Anthony van Dyck and Joshua Reynolds.

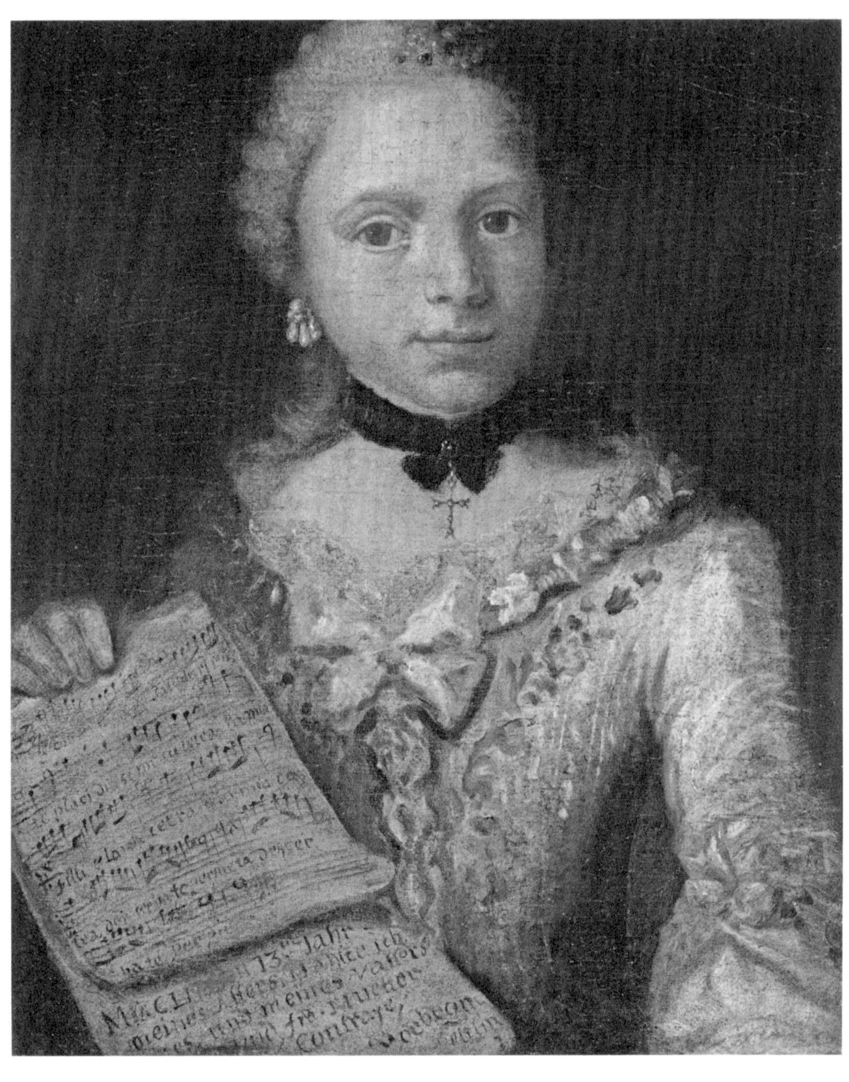

Angelica Kauffman, *Self-Portrait as a Singer*, c. 1753.
Oil on canvas, 49.5 × 40.5 cm (19½ × 16 in.)

In Britain Kauffman encountered attitudes that had the potential to hinder her artistic progress, with institutionalized inequalities between men and women entrenched in the nation's educational practices. Ideas around study of the visual arts were dominated by pseudo-scientific theories, which posited that men were able to learn through watching, whereas women could learn only by undertaking activities themselves.[7] Interestingly, such ideas were not especially reflected in the Renaissance writings that held such sway in the eighteenth century; the Italian courtier Baldassare Castiglione claimed in 1528, for instance, that 'women can understand all things men can understand, and…the intellect of a woman can penetrate wherever a man's can'.[8]

Despite these obstacles the twenty-five-year-old Kauffman managed to set up her own studio in London shortly after her arrival, and she quickly became the talk of the town. Excited letters home to her father seem to confirm her almost immediate success: 'I have finished some portraits which are snapped up by everyone, Mr Reynolds is excessively pleased with them…This morning I had a visit from Mrs Garrick. Milady Spencer was here two days ago. Lord Baltimore also visits me occasionally. The Queen was delivered of a child two days ago, as soon as she is better, I shall be presented to her.'[9]

Not all the talk around town was about Kauffman's art or previous achievements though; much of it related to her private life. Under this gendered and intrusive lens, she was rumoured to be having relationships with many of the fellow artists she had spent time with while practising her art on the Continent. Reynolds was said to have proposed to her, while others talked of a brief flirtation with the printmaker William Wynne Ryland and a possible affair with West. The fact that Kauffman quickly established friendships with the leading artists of the day only added credence to these rumours in people's minds (had they been directed at a male artist, they would no doubt have been viewed in a favourable light).

The quality of Kauffman's art was clearly not uppermost in the thoughts of the British public, who seemed unable to see beyond her gender in conversations about her work. The ongoing besmirching of Kauffman's private life was clearly grounded in incredulity that a woman – moreover an unmarried one – would dare to flout convention with her presence in areas that men felt were their exclusive domain. Kauffman had clearly spent time in Reynolds's studio for instance, as attested by her production of both a study and a subsequent finished portrait of him (fig. 71). While the gossip did not hinder her ability to make art that was appreciated by many aficionados, as long as she continued to operate and earn comparable wages in an arena controlled by men, false rumours regarding her public reputation would continuously be used in what amounted to a smear campaign to undermine her work and social standing. The situation was not helped by Kauffman's marriage just a year after her arrival in England to a man calling himself Count Frederick de Horn, who claimed to be a nobleman of good reputation and sound financial standing. It soon transpired that not only was he already married, he was not even a count, but rather a con artist whose true intention was to remain in England through marriage to Kauffman and no doubt the extortion of money from her family. When the deception was discovered, Kauffman's father had to pay off the con artist to be rid of him, and Horn fled the country soon after.[10]

A year or two before this event, the artist Nathaniel Dance painted a portrait of Kauffman that acknowledged her status as an artist and also her status in society, judging by her sumptuous dress, fringed with lace and furs (fig. 70). The ambiguity of the painting's date means it may have been painted before her arrival in England, as Dance was one of the many British artists abroad on the Grand Tour at this time. Unfortunately, sitting for a man in the privacy of his studio sparked yet another scandal, and it was said that Kauffman and Dance had been engaged in Italy, but that she had broken off the engagement shortly before coming to England. Not surprisingly this story has never been substantiated by any credible facts beyond a dubious and frankly biased letter written by Dance's brother, who sought to blame Kauffman for his brother's disappointment in not securing a relationship with her.[11]

While Kauffman's position as an unmarried woman without children allowed her to devote her time entirely to her profession, the patriarchal society in which she lived still restricted her activities. In this respect Kauffman was a victim of her era, in which the ideals of the classical world and the Renaissance were placed on an intellectual pedestal, and it was believed only men possessed the ability to comprehend such lofty concepts. The artist would spend her creative life trying to prove herself the equal of men in this arena, but the gatekeepers of taste and art institutions were inevitably men, and as the ultimate judges of her work they did not always hold the impartiality deemed essential by the English artist Jonathan Richardson in his 1719 essay *The Science of a Connoisseur*, who reasoned that: 'To be a connoisseur, a man must be as free from all kinds of prejudice as possible; he must moreover have a clear and exact way of thinking and reasoning; he must know how to take in, and manage just ideas; and throughout he must have not only a solid, but unbiased judgement.'[12] Nevertheless, Kauffman was determined to prove through her work that she belonged alongside the men, possibly in the hope she might gain acceptance through merit alone. In a self-portrait (fig. 73) made perhaps five or ten years after the Dance portrait, and based on it compositionally, she again emphasizes her professional status as an artist, but this time depicts herself in semi-classical costume, reflecting the dominant artistic interest in the antique. Yet she was still some considerable distance from being placed on an equal footing with her male counterparts. According to her earliest biographer, Giovanni Gherardo De Rossi, when Kauffman was struggling to choose a profession, a local priest advised that early success in a musical career would be comparatively easy and initially more lucrative, but the life of a performer might present dangers for a young Catholic lady, as it would not allow time for proper religious observance. On the other hand, he argued, while a career in painting would require more training and probably not bring immediate success, this more intellectual and arduous profession could ultimately present greater rewards.[13] This proved to be the case, as just two years after her arrival in England Kauffman became part of the establishment as a founding member of the Royal Academy.

The critical acclaim Kauffman's work received across Europe brought connoisseurs and scholars to Britain. Among them was Helfrich Peter Sturz, an attaché of the German Foreign Office, who accompanied King Christian VII of Denmark and Sweden (r. 1766–1808) on his Grand Tour of Europe in 1768–69, arriving in London in September 1768. A month after visiting Kauffman's London home in Golden Square,

Sturz commented that 'while enjoying one of my most beautiful days at Garrick's country house [I saw] Garrick's portrait, painted by our country-woman Angelica Kauffmann, hung amid a whole collection of paintings of famous actors and actresses who all appear in important scenes of their plays and presented with much expression.'[14] On his visit to Kauffman's studio, Sturz acquired a few prints from the artist, among them an etching of Winckelmann. This was singled out for praise by Sturz, who said that Kauffman had captured the 'flaming gaze' of the renowned Prussian antiquarian, 'which found in Apollo's nose the contempt of the gods, and the Hercules in the Torso'.[15]

Yet it is clear that Sturz also could not separate Kauffman's art from her gender, going on to comment that, 'In her figure and in her paintings, in her speech and her motion, only a single tone is dominant; namely virginal dignity.'[16] These backhanded compliments and lack of objectivity reveal that some prejudices remained firmly entrenched in this seemingly intellectual milieu, and functioned as a barrier to women working in those artistic areas to which male artists claimed exclusive rights, especially the genre of history painting. Despite Kauffman's learned academic approach, Sturz still remarked on her weakness in drawing and her shortcomings in the anatomy of the nude.[17] Still, he acknowledged that her forms were 'full of grace', while also criticizing her rendering of the male figure.[18]

In these statements Sturz was echoing comments made in 1767 by the Swiss painter, art historian and lexicographer Johann Rudolf Füssli, who complained that 'Kauffmann understood the ancients but revealed too much of her own sex in her male figures'.[19] But whether or not Kauffman engendered her male figures with a high degree of effeminacy was beside the point according to Winckelmann, who rushed to her defence by noting in her work the androgynous qualities of ancient Greek sculptures such as the *Apollo Belvedere* and Renaissance sculptures such as Donatello's bronze *David*. The received but invented wisdom surrounding the practice of history painting centred around the idea that the skills and extensive knowledge of literature required to draw the human figure could not be understood or learned by women, and female artists were instead encouraged to restrict themselves to still life, flower painting or portraiture, so-called lesser genres that were considered to require no intellectual engagement or mastery of anatomy. Portrait painting, for instance, was seen as purely mechanical, as it was thought that no imagination was needed to copy what was in front of you. To a certain extent thereafter, critics would attack the entire genre of portraiture, the area in which Kauffman made most of her earnings both while in England and abroad.

Notably, no such criticism was levelled at the drawing of a nude model from life, as seen in Johann Zoffany's 1771–72 painting *The Academicians of the Royal Academy* (fig. 72). This work, set in the Royal Academy's life-drawing room, depicts the Academy's thirty-four male founding members, including Reynolds, gathered around a nude man to draw him (interestingly, a practice for which Renaissance biographers including Bellori had criticized Caravaggio).[20] The inclusion of the two female founder members, Kauffman and Moser, as mere portraits on the wall in the Zoffany painting serves as a graphic realization of the position of women in the so-called enlightened world of British art in the eighteenth century. Similarly in Henry Singleton's painting of 1795, *The Royal Academicians in General Assembly* (fig. 74), they are pushed to the far background. With such prejudices consolidated into establishment practice, women were effectively barred from studying in a life class, with societal norms suggesting that their inclusion would be seen as inappropriate and could undermine their standing in society, an attitude that served to keep them at some distance from the genre of history painting, considered the highest form of art.

Despite these obstacles, Kauffman did work in the genre of history painting, introducing and popularizing British historical subjects. Presenting medieval scenes such as *The Tender Eleanora Sucking the Venom out of the Wound* (p. 240), she sparked a revival of interest in British history that fed into the widespread celebrations of the bicentenary of Shakespeare's birth in 1764. In awakening this renewed interest, Kauffman undoubtedly paved the way for the similar subjects that were produced by the Pre-Raphaelite Brotherhood eighty years later.

Artists and aristocrats in Britain had long held an ambition to incorporate the sheen of academia into the art of painting. For instance, in 1713 Anthony Ashley Cooper, 3rd Earl of Shaftsbury, likened Hercules' choice

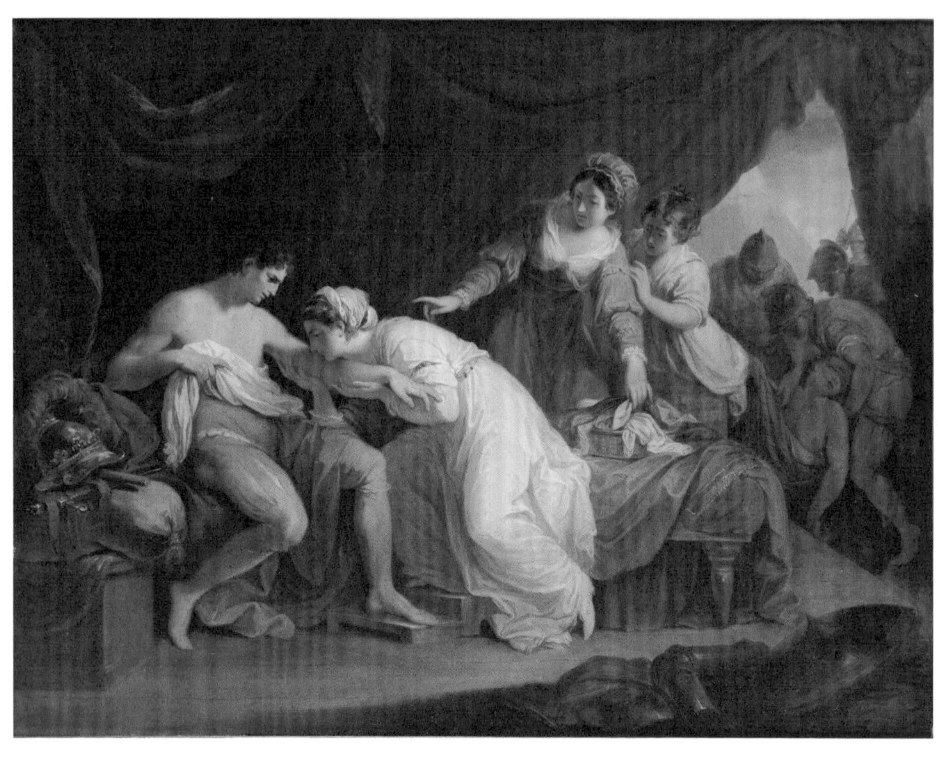

Angelica Kauffman, *The Tender Eleanora Sucking the Venom out of the Wound which Edward I, her Royal Consort, received with a Poisoned Dagger from an Assassin in Palestine*, c. 1780. Oil on canvas, 86.4 × 96.7 cm (34⅛ × 38⅛ in.)

between the easy path of pleasure and the hard path of virtue as similar to the one between a life of pleasure – which could be ascribed to the perceived ease of portrait or still-life painting – versus the virtuous and much harder path of history painting.[21] While the production of historical or mythological subjects was seen as the only way an artist in Britain could be taken seriously by the art establishment of the day, the reality was that portraiture was by far the genre most requested by patrons. Artists and critics were clearly not impressed with its popularity; in 1771 the botanical artist Mary Delany noted: 'This morning we have been to see Mr. West's and Mrs. Angelica's paintings, introduced by Mr Crispin, whom I like extremely. My partiality leans to my sister painter, but I like her history still better than her portraits.'[22]

Although Delany encouraged Kauffman's interest in this genre, there were clearly misgivings around the idea of a woman straying into the field of history painting. One critic though, writing in the *Middlesex Journal* in 1772, proved an exception to the generally negative criticism and acknowledged Kauffman's skill in this area: 'This lady seems to have a peculiar turn for history painting, in which branch of the arts she has long since acquired a very eminent character.'[23] It is clear from the number of surviving portraits painted by Kauffman that the genre made up a substantial part of her income, but it is also clear that it was not this work that won her critical praise.

While a minority in Britain encouraged history painting as a means of demonstrating sophistication to their Continental rivals, the majority of those commissioning art, such as the landed gentry, just wanted pictures of themselves and their possessions, including their wives, land, property and children. On the occasion of a Royal Academy exhibition in May 1775, a critic writing in the *Public Advertiser* noted: 'It has long been a matter of complaint in this Country, that there is very little Encouragement for Historical Painting; and that most Men extend their Ideas of Painting no farther than to get their own Portrait executed, and perhaps that of their Wife, or favourite Child.' Nevertheless, the piece optimistically goes on: 'The public Exhibitions have kindled an Emulation among the Artists; and above all, the ROYAL PATRONAGE AND PROTECTION has set an Example of Encouragement to the Rich and Great; so that at present when artists arise in the historical Line (of such acknowledged Merit as Mr West and Signora Angelica) there can be no doubt of their being fully employed and amply rewarded.'[24]

In 1781 Kauffman decided to leave England. Her departure was seen by some as a great loss to painting in Britain, as expressed by her friend George Keate, poet, painter, and friend of Voltaire. In his *Epistle to Angelica Kauffman* (1781), Keate conjured an image of a grief-stricken nation struggling to come to terms with the loss of one of its own.[25] In the fifteen years she spent in London, Kauffman had been at the very heart of the British art scene and society, achieving much, including the accumulation of a large personal fortune calculated at £14,000.[26]

In leaving Britain, Kauffman did not escape the continued gendered criticism directed at her work, especially the rendering of male figures, as exemplified in the *Lyric Ode to Royal Academicians* penned in 1782 by John Wolcot under the pseudonym 'Peter Pindar':

> Angelica my plaudits gains,
>
> Her art so sweetly stains,
>
> Her Dames, so gracious, give me such delight:
>
> But were she married to such gentle Males,
>
> As figures in her painted tales
>
> I fear she'd find a stupid wedding mate.

The painting, *Zeuxis Selecting Models for Helen of Troy* (fig. 75), made when she was still in England, around 1778, once again demonstrates Kauffman's knowledge and interest in the antique, along with her ability to manipulate the classical story to her own ends. In the scene the models prepare to be judged by the ancient Greek artist Zeuxis, who selects the best features of each one to create the perfect woman. But in Kauffman's rendition, one of the models seems to defy the act of objectification by circumventing Zeuxis to take up the artist's tools behind his back and approach the empty canvas. The painting has often been seen as semi-autobiographical, offering a metaphor for Kauffman's own life. Another piece in the *Public Advertiser*, dating from May 1786, paints a vivid picture of just how ungrateful some of her contemporaries were for her contribution to British painting:

These pictures possess that character which usually constitutes her works, but they do not appear to be either so beautifully conceived, or tasty in their execution, as to drawing characters, or colour, as those which she painted in England. They seem to be done from memory of her former works, and no new beauties have been added to her style by her late tour to Italy. Here perhaps it may be proper to remark that there is now established in this country a school of art much superior to what may be found on any part of the Continent, there being at this moment in England a greater number of living artists, excelling in different branches, envious of each other, and striving with a spirit of enthusiasm, which has left our neighbours far behind. Amongst other foreign artists this country is certainly indebted to Signora Kauffman. She had enriched the cabinets of the curious with many elegant performances, composed and executed in her best time; and though she has withdrawn herself from us, her best works and her taste remain with us.[27]

This writer not only disparagingly refers to Kauffman as a foreigner, despite the fact she is now claimed as a British painter, but also suggests that Britain is somehow superior to the rest of Continental Europe in its approach to art and art appreciation. The statement represents an attitude that continues to be deeply rooted in the British psyche.

Some of Kauffman's most feted history paintings, including *Bacchus and Ariadne* and *Paris and Helen*, were made after she left Britain. This final chapter of her life would be the most celebrated and well documented, principally because a *Memorandum* of her paintings was meticulously maintained by her second husband, the Italian painter Antonio Zucchi, whom she married in 1781, following the death of her first husband.[28] It is likely that they met soon after Kauffman's arrival in London in 1766. Made an Associate of the Royal Academy in 1770, Zucchi had long been established as a successful painter and draughtsman and took an active professional interest in Kauffman's work in the form of his *Memorandum*. The couple married when Zucchi was fifty-five and Kauffman was thirty-nine. Also unusual was their marriage contract, which bestowed Kauffman with complete autonomy over her

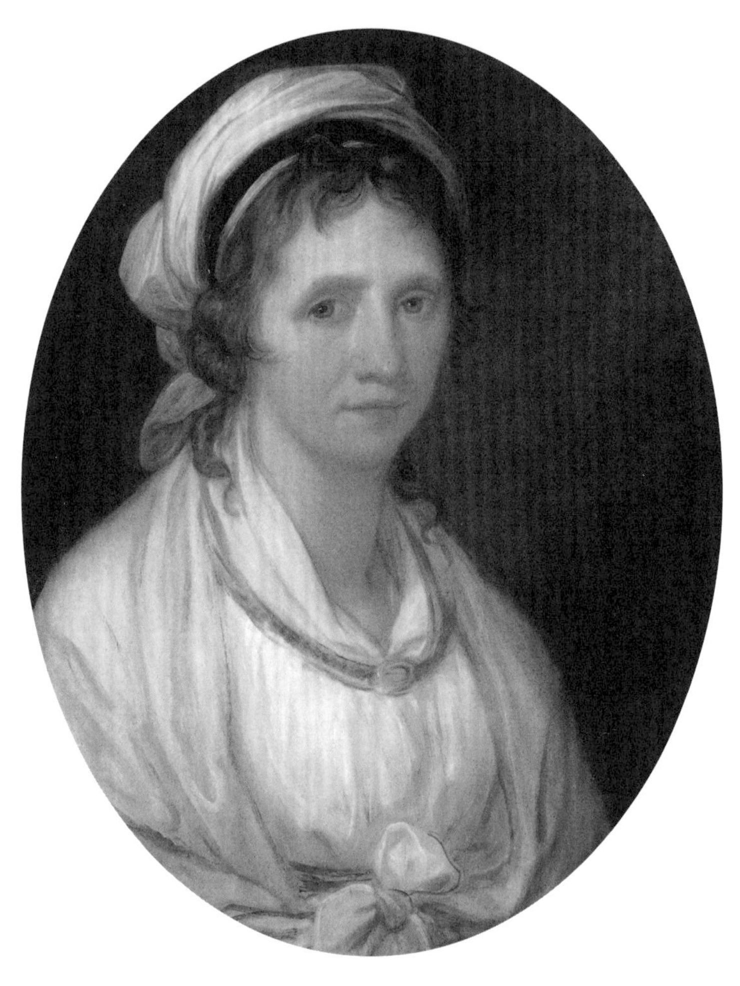

Angelica Kauffman, *Self-Portrait*, *c.* 1800.
Oil on canvas, 60 × 50 cm (23⅝ × 19¾ in.)

own income and even protected her against any debts that Zucchi might incur.[29] Such an extraordinary arrangement, likely intended as a safeguard following the problems of her first marriage, clearly advantaged Kauffman, since she set up their home with a considerably larger income than her husband. One can only imagine that Zucchi must have been a somewhat enlightened man for the period.

Although it is often suggested that Kauffman and Zucchi collaborated on decorative schemes for private houses, there is no real documentary evidence for this, as they painted in their respective studios in London rather than in situ. Set up in 1781 on the via Sistina, the couple's sumptuous house in Rome became a locus for fashionable Grand Tourists from Britain. Among those who visited Kauffman in Rome were her friend the art dealer Thomas Jenkins, whose portrait Kauffman made in 1790, and Thomas Noel Hill, 2nd Baron Berwick, whom Kauffman had painted in 1773. On this occasion Hill commissioned two paintings with themes from Greek mythology, including another version of *Bacchus and Ariadne*, this one painted in 1794.

History painting never really flourished as a popular genre in Britain in quite the way portraiture did and, despite her success as a portraitist, Kauffman's career was somewhat curtailed by the lack of interest in this area in which she clearly wanted to make a name for herself and be seen as having an equal intellect and social standing with her male counterparts. Such art was in demand on the Continent though, both from Italians and from European Grand Tourists, and so her departure to Italy was inevitable. Now away from negative criticism in Britain, Kauffman's painting business flourished, and through her numerous contacts she was able to procure the most lucrative commissions, including from the royal family of Naples, who also employed her to teach drawing. She was so successful that she was even able to turn down a permanent position at the royal household in favour of retaining her independence. This proved to be a shrewd move because it also allowed her to undertake large-scale history painting commissions from influential patrons including Emperor Josef of Austria and Catherine the Great of Russia. Zucchi recorded in his *Memorandum of Paintings* that within a few months of arriving in Venice in October 1781, Angelica had sold three history paintings to the Grand Duke of Russia.

Her move to Italy did not preclude Kauffman from continuing to send paintings to the annual Royal Academy exhibitions; *Bacchus Teaching the Nymphs to make Verses*, for example, was exhibited in 1788, seven years after her departure. Between 1791 and 1794, Kauffman produced two versions of a *Self-Portrait of the Artist hesitating between the Arts of Music and Painting* (fig. 76), in which she depicted through allegory her struggle to decide between the two paths. It is extraordinary to consider that Kauffman, who was in her fifties when she produced these paintings, had perhaps still not yet fully made up her mind about the direction of her professional career, or maybe she was reflecting on the decision she had made so long ago and the path she had subsequently travelled. It is more than likely that these paintings also represent a show of support and homage, because compositionally they closely follow the debut work (also made in 1791) of the twenty-three-year-old French painter Marie-Guillemine Laville-Leroux (fig. 77), who had been trained by the equally talented Elisabeth Vigée Le Brun.

Just a year after completing these paintings, entries to the *Memorandum* ceased with the death of Zucchi in 1795. Kauffman survived her husband by a further twelve years. In one of her final self-portraits, painted 1800, we observe the artist modestly dressed, with no need to declare her status or indeed her profession, because at this stage of her life she had little else to prove (p. 244). She died on 5 November 1807 at the age of sixty-six, and in one of the longest processions the city of Rome had ever seen, friends and members of the Academy of St Luke's accompanied her to her final resting place beside her husband in the Basilica of Sant'Andrea della Fratte.

Kauffman's fame sadly did not continue after her death in the manner that immortalized her male counterparts. Almost a century later, Kauffman's reputation and skill as an artist was still being called into question in certain quarters. In 1905 the writer on art and architecture Walter Shaw Sparrow assembled and edited an overview, *Women Painters of the World*, in which he observed:

> Angelica Kauffman, R.A., though born at Coire, the capital of the
> Grisons, belongs to the British school, and holds in the early history
> of that school a position similar to that which has been assigned in

France to Madame Vigée Le Brun. The art of the two ladies differs widely to be sure, that of Angelica Kauffman having less mirth, less wit, less sprightliness and homeful sincerity; it is quite artificial in spirit, with a strong bias towards the sentimental; but it has for all that considerable charm and ability, qualities, let us remember, that won the admiration of Reynolds and of Goethe. Turner, also, possessed two of her drawings, as I am told by his descendant, Mr Charles Mallord W. Turner…But in recent times Angelica Kauffman has been remembered for the romance of her personal life and treated with cool contempt in all that appertains to her work. Critics have searched in her pictures for manly qualities, and finding there the temperament of a sentimental woman, their judgment has failed them. The very men who would be astonished beyond measure if a prima donna sang to them in a voice like the leading tenor's, do not hesitate to complain when the voice in a woman's painting is one filled with womanhood.[30]

Angelica Kauffman and Mary Moser were never 'elected' as Royal Academicians; they were 'invited' (a technicality because the election system was not yet in place).[31] But following the death of Moser in 1819, no women were elected to the Royal Academy for at least a century. The next was the painter Annie Swynnerton, a supporter of the suffragette movement and friend of the Pankhursts, who was selected in 1922, followed a decade later by Laura Knight.

Like so many who wish to succeed under the dictates of their age, Kauffman subscribed to the conventions of the eighteenth-century artistic establishment, dominated by classical subjects and Renaissance ideals, and like her friend Joshua Reynolds her paintings are products of their time. Yet in the relatively short time she spent in England, she captured in her work an exciting and historically important moment in British society and art history, both in the sitters she portrayed and in her unique take on mythological subjects, in the process, embellishing houses in both Britain and Europe with integral decorative schemes. The pictures she made in England, and those executed after her departure, injected what was seen at the time as European sophistication into British art, and raised the nation's standing on the Continent. Kauffman's competency, skill and contribution to British art has begun to be recognized and appreciated in recent times in the form of exhibitions and the permanent display of her works in major British art institutions. Perhaps this relatively recent reassessment of her work will now recognize her as an artist worthy of being judged on an equal footing within the canon of art history, free from the gender bias and xenophobia that plagued her in the openly patriarchal society in which she lived and worked.

Afterword

Nations with an imperial past (of which there are many) are often shackled by a false sense of superiority and permanency. Such ideas sometimes result in a nostalgic reinvention of an edited past, which can lead to self-righteousness and little acknowledgment of those who came from elsewhere and helped to create and shape the national culture. This attitude frequently presents in a belief that, as a nation, they have achieved all they have with no help from anyone, a false perception of autodidacticism and being 'self-made'. But, as my late mother used to say to my arrogant younger self, 'no man is an island'. As a person of colour born in England, I grew up in a country that did not want me here, or at least sought to emphasize my difference with questions such as 'where are you from? I mean where are you *really* from?', even though this was the only place I knew. Unlike the artists discussed in this book, I had neither the extensive experience of European travel nor the required white skin colour to pass and assimilate without drawing attention and was unable to avoid the otherness imposed on me by the asking of such questions.

The xenophobic and discriminatory attitudes that were levelled at many European artists across the centuries have not dissipated over time but are still very much with us today. If nothing else, my life experiences have given me a fuller appreciation of such attitudes, making me a Brit with a different outlook, with a tendency not to entertain an air of superiority or a lack of appreciation. This is not to say that I haven't on occasion succumbed to the odd bout of self-righteousness myself. There exists in Britain a mindset that is still with us today, described by the British historian Paul Gilroy as 'postcolonial melancholia'. This can be characterized as an inability to accept the end of empire, which manifests in a continued dwelling on a version of the past in which Britain is both triumphant and benevolent. Such melancholia even bleeds into contemporary culture, with constant references to victories in two world wars and a harking back to England's single World Cup victory in 1966. This inability to move on can be seen in sections of the British population who make strident efforts to persecute and ostracize – or at least marginalize – those perceived as incomers, in a desperate attempt to recreate a mythic bygone age. This exclusionary account of British history is but a version of national identity favoured by those with a particular agenda that is rooted in the idea of whiteness as superior.[1]

Despite the very typical discrimination I encountered – and to a large extent still encounter – I continue to be proud of my dual British and Caribbean heritage. Nevertheless, my experiences make me painfully aware of how little, if any, mass public acknowledgment there is of the large number of foreigners in contemporary society and over the centuries who have contributed so much to the culture and infrastructure of Great Britain. Many foreign artists who came to the country were persecuted or seen as a threat, their contributions often forgotten or erased, leading to a skewed and inaccurate historical record. This frequently resulted, of course, from the social mores of the day and the nationalistic agenda of the person writing, the attitudes of whom, in turn, echo down the centuries in relation to a variety of historical situations. This includes the nation's collective amnesia and fear of facing up to Britain's colonial past, which, after all, is a substantial part of our history. As an art historian, I find these self-created holes in the British historical record, born out of guilt, shame, fear and jealousy, deeply problematic, and while I am not saying that anyone can be truly historically objective, we must be aware of how a lack of objectivity can impact our picture of past events and ultimately our current perception of what it is to be British. Having said that, the desire to forget uncomfortable truths from the past, common to many nations, is not new and has a habit of repeating itself.

This pointed amnesia has not gone unchallenged, however; as detailed in the introduction to this book, there were plenty of individuals in the past who went out of their way to acknowledge the debt we owe to foreigners. Their positive commentaries are now part of the British historical record thanks to the research and writing of modern scholars who demonstrate that we can be humble and appreciative of foreign contributions to our culture and economy.[2] But too often such enlightened voices have been drowned out by others, and such arguments are often seen as belonging only to academic discourse rather than mainstream historical knowledge, so that we slip too easily back into an inaccurate but comfortably nostalgia-laden notion of British history.

In the *Public Advertiser* of 1786, cited in Chapter Eleven, the writer describes a situation of homogenous artistic competition in Britain and seeks to promote English artists as superior to their European neighbours. However, in his xenophobic, nationalistic rhetoric, he fails to recognize that the most significant competition had not been among native-born artists but instead between those of foreign heritage, such as Mytens and Van Dyck. As English painting slowly began to mature and the Royal Academy emerged in 1768, the British reliance on foreign-born artists and their descendants began to wane as more native-born artists and architects looked abroad for their training and education, including the architect and portraitist George Dance the Younger, a member of the Accademia di San Luca and Accademia degli Arcadi in Rome, and Joseph Wilton, possibly the first British sculptor to have received his training and education on the Continent. It is clear that British artists and architects were beginning to realize that the experience gained in travelling abroad added substantially to their skill-set. Of the founding members of the Royal Academy, twenty-eight were painters, five were architects and three were sculptors. Significantly only nine had been born in Continental Europe and two in Ireland.[3] In the wake of Benjamin West's death in 1820, the Academy began to see a decline in foreign-born Academicians as Britain formulated a new way of categorizing its output in the British school of art.

It is also interesting to note that some significant American painters made their names in Britain in the eighteenth and nineteenth centuries, following the path set by Benjamin West. The Rhode Island-born Gilbert Stuart, a pupil of West, was seen as the pre-eminent American portrait artist of his day, yet it was judged that he could not attain greatness and career success without travelling to London (and later Dublin), a journey that was seen as a rite of passage for American artists.[4] Stuart's European success gave him credibility in America and enabled him to return to New York, where he was now in a position to gain high-profile commissions from the rich and famous. He was not the only American painter to return home: Charles Willson Peale, who studied in London between 1767 and 1769, went back to Philadelphia and fought in the American Revolutionary War. But revealingly, what these American artists have in common is that both in their time and to this day they are lauded as great British artists by the British and founding fathers of American art by the Americans.

In the final analysis, it is fair to say that all the artists we have encountered throughout this book have enriched Britain's culture and artistic heritage. London, at the epicentre, has particularly flourished as a world arts capital and, although we rarely collectively acknowledge or celebrate this reality, it is immigration that has given both the city and the nation this advantage. It is hard to imagine what British art would look like without the influence of immigrant artists and their offspring. Above all, it is those who settled in Britain and made it their home – Holbein, Gheeraerts, Hollar, Oliver, Van Dyck, Lely – who had the deepest and most lasting impact in changing and remaking the very fabric of the nation's culture with their invention of a style now described as the British school. This art historical designation was born out of internationalism and remains with us to this day, surely a reason to hold national pride in our justly celebrated and constantly changing arts scene.

Notes

INTRODUCTION

1 Yale Center for British Art, Paintings and Sculpture Department: https://britishart.yale.edu/paintings-and-sculpture; Tate, Collection: https://www.tate.org.uk/about-us/collection. Both accessed 25 June 2024.

2 See John T. Paoletti and Gary M. Radke, *Art in Renaissance Italy*, London, 2001, pp. 22–27.

3 Hearn 1996, p. 6.

4 Goose and Luu 2005, p. 137.

5 Ibid., pp. 137–38.

6 Ibid., p. 138.

7 Ibid.

CHAPTER ONE

Hans Holbein the Younger

1 Eire 1986, p. 38, citing Erasmus von Rotterdam, *Ausgewählte Schriften*, vol. 1, ed. Werner Welzig, Darmstadt, 1968, p. 178.

2 Müller 2006, p. 14.

3 Godfrey 1994, p. 15.

4 Harington's 1607 notes to Ludovico Ariosto's *Orlando Furioso in English Heroical Verse*, transl. Sir John Harington, London, 1591: 'Yet I may say thus much without partialitie, for the honour of my country, as mine author hath done for the honour of his, that we haue with vs at this day one that for limming (which I take to be the very perfection of art) is comparable with any of any other countrey.'

5 Edmond 1983, pp. 20–21.

6 Goldring 2019, p. 3.

7 Ibid., pp. 7–8. The borrowing of the word *miniatura* also suggests an Italian tradition in this art form, and the sixteenth-century artist Giulio Clovio was certainly the most celebrated in this case.

8 Reynolds 1999, p. 45.

9 Ashcroft 2017, p. 583.

10 Heard and Whitaker 2011, p. 68.

11 Foister 2006, p. 93.

12 Strong 1983, p. 34.

13 Foister 2006, p. 41.

14 In fact, the word 'journey' originally derived from the French words for day – *jour* and *journée* – which were combined in Middle English to become 'journei'.

15 Müller 2006, pp. 146–47.

16 J. Waterworth (ed. and transl.), *The Canons and Decrees of the Sacred and Oecumenical Council of Trent*, London, 1848, pp. 234–36; see https://history.hanover.edu/texts/trent/ct25.html, accessed 28 May 2024.

17 See Gabriele Paleotti, *Discourse on Sacred and Profane Images*, transl. William McCuaig, Los Angeles, 2012.

18 Müller 2006, p. 194: 'Although only a painted likeness, I am not inferior to the living face; I am instead the counterpart of my master, and distinguished by accurate lines. Just as he completes three intervals each lasting eight years [i.e., is twenty-four years old], this work of art diligently renders his true character. Jo[hannes] Holbein painted Bon[ifacius] Amerbach on 14 October 1519.'

19 Ibid., p. 11.

20 Goldring 2019, pp. 2–3 and 8.

21 Foister 2006, p. 53. Apelles of Kos was the renowned painter of ancient Greece, still seen as an exemplar of artistic practice.

22 Ibid., p. 17.

23 Bätschmann and Griener 1997, p. 160, and Moyle 2021, p. 186.

24 King 2004.

25 Müller 2006, p. 37. On witnessing the scenes of rampant destruction, on 9 May 1529 Erasmus wrote to his friend, the Nuremberg humanist Willibald Pirckheimer, lamenting that 'Nothing was spared, however precious or beautiful'.

26 Foister 2006, p. 41.

27 Foister, Roy and Wyld 1997, pp. 13–14.

28 Foister 2006, p. 137.

CHAPTER TWO
Marcus Gheeraerts the Younger

1 Cooper et al. 2015, p. 204.

2 Vasari 1996, vol. 1, pp. 425–27.

3 See *Encyclopaedia Britannica* online, https://www.britannica.com/ biography/Fernando-Alvarez-de-Toledo-y-Pimentel-3er-duque-de-Alba, accessed 14 October 2023.

4 Cooper et al. 2015, p. 281.

5 Ibid., pp. 178–79.

6 Hearn 2002, p. 11, citing Huguenot Society, Return of Aliens, 1568, iii, p. 395.

7 Cooper et al. 2015, p. 171.

8 Cooper 2010.

9 Cooper et al. 2015, p. 171.

10 Piper 1960, p. 212.

11 Hearn 2002, p. 14.

12 Ibid., pp. 11–12.

13 See the entry for the painting on the Tate website, https://www.tate.org.uk/ art/artworks/gheeraerts-portrait-of-mary-rogers-lady-harington-t01872, accessed 14 October 2023.

14 Kee 2003, p. 35.

15 Hearn 1996, p. 176.

16 Not only did Lee live openly unmarried with his mistress, Anna Vavasour, who bore him an illegitimate child, but Vavasour had previously been the mistress to the married Edward de Vere, 17th Earl of Oxford. She went on to have an illegitimate child with him and thereafter, under the orders of Elizabeth, was imprisoned in the Tower of London. Some months after her release she was banished from court, before finally being forgiven in June 1583.

17 Hearn 2002, pp. 13–14.

18 Orrock 2023, p. 15.

19 Hearn 2002, p. 9.

20 Jaffé 2003, p. 45.

21 See Catharine MacLeod, 'Paintings associated with Guillim Scrots: some technical evidence', National Portrait Gallery, https://www.npg.org.uk/ collections/research/programmes/ making-art-in-tudor-britain/ workshops/workshop-3-abstract-2, accessed 14 October 2023.

22 Hearn 1996, p. 45; Foister 2006, p. 93.

23 Kaufmann 2017, p. 13.

24 See Harrison 1889, p. 14, and Kaufmann 2017, pp. 15–16.

25 Early examples of these ideas can be found in writings such as *De Humana Physiognomonia* (1586) by the Italian scholar and polymath Giovanni Battista della Porta. By the eighteenth and nineteenth centuries they had morphed into now discredited racial theories propounded by physicians and anatomists including Petrus Camper, Carl Linnaeus, Paul Broca, Johann Casper Lavater and Francis Galton, which form the basis of racism in modern times.

26 Fryer 2018, pp. 10–12, citing Acts of the Privy Council of England, n.s. XXVI, 1596, pp. 20–21.
27 Cooper 2010.
28 Piper 1960, p. 214.
29 Ibid., pp. 213–14.
30 See the website of the Bodleian Library, Oxford, the painting's current owner; https://digital.bodleian.ox.ac.uk/objects/672dbf2a-9c8c-41a6-8b54-e1bdceae805c/, accessed 14 October 2023.
31 Strong 1963, p. 150.
32 Piper 1960, p. 212.
33 Hearn 2002, p. 14.
34 Hearn 2009, p. 39.
35 Strong 1963, p. 150.
36 Cooper et al. 2015, pp. 178–79.

CHAPTER THREE
John Bettes to Robert Peake the Elder

1 Waterhouse 1994, p. 23.
2 Foister 2006, p. 116.
3 Edmond 1978–80 suggests that Bettes had died by 1570, based on a reference to his death in John Foxe's *Actes and Monuments* for that year. He may have been the 'Johannes Bett' buried at St Martin-in-the-Field on 24 June 1570.
4 Hearn 1996, p. 107.
5 Town and David 2020, p. 737.
6 Vasari 1996, vol. 2, p. 479.
7 Auerbach 1954, p. 109.
8 Town and David 2020, p. 747.
9 British Museum, Lansdowne MS 105, no. 37, and MS 115, no. 44; see Auerbach 1954, p. 109.
10 Town and David 2020, p. 731.
11 Ibid., p. 737.
12 Hearn 1996, p. 108.
13 Goldring 2019, pp. 8–9.
14 MacLeod 2019, p. 32.
15 See the portrait miniature of a girl, formerly thought to be Queen Elizabeth I as princess (1549), attributed to Teerlinc in the Victoria and Albert Museum, London; https://collections.vam.ac.uk/item/O1067948/a-girl-formerly-thought-to-portrait-miniature-levina-teerlinc/, accessed 29 May 2024.
16 See Town 2014, p. 172; Goldring 2019, p. 75; Chadwick 1990, pp. 105–6.
17 MacLeod 2019, p. 32.
18 Ibid., p. 49.
19 Edmond 1983, pp. 64–65.
20 MacLeod 2019, p. 33.
21 Fryer 2018, p. 9.
22 MacLeod 2019, p. 33.
23 Auerbach 1954, p. 102.
24 MacLeod 2019, pp. 33–34.
25 Goldring 2019, p. 273.
26 Ibid.
27 MacLeod 2019, pp. 11–12.
28 Ibid., p. 1.
29 Goldring 2019, pp. 274–76.
30 Edmond 1983, p. 153.
31 Hearn 1996, p. 185.
32 Edmond 1983, p. 153.
33 Borg 2005, p. 26.
34 Cooper et al. 2015, p. 208.
35 Holmes 1978, p. 29.
36 'Evil May Day: anti-alien riots in 1517', Early Modern Migrations, 1500–1750, https://www.ourmigrationstory.org.uk/oms/londons-evil-may-day-riots, accessed 14 October 2023.
37 See Luu 1996, p. 2.
38 Cooper et al. 2015, p. 215.
39 Ibid., p. 171.
40 Auerbach 1954, pp. 109–10.
41 Ibid., p. 110.
42 Wagner 1949, p. 19.
43 Will 2014, p. 119.
44 Cooper 2010.
45 Auerbach 1954, p. 110.

46 Hearn 1996, p. 166.

47 See Moxey 1989, pp. 31–36.

48 Hearn 1996, p. 166.

CHAPTER FOUR
Orazio and Artemisia Gentileschi

1 Vodret 2003, p. 52.

2 Treves 2016, pp. 13–14.

3 Ibid., p. 97.

4 Ibid.

5 Treves 2020, p. 12.

6 Ibid.

7 Finaldi 1999, p. 13.

8 Langdon 1999, p. 263, citing the translation in Herwarth Röttgen, *Caravaggio. Der Irdische Amor oder Der Sieg der fleischlichen Liebe*, Frankfurt am Main, 1992, pp. 16–22.

9 Langdon 1999, pp. 262–65.

10 Harris 2008, p. 50.

11 Treves 2020, p. 12.

12 Ibid.

13 Bissell 1981, p. 101.

14 Treves 2020, p. 12.

15 Harris 2008, p. 53, citing the translation in Bissell 1999, p. 1.

16 Treves 2020, p. 37.

17 Christiansen and Mann 2001, p. 287.

18 Treves 2020, p. 13.

19 Ibid., p. 14.

20 Ibid., p. 21.

21 Ibid., p. 186.

22 Ibid.

23 Ibid., p. 194.

24 Ibid., p. 189.

25 Ibid., p. 187.

26 Christiansen and Mann 2001, pp. 137 and 288.

27 Ibid., p. 223.

28 Bissell 1981, p. 50.

29 Ibid.

30 Treves 2020, p. 189.

31 Ibid., p. 43.

32 Ibid., pp. 191–93.

33 Ibid., p. 27, citing the translation in Francesco Solinas, Michele Nicolaci and Yuri Primarosa, *Lettere di Artemisia*, Rome, 2011), pp. 124–37.

34 Treves 2020, p. 249.

CHAPTER FIVE
Daniel Mytens

1 Cammaerts 1944, p. 304.

2 Cooper et al. 2015, p. 281.

3 Ibid.

4 Ibid., p. 301, citing Robert Hill, 'Sir Dudley Carleton and his Relations with Dutch Artists 1616–1632', *Leids Kunsthistorisch Jaarboek*, 13 (2003), pp. 255–60.

5 Cooper et al., 2015, pp. 299–301.

6 Mander 1936, pp. 351–52: 'In art, a master that excels deserves to be praised and freed from the spitefulness of others. For this reason, I cannot refrain from commenting on Michiel Jansen Miereveldt. He was gifted in many ways. He was certain to become a painter of portraits. He is a master in this field, and his work proves that he is not equalled or surpassed.'

7 Ibid.: 'There seems to be trouble in our Netherlands, especially at the present time. There is too little for artists to do in making compositions with figures, and young artists have little opportunity to become proficient at painting figures and nudes. Most of the time they have to paint portraits from life. Most artists are attracted by a sweet profit, and, as they have to support themselves, they take this by-path in art – the painting of portraits from life. This kind of portraiture has been done by many of the great masters, and at present our contemporary,

Miereveldt – or Michiel Jansen – is doing it. He has no equal here in the Netherlands.'

8 Cooper et al., 2015, p. 279.
9 Hearn 2009, p. 39.
10 Waterhouse 1994, p. 54.
11 Novikova 1999, p. 72.
12 Stopes 1910, p. 161, citing Accounts of the Treasurer of the Chamber, Audit Office (Bundle 391, Roll 58).
13 Ibid., citing Accounts of the Treasurer of the Chamber, Audit Office (Bundle 391, Rolls 60 and 61).
14 Ibid.
15 Records of large payments found in the court documents include: 'To Danyell Mittens upon the like warrant dated 4th April, 1623, for drawing his Majesty's picture at the length, which was given to Mounsieur Boyschote ambassador from the Arch Dukes £30', and 'To Daniell Mittens upon a warrant dated 9th October, 1623, for a picture of the Prince his Highness drawne at length and delivered to Don Carlos de Colona, the Ambassador from the King of Spaine, £30'; ibid.
16 Wood 2000–1, p. 177.
17 Stopes 1910, p. 161, citing Accounts of the Treasurer of the Chamber, Audit Office (Bundle 391, Rolls 60 and 61).
18 Vaughan 1970, p. 3.
19 Stopes 1910, p. 161, citing Accounts of the Treasurer of the Chamber, Audit Office (Bundle 391, Rolls 60 and 61).
20 Ibid., pp. 160–63, citing Calendar of State Papers, Domestic – Charles I, LXX, 54.
21 Waterhouse 1994, p. 54.
22 Ibid.
23 Town 2014, p. 146.
24 Ibid.

CHAPTER SIX
Peter Paul Rubens

1 Lodovico Guicciardini, *Descrittione di Lodovico Guicciardini Patritio Fiorentino di tutti i Paesi Bassi Altrimenti detti Germania Inferiore*, Antwerp, 1567. The work was republished in English in 1593.
2 Pye 2021, pp. 213–14.
3 Jaffé and Moore Ede 2005, p. 14.
4 Ibid., p. 86.
5 Wood 2002, p. 13.
6 Ibid., p. 33.
7 Jaffé and Moore Ede 2005, p. 17.
8 Magurn 1971, pp. 52–53, translation of Rubens's letter to Johann Faber, 10 April 1609.
9 Ibid., p. 123, translation of Rubens's letter to Palamède Fabri de Valavez, written from Laeken, outside Brussels, 26 December 1625.
10 Brejon de Lavergnée 2004, p. 179.
11 Vander Auwera and Van Sprang 2007, citing a lost letter of 13 September 1621.
12 Wedgwood 1975, p. 10.
13 Ibid.
14 Magurn 1971, p. 279, translation of Rubens's letter to Pierre Dupuy, 10 August 1628.
15 Vergara 1999, pp. 110–11.
16 Davis 2020, p. 13.
17 Ibid.
18 Ibid., pp. 20–21.
19 Magurn 1971, pp. 404–6, translation of Rubens's letter to Nicolas Claude Fabri de Peiresc, written from Castle Steen, 4 September 1636: 'To tell the truth I have been living somewhat in retirement for several months, in a country house which is rather far from Antwerp and off the main roads. This makes it very difficult for me to receive letters and also to send them.'

20 See ibid., pp. 392–93, translation of Rubens's letter to Nicolas Claude Fabri de Peiresc, 18 December 1634.

21 Ibid., pp. 320–21, translation of Rubens's letter to Pierre Dupuy, 8 August 1629: 'To see so many varied countries and courts, in so short a time, would have been more fitting and useful to me in my youth than at my present age…my mind would have been able to prepare itself, by experience and familiarity with the diverse peoples, for greater things in the future.'

22 Davis 2020, pp. 84–88.

CHAPTER SEVEN
Anthony van Dyck

1 Kirby 1999, p. 7.

2 See https://www.rubenshuis.be/en/page/anthony-van-dyck-3, accessed 15 January 2024.

3 Kirby 1999, p. 5.

4 Hearn 2009, p. 40, citing Mary F. S. Hervey, *The Life, correspondence & collections of Thomas Howard, Earl of Arundel*, Cambridge, 1921, p. 176.

5 Hearn 2009, p. 19.

6 Bellori 2009, p. 216.

7 Howarth 1990.

8 Alsteens and Eaker 2016, p. 55.

9 Hearn 2009, p. 40.

10 Ibid.

11 Ibid., pp. 19–22.

12 Bellori 2009, p. 216.

13 Hearn 2009, p. 40.

14 Martin 1970, pp. 58–59: 'The negro's head and the right-hand half of the head on the right are thinly painted and somewhat retouched. The handling of the principal sitter, especially his flesh, seems to differ from that of the other two men. But all the flesh, although flattened in the case of the main sitter, and worn in the case of the negro and man on the right, is coarse and clumsy in different ways.'

15 See https://www.nationalgallery.org.uk/paintings/anthony-van-dyck-portrait-of-george-gage-with-two-attendants, accessed 15 January 2024: 'Van Dyck has depicted Gage as an elegant figure in the midst of a negotiation with a dealer in classical antiques. The dealer looks intently at him as he gestures towards the sculpture; while Gage may look diffident, he returns his gaze and seems about to speak. The figure in the background looks across them and directly at us. He holds the sculpture and is also pointing at it.'

16 Shawe-Taylor and Rumberg 2018, pp. 100–1.

17 Jaffé 2003, p. 22.

18 Shawe-Taylor and Rumberg 2018, pp. 100–1.

19 Hearn 2009, p. 40.

20 Alsteens and Eaker 2016, p. 104.

21 Royal Collection Trust, https://lostcollection.rct.uk/charles-i/mantua-purchase, accessed 15 January 2024.

22 Shawe-Taylor and Rumberg 2018, p. 30.

23 National Archives, E403/2567; National Archives, Privy Seal Office, 2/104.

24 Alsteens and Eaker 2016, p. 194.

25 Hearn 2009, p. 70.

26 Shawe-Taylor and Rumberg 2018, p. 30.

27 Hearn 2009, p. 153.

28 Carey-Thomas 2013, p. 17.

29 Howarth 1993, pp. 34–39.

30 Alsteens and Eaker 2016, p. 103.

31 Hearn 2009, p. 153.

32 Ibid., pp. 153–54.

33 Roettgen 1993, p. 14.

34 Penny 2008, pp. 219–20; Baker and Henry 1996, p. 669.

35 National Archives, SP 16/406, 4, T.56/4, fol. 206; see Hearn 2009, p. 66.

36 See https://www.rct.uk/collection/402531/margaret-lemon-fl-1635-1640, accessed 28 January 2024.

37 Vaughan 1999, p. 72.

CHAPTER EIGHT
Wenceslaus Hollar

1 Godfrey 1994, p. 14.

2 Griffiths and Kesnerová 1983, p. 5.

3 'Hollar, Wenceslaus (1607–1677)', *Oxford Dictionary of National Biography*.

4 Parry 1980, pl. 26.

5 Tindall 2002, pp. 9–10.

6 Vertue 1759, p. 137.

7 Aubrey 2016, p. 162.

8 Van Eerde 1970, p. 6.

9 Griffiths and Kesnerová 1983, p. 6.

10 Van Eerde 1970, p. 8.

11 Vertue 1759, p. 137.

12 Hartley 1991, pp. 256–59.

13 Landau and Parshall 1994, pp. 23–27.

14 Chadwick 2021.

15 Royal Collection Trust, https://www.rct.uk/collection/804323/head-of-a-youngnbspblack-boy, accessed 23 February 2024.

16 Kolfin and Runia 2020, p. 34.

17 Parry 1980, p. 13.

18 Ibid.

19 Ibid., p. 15.

20 British Library, Add. MS 15970, letter from the Earl of Arundel to the Reverend William Petty, May 1636.

21 Godfrey 1978, p. 20.

22 Parry 1980, p. 26.

23 Godfrey 1994, p. 11.

24 Griffiths 1998, p. 44.

25 Vertue 1759, pp. 141–42.

26 Aubrey 2016, p. 163.

27 Heard and Whitaker 2011, pp. 178–81.

28 Debrett's College of Arms, https://debretts.com/peerage/college-of-arms/, accessed 23 February 2024: 'The heralds are a part of The Queen's Household and have royal duties such as publicly reading royal proclamations at the succession of a new Sovereign. They also take part in Coronations, the State Opening of Parliament, the introduction of new peers into the House of Lords, and at the rites associated with the Orders of Chivalry'.

29 Griffiths and Kesnerová 1983, pp. 62–63.

30 Ibid.

31 Howarth 1993, p. 59.

32 Griffiths and Kesnerová 1983, p. 63.

33 Godfrey 1994, p. 27.

34 Ibid.

35 Vertue 1759, p. 147.

36 Aubrey 2016, p. 163.

CHAPTER NINE
William Hogarth

1 Riding 2021, pp. 45–48.

2 Hallett and Riding 2006, p. 15.

3 Paulson 1971, vol. I, p. 43, citing British Library, Registry of Apprentices of the Merchant Taylors' Company, 2 February [1713 or 1714].

4 Hogarth 1833, p. 3.

5 Dabydeen 1978, p. 11.

6 Fryer 2018, p. 74.

7 Gerzina 2020, pp. 84–85.

8 Myers 1996, p. 19.

9 Murray 1976, p. 219; Vaughan 1999, p. 34.

10 Hogarth 1833, pp. 4–5.

11 Pears 1988, p. 124, citing John Ireland, *Hogarth Illustrated*, London, 1791.

12 Pears 1988, p. 124.

13 Ibid., citing Ireland, *Hogarth Illustrated*.

14 Waterhouse 1994, p. 142.

15 Hallett and Riding 2006, pp. 16-17.

16 Waterhouse 1994, pp. 168–69.

17 Hogarth 1833, pp. 8–9.
18 Hallett and Riding 2006, p. 80.
19 Sander 2013, pp. 236–37.
20 Ibid., p. 73.
21 Hallett and Riding 2006, p. 162.
22 Reynolds 1997, p. 51.
23 Hallett and Riding 2006, p. 190.

CHAPTER TEN
Joshua Reynolds
1 James Cook, Journal of HMS *Endeavour*, 1768–1771, State Library of New South Wales.
2 Joseph Banks, *Endeavour* journal, 15 August 1769–12 July 1771, entry of 12 July 1769: 'This morn Tupia came on board, he had renewd his resolves of going with us to England, a circumstance which gives me much satisfaction…but what makes him more than any thing else desireable is his experience in the navigation of these people and knowledge of the Islands in these seas…I therefore have resolvd to take him. Thank heaven I have a sufficiency and I do not know why I may not keep him as a curiosity, as well as some of my neighbours do lions and tygers at a larger expence than he will probably ever put me to; the amusement I shall have in his future conversation and the benefit he will be of to this ship, as well as what he may be if another should be sent into these seas, will I think fully repay me.'
3 Parsons 2015, p. 150.
4 Philip Dormer Stanhope, *Letters to His Son on the Art of Becoming a Man of the World and a Gentleman* (1774).
5 Postle 2005, p. 216.
6 Fowler 2020, pp. 232–33.
7 Papers of Sir Joseph Banks, National Library of Australia, MS 9, appendix IV, 'Thoughts on the Manners of Otaheite' (1773).
8 Turner 2001, p. 26.
9 Ibid.
10 https://www.npg.org.uk/collections/search/portrait/mw69742/Mai-Omai-Sir-Joseph-Banks-and-Daniel-Solander?LinkID=mp00240&role=sit&rNo=1, accessed 4 April 2024.
11 See also the discussion of the painting on the Art UK website, https://artuk.org/discover/artworks/omai-c-1753c-17761777-sir-joseph-banks-17431820-and-dr-daniel-solander-17361782-10128, accessed 4 April 2024.
12 Turner 2001, p. 26.
13 Ibid.
14 Ibid., p. 23.
15 McCormick 1977, pp. 53 and 125.
16 Ibid., p. 102.
17 Postle 2005, p. 218, citing Annie Raine Ellis (ed.), *The Early Diary of Frances Burney 1768–1778*, London, 1913, vol. 1, p. 334.
18 Fryer 2018, p. 74.
19 Fullagar 2010, p. 198.
20 Reynolds 1997, p. 72.
21 Ibid., p. 59.
22 Ibid.
23 See Postle 2005, p. 216, and Turner 2001, p. 26.
24 Reynolds 1997, p. 137.
25 Ibid., p. 88.
26 Ibid., p. 140.
27 Ibid., p. 171.
28 Alberti 1991, p. 74.
29 Turner 2001, p. 32, citing J. C. Beaglehole (ed.), *The Journals of Captain James Cook on his Voyages of Discovery. Volume 3: The Voyage of the Resolution and the Discovery, 1776–1780*, part 2, Cambridge, 1967, pp. 1514–15.
30 Turner 2001, p. 32, citing George

Forster, *A Voyage Round the World,
Performed in His Britannic Majesty's Ships
the Resolution and Adventure, in the Years
1772, 1773, 1774 and 1775*, London, 1777.

CHAPTER ELEVEN
Angelica Kauffman

1 Bermingham 1993, p. 3.
2 Chadwick 1990, pp. 142–43.
3 Baumgärtel 2020, p. 10.
4 Roettgen 1993, p. 15.
5 Roworth 1992, p. 17.
6 Chadwick 1990, p. 144.
7 Bermingham 1993, p. 3.
8 Castiglione 1959, p. 204.
9 Uglow 2020.
10 Roworth 1992, p. 14.
11 Rosenthal 2006, pp. 117–18.
12 Jonathan Richardson, *The Works of
Mr. Jonathan Richardson*, Hildesheim,
1773, p. 267.
13 Roworth 1992, p. 15.
14 Rosenthal 2006, pp. 189–90, citing
Helfrich Peter Sturz, *Schriften* (1779),
vol. 1, pp. 120 and 122–23.
15 Ibid., p. 189, citing Sturz, *Schriften.*
16 Rosenthal 2006, p. 190, citing Johann
Rudolf Füssli, *Allgemeines
Künstlerlexikon, 1763–76, 3. Suppl.*,
Zurich, 1777, p. 106.
17 Rosenthal 2006, p. 190.
18 Ibid.
19 Rosenthal 2006, p. 190, citing Füssli,
Allgemeines Künstlerlexikon.
20 Bellori 2009, pp. 184–85.
21 Roworth 1992, p. 22, citing Anthony
Ashley Cooper, 3rd Earl of Shaftsbury,
*A Notion of the Historical Draught of
Tablature of the Judgement of Hercules*
(1713).
22 Manners and Williamson 1924, p. 38.
23 *Middlesex Journal* (25 April 1772), p. 4.
24 *Public Advertiser* (2 May 1775), p. 2.

25 Roworth 1992, p. 11.
26 Ibid., p. 12.
27 *Public Advertiser* (22 May 1786), p. 2.
28 Roworth 1992, p. 12.
29 Baumgärtel 2020, p. 15.
30 Sparrow 1905, p. 59.
31 The very first Royal Academy
Nominations Book, in which proposed
candidates' names are first inscribed,
dates from 1866 to 1907, so presumably
no members were officially made
Academicians before the process was
formalized. See https://www.
royalacademy.org.uk/article/how-do-
academicians-get-elected, accessed
7 June 2024.

AFTERWORD

1 See Zakia Sewell (presenter),
'Four Hundred Years', *My Albion*, BBC
Radio 4, broadcast 1 December 2020;
https://www.bbc.co.uk/sounds/play/
m000pxpb, accessed 27 June 2024.
2 See, for instance, Goose and Luu 2005.
3 Holger Hoock, 'Founders of the Royal
Academy of Arts (act. 1768–1825)',
Oxford Dictionary of National Biography,
https://doi.org/10.1093/ref:odnb/94593,
accessed 27 June 2024.
4 Carrie Rebora Barratt, 'Gilbert Stuart
(1755–1828)', *Heilbrunn Timeline of Art
History*, http://www.metmuseum.org/
toah/hd/stua/hd_stua.htm, accessed
27 June 2024.

Bibliography

Adi, Hakim, *African and Caribbean People in Britain: A History*, London, 2022

Alberti, Leon Battista, *On Painting* (Penguin Classics), transl. Cecil Grayson, London, 1991

Alsteens, Stijn and Adam Eaker, *Van Dyck: The Anatomy of Portraiture*, New Haven and London, 2016

Ashcroft, Jeffrey, *Albrecht Dürer: Documentary Biography*, New Haven and London, 2017

Aubrey, John, *Aubrey's Brief Lives*, ed. Oliver Lawson Dick, London, 2016

Auerbach, Erna, *Tudor Artists: A Study of Painters in the Royal Service and of Portraiture on Illuminated Documents from the Accession of Henry VIII to the Death of Elizabeth I*, London, 1954

Baker, Christopher and Tom Henry, *The National Gallery Complete Illustrated Catalogue*, London, 1996

Bätschmann, Oskar and Pascal Griener, *Hans Holbein*, London, 1997

Baumgärtel, Bettina (ed.), *Angelica Kauffman*, Munich, 2020

Bellori, Giovan Pietro, *The Lives of the Modern Painters, Sculptors and Architects: A New Translation and Critical Edition*, transl. Alice Sedgwick Wohl, Cambridge, 2009

Bermingham, Ann, 'The Aesthetics of Ignorance: The Accomplished Woman in the Culture of Connoisseurship', *Oxford Art Journal*, 16:2 (1993), pp. 3–20

Bissell, Raymond Ward, *Orazio Gentileschi and the Poetic Tradition in Caravaggesque Painting*, University Park, PA, 1981

Bissell, Raymond Ward, *Artemisia Gentileschi and the Authority of Art*, University Park, PA, 1999

Borg, Alan, *The History of the Worshipful Company of Painters, otherwise Painter-Stainers*, London, 2005

Brejon de Lavergnée, Arnauld (ed.), *Rubens*, exh. cat., Lille, Palais des Beaux-Arts, 2004

Brown, Beverley Louise (ed.), *The Genius of Rome 1592–1693*, exh. cat., London, Royal Academy of Arts, 2001

Brown, Christopher and Hans Vlieghe, *Van Dyck 1599–1641*, exh. cat., Antwerp, Koninklijk Museum voor Schone Kunsten, and London, Royal Academy of Arts, 1999

Burnard, Trevor, 'A New Look at the Zong Case of 1783', *XVII–XVIII*, 79 (2019), doi.org/10.4000/1718.1808

Calvocoressi, Peter, *Who's Who in the Bible*, London, 1990

Cammaerts, Emile, 'The Flemish Predecessors of van Dyck in England', *Burlington Magazine*, 85:501 (1944), pp. 302–7

Campbell, Lorne, *The Early Flemish Pictures in the Collection of Her Majesty the Queen*, Cambridge, 1985

Carey-Thomas, Lizzie (ed.), *Migrations: Journeys into British Art*, London, 2013

Castiglione, Baldassare, *The Book of the Courtier*, transl. Charles S. Singleton, New York, 1959

Chadwick, Esther, 'A Platter of Turnips', *London Review of Books*, 43:1 (January 2021), www.lrb.co.uk/the-paper/v43/n01/esther-chadwick/a-platter-of-turnips

Chadwick, Whitney, *Women, Art and Society*, London and New York, 1990

Christiansen, Keith and Judith W. Mann, *Orazio and Artemisia Gentileschi*, exh. cat., New York, Metropolitan Museum of Art, 2001

Cleland, Elizabeth and Adam Eaker, *The Tudors: Art and Majesty in Renaissance England*, exh. cat., New York, Metropolitan Museum of Art, 2022

Cooper, Tarnya, 'Foreign Artists in 16th Century London', transcript of lecture given on 1 March 2010, https://www.gresham.ac.uk/watch-now/foreign-artists-16th-century-london

Cooper, Tarnya et al. (eds), *Painting in Britain 1500–1630: Production, Influences and Patronage*, Oxford, 2015

Dabydeen, David, *Hogarth's Blacks: Images of Blacks in Eighteenth Century English Art*, Manchester, 1978

Dabydeen, David, John Gilmore and Cecily Jones (eds), *The Oxford Companion to Black British History*, Oxford, 2007

Davis, Lucy, *Rubens: The Two Great Landscapes*, London, 2020

Edmond, Mary, 'Limners and Picturemakers', *The Volume of the Walpole Society*, 47 (1978–80), pp. 60–242

Edmond, Mary, *Hilliard and Oliver: The Lives and Works of Two Great Miniaturists*, London, 1983

Egerton, Judy, *The British Paintings* (National Gallery Catalogues), London, 2000

Eire, Carlos M. N., *War against the Idols: The Reformation of Worship from Erasmus to Calvin*, Cambridge, 1986

Finaldi, Gabriele (ed.), *Orazio Gentileschi at the Court of Charles I*, exh. cat., London, National Gallery, 1999

Foister, Susan, *Holbein in England*, London, 2006

Foister, Susan, Ashok Roy and Martin Wyld, *Making and Meaning: Holbein's Ambassadors*, London, 1997

Fowler, Corinne, *Green Unpleasant Land: Creative Responses to Rural England's Colonial Connections*, Leeds, 2020

Fryer, Peter, *Staying Power: The History of Black People in Britain*, London, 2018

Fullagar, Kate, 'Reynolds' New Masterpiece: From Experiment in Savagery to Icon of the Eighteenth Century', *Cultural and Social History*, 7:2 (2010), pp. 191–212

Gerzina, Gretchen (ed.), *Britain's Black Past*, Liverpool, 2020

Godfrey, Richard T., *Printmaking in Britain: A General History from Its Beginnings to the Present Day*, Oxford and New York, 1978

Godfrey, Richard T., *Wenceslaus Hollar: A Bohemian Artist in England*, New Haven and London, 1994

Goldring, Elizabeth, *Nicholas Hilliard: Life of an Artist*, New Haven and London, 2019

Goose, Nigel and Lien Luu (eds), *Immigrants in Tudor and Early Stuart England*, Eastbourne, 2005

Griffiths, Antony, *The Print in Stuart Britain, 1603–1689*, London, 1998

Griffiths, Antony and Gabriela Kesnerová, *Wenceslaus Hollar: Prints and Drawings*, London, 1983

Hallett, Mark and Christine Riding, *Hogarth*, London, 2006

Hallett, Robin, 'The European Approach to the Interior of Africa in the Eighteenth Century', *Journal of African History*, 4:2 (1963), pp. 191–206

Harris, Ann Sutherland, *Seventeenth Century Art & Architecture*, London, 2008

Harrison, William, Elizabethan England: From a Description of England, London, 1889

Hartley, Craig, 'The Young Hollar in Prague: A Group of New Attributions',

Print Quarterly, 8:3 (September 1991), pp. 252–74

Heard, Kate and Lucy Whitaker, *The Northern Renaissance: Dürer to Holbein*, London, 2011

Hearn, Karen (ed.), *Dynasties: Painting in Tudor and Jacobean England 1530–1630*, New York, 1996

Hearn, Karen, *Marcus Gheeraerts II: Elizabethan Artist in Focus*, London, 2002

Hearn, Karen (ed.), *Van Dyck and Britain*, London, 2009

Hogarth, William, *Anecdotes of William Hogarth, Written by Himself*, ed. J. B. Nichols, London, 1833

Holmes, Colin (ed.), *Immigrants and Minorities in British Society*, London and New York, 1978

Howarth, David, 'The Arrival of Van Dyck in England', *Burlington Magazine*, 132:1051 (1990), pp. 709–10

Howarth, David (ed.), *Art and Patronage in the Caroline Courts*, Cambridge, 1993

Jaffé, David (ed.), *Titian*, London, 2003

Jaffé, David and Minna Moore Ede, *Rubens: A Master in the Making*, London, 2005

Joppien, Rüdiger, *James Cook and the Exploration of the Pacific*, London and New York, 2009

Kaufmann, Miranda, *Black Tudors: The Untold Story*, London, 2017

Kee, Robert, *Ireland: A History*, rev. edn, London, 2003

King, David J., 'Who was Holbein's lady with a squirrel and a starling?', *Apollo*, 159:507 (May 2004), pp. 165–75

Kirby, Jo, 'The Painter's Trade in the Seventeenth Century: Theory and Practice', *National Gallery Technical Bulletin*, 20 (1999), pp. 5–49

Kitson, Michael, 'Hogarth's "Apology for Painters"', *The Volume of the Walpole Society*, 41 (1966–68), pp. 46–111

Kolfin, Elmer and Epco Runia (eds), *Black in Rembrandt's Time*, exh. cat., Amsterdam, Rembrandt House Museum, 2020

Landau, David and Peter Parshall, *The Renaissance Print 1470–1550*, New Haven and London, 1994

Langdon, Helen, *Caravaggio: A Life*, London, 1999

Luu, Lien Bich, 'Migration and Change: Religious Refugees and the London Economy, 1550–1600', *Critical Survey*, 8:1 (1996), pp. 93–102

Lyon, J. Vanessa, 'A Psalm for King James: Rubens's *Peace Embracing Plenty* and the Virtues of Female Affection at Whitehall', *Art History*, 40 (2017), pp. 38–67

MacLeod, Catharine, *Elizabethan Treasures: Miniatures by Hilliard and Oliver*, London, 2019

McCormick, E. H., *Omai: Pacific Envoy*, Auckland and Oxford, 1977

McGrath, Elizabeth, 'Rubens's Arch of the Mint', *Journal of the Warburg and Courtauld Institutes*, 37 (1974), pp. 191–217

Magurn, Ruth Saunders (ed.), *The Letters of Peter Paul Rubens*, Cambridge, MA, 1971

Mander, Carel van, *Dutch and Flemish Painters*, transl. from the *Schilderboeck* and intr. Constant van de Wall, New York, 1936

Manners, Lady Victoria and G. C. Williamson, *Angelica Kauffmann, RA: Her Life and her Works*, London, 1924

Martin, Gregory, *The Flemish School: 1600–1900* (National Gallery Catalogues), London, 1970, reprinted 1986

Millar, Oliver, *Van Dyck in England*, London, 1983

Montrose, Louis A., 'Idols of the Queen: Policy, Gender, and the Picturing of Elizabeth I', *Representations*, 68 (1999), pp. 108–61

Moxey, Keith, 'Interpreting Pieter Aertsen: The Problem of "Hidden Symbolism"', *Nederlands Kunsthistorisch Jaarboek*, 40 (1989), pp. 29–39

Moyle, Franny, *The King's Painter: The Life and Times of Hans Holbein*, London, 2021

Müller, Christian (ed.), *Hans Holbein the Younger: The Basel Years 1515–1532*, Munich, 2006

Murray, Peter and Linda, *The Penguin Dictionary of Art and Artists*, 4th edn, New York and London, 1976

Myers, Norma, *Reconstructing the Black Past: Blacks in Britain 1780–1830*, London and Portland, OR, 1996

Novikova, Anastassia, 'The Marriage of Signs, or the Signs of Marriage, or the Ideal Marriage of the Arundels', *Object: Postgraduate Research and Reviews in the History of Art and Visual Culture*, 2 (1999)

Orrock, Amy, with contributions by Edward Town, *Tudor Mystery: The Master of the Countess of Warwick*, exh. cat., Compton Verney Art Gallery, 2023

Parry, Graham, *Hollar's England: A Mid-seventeenth Century View*, Wilton, 1980

Parsons, Harriet, 'British–Tahitian collaborative drawing strategies on Cook's *Endeavour* voyage', in Shino Konishi et al. (eds), *Indigenous Intermediaries: New Perspectives on Exploration Archives*, Canberra, 2015, pp. 147–67

Paulson, Ronald, *Hogarth: His Life, Art, and Times*, New Haven and London, 1971

Pears, Iain, *The Discovery of Painting: The Growth of Interest in the Arts in England, 1680–1768*, New Haven and London, 1988

Penny, Nicholas, *The Sixteenth Century Italian Paintings, Volume II: Venice 1540–1600* (National Gallery Catalogues), London, 2008

Piper, David, 'Some Portraits by Marcus Gheeraerts II and John de Critz Reconsidered', *Proceedings of the Huguenot Society of London*, 20:2 (1960), pp. 177–94

Postle, Martin, *Joshua Reynolds: The Creation of Celebrity*, London, 2005

Pye, Michael, *Antwerp: The Glory Years*, London, 2021

Reynolds, Anna, Lucy Peter and Martin Clayton, *Portrait of the Artist*, London, 2016

Reynolds, Graham, *The Sixteenth- and Seventeenth-Century Miniatures in the Collection of Her Majesty The Queen*, London, 1999

Reynolds, Sir Joshua, *Discourses on Art*, ed. Robert R. Wark, New Haven and London, 1997

Riding, Jacqueline, *Hogarth: Life in Progress*, London, 2021

Roettgen, Steffi, *Anton Raphael Mengs 1728–1779 and his British Patrons*, London, 1993

Rosenthal, Angela, *Angelica Kauffman: Art and Sensibility*, New Haven and London, 2006

Roworth, Wendy Wassyng (ed.), *Angelica Kauffman: A Continental Artist in Georgian England*, London, 1992

Ruiz Gómez, Leticia (ed.), *A Tale of Two Women Painters: Sofonisba Anguissola and Lavinia Fontana*, exh. cat., Madrid, Museo Nacional del Prado, 2019

Sander, Jochen (ed.), *Albrecht Dürer: His Art in Context*, exh. cat., Frankfurt, Städel Museum, 2013

Shawe-Taylor, Desmond and Per Rumberg (eds), *Charles I: King and Collector*, exh. cat., London, Royal Academy of Arts, 2018

Sparrow, Walter Shaw (ed.), *Women Painters of the World: From the Time of Caterina Vigri, 1413–1463, to Rosa Bonheur and the Present Day*, London, 1905

Stopes, Charlotte C., 'Daniel Mytens in England', *Burlington Magazine*, 17:87 (1910), pp. 160–3

Strong, Roy C., 'Elizabethan Painting: An Approach Through Inscriptions – III Marcus Gheeraerts the Younger', *Burlington Magazine*, 105:721 (1963), pp. 149–59

Strong, Roy, *Artists of the Tudor Court: The Portrait Miniature Rediscovered 1520–1620*, exh. cat., London, Victoria and Albert Museum, 1983

Tindall, Gillian, *The Man Who Drew London: Wenceslaus Hollar in Reality and Imagination*, London, 2002

Town, Edward, 'A Biographical Dictionary of London Painters, 1547–1625', *The Volume of the Walpole Society*, 76 (2014), pp. 1–235

Town, Edward and Jessica David, 'George Gower: Portraitist, Mercer, Serjeant Painter', *Burlington Magazine*, 162:1410 (2020), pp. 739–55

Treves, Letizia, *Beyond Caravaggio*, London, 2016

Treves, Letizia (ed.), *Artemisia*, exh. cat., London, National Gallery, 2020

Turner, Caroline, 'Images of Mai', in *Cook & Omai: The Cult of the South Seas*, Canberra, 2001, pp. 23–30

Ungerer, Gustav, 'Recovering a Black African's Voice in an English Lawsuit: Jacques Francis and the Salvage Operations of the *Mary Rose* and the *Sancta Maria and Sanctus Edwardus*, 1545–ca 1550', *Medieval & Renaissance Drama in England*, 17 (2005), pp. 255–71

Uglow, Jenny, 'The Meteoric Rise of Angelica Kauffman RA', *RA Magazine* (Summer 2020), https://www.royalacademy.org.uk/article/ra-magazine-jenny-uglow-angelica-kauffman-ra

Van Eerde, Katherine S., *Wenceslaus Hollar – Delineator of His Time*, Charlottesville, VA, 1970

Vander Auwera, Joost and Sabine van Sprang, *Rubens: A Genius at Work*, Tielt, 2007

Vasari, Giorgio, *Lives of the Painters, Sculptors and Architects* (Everyman's Library), transl. Gaston du C. De Vere, 2 vols, New York, 1996

Vaughan, William, *Endymion Porter & William Dobson*, London, 1970

Vaughan, William, *British Painting: The Golden Age from Hogarth to Turner*, New York and London, 1999

Vergara, Alexander, *Rubens and His Spanish Patrons*, Cambridge and New York, 1999

Vertue, George, *A Description of the Works of the Ingenious Delineator and Engraver Wenceslaus Hollar, Disposed into Classes of Different Sorts; With some Account of His Life*, 2nd edn with additions, London, 1759

Vodret, Rossella, 'The Spread of Caravaggio's Influence: Caravaggism in Italy', in *Darkness & Light: Caravaggio and his World*, exh. cat., Sydney, Art Gallery of New South Wales, and Melbourne, National Gallery of Victoria, 2003

Wagner, Anthony, *Heraldry in England*, London, 1949

Walpole, Horatio, *The Works of Horatio Walpole, Earl of Orford, vol. 4*, London, 1798

Waterfield, Giles and Anne French, *Below Stairs: 400 Years of Servants' Portraits*, London, 2003

Waterhouse, Ellis K., *Painting in Britain 1530–1790*, 4th edn, London, 1994

Wedgwood, C. V., *The Political Career of Peter Paul Rubens*, London and New York, 1975

Weissbourd, Emily, '"Those in Their Possession": Race, Slavery, and Queen Elizabeth's "Edicts of Expulsion"', *Huntington Library Quarterly*, 78:1 (Spring 2015), pp. 1–19

Will, Kathryn Karen, 'Cultivating Heraldic Histories in Early Modern English Literature', DPhil dissertation, University of Michigan, 2014

Wood, Jeremy, 'Orazio Gentileschi and Some Netherlandish Artists in London: The Patronage of the Duke of Buckingham, Charles I and Henrietta Maria', *Simiolus: Netherlands Quarterly for the History of Art*, 28:3 (2000–1), pp. 103–28

Wood, Jeremy, *Rubens: Drawing on Italy*, exh. cat., Edinburgh, National Gallery of Scotland, 2002

ONLINE RESOURCES

Art UK: artuk.org

Bank of England, Inflation Calculator: www.bankofengland.co.uk/monetary-policy/inflation/inflation-calculator

Bodleian Library, Oxford: digital.bodleian.ox.ac.uk

Encyclopaedia Britannica: www.britannica.com

English Heritage: www.english-heritage.org.uk

National Gallery, London: www.nationalgallery.org.uk

National Portrait Gallery, London: www.npg.org.uk

Our Migration Story: The Making of Britain: www.ourmigrationstory.org.uk

Oxford Dictionary of National Biography: www.oxforddnb.com

Royal Academy, London: www.royalacademy.org.uk

Royal Albert Memorial Museum and Art Gallery, Exeter: rammuseum.org.uk

Royal Collection Trust: www.rct.uk

Rubenshuis, Antwerp: rubenshuis.be

Tate: www.tate.org.uk

Understanding Slavery: understandingslavery.com

Westminster Abbey, London: www.westminster-abbey.org

Acknowledgments

My journey to writing this book has owed a lot to those that helped and inspired me from the world of art history, and many others beyond it. The first person I want to acknowledge for their help is the archaeologist and academic Peter James, whom I have known as a friend since my early twenties. He recognized my interest in art, which had been growing steadily over several years, and encouraged me to try my luck at working in my favourite repository of art, the National Gallery. His strategy for circumventing my lack of qualifications was to seek out a job in the National Gallery shop, as he had done at the British Museum while he was studying. It worked: after moving from there to the information department, I found myself among individuals that were also interested in art. There I met Jane McCarthy, who taught me how to use PowerPoint, which I still use to this day to assist me in my role as a public speaker, so I want to thank Jane for that important start. For my art history studies, I want thank Francis Ames-Lewis, now Emeritus Professor in Art History at Birkbeck College, University of London, who had a profound impact on my studies at Birkbeck. Naturally, the paintings I chose to study during my undergraduate degree were those from the National Gallery's permanent collection. This was done from my new post as a member of front of house information staff. From this new post I attended as many talks as possible by the curators and the then director, Neil MacGregor. It is Neil I want to acknowledge next, because he immediately recognized that I needed help and introduced me to the National Gallery Archive and its staff, whom he instructed to assist me in my endeavours. Neil MacGregor continues to be an inspiration to me. But during my evening studies at Birkbeck, my life at the National Gallery would continue to throw up surprises, because the next person I want to acknowledge was the then head of education, Kathy Adler, who took it upon herself to appoint me as a National Gallery lecturer while I was still an undergraduate. The next of the Birkbeck cohorts I would like to thank is Simon Shaw-Miller, who discovered my dyslexia during the first year of my undergraduate studies; the Birkbeck Disabilities Officer, Mark Pimm; and the independent dyslexia tutor and coach Bernadette Kirwan. I would like to acknowledge Vivienne Loren for believing in me and recommending me for my very first teaching post in 2005 at Reading University. These amazing individuals helped me to flourish as an undergraduate student, along with the other notable Birkbeck teachers such as Peter Draper, William Vaughan, Laura Jacobus and Dorigen Caldwell. I would also like to thank my ever-supportive agent, Leslie Gardner at Artellus, and the team at Thames & Hudson, including Roger Thorp, Mohara Gill and especially Felicity Maunder for her hard work, diligence and intelligence when knocking this book into shape. Likewise Peter Burgess and Agatha Smith for their work on the inside design and cover, respectively; picture researcher Jennifer McHugh and production controller Celia Falconer; and project manager Phoebe Colley.

I would also like to thank the love of my life, Clair O'Leary. We had much in common when we met at a private view afterparty over twenty years ago. We had both studied photography, and we were both working in galleries. But most importantly, she was not English; she had emigrated from Cork in the Irish Republic in the mid-1980s, meaning we both understood what it was like to be an outsider. We both understood what it was like to experience discrimination, not just on her part in terms of misogyny, but also discrimination against the Irish, which was rife in England at that time. I understood discrimination because although I am English, throughout my life many white English people did not see me as such – some still do not. Clair supported me through the rest of the undergraduate degree and through my postgraduate degree, despite me revealing very early on in our relationship that I was almost £20,000 in debt due to the ongoing cost of my studies. But more importantly, Clair has been instrumental in getting me to the point of writing of this book.

Finally, I would like to thank my mother, Olive, who lived long enough to attend my undergraduate celebration day with Clair, but not my postgraduate ceremony, as she sadly died in June 2012. Having left her home country of Guyana as a teenager, I am saddened that she experienced so much discrimination and prejudice upon her arrival in England and throughout her time here. I am also saddened that her small contribution to this country was never really acknowledged by the society in which she lived, or by me. So, it is with much regret that I want to belatedly thank her for all she did for me, all her struggles with me, and for all I am. Strong women are what the world needs, and more power to them.

Picture Credits

Sources of colour illustrations by figure number:

1 Augsburg State Gallery. Photo Maurice Babey/akg-images; **2** Kunstmuseum Basel, Amerbach-Kabinett; **3** Kunstmuseum Basel, Amerbach-Kabinett; **4** Würth Collection, Künzelsau; **5** National Gallery, London; **6** Museo Thyssen-Bornemisza, Madrid; **7** Kunsthistorisiches Museum, Vienna; **8** National Gallery, London; **9** National Gallery, London; **10** Tate Britain, London; **11** National Portrait Gallery, London; **12** Hatfield House; **13** Folger Shakespeare Library, Washington, DC, with permission of Folger Shakespeare Library, Washington, DC; **14** Tate Britain, London. Photo akg-images; **15** National Portrait Gallery, London; **16** National Portrait Gallery, London. Purchased with help from the Wolfson Foundation and HM Government, 1971. Photo National Portrait Gallery, London; **17** Metropolitan Museum of Art, New York, purchased by Joseph Pulitzer Bequest, 1944; **18** National Gallery, London. Photo Bridgeman Images; **19** Tate Britain, London; **20** Schloss Weissenstein, Pommersfelden; **21** Museo Reale Bosco Nazionale di Capodimonte Napoli; **22** National Gallery, London. Photo The National Gallery, London/Scala, Florence; **23** Kunsthistorisches Museum, Vienna; **24** Palazzo Doria Pamphilj, Rome. Photo DeAgostini Picture Library/Scala, Florence; **25** J. Paul Getty Museum, Los Angeles; **26** J. Paul Getty Museum, Los Angeles; **27** Royal Collection Trust, London; **28** Royal Collection/Hampton Court Palace; **29** Polo Museale dell'Emilia Romagna, Collezioni della Pinacoteca Nazionale Bologna; **30** Ashmolean Museum, Oxford, presented by the children of Janet Carleton through the Art Fund, 2003. Photo Ashmolean Museum/Bridgeman Images; **31** National Portrait Gallery, London; **32** National Portrait Gallery, London; **33** Private Collection; **34** Tate Britain, London; **35** Tate Britain, London, Photo akg-images; **36** Scottish National Portrait Gallery, purchased with help from Art Fund, the National Heritage Memorial Fund and the Pilgrims Trust, 1987. Photo Artepics/agefotostock/SuperStock; **37** National Portrait Gallery, London; **38** Royal Collection Trust, London; **39** National Gallery of Art, Washington, DC, Samuel H. Kress Collection; **40** Cathedral of Our Lady, Antwerp; **41** Santa Maria Gloriosa Dei Frari, Venice; **42** Royal Museum of Fine Arts of Belgium, Brussels; **43** National Gallery, London; **44** National Gallery, London; **45** Banqueting House, Whitehall, London. Photo image/Alamy Stock Photo; **46** Rubenshuis, Antwerp. Photo Heritage Images/Getty Images; **47** National Gallery, London. Photo National Gallery, London/akg-images; **48** Rubenshuis, Antwerp; **49** National Gallery, London; **50** Olomouc Museum of Art, Archdiocesan Museum Kroměříž, Czech Republic. Photo Zdeněk Sodoma; **51** Olomouc Museum of Art, Archdiocesan Museum Kroměříž, Czech Republic. Photo Zdeněk Sodoma; **52** Royal Collection Trust, London. Photo Royal Collection Trust 2022/Bridgeman Images; **53** Royal

Collection Trust, London. Photo Royal Collection Trust 2022/Bridgeman Images; **54** National Portrait Gallery, London; **55** The Huntington Library, Art Museum and Botanical Gardens; **56** Yale Center for British Art, New Haven, Paul Mellon Collection; **57** Royal Collection Trust, London. Photo Royal Collection Trust 2022/Bridgeman Images; **58** Rijksmuseum Amsterdam, The Netherlands. Photo Bridgeman Images; **59** Metropolitan Museum of Art, New York, Elisha Whittelsey Collection, Elisha Whittelsey Fund, 1949; **60** Tate Britain, London; **61** National Gallery, London; **62** Foundling Museum, London; **63** National Portrait Gallery, London, and Getty, Los Angeles; **64** National Maritime Museum, Greenwich, London; **65** Co-owners: National Portrait Gallery, London; Captain Cook Memorial Museum, Whitby; National Museum of Wales. Photo National Museums and Galleries of Wales/Bridgeman Images; **66** Gilcrease Museum, Tulsa, gift of the Thomas Gilcrease Foundation, 1964; **67** National Maritime Museum, Greenwich, London, Caird Collection; **68** Royal Pavilion Museums, Brighton and Hove; **69** Tiroler Landesmuseum Ferdinandeum, Innsbruck; **70** Burghley House Collection, Stamford; **71** National Trust, Saltram Collection, Devon; **72** Royal Collection Trust, London. Photo Royal Collection Trust 2024/Bridgeman Images; **73** National Portrait Gallery, London; **74** Royal Academy of Arts, London; **75** Brown University, Ann-Mary Brown Collection, Providence; **76** National Trust, Nostell Priory, West Yorkshire; **77** Private Collection.

Sources of b&w illustrations by page number:

Frontispiece: Rubenshuis, Antwerp. Photo Heritage Images/Getty Images; **17** Kupferstichkabinett: Staatliche Museen zu Berlin. Photo The Picture Art Collection/Alamy Stock Photo; **18a** Royal Collection Trust, London. Photo Royal Collection Trust 2023/Bridgeman Images; **18b** Royal Collection Trust, London. Photo Royal Collection Trust 2023/Bridgeman Images; **24** Metropolitan Museum of Art. Rogers Fund, aided by subscribers, 1906; **30** National Gallery, London; **43** Tate Britain, London; **45** Viscount L'Isle, Penshurst Place. Private Collection; **48** National Portrait Gallery, London; **53** Bodleian Library, Oxford; **54** Private Collection; **59** Private Collection, by descent Earls of Fitzwilliam, possibly associated with the collection of Lady Juliet Tadgell; **62** Tate Britain, London. Photo akg-images; **63** Tate Britain, London. Photo akg-images; **64** Private Collection. Photo Mark Fiennes Archive/Bridgeman Images; **69a** National Portrait Gallery, London. Photo National Portrait Gallery, London; **69b** Private Collection. Photo The Weiss Gallery, London; **78** National Maritime Museum, Greenwich. Photo Fine Art Images/Diomedia; **89** Detroit Institute of Arts, Michigan, gift of Mr Leslie H. Green; **90** Metropolitan Museum of Art, New York, gift of Elinor Dorrance Ingersoll, 1969; **96** National Gallery, London; **97** Museo Nacional del Prado, Madrid; **106** National Portrait Gallery, London. Photo Granger Historical Picture Archive/Alamy Stock Photo; **107** National Portrait Gallery, London; **108** National Maritime Museum, Greenwich; **109** National Maritime Museum, Greenwich, Caird Fund;

115 The Harley Foundation, Portland;
116 National Portrait Gallery, London;
117 Metropolitan Museum of Art, New York, gift of George A. Hearn, 1906; **123** Museo Nacional del Prado. Photo MNP/Scala, Florence; **124** Galleria Palatina, Palazzo Pitti, Firenze; **128** Alte Pinakothek, Munich; **129** Sammlungen des Fürsten von und zu Liechtenstein, Vaduz, Wien; **130** National Gallery of Canada, Ottawa; **131** Pinacoteca, Vatican; **137** Metropolitan Museum of Art, New York, gift of Mr and Mrs Charles Wrightsman, in honour of Sir John Pope-Hennessy, 1981; **138** Wallace Collection, London. Photo Wallace Collection, London/Bridgeman Images; 140 National Gallery, London; **147** J. Paul Getty Museum, Los Angeles; **148** Metropolitan Museum of Art, New York, Jules Bache Collection, 1949; **149** State Hermitage Museum, St Petersburg; **150** Galleria Palatina, Palazzo Pitti, Firenze; **153** Wallace Collection, London. Photo Wallace Collection, London/Bridgeman Images;
154 Kunsthistorisiches Museum Wien, Gemäldegalerie; **156** Museo Nacional del Prado, Madrid; **163** Museo Nacional del Prado, Madrid; **168** Metropolitan Museum of Art, New York, gift of Carl J. Ulmann, 1924; **175** Yale Center for British Art, New Haven, Paul Mellon Collection;
178–79 British Museum, London. Photo The Trustees of the British Museum;
178 Metropolitan Museum of Art, New York. Harris Brisbane Dick Fund, 1917;
179 Metropolitan Museum of Art, New York. Harris Brisbane Dick Fund, 1917;
181 Royal Collection Trust, London. Photo Royal Collection Trust 2022/Bridgeman Images; **182** Metropolitan Museum of Art, New York, gift of Leo Steinberg, 1991;
186a British Museum, London. Photo The Trustees of the British Museum;

186b Metropolitan Museum of Art, New York, Elisha Whittelsey Collection, Elisha Whittelsey Fund, 1956; **190** National Maritime Museum, Greenwich, Caird Collection; **199** National Gallery of Art, Washington, DC, Paul Mellon Collection;
200 Metropolitan Museum of Art, New York, gift of Sarah Lazarus, 1891;
206 Metropolitan Museum of Art, New York, Harris Brisbane Dick Fund, 1932;
207 Metropolitan Museum of Art, New York, gift of Sarah Lazarus, 1891;
211 National Library of Australia, Canberra;
215 National Library of Australia, Canberra;
216 National Library of Australia, Canberra;
221 National Gallery of Australia, Canberra, purchased 2006; **222a** Yale University Art Gallery, gifts of the Associates in Fine Arts;
222b National Library of Australia, Canberra; **228** Captain Cook Birthplace Museum, Marton, Middlesbrough Council. Photo British Library; **234** Tiroler Landesmuseum Ferdinandeum, Innsbruck;
240 The Huntington Library, Art Museum, and Botanical Gardens, purchased with funds from the Art Collectors' Council and Ann and Dale Fowler; **244** Private Collection.

Index